BEST-LAID PLANS

BEST-LAID PLANS

THE PROMISES AND PITFALLS OF THE NEW DEAL GREENBELT TOWNS

JULIE D. TURNER

University of
CINCINNATI | PRESS

About the University of Cincinnati Press

The University of Cincinnati Press is committed to publishing rigorous, peer-reviewed, leading scholarship accessibly to stimulate dialog among the academy, public intellectuals, and lay practitioners. The Press endeavors to erase disciplinary boundaries in order to cast fresh light on common problems in our global community. Building on the university's long-standing tradition of social responsibility to the citizens of Cincinnati, state of Ohio, and the world, the Press publishes books on topics that expose and resolve disparities at every level of society and have local, national, and global impact.

University of Cincinnati Press Copyright © 2022

All rights reserved. No part of this book may be reproduced or utilized in any form or by any means, electronic or mechanical, or by any information storage and retrieval system, without written permission from the publisher. Requests for permission to reproduce material from this work should be sent to University of Cincinnati Press, Langsam Library, 2911 Woodside Drive, Cincinnati, Ohio 45221
ucincinnatipress.uc.edu

ISBN (hardback) 9781947602458
ISBN (e-book, PDF) 9781947602472
ISBN (e-book, EPUB) 9781947602465
Library of Congress Cataloging-in-Publication Data
Names: Turner, Julie D., author.
Title: Best-Laid Plans : the promises and pitfalls of the New Deal's Greenbelt towns / Julie D. Turner.
Description: Cincinnati, Ohio : University of Cincinnati Press, [2022] | Includes bibliographical references and index.
Identifiers: LCCN 2022005304 (print) | LCCN 2022005305 (ebook) | ISBN 9781947602458 (hardback) | ISBN 9781947602465 (epub) | ISBN 9781947602472 (pdf)
Subjects: LCSH: Housing development—United States—History—20th century. | Housing policy—United States—History—20th century. | City planning—United States—History—20th century. | Greenbelts—United States—History—20th century. | Suburbs—United States—History—20th century.
Classification: LCC HD7293 .T7795 2022 (print) | LCC HD7293 (ebook) | DDC 333.73/150973—dc23/eng/20220207
LC record available at https://lccn.loc.gov/2022005304
LC ebook record available at https://lccn.loc.gov/2022005305

Designed and produced for UC Press by Alisa Strauss
Typeset in Garamond Premier Pro and Avenir Next
Printed in the United States of America
First Printing

For Jeff, Ben, and Nic,
who never asked why I bother.

TABLE OF CONTENTS

INTRODUCTION

I don't remember noticing much about my new school as I entered the seventh grade. A rather shy introvert recently relocated from Kansas to Ohio, I felt wholly out of place, and undoubtedly focused much more on myself and my new classmates' reactions to me than on the architecture or decoration of the building. I likely paid scant attention to the hand-painted murals on the walls of the school's library or the bas-relief decoration behind the basketball hoop in the gym. I do remember the brilliant whiteness of the building as my bus pulled up in front of it every morning. I recall finding the rows of theater-style seats in an upstairs balcony overlooking the gym rather odd. But at that point nothing felt quite normal. Possibly I felt that, like me, this school seemed conspicuously out of sync with the daily crush of noisy, bustling students. Compared to my modern elementary school back in Kansas, this building bore an obvious patina of age, a history that the throng filling its halls surely failed to register or understand.

Figure Intro.1. Greenhills school/community building as it looked in 1938. It looked much the same in the mid-1970s when it served as Greenhills Middle School. Library of Congress, Prints and Photographs Division, FSA-OWI Collection.

Other signs of the past abounded nearby. My friend Linda[1] lived just a block or so from the school, but when I visited her home I didn't notice the architecture or the way the structures had been grouped together; rather, the impression I recall is how extremely cramped the home felt. Linda, her many siblings, and her parents filled a space less than half the size of the roomy house my much smaller family occupied just a couple of miles away. And inside, her home seemed old, tired, as though many other families had packed themselves into it over the decades, each leaving it a bit more faded and spent. Her house intrigued me, but also made me slightly uneasy. Was Linda's family *poor*? I eventually understood that no, her family wasn't poor, but her living situation was not quite in line with the suburban American dream of the late 1970s, not the middle-class lifestyle we saw weekly on TV and in my own nearby neighborhood.

Figure Intro.2. Greenhills rowhouses, 1938. The homes had aged by the time my friend Linda's family lived in one. Library of Congress, Prints and Photographs Division, FSA-OWI Collection.

My school and its immediate surroundings, integral backdrops to my adolescence, were in Greenhills, Ohio, a community constructed in the 1930s as just one project of the sprawling and unwieldy New Deal. Over time I would feel drawn to learn more about how this place came to be. I have always felt a strong connection to the 1930s, as well as to vintage architecture and design. I love old photographs, which, it turns out, the agencies responsible for the town had produced in ample quantity.[2] As I learned more about this place and the program that created it, it seemed the perfect subject for my own historical exploration. The places I haunted as a young teen led me to years of research into the era when my grandparents were newlyweds, into the mood of the nation during the Great Depression, and into one extraordinary experiment in town design.

A NEW DEAL FOR AMERICA

The Great Depression was more than just an economic crisis. The widespread unemployment, the home foreclosures, and the business collapses all unnerved the people of the United States—not for months or a few years, but for a decade. The symptoms of possible economic trouble began to show in the 1920s as mining and farming slumped, but those warning signs went almost entirely unnoticed as the overall economy soared. The stock market crash in 1929, rather than being the cause of the Depression, was merely the most obvious sign that something had gone horribly wrong. It took months for most Americans to realize just how bad the situation would become. Those who did not immediately lose their jobs watched anxiously to see whether their luck would hold. Stories of friends, relatives, and neighbors suddenly unemployed or homeless left many feeling unmoored, wondering if security—financial or emotional—was just an illusion.

Paradoxically, the Depression also brought hope, an unprecedented opportunity to reassess old assumptions and imagine a different future. As columnist Walter Lippmann explained in 1933: "There are good crises and there are bad crises. Every crisis breaks a deadlock and sets events in motion. It is either a disaster or an opportunity." Lippmann's conclusion: "The present crisis is a good crisis."[3] For many the Depression, as horrendous as it was, offered the prospect of correcting longstanding economic and social ills, of setting the nation on a better path. The depth of the calamity opened minds to new ideas and fresh possibilities.

In the early years of the Depression, President Herbert Hoover failed miserably at bringing either relief or hope to the American people. He was, quite simply, the wrong leader for this fraught time. An intelligent man, and not unfeeling, Hoover believed to his very core that to give people anything approaching a handout would forever destroy the independent spirit that had built the nation. His unwillingness to budge on this stance would cost him the presidency; in 1933 Franklin Delano Roosevelt (FDR), an upper-crust country squire who claimed to understand the suffering of ordinary citizens, swept into the White House, a refreshing breeze promising to disperse the heavy clouds that hung over the nation.

Roosevelt, in truth, had no more idea of how to solve the economic crisis than Hoover had, but FDR exuded confidence and charm, and calmed a nervous population—at least temporarily. Although he did not have a single, clear plan, he did have ideas. Historians disagree over just how many of the strategies to save the US economy he had already mapped out when he took office, but he stated definitively that "letting things alone" was not an acceptable option. He particularly dismissed the notion that "if we make the rich richer, somehow they will let a part of their prosperity trickle down to the rest of us" (exactly the economic plan that Ronald Reagan would enthusiastically promote some fifty years later). Instead, FDR urged "social justice through social action"—specifically, "the reduction of poverty."[4] The New Deal—a term adopted by journalists from a throwaway line in FRD's Democratic nomination acceptance speech—offered a vast array of optimistic plans, some quite modest and some immensely ambitious, an "alphabet soup" of newly formed agencies casting about for the magic formula that would set things right.

One agency in the New Deal pantheon was the Resettlement Administration (RA).[5] Greenhills, along with its sister cities of Greendale, Wisconsin, and Greenbelt, Maryland, was part of the RA's most ambitious and expensive project: the Greenbelt towns program. This effort offers an intriguing window into the audacity, the optimism, and, too often, the hubris of the New Deal.

Roosevelt's plan to turn the economy around centered on harnessing the power of experts. Historians have long observed that FDR not only called on specialists to recommend policy, but often adopted proposals from those with opposing views, allowing each plan to triumph or perish on its own merits, a policy version of survival of the fittest. Willing to experiment, Roosevelt gathered around him a cadre of educated men and women, pressing them to find creative solutions to the calamity that had befallen the nation. He wanted people by his side who could execute bold strategies, who were unencumbered by traditional modes of thinking.

Dr. Rexford Guy Tugwell was one such unorthodox expert. He burst onto the American scene as a member of Roosevelt's Brain Trust, the group of specialists from a variety of fields who helped put FDR into the White House. By training an economist, and by inclination a reformer, he had studied at the prestigious Wharton School of Economics and was working as a professor at Columbia University when Roosevelt chose him as an adviser on economic and agricultural issues. In 1934 Tugwell became undersecretary of agriculture, and in 1935 head of the newly created Resettlement Administration.

Good-looking and always well-dressed, the intellectual Tugwell could be quite charming, but also exhibited a tendency to be outspoken to the point of bluntness. Many bristled at his direct manner and interpreted his self-assurance as arrogance. These characteristics earned him the reputation of being an ivory-tower elitist. Although the public often perceived him as being woefully out of touch with the common man and unable to conceive of the everyday struggles of ordinary Americans, in fact he had grown up among the fruit orchards from which his father earned a living, and he understood the precarious nature of life for farmers and other workers. He observed the economic inequality within the United States and came to believe that this national defect might be mitigated by rational policy decisions if only the right people could be placed in charge at the federal level. The new president's faith in Tugwell's opinions offered the progressive-minded economist a once-in-a-lifetime opportunity to shape such decisions, to try to repair this fatal flaw.

THE GREENBELT PROGRAM

In March of 1935 Tugwell presented FDR with the proposal that would result in the Greenbelt towns. He described in his diary later that day how he had suggested to the president that the federal government should "go just outside centers of population, pick up cheap land, build a whole community and entice people into it. Then go back into cities and tear down slums and make parks of them."[6] The idea intrigued Roosevelt. Such a program offered the opportunity to put men to work while also getting people out of blighted neighborhoods in the nation's cities. The president approved the plan and placed Tugwell at the head of the newly conceived Resettlement Administration, which would oversee this and many other projects. The same diary entry notes that the two men then drove to Beltsville, Maryland, about ten miles from the capital, to look at a promising site for such a town, Tugwell observing that FDR "was much surprised at its scale and took great interest in everything." He noted that "one of [the president's] saving qualities is an enormous interest in physical construction and growth."[7] The seeds for the Greenbelt towns had been planted.

But planting the seeds gave no guarantee that they would germinate or thrive. After approving the project, FDR seems to have offered minimal input on the towns. His wife, Eleanor, found the project intriguing and worthwhile, but she, too, had little direct influence on the unfolding experiment. Tugwell took a keen interest in the plans early in the process, and inserted his ideas for improving American society into the overall goals for the communities, but his tenure as head of the RA lasted just nineteen months; he would be long gone before the towns were completed. The planning would fall to those lower on the food chain, but these were experts in their fields. Administrators below Tugwell brought their own expectations into the mix, as did the design teams, one for each of the four towns initially funded (though only three were actually built). The Greenbelt program found staunch supporters in the men and women charged with seeing the plans to fruition.

The various expectations of so many different players, understandably, sometimes clashed. The program suffered from having "too many cooks," who then, as the saying suggests, might spoil the broth. Roosevelt wanted to create jobs; clawing the nation out of the Depression topped his agenda. Tugwell longed to improve the living conditions of the nation's underclass, and he hoped that the Greenbelt towns might offer a template for a substantial realignment between the haves and have-nots. Administrators, planners, and architects each brought their own wish list: to end the Depression or serve their president or aid the poor or introduce innovative urban design. These bright and talented individuals necessarily carried their own—sometimes conflicting—hopes into the project. Each town represents a melding of ideals, optimism, and cold, hard political and economic realities. Possibly the program could have benefited from having a more centralized authority making all decisions, but then the towns would almost certainly have been less innovative, the designers less free to be creative.

The flagship of the program, the quiet town of Greenbelt, Maryland, lies just outside Washington, DC, where today the Capital Beltway intersects the Baltimore–Washington Parkway.[8] Greenbelt looks like no other nearby community, neither steeped in tradition nor any longer new. Most homes are of either minimalist white block or a somewhat more traditional red brick, most arranged in neat clusters around courtyards and cul-de-sacs. The commercial center, like many of the homes, is bright white, reflecting the popular Art Deco style of the early twentieth century. At one corner of the commercial hub sits a small movie theater that once showed the films of Shirley Temple and Clark Gable. From the town's center, pedestrian walkways wind and curve through residential areas, connecting public and private spaces. The town now serves as a relatively affordable housing option for those working in the nation's capital. It is today more culturally diverse than its creators ever imagined, yet the carefully planned mix of homes, shopping, educational facilities, and green spaces continues to shape the lives of Greenbelt's residents, creating a community in the truest sense of the word.

Six hundred and forty miles northwest of Greenbelt, just outside of Milwaukee, the town of Greendale, Wisconsin, too, infuses its residents with a sense of being someplace unique. Although its commercial center is of red brick and traditional in style, and its municipal administration building would look just as natural sitting in a colonial village as in a New Deal town, this community is nonetheless unmistakably related to Greenbelt. The use of white block for many of the homes, the meandering paths, the generous inclusion of green spaces throughout, all echo the design of the Maryland town even as Greendale has its own look and feel. This is a place built to be much more than just a collection of houses; it was meant, above all, to bring residents together in a shared community experience.

Southeast of Greendale, and nearly due west of Greenbelt, in the rolling Ohio valley landscape eleven miles north of Cincinnati, sits Greenhills, Ohio, the place of my middle-school memories. Not exactly like Greenbelt or Greendale, this community is nonetheless obviously a sibling to the other two towns. Here a shopping center, a community swimming pool, and the gleaming white community center that once housed my school serve families living in homes arranged in rows of townhouses, blocks of apartments, and a handful of single-family dwellings. This town features a variety of architectural styles, but the straight lines and minimalism of 1930s modern design form a prominent theme. Here, too, the community is interwoven with ample green space. The feeling once again is that this is no ordinary suburb.

Each of these towns has grown over the decades, and each now includes a substantial band of more recent housing encapsulating the 1930s village. But the original cores of all three communities represent a bold experiment, a program that promised a bright beacon of hope during the dark days of the Great Depression. It is difficult to imagine today just how sweeping a project it took to bring these communities to life, and equally difficult to believe that this program once sparked alarmed warnings among critics that the Greenbelt plan represented dangerous, "un-American" ideas.

To set the program into motion, not long after Tugwell shared his vision with President Roosevelt, the RA began purchasing plots of land near larger cities, which would theoretically provide employment for the residents of the new towns. The planners also hoped that industries might eventually be lured to the outer edges of the communities, thus providing even more convenient proximity between home and work. According to the original plan, the population would be primarily low-income and working class. The housing would be affordable rental property with the towns initially owned by the federal government and then turned over to a private entity once fully established. Each would include not just homes, but also a local commercial center for retail businesses, ample recreational and community facilities, and a band of green land, largely undeveloped but including some agricultural use, to encircle the community and shield it from outside encroachment and undesirable sprawl. (As it turned out, no industries could be enticed to locate close enough to the towns to provide employment, and because no private buyer could be found the federal government continued in the role of landlord until the late 1940s.)

This ambitious goal of creating entire towns sets the Greenbelt experiment apart from other New Deal building projects. Norris, Tennessee probably offers the closest parallel, but it was built to house Tennessee Valley Authority (TVA) workers constructing dams and hydroelectric plants, not to serve as a model of modern community building. Other housing projects provided homes, but not the infrastructure for entire towns. The Greenbelts went beyond other New Deal residential programs, offering housing, but also acting as examples of what expert planning could accomplish to aid the nation's working class by providing better homes and superior communities.

Like many of Franklin Roosevelt's experiments in jump-starting the economy, this effort faced heated opposition, inciting various charges including that of its being socialist—after all, it proposed to use federal funds to provide homes for needy citizens. It also introduced innovative ideas meant to address both a chronic housing crisis and an acute need to put men to work. The program sparked criticism as it delved into economic endeavors previously reserved for private enterprise. For those skeptical of FDR's motives, the Greenbelt project also appeared to aim at nothing less than a full-scale redefinition of American community and family life. This was a bold experiment not just in housing or work-relief, not just in using public funds to ease private need. It represents a moment when the federal government became involved in city planning and, as many critics saw it—though at that time the term barely existed to describe it—social engineering.

We can see now, in hindsight, that many of the program's specific goals were virtually doomed to fail from the outset. This is not to say that the towns failed to provide good neighborhoods and homes, because they surely did accomplish that. But they did so only after administrators acknowledged the need for federal subsidies to make rents affordable, and even then the target families were far closer to the middle class than to the working class for whom the towns were purportedly created. They failed at proving that affordable housing could also be good housing. They failed at pointing the way for future government town-building.

This project suffered under the burden of too many competing goals: maximum job creation at minimal cost, exquisite town planning that would provide modest residences for low-income families, progressive innovation that would serve to honor and reinforce traditional American values. In addition to these opposing goals, the Greenbelt experiment faced the derision of conservative politicians and members of the media who vented their hostility toward FDR and the New Deal, as well as toward Tugwell and anything he touched. The program was huge and expensive, and in the end provided benefits to just a tiny portion of the population. All of this provided ample ammunition for hostile observers.

THE GREENBELTS AS HISTORICAL SUBJECTS

Although the Depression and New Deal have been analyzed in great depth by historians (more on this in Chapter 3), the Greenbelt towns have inspired surprisingly little scholarship. The two most important books that cover the program as a whole, one published in 1959 and one in 1971, offer detailed chronologies of and commentary on the three towns and how they came into being.[9] But they do little to anchor their discussions within the broader cultural and social issues of the era. These books, while extremely useful resources, leave the reader wondering why such a huge expenditure seemed necessary, why housing and urbanization and leisure sparked such concern that the government would embark on such a costly and audacious project.

Best-Laid Plans seeks to provide that context alongside its focus on the towns. We cannot truly understand this sweeping experiment without a sense of what else was happening at the time. New Deal agencies tackled American problems large and small. This was just one such effort, but one that allows us to step back in time and understand why these towns were perceived as necessary, why they were designed as they were, and what they accomplished—or failed to accomplish.

This book also differs from most earlier studies of the towns in a number of other ways. For example, previous works have tended to paint the Greenbelt program as facing a great deal of opposition. Some authors have been more tethered to this argument than others, but overall the concept that this was a widely unpopular venture has permeated much of the research on the towns. In reality, it seems that critics of the program managed to make a great deal of noise and fuss while average Americans went about their business unconcerned about this, just one project of so many born in this era. It is all too easy to be distracted by opponents' clamor and miss the curiosity and acceptance frequently expressed by the population at large. The New Deal was itself controversial, of course, but it does not appear that the Greenbelt towns sparked any more division than FDR's other experiments.

Previous scholarship gave scant attention to certain aspects of the program. Some earlier scholars noted in a paragraph or a page that planners included swimming pools, playgrounds, movie theaters, and civic art in the towns, but did not question the purpose of these inclusions. Why did the government spend precious money on sculptures and murals in communities meant for low-income workers? Why provide swimming pools rather than additional housing units? What vision, what assessment of the needs for American workers, guided the planners in shaping these places?

Those who have studied this program have often depicted it as an outlier in the America of the 1930s, a project that stood apart from the rest of the New Deal. It certainly was bold in its scope and innovative goals, but no more so than many other entirely new concepts introduced during these years. The program arose, to a large extent, out of deep fears about the swiftly changing nature of home and family life in the United States, about rapid urbanization and the shifting nature of the workplace. The RA employed educated experts to try to solve the problems facing ordinary working Americans; in the process it raised concerns about government overreach and made plain the wide partisan divide in the nation. The towns' planners tried to honor a revered, often misremembered and mischaracterized past while at the same time anticipating an unknown and unknowable future.

These are all key themes of the Depression era as well. Rather than being an outlier, the Greenbelt program is actually, in some ways, emblematic of the New Deal: it was large, messy, and complex. For some it seemed perfectly reasonable, for others it appeared as a harbinger of dangerous, perhaps even un-American ideologies, and for still others it seemed only a weak effort when bolder action might have truly solved some of the nation's most pressing challenges. It helped some Americans, but it was also expensive and easily repudiated as that most hated kind of frivolous and pricy experiment: a "boondoggle." The idea was grand in scope, but was slowly diluted, swallowed up by the political and economic realities that so often hinder change in a democracy. Both the New Deal and the Greenbelt program pitted government largess against the interests of private enterprise, public benefit against public cost, the promise of a more equitable America against deeply entrenched traditions and strongly held—if often unacknowledged—prejudices.

In other ways, the Greenbelt project stands out among the mass of New Deal activities. Those agencies and experiments that found the most favor upheld longstanding beliefs about the rewards of hard work and did not challenge existing ideas about who deserved help. In building entire towns, complete with all the modern amenities, and at enormous cost, the Greenbelt program raised serious and not unreasonable questions about whether the government had traveled too far down the path of wishful, wasteful experimentation.

Best-Laid Plans uses the Greenbelt program as a lens through which we can examine both the New Deal's goals and efficacy and American society and culture in the 1930s. This single experiment in housing—the ways administrators envisioned and implemented the program, and the ways the public and the eventual residents responded—demonstrates the struggles of ordinary Americans during the Great Depression, and how the government met their needs, or failed to.

The Greenbelt towns represent a noble and ambitious effort—in the end, overly ambitious. This quixotic program—the brainchild of a controversial presidential adviser, the laboratory of a group of talented planners and designers, the target of conservative pundits—also became the salvation of hundreds of American families desperately longing for a better life, a safe home, a neighborly community. Like the era that spawned them, the towns represent a jumble of hopes and fears, the best and, some feared, the worst that the federal government had to offer.

1

THE NEED

If a nation wants good citizens, it must see that they have good housing.

—Edith Elmer Wood, 1935

Few concepts have been romanticized in American culture quite so much as the idea of "home." Despite the fact that throughout the history of the United States many of its residents lived in horrid surroundings, they were still told to believe in "home, sweet home," to see the American home as a nearly sacred ideal. Yet why would this be so? Why should a collection of boards and bricks be held so dearly in the national consciousness? Something about where Americans live, and in turn how they live, has long seemed uniquely suited to illustrating the character of the people, and the nation.

In 1918 architectural writer and critic Charles Harris Whitaker offered his perspective: A house "is the prime element of national growth. It is the soil whence springs that eagerness in the heart of every man for a home of his own. It is, after all, the physical attribute of life upon the possession or retention of which most of our energy is directed. Because of these things, it is the backbone of the nation. By the quality of its appearance, its convenience, its durability, one may infallibly determine the real degree of a nation's prosperity and civilization."[1]

The following year housing expert Edith Elmer Wood echoed Whitaker's sentiments, insisting that "no nation can rise higher than the level of its homes." She went on to issue a challenge: "Good citizenship is a product of normal family life. The other nations of the world are seeing to the housing of their people. Can we alone afford to neglect it?"[2] This was, for Wood and many others, a matter of national pride symbolizing the vigor of the nation and its people in an increasingly competitive world.

Yet if national status depended on decent housing, many argued, it logically followed that the nation itself bore a responsibility to help provide such homes. Architect and city planner Henry Wright said as much in 1916, contending that "for self-preservation the city and the state must develop and preserve the home."[3] At the time this proposition went strongly against American expectations of self-sufficiency and belief in the power of the free market, but economic factors through the nineteen-twenties and thirties would demonstrate the shortcomings of such attitudes.

Many understood that a crisis in housing was coming. American planner and reformer Catherine Bauer observed, "By 1900 any fairly acute person might have realized that this matter of housing, in its largest sense as average human environment, was bound to be one of the pivotal questions of the twentieth century."[4] She was correct, although nobody in 1900 could have imagined the two world wars and decade-long economic depression that would compound and complicate this issue.

The home stood as a symbol of conscientiousness, independence, and stability. Homeowners were seen as solid, reliable members of society. As one recent historian notes: "The multi-faceted role of the house and home in the 1920s, particularly their symbolic roles... became aspects in the vulnerability that grew exponentially as the Great Depression took hold."[5] As a growing housing crisis emerged in the twenties, experts debated how to address the rising challenges. The situation would worsen considerably in the thirties, as hundreds of thousands of Americans lost their homes to foreclosure. The crisis called into question American ideas about homeownership and permanence, and who should be considered a solid, responsible citizen.

SHORTAGE

Historically, great cities have tended to contain both enormous wealth and abject poverty. Until the late nineteenth century, however, the middle and upper classes paid little attention to America's urban slums, believing that those who lived in squalor somehow deserved their fate, that the moral failings of the poor had created the dismal environments in which they lived.

During the Progressive Era, at the end of the nineteenth and start of the twentieth century, many began questioning this logic. Experts began to argue that poor living conditions created degraded lifestyles, rather than the other way around, a concept known as "environmental determinism." How, they asked, could anyone living in squalor ever rise above the lowliest station in life? If the slums ensnared the lower classes, what could be done to release them and allow them to improve their lot? Reformers called for better residential conditions as one possible solution to poverty and its attendant evils, though exactly how to accomplish such an enormous task eluded them.

Meanwhile, many Progressives were equally determined to help—or to push—immigrants and the poor into "respectability" as defined by the White middle class. They called for improved sanitation and better housing construction, but by the First World War they had little to show for their efforts. Zoning codes, a new innovation in the first decades of the twentieth century, made some aspects of city life better, but the overall state of housing for working-class and poor Americans remained appalling.[6]

Experts pointed to rapid urbanization as the primary culprit in the worsening housing situation. The 1910 US Census had reported 45.6 percent of the population as urban (living in an area having 2,500 or more residents) and 54.4 percent as rural. In 1920, for the first time in the nation's history, a majority of the population—51.2 percent—were classified as urban, and by 1930 the proportion reached 56.1 percent.[7] From 1880 to 1939 the urban population had nearly doubled.[8] (Interestingly, 1930–32 would see a substantial reduction in urban population, with city-dwellers rebounding to 56.6 percent only by 1940. This was primarily because during the early years of the Depression cities no longer offered the abundant job opportunities that had for decades drawn people in from the countryside.)

This influx of new city-dwellers led to catastrophic living conditions in the poorest neighborhoods. Traditionally, workers' housing in and near the cities had come about primarily in one of two ways. Often, housing that had originally been built for the more well-off members of the population would be left behind by that class as they moved to new, more fashionable areas. As their old neighborhoods slipped in prestige, their discarded homes would be purchased for use as housing for the poor, often subdivided in whatever way would yield the most rent-producing units. Large single rooms might be divided into several smaller ones, even if this meant that some would have no windows for natural light and airflow. Conditions in such dwellings were almost universally substandard, and far too frequently utterly deplorable.

At the same time, cheap houses, apartment buildings, and tenements were constructed specifically for the working class. These newly built homes for the lower classes, although generally held to be more desirable than subdivided existing homes, were also decried by housing reformers. One criticism leveled at low-income residential buildings—both within the cities and on their peripheries—was that to make construction cost-effective and profitable, the expense had to be kept to a minimum and, as a consequence, the quality of both workmanship and materials suffered, resulting in a wholly inadequate final product. Speculation in low-rent housing proved unattractive to many builders and landlords because, even with cost-cutting measures in place, profits were likely to be slim. This meant that there was rarely enough new construction in working-class neighborhoods, even of an inadequate nature. As cities began to impose building codes and zoning laws in the early decades of the twentieth century, ensuring basic levels of safety, light, and ventilation, home-building within these cities became more expensive, making construction of low-income housing seem an even less appealing investment.

The result was a massive housing shortage. Through the last three decades of the nineteenth century and up to the start of the First World War, housing construction in cities provided approximately one new dwelling for every three recently arrived urban residents, and so theoretically kept up with the influx of people to the cities.[9] Yet because it was profit-driven, and there was little profit to be made in housing the needier members of society, most of this construction was aimed at the middle class and above. The working class and the poor, on the other hand, faced a growing shortage of decent, affordable housing.[10] Other factors also helped fuel the shortage. The expense of home construction, for example, rose throughout the decades just before and after the turn of the twentieth century. Between 1895 and 1914 residential construction costs went up by 50 percent, largely due to the increased expense of building materials, particularly lumber.[11]

The First World War brought the worsening situation to the attention of the federal government as workers flooded into cities seeking defense jobs, triggering an acute housing shortage that was impossible to ignore. The population of Washington, DC—admittedly an extreme example—mushroomed from 300,000 to 1.5 million during the war.[12] Private enterprise could not keep up with the enormous demand, and so the federal government, in an unprecedented move for the United States, took on the role of providing housing for its workers. Federal officials limited their efforts to areas where the need was greatest in relation to the war effort, such as near facilities producing ships and armaments. They intended the program strictly as an emergency wartime measure. Housing reformers lamented the fact that, unlike in much of Europe, in the United States this endeavor ended abruptly with the return of peace.[13]

Yet by the end of the war the housing problem was worsening, and as the numbers of those affected rose, fewer Americans could shrug off the problem. When, in 1890, Jacob Riis had documented the environments of the urban poor, "the other half" still meant primarily African Americans and recent immigrants.[14] This had ceased to be the case by the 1920s, when the problem of inadequate housing exploded, no longer just the misfortune of those ethnically or racially outside the perceived American norm, but increasingly affecting larger numbers of native-born Whites.

The reason was simple: in the past, as one wave of newcomers moved into the cheapest and most horrid dwellings, the wave that had come before them, now slightly more settled and prosperous, moved on to something better. And so it went up the economic ladder, with the poorest crowding in at the bottom and the slightly wealthier ascending to more desirable homes.[15] (While this trend was common for immigrants, it did not hold true for African Americans, who were far more likely to remain trapped in the worst racially segregated neighborhoods generation after generation.) During World War I, wartime disruption slowed the incoming flow of immigrants. Then, in the 1920s and 30s, severe immigration restrictions virtually halted this chain reaction of upward mobility as no newer, more desperate foreign arrivals competed for these deplorable dwellings. With fewer impoverished recent immigrants feeding the system from below, those living in poor conditions found it increasingly difficult to escape to better neighborhoods. As Wood noted, "The way [up and out] is still open to the exceptionally gifted. But most people are not exceptionally gifted."[16] As a result, native-born Whites began to make up an increasing portion of those living in these miserable environments, a fact that alarmed reformers and made the problem seem much more urgent than it had ever been before.

Up to this point, White Americans had found it easy to say, with a sad shake of the head, that there was only so much that could be done to elevate the immigrant or "Negro" poor. But when the native White working class also began to suffer appalling housing conditions, and the rest of the American public became increasingly aware of the situation thanks to journalists and progressive reformers, new questions arose concerning the larger implications of inferior housing. Experts worriedly noted the shrinking supply of housing for the nation's poor.[17] Meanwhile, housing shortages continued to drive rents higher, leaving even fewer options for workers who needed to remain in the cities and close to their places of employment.

The highly touted economic prosperity of the 1920s brought little relief. In 1925, a year of enormous housing gains, residential building in 257 cities with populations of 25,000 or more accounted for permit values totaling over $3.8 billion; by 1929 the amount had fallen to $2.58 billion.[18] And little of that was intended for the lower classes. Architect and town planner Clarence Stein made plain the dismal situation in 1932, writing, "There is a fairy story about housing that all Americans like to believe. It tells us that any American of sound character and industrious habits can provide himself with 'the house of his heart's desire.'" However, Stein lamented, "The hard facts are quite different from the fairy story...Housing for the well-to-do is a good business, but housing for two-thirds of our citizens is nobody's business."[19] And even for those who saw low-income housing as their business, it was a purely capitalistic enterprise, driven by the quest for personal gain above public benefit, profit above livability.

Economic gains in the 1920s primarily favored the better off. Estimates show a growth of income of between 29 percent and 34 percent for the wealthiest 5 percent of the population during the 1920s, while industrial workers' incomes remained relatively stagnant after 1923.[20] Between 1910 and 1919 wages for industrial manufacturing workers had risen from an average of $558 per year to $1,158, an impressive increase. In contrast, between 1919 and 1928 wages rose only slightly higher, to $1,325.[21] At the same time housing costs soared, making it increasingly difficult for much of the population to afford a decent place to live.

By the end of the 1920s there were 27.5 million families in the United States, of whom 12 million (or 43.6 percent) lived below the poverty line as defined by the federal government: $1,500 per year for a family of four.[22] Washington's Brookings Institution, which calculated the minimum income necessary to provide the "basic necessities" to be higher, at $2,000 per year, found that 60 percent of American families failed to meet this minimum standard.[23] The post–World War II situation, in which a strong economy elevated a huge number of Americans to the middle class, still lay decades in the future. In the early twentieth century an enormous portion of the population was by most calculations "poor," a situation that only worsened with the coming of the Depression.

In the summer of 1930, just months after the 1929 stock market crash, President Herbert Hoover turned his attention to the problem of the American home. It seems a somewhat mystifying topic for a man who had more than enough to occupy his mind just then. Nobody knew whether the economy would quickly bounce back or decline still further.

In hindsight, it seems like an unnecessary distraction for the president at that particular moment, but for Hoover and many others of the era, the question of where and how Americans lived appeared to be one of the most pressing matters of the day. Citizens' residential environments and levels of home ownership seemed ultimately to signify the character of the people, even of the nation itself. Experts warned that unless its citizens had good homes, the United States would face far more troubling problems than a (hopefully short-lived) economic slide.

The question of how to improve housing and promote homeownership thus appeared to be urgent enough to warrant the president's attention. Before he became a politician, Hoover had been an engineer, and he approached the troubles of the nation, including growing concerns over housing, with an engineer's mindset. He believed in the power of facts, experts, and rational solutions, and he applied his usual pragmatic approach to this topic by convening a group of specialists to study the situation and propose solutions. He called for a massive endeavor to understand the housing problem; as a result, the President's Conference on Home Building and Home Ownership took place in December 1931. Some four hundred people helped conduct the research for the conference, a year-long inquiry that studied all forty-eight states. Twenty-five committees submitted findings; the published reports filled eleven volumes.

In his opening address to the conference Hoover asserted that "next to food and clothing the housing of a nation is its most vital social and economic problem."[24] In explaining why this subject deserved such a deep level of expert attention, the president argued: "Adequate housing goes to the very roots of well-being of the family, and the family is the social unit of the Nation. The question involves important aspects of health, morals, education, and efficiency. *Nothing contributes more to social stability and the happiness of our people than the surroundings of their homes*" (emphasis added).[25] This was hardly an original or startling claim; in this statement the president merely echoed views shared by a large portion of the American population.

The issue had seemingly become urgent by this point because so much housing failed to live up to society's expectations. One report from the conference lamented that "the great majority of the homes that are being built in this country today are not worthy of the American people."[26] The home, the base upon which the nation had been built, now appeared to sit atop a creaking, unstable foundation.

QUANTIFYING THE PROBLEM

The President's Conference reports were among the most ambitious studies, but not the only, or even the first, effort to explain and quantify the challenges at hand.[27] Sociologists Robert and Helen Lynd found in the mid-1920s that in Muncie, Indiana—the true location of the "Middletown" studied in their groundbreaking book by that title—just two-thirds of the homes were connected to sewer lines and just 75 percent had running water.[28] *Literary Digest* published the results of a study of living conditions in Zanesville, Ohio in 1927. The city of roughly 30,000 residents had been chosen because it was so "typical" of ordinary America (itself a telling claim: 95 percent of the city's residents were native-born Whites, compared to just 78.4 percent nationally in 1920 and 81.1 percent in 1930).[29] More than 38 percent of the homes in Zanesville lacked bathrooms, and nearly 10 percent were without running water.[30] Such studies show that many Americans lived without amenities that were increasingly identified as basic necessities of modern life.

The poorer residents of larger cities fared far worse than those in Muncie or Zanesville. The editors of *Fortune* magazine enumerated some of the problems encountered in urban residential areas. They found that in 1929, in Philadelphia's poor districts, 95 percent of the dwellings were heated only by a stove and 90 percent had outdoor toilets.[31] In a survey of nearly 6,000 apartments in Cincinnati's "malodorous 'Basin' district," which housed approximately one-fourth of the city's population, researchers discovered that 70 percent lacked indoor toilets, with residents relying instead on outdoor facilities shared by as many as nine families. The entire district boasted just eighty bathtubs. As many as seventeen people might occupy a two-room apartment.[32] They summed up their discouraging findings by noting, "and so the story runs, in one degree of filth or another, for most of the industrial cities of the continent."[33]

Fortune published its findings in 1932. Among the discoveries: in the worst areas one could find "toilets shared by as many as twenty-five people and cleaned by none of them so that the resulting fetor will be literally indescribable within the limits of printable English. Hallways and stairs will be filthy and stinking and black." The living spaces, the writers observed, offered little comfort and no privacy. "An investigator may find any kind of human misery he desires," the report continued, noting:

> A three-room apartment will house eleven people, the baby sleeping in a cheap baby carriage, the husband and wife and the next youngest child in a three-quarters bed in the bedroom, five older children in another three-quarters bed in the dining room, another child on a bed of boards and chairs in the same room, and a boarder on a folding cot in the kitchen.

In another example, the report noted that

> nine people will live in a three-room apartment (originally
> designed for coal bins and storage lockers) with one windowless
> room, one room with a window on an areaway and so dark that
> not even a flashlight photograph could be taken, and one win-
> dow looking out at the shoe-soles of passers-by.[34]

Reformers insisted that fresh air, sunshine, and privacy were essential for
physical, mental, and moral wellbeing, and far too many tenement living
conditions clearly fell far short.

Between 1934 and 1936 the Works Projects Administration (WPA)
conducted inventories of city housing based on exhaustive surveys of 203 of
America's urban areas. The resultant data corresponded with the findings of
earlier studies and provided New Deal housing reformers with evidence of
the atrocious state of workers' residential environments. The report stated
that 15 percent of the surveyed dwellings lacked private, modern, indoor
flush toilets. Twenty percent had neither a bathtub nor a shower. Forty percent were without central heating. Overall (excluding New York City), the
report deemed 16 percent of homes to be either in need of major repairs or
completely unfit for habitation.[35]

As social critic and city planning advocate Lewis Mumford noted in
1934, "American housing, ever since the period of industrialization, has
never reached the lower half of the existing income groups except in the
form of low-grade inferior dwellings, badly planned and badly built, slums
in conception as well as in final result."[36] Plentiful evidence supported
Mumford's claim.

Despite the common impression that most of the urban poor and
working class occupied tiny apartments in dilapidated tenements, in truth
only the most desperate residents of the largest cities lived in such buildings.
Apart from places such as New York City and Washington, DC, smaller,
newer, multifamily or small single-family dwellings housed a much larger
portion of those in the lower income groups.[37] Few zoning codes existed
outside the cities, and so the near-outer urban perimeter became a favored
place for developers and speculators to construct working-class housing
free from cumbersome and expensive regulations.

Such homes were generally superior to the tenements in urban slums, but as the editors of *Fortune* noted, even homes on the urban periphery, even those that looked respectable, in reality failed to meet "a minimum standard of decency."[38] They blamed the situation on "the inertia of mediocrity."[39] Adding comforts or using more sturdy construction methods and materials would have increased costs and reduced builders' profits. Landlords and developers argued that this would cause rents to rise to a point beyond the economic reach of much, if not most, of the working class.

As a result, huge numbers of urban workers lived in cheaply built, relatively crowded, aesthetically uninspired housing on the cities' fringes, often within sight and smell of the warehouses and factories in which they labored. As one housing expert put it, "American housing [was] one of the anachronisms of the twentieth century."[40] In a modern, technologically advanced nation, such living conditions served as an unwelcome and embarrassing reminder of the limits of the free market.

The *Fortune* editors noted, "If the tenants are frequently to blame for the condition of their homes, it is nevertheless a question whether the beastly tenant begets the bad housing or the bad housing begets the beastly tenant."[41] Those who applied the new perspective of environmental determinism declared that bad housing did indeed spawn "beastly tenants." Some reformers then took the argument further, contending that builders and landlords seeking maximum profit, by constructing and managing inadequate homes in deteriorating neighborhoods, bore the ultimate responsibility for the degradation of the poor. Few, however, could formulate a viable solution.

PROPER TYPES OF HOMES

Prominent planner John Nolen asserted in 1930 that "a modern house should be, first of all, safe and healthful." This meant that it must be "easy to clean, convenient, and comfortable" and that it should provide "fresh air through the right orientation of rooms for prevailing winds and cross ventilation [and] a place in the sun." But beyond these basic needs, he believed that "the modern family also demands a house that satisfies the widespread and increasing desire for play and gayety, for pleasure, and for old and new forms of beauty." Families, he believed, wanted "the amenities of life—freedom from clatter and noise." Nolen cautioned, however, that this "discussion must be limited to families having an income of... $3,000 to $5,000 a year"—well above the average for the working class.[42]

Nolen had attempted to provide housing for lower-income groups, perhaps most notably in Mariemont, a community he planned just outside Cincinnati in the 1920s. In this project he tried to improve standards, but as with so many other efforts at building working-class homes, the expense of creating the town, in the end, drove housing costs out of reach of the "workingmen" for whom it was intended. It became instead a fairly middle-class suburb. Because of this experience, Nolen was well aware of the obstacles to providing such standards for America's workers.[43]

In their efforts to define the characteristics of a proper home, reformers also expressed strong opinions about the best type and arrangement of dwelling units. Popular sentiment in the United States held up the single-family home as the ideal; anything else was often deemed inferior.[44] Experts even voiced uneasiness over the increasing numbers of middle- and upper-class apartment buildings in upscale city neighborhoods. The President's Conference reported, for example, "Occupants of one-family houses, whether owned or rented, tend to have greater stability [and] a greater concern in the character of their neighborhood."[45] Many suspected that apartment-dwellers must be less than completely committed citizens.

Reformers especially worried about the possible detrimental effect on children deprived of a single-family home with at least a bit of yard. A President's Conference report declared the ideal home for raising children to be a single-family detached house with a yard; perceived conditions for the nation's youth trended downward as homes became more multifamily and more crowded.[46] This focus on the need for individual yards, and the fact that fewer and fewer urban dwellings had such space, was one factor in movements to provide urban parks and playgrounds, efforts to deliver what the average urban residence no longer could.

An increasing portion of the population simply could not afford a detached house with a yard. Although in 1930 over three-quarters of Americans still lived in single-family rather than multifamily dwellings, in the city centers the proportion was lower, at 63.3 percent, and experts feared that eventually apartments would outnumber traditional single-family homes.[47] In Chicago, for example, construction of multifamily dwellings accounted for up to 80 percent of residential building during the 1920s.[48] Whether desirable or not, increasing numbers of urban Americans simply had no choice but to live in multiple-family structures.

A small handful of experts, most notably Henry Wright, challenged the general consensus that single-family homes should be the goal for every family. In 1933 Wright argued that "the fantasy of the snug and cozy little home that the typical American will own... on his own lot, is indeed one of the most highly paid fairy tales the advertising man ever managed to float."[49] He endorsed low-cost housing built to adequate standards that would serve residents well and would hold up over time; whether these were single- or multiple-family dwellings mattered little if they met other considerations of livability. Mumford cited Wright's work as demonstrating that "the individual free-standing house has become a luxury for the greater part of the population."[50] Lower-paid urban workers, both men argued, could not expect—and need not aspire to—individual detached homes.

Economic realities left the working class and poor with few housing options. Experts calculated that a family of limited income could spend no more than 20 percent of its earnings on housing "without impairing health by undue economy on food and clothing."[51] Yet Chicago families in the lowest twenty-fifth percentile income bracket spent on average 36 percent of their earnings on housing. Even relinquishing over one-third of their funds on rent did not ensure decent lodgings. A typical apartment might consist of a living room, two bedrooms, and a kitchen arranged in a long row of dim, or even windowless, rooms, the only plumbing a cold-water kitchen tap and a toilet tucked into a small space nearby.[52] These were strictly utilitarian dwellings—no comforts, no conveniences, no frills.

Even sorrier conditions prevailed in Washington, DC, which was among the worst cities in the nation in terms of livable low-cost residential space. The Final Report on Greenbelt, Maryland (1938), offered evidence of the depth of the crisis by breaking down rental costs in the capital. One-fourth of federal employees earned under $1,500 annually. Using the guideline that no more than 20 percent of a family's income should be spent on housing, a family earning $1,500 per year should have spent no more than $25 a month on rent. Yet a typical District apartment building intended for White residents might offer one room and a bath, with no kitchen, for $25 to $30 per month (note that this is one *room*, not one bedroom). One room with both a bath and a kitchen cost $30 to $50 a month. Larger families needing more space had a particularly difficult time: three rooms with a bath and kitchen commanded $60 to $90 per month. Given that 61 percent of federal employees earned $2,000 or less annually, under the prevailing formula their housing costs should have been no more than $33 per month—approximately the price of one room, a bath, and a kitchen.[53]

The Greenbelt report stated:

> A chronic house famine has pushed rents [in DC] a third higher than the national average, and is forcing low-waged government workers to pay as much as half of their salaries to keep any kind of roof over their heads... The majority of federal employees in Washington fall definitely within the low income groups... Federal employees, however, are living on velvet in comparison with the city's lower-paid laborers.[54]

Experts wondered how families paying such a high proportion of their incomes in rent could ever amass any surplus. How could they achieve the American dream of upward mobility? How could America's workers move into the middle class?

Some experts argued that these problems could not be solved on a family-by-family basis. Sociologist Ernest Groves wrote in 1927 that "from whatever angle one views it, housing becomes a community problem, not a matter of mere individual taste as the complacent American is so likely to regard it." He went on: "It is as contrary to public policy to tolerate the slums as it is to permit a carrier of disease infection to deliver milk."[55] Better homes, and better home life, most experts agreed, would benefit everyone.

As a result of these deep concerns about the housing situation, in 1934 the National Association of Housing Officials concluded that a minimum standard for decent housing was vital to society and the economy. Their report stated, "The community cannot afford the continuing degeneration of the living standards, the discontent, and the expense thrown upon public services... which follow any failure to maintain such a standard in housing." And, they concluded, private enterprise was clearly failing to provide decent homes for the working class and poor. "Consequently," they declared, "the duty of securing the *standard* must be regarded as a public responsibility, and, as in the case of education and water supply, must be undertaken as a public service."[56] The idea that this might be the proper role of the government was new to most Americans, and struck many as a radical departure from the nation's celebrated ideal of self-sufficiency. Yet those urging housing reform in this country only needed to look across the Atlantic to find a model for the improvements they envisioned.

THE EUROPEAN MODEL

Following World War I, several European nations extended their wartime efforts, continuing to pursue national housing programs for low-income groups. This activity was not limited to those places that had experienced physical devastation during the war and thus needed to rebuild, but also included those for whom the residential shortages of the war had forced a recognition of an ongoing housing crisis. Governments in Great Britain, France, Belgium, Italy, Sweden, Denmark, the Netherlands, Germany, and Austria sponsored public housing developments in the 1920s. In many cases government support took the form of loans and reduced taxes for builders of low-cost housing, but almost 30 percent of this housing was constructed by governmental action (though not always at the national level) on munic-ipally owned land.[57] As a result, low-rent workers' housing in these nations increased enormously from the end of the war to the start of the Depression. In Cologne, Germany, for example, between 1919 and 1932 private builders supplied just 1,000 homes; the remainder of the 22,000 homes constructed in that period relied on some form of government aid.[58]

Raymond Unwin, a leading British city planner with a popular fol-lowing in the United States, strongly advocated such governmental assis-tance, writing that "the provision of a minimum standard of housing for the lower paid sections of the people at rents which they can afford to pay must be accepted as a community responsibility and a public service."[59] American architect and planner Clarence Stein, an admirer of Unwin, also promoted this idea, stating,

> Housing for the lower income groups must become a direct gov-ernmental service—in my opinion a service far more important than the building of roads, utilities, transportation, even more important than schools... Inadequate incomes will never pay for adequate homes.[60]

The idea of government involvement in housing, however, and particularly the possibility of subsidies, was met with staunch resistance in the United States. Many felt that the effort would be too expensive, or they opposed the idea of giving handouts, or both.

A PUBLIC PROBLEM, A PUBLIC SOLUTION?

American reformers calling for better housing for the working class and poor must have understood that they were swimming against a national tide of complacency and perceived self-reliance. So, rather than simply depending on others' humanitarian instincts, they often presented their arguments by highlighting the ripple effect bad housing could have on all citizens, and on the nation as a whole. The Federal Emergency Administration of Public Works concluded in 1937, for example, that everyone paid higher taxes due to the disease, crime, and other menaces emanating from slum districts.[61]

Others made similar observations. Edith Elmer Wood, still advocating for improved housing in 1940, urged that improvements in homes and neighborhoods were vital "if we are to maintain a successful urban civilization."[62] The nation needed to take action to provide better homes for its needier citizens, even if only as an act of societal self-preservation.

Although in the 1920s most Americans likely would have been unwilling to accept the concept of federally provided housing, during the early years of FDR's presidency resistance weakened as citizens demanded that their government come to their aid. Between the social and economic crisis of the Depression on the one hand, and the strong emotional ties Americans had to the sanctity and centrality of the home on the other, housing experts now seized the opportunity to act. This issue, they argued, could both help relieve some of the suffering brought on by the Depression and ensure the future vitality of the nation.

It should come as no surprise that one New Deal program after another attempted to tackle this problem, resulting in dozens of housing projects undertaken by various agencies. For those who had long called for rationally planned residential building programs for the masses, the New Deal offered the promise—finally—of forceful, positive action in providing adequate residential environments for the nation's working class. The combination of citizens' desperation, urgent calls for action, the eagerness of experts to give their advice, and a temporary willingness among federal and local officials to work together and experiment all aligned perfectly, if only for a brief moment.

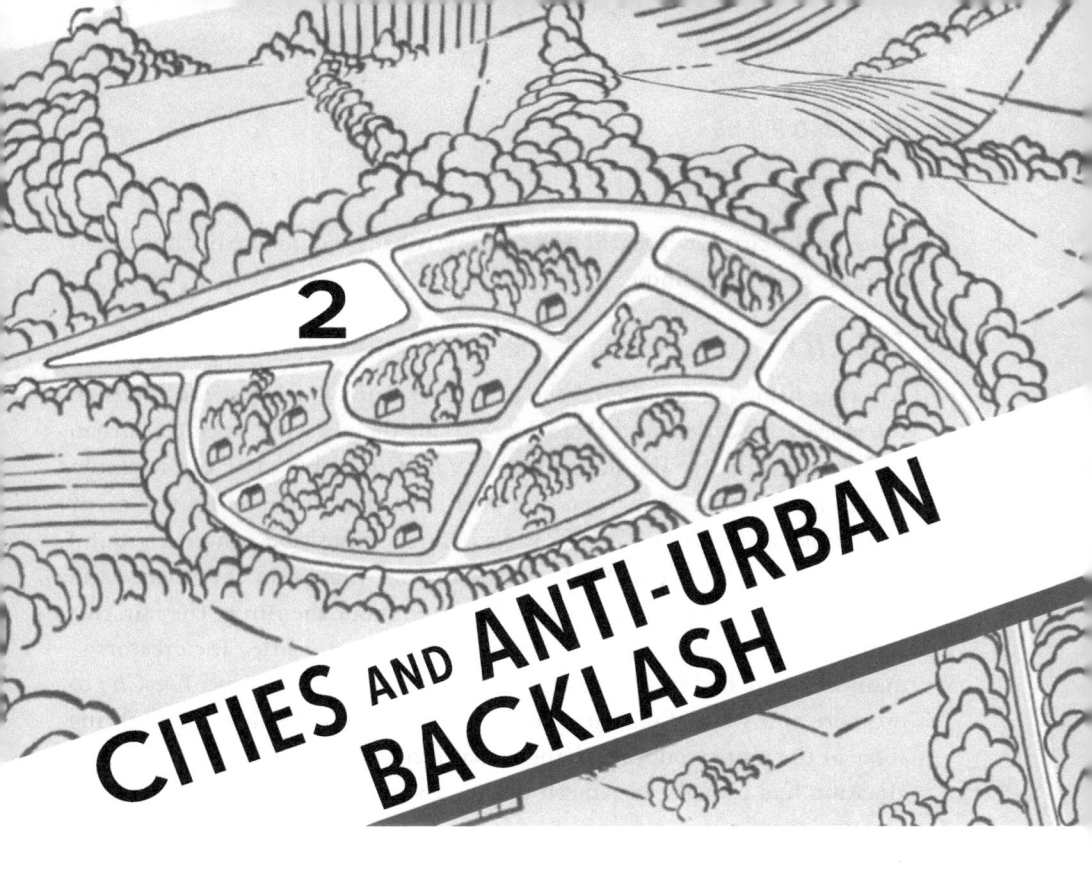

2
CITIES AND ANTI-URBAN BACKLASH

Few fail to find a certain degree of
unwholesomeness in city life.

—Niles Carpenter, 1931

The 1930s closed with two blockbuster motion pictures, each the tale of a young woman with strong ties to her family home. At the end of *Gone with the Wind*, Scarlett O'Hara finds a new determination and a new direction following the ravages of the Civil War. When she vows to survive and triumph, when she finds her greatest strength, she is, significantly, at Tara, her family's beloved plantation. In 1939's other outstanding hit, *The Wizard of Oz*, Dorothy strives throughout the film to get back to the house belonging to Auntie Em and Uncle Henry. "There's no place like home," Dorothy repeats to unleash the enchantment that will whisk her back to Kansas. Tellingly, during their cinematic adventures each of these heroines has visited the big city, has witnessed the drama and turmoil of life among crowds of strangers, and, in the end, yearns to return to the one place she truly belongs. Each sees the countryside as the antidote to the chaos of the city. Each yearns to find her way back, not just to her home, but to a tranquil, *rural* home.

THE CITY

Another film that premiered the same year, with much less fanfare than the stories of Scarlett and Dorothy, laid out the negative aspects of urban life more explicitly. The documentary *The City* debuted at the Museum of Modern Art in May 1939, and was later that year among the many attractions at the New York World's Fair, an exposition centered around the theme "Building the World of Tomorrow."[1] Shown in the Science and Education building several times a day throughout the run of the fair, this film is undeniably propaganda, its agenda far from subtle. The creators— many of whom had ties to the recent Greenbelt program—used *The City* to promote new ways of planning towns while at the same time highlighting some of the more troubling changes that recent urbanization and industrialization had brought to American life. The majority of the documentary juxtaposes existence in hectic modern cities with the promise of better living in quiet, rationally planned suburban communities.

The opening of the film features an image of sunlight reflecting on rippling water, with the caption: "Year by year our cities grow more complex and less fit for living. The age of rebuilding is here. We must remould our old cities and build new communities better suited to our needs."[2] As depicted in this film, the United States, once a nation of cooperative and friendly villages, had increasingly become a land of industrial regimentation in cities populated by seas of nameless, harried drones. Now pitiable workers seemingly exist only to keep the machines running; they find no satisfaction in their work and obtain no respite in a quiet home at day's end—unless, that is, they are fortunate enough to inhabit one of the new planned communities designed to combat the strains of frenzied modern life. While most of the 1939 New York World's Fair celebrated the technological triumphs of the recent American past, *The City* expressed grave doubts about an urban future left to unfold without careful direction and expert planning.[3]

After the film's rural opening, the next several minutes contrast the pandemonium of a modern metropolis with the bucolic tranquility of a

New England village of "a century or two ago."[4] Quick-cut shots of city hurry, dirt, and danger, set to an urgent musical score composed by Aaron Copland, set the tone for the film's urban segments. The rapid-fire narration explicitly lays out the negative outcomes of mechanization:

> Machines, inventions, power! Black out the past, forget the quiet cities! Bring in the steam and steel, the iron men, the giants! Open the throttle! All aboard! The promised land! Pillars of smoke by day, pillars of fire by night! Pillars of progress! Machines to make machines! Production to expand production! ... Faster and faster, better and better!

The images depict a modern, industrial city nearly beyond the control of the humans living within it.

Later in the film we see images of dams and power lines and a wave of people moving like a massive herd of sheep (suspiciously similar to the opening scene to Charlie Chaplin's 1936 film *Modern Times*) and then working at repetitive jobs like mindless automatons. The tone of the narrator is urgent: "The spectacle of human power—immense but misplaced—disorder turned to steel and stone. A million mechanisms, almost human, superhuman in speed. Men and women losing their jobs, losing their grip unless they imitate machines, live like machines. Cities unrolling ticker-tape instead of life. Cities where people count the seconds and lose the days. Cities where Mr. and Mrs. Zero cannot move or act until a million other zeros do. Cities where people are always getting ready to live, some other time, some other place, getting ready—never getting there."

We can only guess at how individual audience members responded to the documentary. One reviewer, however, praised it with gusto. Archer Winsten, film critic for the *New York Post*, gushed: "If there is nothing else worth seeing at the fair, this picture would justify the trip and all the exhaustion;" he recommended that "no one should do himself the injury of missing *The City*."[5] Winsten's enthusiasm, of course, may have represented a commentary on the filmmaking more than on the film's message, but he found the message acceptable enough to urge all fair attendees to share in the experience. Although we cannot know what viewers at the time thought of it, today *The City* is counted among the most iconic documentaries of the 1930s.

Although the film never names the idyllic community presented as the antidote to urban life, most of the scenes of modern suburban calm and contentment were in fact filmed in Greenbelt, Maryland.[6] Camera crews had descended on the recently completed town, using local residents to show vignettes of unhurried tranquility, offering the community as a model of what the future could hold.[7] In these new residential havens, we are told, families could recapture the kind of community and home life that seemed to be disappearing from the nation. The film perhaps exaggerated the defects of cities, yet it tapped into very real concerns about the detrimental qualities of urban life and presented a highly alluring alternative.

URBANIZATION

Even by the 1930s, when more than half of the nation's population lived in areas defined as urban, the American people continued to implicitly accept the idea that the healthiest, most spiritually and morally uplifting life could only be found away from cities.[8] In 1931 sociologist Warren S. Thompson noted a growing sense that large cities represented "an experiment in human association [that] is turning out badly."[9] Urban living, although in many ways highly desirable, connoted mobility; city-dwellers seemed to be modern vagabonds, never settling in one place for long, never putting down deep roots, never fully integrating into local life, never committing to the larger community. Close-knit villages and family farms, on the other hand, represented stability and a reverence for tradition. Even as city populations surged, doubts about the meaning of an urban America persisted. As one twenty-first-century historian has noted, "We are a nation reliant on the engines of our cities, populated with people who do not like cities very much."[10]

National leaders in the first half of the twentieth century frequently expressed deep concerns over urbanization. In a 1909 speech, President Theodore Roosevelt warned,

> The great recent progress made in city life is not a full measure of our civilization; for our civilization rests at bottom on the wholesomeness, the attractiveness, and the completeness, as well as the prosperity, of life in the country. The men and women on the farms stand for what is fundamentally best and most needed in our American life.[11]

Whether he truly believed this or was simply pandering to the rural citizens who at that point still made up a slight majority of the nation's inhabitants, his speech bears witness to an enduring reverence for the American farmer and the rural life. But the trend toward urbanization would not be stopped. In the same year that Roosevelt spoke these words, American city planner Benjamin Clark Marsh astutely predicted that "the drift to the city is inevitable."[12] This drift, though inevitable, also struck some as both undesirable and unnatural.

Even by 1931, more than a decade after the Census Bureau proclaimed that the majority of Americans were inhabiting cities, this notion persisted. In that year another prominent politician asserted that

> the country has added advantages that the city cannot duplicate in opportunities for healthful and natural living. There is space, freedom and room for free movement. There is contact with earth and with nature and the restful privilege of getting away from pavements and from noise. There is an opportunity for permanency of abode, a chance to establish a real home in the traditional American sense.

The speaker was New York governor, and presidential candidate, Franklin Delano Roosevelt, sounding much like his distant relation (and his wife's uncle) Theodore more than two decades earlier.[13]

But by this time the ongoing migration into the nation's cities was irreversibly reshaping much of American society. While popular culture continued to depict farm life as the ideal in books, movies, art, and song (while at the same time playing up the stereotype of the country hick), in reality the pull of the cities proved far more compelling.[14]

Fears about urbanization were not completely unfounded. Undeniably noisy, dirty places, the worst sections of America's cities in the early twentieth century hardly represented the zenith of modern civilization. Factories polluted the air. Too much humanity seemed pressed into too small a space, and too much of that space was made up of crumbling, decaying slums. The suspicion that rural life represented virtue, and city life depravity, seemed to be borne out by the overcrowding and squalor of the most degraded urban districts.

Prominent sociologist William Fielding Ogburn expressed rather hyperbolic alarm in 1934—though giving absolutely no evidence for his claims—warning:

> The city has done things to us. More crimes are committed in the city than in the country. Not so many people get married. Families have fewer children. More women are employed outside the home. Suicides are more frequent in cities. City people are more nervous and more of them go insane... Cities have made man a different person.[15]

Such assertions hardly met the standards of scientific rigor, yet coming from a respected academic these words must nonetheless have carried some weight with readers.

DELINQUENCY

If cities were fundamentally changing the populace, fears about the corrupting influences of cities on the nation's youth took on particular importance. One study reported that, despite the fact that experts differed over whether delinquency was actually increasing or decreasing, worry about delinquency was decidedly on the rise.[16]

For most White middle-class Americans the urban environment appeared anything but conducive to raising morally wholesome youth.[17] In 1925, sociologist Robert E. Park noted that the roots of delinquency lay in a child's social group, which in turn would naturally depend on where that group lived.[18] Edith Elmer Wood also touched on the influence of the living environment in several of her publications. She contended that as it had become more difficult for families to escape slum districts many children saw "small likelihood of getting away" other than by "the easy short-cut of crime."[19] And the natural assumption was that criminal youth would grow into criminal adults.

Unlike many of her predecessors and contemporaries, though, Wood was unwilling to accept the notion that high crime levels in some urban areas were due to "the inherently criminal tendencies of racial groups living there."[20] Like Park, Wood stressed the importance of friends and neighbors in shaping children's behaviors.[21] But she believed also that the physical surroundings themselves played a significant role in determining a child's future character. She pointed out, for instance, that children living in neighborhoods lacking adequate play space would resort to the streets for their amusement; left to their own devices and beyond the watchful supervision of their mothers, these children of the streets were much more likely to get into mischief—or worse.[22]

Despite the near impossibility of separating cause from effect, many experts made sweeping claims that city environments led to delinquency. A 1930 study conducted by the New York Crime Commission reported, "No direct relationship between congestion of population and degree of delinquency could be found." But it nonetheless went on to claim, "There is a growing body of evidence that the slum has easy, lax standards, obtuse moral perceptions, uncoordinated and chaotic strivings." The explanation the commission offered for such an alarming state: slums are "composed, to a great extent, of persons endowed with poor intelligence, who lack the capacity to consider a large number of details in making a decision, lack foresight, and cannot make fine ethical discriminations."[23] Experts agreed that delinquency was more prevalent and problematic in cities, particularly in the most impoverished areas, but beyond that, when they tried to ascertain why this was the case, the issue became muddied. No study could determine exactly which factors had the greatest detrimental influence; many who commented on the situation simply fell back on old assumptions about the moral character of those who lived in such degraded and degrading surroundings.

ALIENATION

Another aspect of city life stood out as a particularly modern danger: urban alienation. American town planner Clarence Perry contended in 1929 that, because city dwellers so seldom formed connections with their neighbors, they were unlikely to know local political candidates or to be able to form educated political opinions.[24] Perry and others who shared his views believed that democracy could only flourish in close-knit communities, and they worried that such communities were absent in contemporary American cities.

Those who discussed this idea of urban alienation pointed out that, paradoxically, the very denseness of cities made it more difficult to truly connect with other people. In 1938 sociologist Louis Wirth expressed this idea by noting that "the contacts of the city may indeed be face to face, but they are nevertheless impersonal, superficial, transitory, and segmental."[25] This idea persisted, it seems, because so many who lived or worked in large cities truly felt this sense of being alone in the crowd, of being disconnected from the throng around them.

If they largely accepted this as reality, experts differed on the precise causes. Some shared Perry's view that small communities represented the ideal environments in which to establish and maintain close ties. Such bonds, they claimed, were more difficult to form in larger cities due to the absence of the old mutual obligations and trust of the village. Others, including Wirth, pointed to the transitory nature of urban life; people in cities barely bothered to know their neighbors because the population of the neighborhood so frequently reshuffled itself.

Still others argued that the heterogeneous nature of urban districts posed an obstacle to forming close ties, that people of differing backgrounds were unlikely to be able—or to desire—to get to know neighbors of differing cultural traditions. Wirth made this argument as well, arguing that "wherever large numbers of differently constituted individuals congregate, the process of depersonalization also enters."[26] Today's multiculturalism seems to have been unimaginable; most Americans believed that those who were different from themselves could never truly be neighbors in the best sense of the word.

Fears of racial or ethnic "contagion," or of actual contagion, or a host of other perceived problems became associated with urban environments. Politicians and educated experts often reinforced this apprehension about urbanization, promulgating negative images of the city and those who lived there, believing that, even as increasing numbers of Americans chose urban life, this choice was sapping the strength from the nation.[27] Landscape architect Charles Downing Lay summed up many of the anxieties concerning urbanization:

> The city is full of shocks for the person of refinement, sights that sicken him, and contacts with fellow men that make him cringe. It is a constant repetition of annoyances for the sensitive; the clamor of the streets, the interruptions of many people demanding a hearing, the discords in time and place, keep his nerves ever on edge.[28]

GARDEN CITIES

These concerns, of course, did not suddenly arise in the early twentieth century. Some form of anti-urban sentiment has probably existed for as long as cities themselves have existed. By the end of the nineteenth century, however, many on both sides of the Atlantic had begun to truly worry about what city life meant for industrial workers, and for the larger society of which they were a part.

Among those focusing on the living conditions of the working class at this time, Ebenezer Howard became one of the best known. He has been heralded as the creator of the British garden city idea, and his concept caught the attention of social reformers and city planners including, eventually, Rexford Tugwell and the designers of the Greenbelt towns. Howard was not himself an architect or city planner; he was a stenographer with a keen interest in organizing society in innovative ways designed to improve the lives of industrial workers. His ideas eventually earned him a reputation as a visionary in the field of city planning. He was certainly not the only one to propose such new ideas; yet the fact remains that, although Howard's concepts were not unique, his promotion of them brought international attention to the garden city model.

Howard was deeply interested in the problems of modern society and the ways in which new town concepts might help to alleviate them. In 1898 he published his one and only book, *To-morrow: A Peaceful Path to Real Reform*, later reissued under the more commonly known title *Garden Cities of To-morrow*. Although today Howard is most remembered as the founder of the garden city design, it was in fact the social, political, and economic concepts—the ways in which such cities might transform life for workers and how the projects could be financed and undertaken—that were his primary interests. He envisioned the municipality itself as being "sole landlord," and therefore able to control the economic activities that could be undertaken in the towns. In particular, he suggested the regulation (though not complete elimination) of the liquor trade as a way to improve community life.[29]

Although Howard's primary interest was administrative, he also offered a potential design for the physical layout of the towns, though he stressed that this was merely one possible configuration. He conceptualized the garden city as a series of concentric circles. The innermost was to be a park, encompassed by residential spaces including houses and private gardens, surrounded by a "grand avenue," and then another encircling band of residential space. His design included industry at the outer edge, allowing residents to work close to home, thus eliminating the need to commute to and from the city each day. The outermost area would be designated for agriculture so that nearby farmers would have a ready market for their products and workers within the city would have a constant supply of fresh and wholesome food. The outer ring would also supply a rural setting for such institutions as agricultural colleges and convalescent homes.

Howard deemed the inclusion of this "green belt" around the perimeter of the towns as vitally important. This swath of less-developed land would prevent urban sprawl, keeping the garden cities within manageable space and population limits. As these communities filled up, others would be constructed farther out, encircling the larger central city as so many interconnected spokes on a wheel, each perhaps eventually spawning its own satellites in turn (though in fact the designation of "satellite town" was not adopted for this scheme until many years later).

The name "garden city" has been applied, and misapplied, to countless communities in the years since Howard first introduced the concept. Howard acknowledged that the actual design of the towns might differ from his concentric-circle plan, but the original conception of the garden city was defined by several specific elements: the combination of parks, residential space, industry, transportation, and the surrounding greenbelt, all close to—but deliberately separated from—a larger urban center. Few of the experimental "garden cities" that followed met all of these criteria; in England those that came closest were the towns of Letchworth, begun in 1903 by Howard devotees Raymond Unwin and Barry Parker, and Welwyn, begun in 1919.

Howard hoped that, by applying his ideas, "the old, crowded, chaotic slum towns of the past" would "be effectually checked, and the current of populations set in precisely the opposite direction—to the new towns, bright and fair, wholesome and beautiful."[30] But he intended the garden city to be much more than simply a way to give a handful of industrial workers pretty environments. Howard wanted to launch a revolution in residential town building. Near the end of his book, after laying out how such a venture might be accomplished, he made clear the scope he had in mind; he hope that "the true path of reform, once discovered, will, if resolutely followed, lead society on to a far higher destiny than it has ever yet ventured to hope for.[31] Despite his intentions, it is not the social reform aspect, but the physical design of the cities—or, more accurately, a rather imprecise interpretation of this design—for which Howard is best remembered.

The garden city idea in its broadest form was, in the 1920s and 1930s, seen by many planners as the best hope for American housing for the future, a way of recapturing past social modes in spaces tailored for the industrial era. Lewis Mumford wrote in 1924, "Far from being a strange importation from Europe, the garden-city is nothing more or less than a sophisticated recovery of a form that we once enjoyed on our Atlantic seaboard."[32] This basic garden city concept, adapted to fit the new machine age, laid the groundwork in the early twentieth century for what was known as the "new town" movement in the United States, an important influence in community planning by the 1930s. Among the most ambitious endeavors to utilize some of the garden city's key ideas, the Greenbelt towns had to address new issues that Howard could not have imagined, most important among them how to accommodate this urban–rural concept to the rapidly changing realities of an age defined by mass-production, machine technology, and the automobile.

SUBURBS

One might be tempted to argue that the garden city idea amounted to nothing more than a glorified suburb. Howard was certainly correct in believing that workers would prefer to live away from the overcrowded city if they had the choice. But in Howard's day, and for decades after, suburbs were reserved for the middle and upper classes. Those in the working class and below could not hope to live farther away than walking distance from the plentiful employment opportunities of the city unless, as in the garden city model, jobs could be drawn away from the city and closer to wholesome environs in the countryside. Even public transportation in the form of streetcars generally came at too dear a price for most industrial or menial workers, so proximity to work was paramount.

Many cities thus melt almost seamlessly into the working-class residential districts that surround them. In the 1920s and 1930s, such areas housed workers who could afford to live outside of the worst inner-city neighborhoods, perhaps renting or even buying cheap homes on the urban periphery. Some classified these as working-class suburbs, but others reserved the term "suburb" for something more removed from the city, more closely related to pseudo-rural living.

However one defined them, suburbs attracted large numbers of Americans, a trend that seemed likely to persist for some time to come, though rarely an option for industrial and other unskilled workers.[33] As Harlan Paul Douglass explained in 1925, the suburb

> is the push of the city outward. It makes physical compromises with country ways but few compromises of spirit. It is the city trying to escape the consequences of being a city while still remaining a city. It is urban society trying to eat its cake and keep it, too.[34]

Suburbanites might want to reside away from the city, but few wished to sever all connections to it. As services such as metropolitan sewer districts and water supplies brought the conveniences of urban life to the wider surrounding areas in the early twentieth century, suburban living became increasingly attractive to those who had the financial resources to achieve it.[35]

A turning point in the move toward more widespread suburbanization came in the 1920s, when increased car ownership opened to a much larger portion of the population the possibility of commuting into and out of cities. Yet cars were expensive enough to purchase and maintain that true suburbs still remained beyond the economic reach of most working-class Americans. Public transportation served many outlying communities, but not all.

And the suburban homes themselves were hardly inexpensive. With balloon-frame construction and the popularity of the bungalow style, houses in the borderlands did become somewhat more affordable during this period, but even with these innovations the cost of a suburban home generally excluded those below the middle class. Prior to the twentieth century, home construction or purchase costs were expected to be paid in cash. If potential homeowners had to borrow the money, they usually turned to friends and family. In the early twentieth century this began to change, as building and loan companies started offering financing, but credit required a down payment, good references, and steady employment. In this era factories routinely laid off workers to retool the machinery or to allow demand to catch up to supply; "steady" employment eluded many in the working class. Thus, even as less-expensive housing options and financing became more available, suburbs largely remained the realm of the skilled and managerial classes.[36] Those of lower status had to make do with the often-substandard housing and neighborhoods available in and very near the cities.

Yet experts and reformers saw the benefits of extending the suburban dream. Marsh had urged as early as 1909 that because of increased urban crowding, homes should be constructed "in all the outlying districts."[37] Douglass warned in 1925 that "a crowded world must be either suburban or savage."[38] As experts worried about the deleterious effects of city life, particularly on the nation's children, widespread home ownership in the suburbs appeared to present the perfect solution. Yet the very large and seemingly intractable impediment of cost remained.

Suburbs presented attractions beyond just additional space and fresher air. When Louis Wirth pointed out that depersonalization resulted "wherever large numbers of differently constituted individuals congregate," he hit on the reason many Americans sought suburban life. This concern about "differently constituted individuals"—different in race, ethnicity, religion, tastes, education, income level—played a major role in fueling suburbanization, as people sought communities made up of others like themselves and as they fled from those who seemed increasingly and disturbingly different.

This homogeneity, in addition to drawing residents out of the cities, appealed to many reformers as well. Douglass, for example, wrote in 1925:

> Because they are largely composed of like-minded people to whom cooperation should not be difficult, and because of the environmental advantages of roominess, the suburbs, in spite of their limitations, are the most promising aspect of urban civilization... Formed out of the dust of cities, [suburbs] wait to have breathed into them the breath of community sentiment, of neighborly fraternity and peace.[39]

In 1930 sociologist Ray E. Baber made the case that "family solidarity is most easily maintained in a fellowship with other families all having common acquaintance and interests."[40] For many experts, suburban communities made up of Americans of similar backgrounds appeared to offer the best hope for rekindling the neighborly, cooperative, democratic spirit.

Yet the sameness of suburbia also came in for criticism. Perhaps the most well-known and biting satire came from Sinclair Lewis, whose novels *Main Street* and *Babbitt* exposed the banality, the smallness, of small-town and suburban life. Some experts also believed that in at least one way suburbs offered no improvement over cities. Housing expert Carol Aronovici noted that "more and more it is found that local communities are merely stopping places in the shuttling between the bedroom and the office or factory, and are not, in the strictest sense of the word, communities or neighborhoods."[41] If a suburb became merely a place to sleep at night, if it failed to create a true neighborliness and community spirit, some argued, it served not to address the real problem, but only to paper over the alienation so pervasive in modern America with a pretty covering.

If cities should theoretically be avoided, and suburbs proved too expensive for most of the lower-middle and working classes, what could be done to bridge the divide between affordability and livability? A smattering of philanthropic efforts at affordable housing had been made in the early twentieth century, but they had largely run up against the unyielding reality that low cost necessitated low quality.[42] As a result, some reformers began to argue that the United States needed to follow the European lead and provide housing by implementing a tool that many ordinary citizens saw as distinctly un-American, and very likely socialist: government subsidy. It would take an economic crisis of never-before-imagined proportions to open even the possibility of such a plan.

3

THE NEW DEAL

Let it be from now on the task of our Party to break foolish traditions.

—Franklin Delano Roosevelt, 1932

The Depression had worsened steadily after the stock market crash, and Herbert Hoover had adamantly defended his belief that any sort of direct relief from the government would set the nation on a path toward its own destruction. By the 1932 presidential race it was clear that the people wanted someone new, someone with fresh ideas, someone willing to take risks to set the economy right.

On July 2 of that year Franklin Roosevelt accepted the Democrats' call to be their presidential nominee. Breaking with tradition, he appeared in person at the party's convention to accept this honor, and gave a speech that raised the spirits of people ground down by years of uncertainty. He stated:

> Throughout the Nation, men and women, forgotten in the political philosophy of the Government of the last years look to us

here for guidance and for more equitable opportunity to share in the distribution of national wealth.

On the farms, in the large metropolitan areas, in the smaller cities and in the villages, millions of our citizens cherish the hope that their old standards of living and of thought have not gone forever. Those millions cannot and shall not hope in vain.

I pledge you, I pledge myself, to a new deal for the American people. Let us all here assembled constitute ourselves prophets of a new order of competence and of courage. This is more than a political campaign; it is a call to arms. Give me your help, not to win votes alone, but to win in this crusade to restore America to its own people.[1]

A "new deal"—the phrase caught the ear of the press and the imagination of the country. Exactly what this new deal would entail was a mystery, but it sounded better than the waiting and worrying that had defined the Depression up to that point.

Whatever one thinks of his politics and policies, FDR undeniably boosted the American mood with his buoyant confidence. His early pronouncements were virtually devoid of concrete details on how he might steer the nation out of its crisis, yet somehow his nebulous promises gave people hope. He did not pretend that recovery would be easy. In his first inaugural address he admitted, "Only a foolish optimist can deny the dark realities of the moment." But he also famously insisted that "the only thing we have to fear is fear itself—nameless, unreasoning, unjustified terror which paralyzes needed efforts to convert retreat into advance." To bring the nation into the light, he would need help. "If we are to go forward, we must move as a trained and loyal army," he asserted. And if he failed to say exactly what form that forward movement might take, the public took comfort in the prospect of deliverance from the crisis. Their new president spoke, it seemed, directly to each of them: "This Nation asks for action, and action now. Our greatest primary task is to put people to work. This is not an unsolvable problem if we face it wisely and courageously." And the nation, for the moment, believed.[2]

In 1967, Rexford Tugwell published *FDR: Architect of an Era*. In it he tried to explain his enigmatic former boss. Franklin Roosevelt had grown up the only son of a wealthy family on an estate on the Hudson River in New York. Franklin's parents had instilled in him the concept of *noblesse oblige*, the responsibility of the fortunate upper class to help the lower classes, though they might have clarified this definition: "help *within reason*." The wealthy certainly did not feel the need to redistribute their fortunes to the poor, or even to associate with those beneath them in social and economic rank. Rather, they believed that donations to appropriate charities catering to the deserving poor satisfied their obligations.

Not so for Franklin Roosevelt, according to Tugwell, who argued that FDR had possessed a generous character; FDR had believed in a much more egalitarian society and that he had a personal responsibility to bring it about. This caused other American aristocrats to see Roosevelt as "a traitor to his class." Tugwell may have given more credit than was due; it is in fact difficult to know where FDR's true ethical beliefs ended and his carefully cultivated political persona began. Still, he undoubtedly helped the underprivileged, and would eventually be held up as a savior by millions ravaged by the Depression.[3]

Franklin had been inspired by his distant cousin Theodore's political career. He proved to be every bit as ambitious and successful, becoming a state senator, assistant secretary of the navy, and governor of New York before becoming the Democratic presidential nominee. The polio that had slowed down his political ascent may have been the one thing in his pampered life that taught him empathy and a level of humility. It also taught him that many faced hardships not of their own making, a lesson he took to heart.

Franklin Roosevelt began his presidency in 1933 facing a nationwide calamity. Fourteen million Americans were out of work, businesses had closed, families had lost homes, and the US banking industry teetered on the edge of absolute collapse.[4] But he also enjoyed some huge advantages: his Democratic party controlled both houses of Congress, he had won by a comfortable margin over the widely discredited Hoover, and the people looked to him with a desperation that allowed for audacious actions. His initial support essentially forced those legislators who normally would have been among his fiercest opponents to go along with his plans for the moment. But eventually the honeymoon period would come to an end.

At that point, he still commanded the admiration of much of the nation, and the people generally placed their faith in him. Yet the passage of time allowed Republicans and other conservatives across the United States to express their disdain for his experimentation more freely, particularly as it became increasingly obvious that none of his programs held the magic formula for ending the Depression.

This was a politically charged and polarized era. Conservatives feared that the nation was being taken in a radical new direction, a concern that predated FDR's presidency, going back at least to the Progressive Era, when reformers and dreamers of all sorts began calling on the federal government to take on roles never expected of it previously. Debates roiled over how far to extend federal authority and obligation.

The period between the two world wars brought new political uneasiness and upheaval. Following World War I, Russia's turn to communisim seemed, to most Americans, an ominous development. In the years just after the war the United States experienced bombings, a Red Scare, and an increase in anarchist and other "subversive" movements. A series of labor strikes gave rise to fears of growing socialist influence, which in turn sparked a backlash aimed at unions and other seemingly dangerous organizations. As Frederick Lewis Allen explained in his 1931 book *Only Yesterday: An Informal History of the 1920s*, Americans

> were listening to ugly rumors of a huge radical conspiracy against the government and the institutions of the United States. They had their ears cocked for the detonation of bombs and the tramp of Bolshevist armies. They seriously thought—or at least millions of them did, millions of otherwise reasonable citizens— that a Red revolution might begin in the United States the next month or next week.[5]

The fact that the revolution did not come only partially quieted the fears.

The Depression heightened the national level of anxiety. Labor strikes continued throughout the 1930s; even when jobs were scarce, workers fought for better treatment, shorter hours, fairer pay. Their frustration in the face of nationwide economic uncertainty spilled over at times, with dissatisfied laborers staging sit-down strikes and otherwise resisting what appeared to be an increasingly heartless system. As a result, union leaders, strikers, and others expressing discontent with the status quo regularly faced accusations of being socialists, communists, anarchists, and any number of other types of dangerous agitators.

The threat of radicalism in the 1930s may have been somewhat overblown, but it was not wholly imagined. Authors served up books on why America should become fascist or socialist.[6] Some asked whether the nation would benefit from making Roosevelt a dictator, or whether, in fact, he already was one.[7] Lewis Mumford called for "basic communism," meaning not communism in the Soviet mold, but a form of governmental oversight of the economy.[8] *The Annals of the American Academy of Political and Social Science* in 1935 devoted an entire issue to the debate over the possibility of the nation turning to communism, socialism, fascism, or dictatorship.[9]

Many feared the coming of a second American Revolution, fueled by the highly combustible combination of radicalism and desperation. Rexford Tugwell worried that just such an upheaval might burst to life under growing social and class antagonisms. Roosevelt, he believed, was well equipped to calm these insurgent tendencies, but, he warned, "another Harding, another Coolidge, another Hoover entrusted with leadership now would set us back... and at the end of it there might not be another leader with the genius to avert a revolution."[10] A 1932 study involving both employed and unemployed engineers asked for responses to the statement: "A revolution might be a very good thing for this country." Six percent of the employed men and 23 percent of the unemployed men polled either agreed or strongly agreed.[11] To the statement "What we need in this country is a good strong dictator," 19 percent of the employed and 34 percent of the unemployed gave approving responses.[12] It is little wonder that people already stunned by what seemed to be the complete breakdown of the nation's economy also feared the potential crumbling of its political system and democratic institutions.

Yet we must be cautious about taking such attitudes as a sign that revolution was truly imminent. Fifty-six percent of the unemployed and 61 percent of the employed men also affirmed that "the United States comes closer to being an ideal country than any other" (it is worth noting here that a larger portion of the unemployed men were immigrants, so even though they had cause to feel anxious about their futures, they also had a deep personal investment in the United States). A full 82 percent of the unemployed and 89 percent of the employed men asserted that "after all, this is a pretty good country."[13]

The frustrations arising from uncertainty undoubtedly pushed some to seek unorthodox solutions. If a strong dictator or a revolution could bring about the economic stability they longed for, it was a price that, in theory at least, some were willing to pay. Although it was easy to express such views in the low-stakes realm of a survey answer, there is no evidence that many actually would have condoned a true revolution or the efforts of a dictator to take power. One telling response to the survey demonstrated a more conventional American attitude: among both employed and unemployed men, 73 percent agreed or strongly agreed with the sentiment that "hard luck should only spur a man to do better."[14] It seems likely that, as this response indicated, rugged individualism still trumped collective action in the minds of most Americans in 1932.

Still, the scope of bleak suffering made many pundits worry. Spencer Miller, Jr., an advocate for labor education and future assistant secretary of labor, summed up the theory in 1933, writing, "Across the whole economic field… there stretches today the vast problem of unemployment as a criticism of our economic system, if not as a threat to the very stability of our social order."[15] Desperate people, many feared, might commit desperate acts. Job creation was therefore crucial to the New Deal.

As the Depression continued, Americans of every social and economic stripe tried to identify the boundary between necessary governmental assistance and dangerous overreach, fiercely disagreeing over where that line should be drawn. Some worried that federal relief, even in times of crisis, would breed weakness, chipping away at the core independent American character. Others demanded that their government throw a life preserver to those being dragged under by the economic maelstrom.

Many scholars have extensively examined the New Deal; it need not be covered in depth here. A brief discussion of a few pertinent ideas will suffice. Some of Roosevelt's new agencies and policies were tremendously popular, while others sparked debate, or even outrage, on the part of his critics. Those programs that offered obvious benefits to the nation as a whole, rather than to just a handful of individuals, tended to be welcomed by the American people. Those that shored up traditional ideas—the value of hard work, for example—generally found favor as well, while those that seemed more like unearned handouts were far more likely to face stiff opposition.

The Civilian Conservation Corps (CCC) offers perhaps the best example of a popular New Deal agency. This program took young men and gave them meaningful work. It was well understood that a large population of dissatisfied, directionless, unemployed young men could pose a huge danger to society. The CCC took this potentially destabilizing group and gave them a purpose. They were organized into military-style camps and sent across the nation to do useful work in reforestation, conservation, and the improvement of public lands. The men worked hard, and most of their pay was sent to their families back home. It was a program that benefited those who took part, their families, and the economy fed by the purchases those families were then able to make. It also benefited the nation by providing environmental conservation and improved recreational facilities that are still being used today. The CCC, like all New Deal programs, had critics, but for most Americans there seemed to be little to complain about (the CCC, however, did not include women and it almost always segregated minorities into separate units). It seemed to be an example of the concept of public works at its best.[16]

Other programs sparked far more controversy, either because of their cost or their aims or methods. The Agricultural Adjustment Act and its corresponding agency, the Agricultural Adjustment Administration (AAA) fall into this category. Farmers had begun to feel the oncoming depression years before the rest of the nation. Following the First World War they saw great profits as a devastated Europe purchased its food from the United States. Many bought equipment and land on credit, but as European agriculture recovered, US profits began to fall. By the 1929 stock market crash, the nation's farmers were already in extreme economic distress. If the CCC was a fairly straightforward concept, the AAA was the opposite, with a complex set of programs and policies aimed at helping farmers weather the crisis.

A particularly controversial policy paid farmers to leave land unplanted in order to increase scarcity and drive up prices for crops. Although this helped farmers, it occurred at a time of great need and rampant hunger. Many found the idea of *not* growing more food ill-conceived, almost evil. More controversial still was the decision that, since the growing and livestock-birthing season had already begun, the only way to ensure lower supply was to destroy some of what already existed. The federal government bought piglets and slaughtered them, and paid cotton farmers to plow their already-growing fields under. Much of the American public was outraged by the deliberate destruction of food and crops, but administrators believed it was necessary to drive up agricultural prices.

The idea of the federal government telling anyone how much they should grow seemed, to many, frankly un-American. It represented a blatant interference in the near-gospel law of supply and demand. Additionally, the payments went to the landowners, meaning that absentee landlords received payments for leaving fields fallow, but their tenants were left with no money and no way to earn it. This hit poor White and African American families in the South particularly hard. Moreover, if anyone expected the AAA to single-handedly save farmers from their economic plight, they were sorely disappointed. In the end, the program did help, but it was not a miracle cure.[17]

The idea of work relief—putting people to work rather than simply giving them a handout—and public works projects—the use of federal funds to build infrastructure and other endeavors for public benefit—became a less-controversial cornerstone of the New Deal. Two agencies came to dominate the area of public works: the Public Works Administration (PWA) and the Works Progress Administration (WPA). Along with the TVA, these account for the majority of the era's major building efforts.

These two programs are too important and too large to cover in any meaningful way here, but to oversimplify: The PWA was aimed mainly at reviving industry through building projects that coincidentally put people to work, while the WPA was more directly and purely work relief. The PWA began in 1933. The primary idea behind it was to stimulate the economy by creating a need for building supplies, though the results went well beyond this narrow goal. Among its accomplishments, it produced roads, highways, bridges, airports, schools, libraries, post offices and other federal or municipal buildings, hospitals, and housing, mainly in the form of low-income slum clearance projects.[18]

Two somewhat competing ideas defined earlier programs such as the PWA: "pump-priming" and "self-liquidation." The rationale behind many New Deal agencies relied on the pump-priming analogy. Before the widespread construction of public water systems, most rural and urban residents got their water from wells; in the nineteenth century this procedure was aided by metal hand-operated pumps. These pumps had leather gaskets to ensure the tight fit that would create the suction to raise the water. If the gasket was too dry, the fit would be loose and the pump would not operate. The apparatus first had to be primed by pouring a bit of water into it to wet the leather. This lay behind the metaphor of "priming the pump" in economics. First a bit of money had to be spent in order to get the mechanism, which had sat idle for too long, working again. The principle was sound, but the second concept often negated any potential benefits.

The second idea, one that was all but sacrosanct before the New Deal, was that all public works projects must be self-liquidating. This meant that they would eventually recoup the expense that went into them, either through usage fees (rents, tolls, and such) or taxation. By 1935 it had become clear that this model was too limited to meet the dire needs of the Depression. Historians have identified the period beginning in this year as the "second New Deal"—a time when the need to be self-liquidating was all but discarded, although many conservatives insisted that this was a grave mistake. Thus projects such as the Greenbelt towns could proceed without the expectation that rents generated by the homes would eventually cover the costs of planning and construction. The expense would be written off as essential, the only way to get people back to work, which was in turn the only way to get the economy running smoothly again.

The WPA was a product of this second New Deal. Created in 1935, this agency oversaw the construction of the same sorts of projects as the PWA with the exception of housing. The key difference lay in the emphasis: the PWA had, at its core, used loans to encourage building projects that would jump-start the industries supplying construction materials. The WPA, in contrast, used building projects as a way to directly put people to work. In addition to paying workers to build libraries, schools, and other public projects useful to the general population, the agency also employed artists (more on this in Chapter 7) and writers. By this time the American people had largely accepted the fact that the government would need to spend, and spend big, to restart the economy. For the most part they saw the benefit of creating jobs while also creating lasting works for the public good.

One recent scholar has called the PWA and WPA together "a public works revolution."[19] It is easy to see why: the programs oversaw the construction of nearly five hundred airports, nearly eighty thousand bridges, and nearly forty thousand public buildings, to name just a few of the types of facilities the programs provided.[20]

OPPOSITION TO FDR AND THE NEW DEAL

The Great Depression, then, spawned the most stunning era of experimentation that the United States had known since the days of the early republic. Historians and pundits would spend the coming decades debating FDR's competence and effectiveness in trying to stem the economic crisis, but there is no doubt that, for better or worse, he took the nation in a new direction. For his critics, that was precisely the danger.

Perhaps the most ominous predictions saw the president's growing power and the New Deal overall as tending toward dictatorship.[21] Yet exactly what would count as an American dictatorship was open to debate. An editorial appearing in a 1933 issue of *Barron's* addressed the topic:

> More or less furtive suggestions of more or less dictatorship after March 4 [FDR's inauguration] continue to crop up here and there from time to time. Of course we all realize that dictatorships and even semi-dictatorships in peace time are quite contrary to the spirit of American institutions and all that. And yet—well, a genial and lighthearted dictator might be a relief from the pompous futility of such a Congress as we have recently had.[22]

The author stated that it was becoming clear that any efforts at solving the Depression "will be done by Executive order under a grant of emergency powers or it will not be done at all. So we return repeatedly to the thought that a mild species of dictatorship will help us over the roughest spots in the road ahead."[23]

Not surprisingly, many Americans were far less sanguine. According to an editorial in the *Catholic World* in April 1934, an invitation to critics to come "fire away" at Roosevelt and the New Deal "filled five large auditoriums and every critic had his say, from wild-eyed communists who blamed the administration for timidity, to timorous conservatives who feel that the Constitution has been jettisoned and that the Republic is already on the rocks." Yet the author of this editorial sought to calm fears of an American dictatorship, pointing out that the simple fact that freedom of speech and freedom of the press allowed FDR's critics to voice their opposition constituted evidence that the president was no dictator.[24]

A close corollary to fears of a dictatorship held that increasing federal dominance represented the first move toward creating a fascist state.[25] E. Francis Brown, a historian and editor of *Current History*, addressed this concern in a 1933 article entitled "The American Road to Fascism." Brown saw fascism as specifically driven by class struggle. Roosevelt had, he said,

> appealed to the country in a campaign that had featured a mysterious something called the new deal. The mass of voters had little understanding of what constituted the new deal; they wanted only a change—a change for the better, of course—but revolutionary movements are seldom specific.

Brown acknowledged that FDR was hardly a fascist in the same vein as Mussolini or Hitler, and that the president came by his powers through legitimate democratic channels, yet still exhibited disturbing tendencies.[26]

Throughout 1934 and 1935 others voiced similar concerns about the potential correlation between Roosevelt, the New Deal, and fascism. Pastor Hugh Stevenson Tigner wrote an article for the *Christian Century* in May 1934 that asked the question, "Will America Go Fascist?" Tigner argued that Americans had in the past overreacted to perceived radical threats. "Everyone who had any understanding of the American scene knew perfectly well at the time that our post-war 'red menace' was a ridiculous though vicious piece of fiction," he wrote. Yet he saw the current situation as more dangerous, and contended that a fascist future for the United States was entirely possible. Admitting that he was uncertain, he concluded: "If I seem to think that [factors] are stacked in favor of fascism, I hope I am wrong and I will be the first to rejoice over my error."[27]

An article a month later by Joseph Brown Matthews, a politically active author and educator, and Ruth Enalda Shallcross, a political economist, asked "Must America Go Fascist?" "No country on earth," they wrote, "has a richer assortment of hatreds which are available for demagogic exploitation for political purposes."[28] The economic and political divides that had seemed so vast by the end of the nineteenth century seemed, in the

Depression, all the more insurmountable, and the fears they raised seem all too familiar today.

Author George Soule, too, identified the disorder and disunion of the nation as inviting fascist tendencies. In *The Coming American Revolution* he warned:

> Anyone can see with half an eye that many of the raw materials of Fascism are lying about within the United States. We have the suffering ranks of unemployed and veterans and farmers, the dwindling numbers of small business men fighting a losing battle against monopoly, the tradition of bumptious nationalism, the racial and religious prejudices, the tendency to violence and brutality, the proneness to organize about vague and mystical slogans.[29]

Although not targeting Roosevelt specifically, Soule clearly saw political trends as heading in a dangerous direction.

A small number of Americans welcomed the possibility of major upheaval in the political system. Lawrence Dennis, a leading proponent of fascism in America, published an article in July 1935 in which he stated that the United States was "headed towards fascism, communism, or chaos."[30] The following year he released *The Coming American Fascism*. In it he predicted that fascism would "triumph" because "it is, among other things, a formula of fulfillment, which people are happy to turn to from the liberal formulas of defeat, frustration, and inhibition both of governmental and private initiatives."[31] Unlike most commentators, Dennis saw these outcomes as entirely beneficial to the nation and its people.

Some experts correctly pointed out that, regardless of how far from traditional democracy the New Deal seemed to have moved, it was much further still from a fascist coup.[32] Journalist Raymond Gram Swing gave FDR the benefit of the doubt. "The President might easily become a fascist leader if it lay in his nature to make this kind of appeal," he wrote. But he went on the say, "Fortunately it does not."[33]

As they first nervously watched the New Deal unfold, and then eventually denounced it, critics expressed concerns about the lasting effects on democracy of growing federal influence and government assistance. Despite the flurry of warnings about possible American fascism in 1934 and 1935, most opponents believed that socialism and communism presented more plausible threats. (Few Americans made any distinction between the two, so most discussions used the terms more or less interchangeably.)

These doctrines did, in fact, find more support in the United States during the Depression than at any other time in its history. When a population is desperate, doctrines that promise to equalize society are bound to spark interest and attract followers. Some Americans did drift toward these ideologies, particularly as unemployment rose. If capitalism had faltered, perhaps it was time to look to other systems. Possibly some unexpected spark might unleash full-scale repudiation of national economic and political institutions—a possibility that sparked longing in some and terror in others. Although few Americans actually joined, or even seriously considered joining, such organizations as the Communist Party, many at least questioned whether laissez-faire capitalism, or even democracy, had outlived their usefulness.[34] The feared revolution never materialized, and in hindsight seems to have been immensely unlikely, but the fear of *potential* radicalism on both left and right was quite real.

PRESSURE TO ACT MORE BOLDLY

FDR's move toward more audacious experiments arose not just from the slow pace of recovery, but also from increasing pressure from the American people. He no longer felt the need to placate big business, as he had already done much to alienate the captains of finance and industry. But he did need to court voters as he looked toward the 1936 presidential campaign. Although it was unlikely that the Republicans could make a strong showing, Roosevelt had to worry about political opponents and popular public figures who developed strong followings by promising more than the president could.

Louisiana governor Huey Long became nationally known for his vocal disgust with big business and his almost equal dislike of FDR. In creating a program he named "Share Our Wealth," he introduced an idea that he claimed would go much further to redistribute American wealth than anything Roosevelt had imagined. He called for the federal government to give every family a yearly income of $5,000—far above what most families earned—and to place caps on inheritance and income. Such a scheme was far too radical for the politics of the era, and was not at all economically feasible, but it garnered enough favorable attention among desperate Americans that FDR had to take notice. Long was a colorful character with an insatiable ambition; these traits caught up with him when, in 1936, he was assassinated.

Another man seemed an unlikely rival to the president: Father Charles Coughlin. A Catholic priest with a popular radio broadcast that reached tens of millions, he initially talked about religion in his broadcasts, but after 1930 he increasingly turned his attention to politics. As the Depression worsened, his popularity rose; his focus on the economic welfare of the downtrodden offered a welcome contrast to then-president Hoover's apparent lack of empathy. He blamed the Depression on wealthy businessmen, but this was hardly a unique stance. A one-time supporter of Roosevelt, Coughlin eventually pushed a much more reform-minded agenda for what he termed "social justice." Like Huey Long, it seems that Coughlin's main motivation was less a concern for his fellow Americans and more an almost pathological desire for fame and influence.

Coughlin's popularity dwindled over time as it became clear that his goals had less to do with social justice than with his own thirst for power and adoration. His political philosophy did not fit the typical American reverence for democracy; by 1938 he was praising Mussolini, and by 1940 he had kind words for Hitler. His "social justice" seemed increasingly like an endorsement for authoritarianism, and eventually his popularity flickered out. Still, between Coughlin and Long, Roosevelt could not help but see how a populist with a huge following making impossible promises could undermine his own political ambitions.[35]

One other man had a tremendous impact on FDR and very likely pushed him toward one of his most long-lasting policies. Dr. Francis Townsend advocated for a nationwide old-age pension. Prior to this, the elderly in America more often than not faced the final years of their lives in poverty and insecurity. Townsend, a retired physician, proposed what became known as the Townsend Plan, but was actually named Old-Age Revolving Pensions. Every American over age sixty would get a monthly payment of $200, which they must then spend before the next month. This, he claimed, would rescue the elderly from destitution while also stimulating the economy through their spending. As a bonus, it would remove those over sixty from the workforce, opening up more jobs for younger Americans. It would be paid for by a new "transaction tax," which was in reality just a sales tax. As with Long's plan, the math simply did not work out; the proposed tax would never cover the enormous cost of the pensions to be paid.

Despite the logistical problems of his plan, fans formed Townsend Clubs all across the country. In early 1935 Dr. Townsend claimed that there were some three thousand clubs, representing 450,000 members, though he never provided any evidence to back up these numbers.[36] His followers loved him and his idea, but he could never provide a coherent blueprint for how it could actually work. His immense popularity almost certainly pushed FDR toward the creation of Social Security.

FDR, then, faced accusations of being a socialist or communist who wished to redistribute the nation's wealth. Others claimed that he was a secret fascist or a would-be dictator. Still others called him a tool of big business, unconcerned with the economic struggles of ordinary people. Trying to find policy positions that would hopefully disprove each of these took quite a bit of political skill.

Although he sparked harsh criticism at the time, today it seems that FDR was more the smooth politician than a Machiavellian mastermind or clueless puppet. He sought to end the Depression out of true concern for his fellow Americans, but not coincidentally, success would earn him the devotion of the people and ensure him a stellar political legacy. He was certainly not burdened by an overabundance of ideology. His New Deal represented something of a hodgepodge of approaches and experiments aimed at alleviating a wide array of economic issues including slumping farm profits, an unstable banking system, foreclosures, hunger, industrial overproduction, and, of course, massive unemployment. His advisers offered one theory after another on the causes and cures, resulting in a sweeping and confusing program of governmental trial and error.

HOW HISTORIANS HAVE TALKED ABOUT THE NEW DEAL

The Great Depression and New Deal have inspired considerable historical study. As is true for most topics in history, experts disagree on key interpretations, on exactly why events unfolded as they did, and what the lasting impact and legacies have been. Although on occasion cultural critics decry historical "revisionism," this is in fact the work of all historians, to take the sometimes contested facts, add newly uncovered evidence or fresh perspectives, and attempt a more precise interpretation. When it is done thoughtfully and with as little bias as possible, such historical revision is no more radical or subversive than the revision of scientific knowledge as new discoveries come to light.

Most historical topics have seen waves of revision, and the New Deal is no different, sparking debate among historians almost from the moment it ended.[37] Although not all historians fit perfectly into the paradigms that dominate their times, there are some overarching trends. Those analyzing and writing about the past cannot help but be influenced by the issues of their own era.

In the late 1940s the trend was toward what has come to be known as "progressive" history, or the belief that the New Deal served as a continuation of the reform spirit of the late nineteenth and early twentieth centuries' Progressive Era. Historians in this school of thought shared a propensity to see the story of the United States as one of continuing progress toward an ever-expanding democracy, a "more perfect union." In this view, the nation had always faced its difficulties in a way that moved the collective polity, society, and culture forward. The 1930s, in this model, revolved around the personality and policies of Franklin Roosevelt. Progressive historians viewed FDR as a leader who helped the population during extremely challenging times. Class struggle was key. The New Deal stood up for ordinary Americans against the wealthy and powerful, just as Progressive Era reformers had fought on behalf of workers, immigrants, and others who did not have the means to fight for themselves.

In this view, the federal government and the New Deal, with Roosevelt at the helm, offered a way out of the national crisis and toward a better future. It should come as little surprise that scholars would take such a hopeful attitude immediately following the Second World War, a titanic struggle for the soul not just of the nation, but of the world. There was at this time a strong urge to find and hold onto hope.

Progressive views of history gave way in the 1950s to what has been termed "consensus history." Scholars in this category challenged the progressive model of continuous struggle and progress with their own vision: the nation as defined, for the most part, by unity, by consensus. Setbacks such as the Depression, they argued, helped the United States not by propelling it toward some goal of perfection but by bringing Americans together as a people. The consensus historians were less enamored with FDR. They saw him not as a progressive-minded savior but as a wily, largely self-interested politician.

This school of thought saw the rugged individualism and personal responsibility engrained in the American character as binding the people together in a shared identity. These historians largely ignored the very real fractures that had always run through American society—chasms of race, economic inequality, patriarchy, and xenophobia. This history placed little emphasis on marginalized groups, and much importance on the alleged American identity—one centered on White men.

Just as the progressive interpretation of the 1940s grew out of a cautious optimism, the consensus view was grounded firmly in the conformity of the 1950s, a time when the nation needed to stand together against terrifying, but often nebulous, threats. Our one-time ally, the Soviet Union, was now a deadly foe, and one with nuclear weapons at that. Americans wondered whether their neighbors might harbor communist sympathies; spies and enemies could be anywhere. For consensus scholars, the Depression, if it were to have any deep meaning, must be seen as a test of the nation's mettle. Conflicts that threatened to tear the United States apart were pushed to the background, and "the people" were defined narrowly in order to allow for a sense of common cause and unity of purpose.

The late 1960s and early 1970s saw yet another wave of revision. As one recent scholar has noted, "If there ever had been a consensus or a shared national experience it unraveled" in the 1960s.[38] Strongly influenced by the turmoil and social movements of the times, historians labeled as belonging to the "New Left" brought the concept of struggle back into the conversation, but not just class struggle. They looked at the 1930s and saw the same issues that surrounded them in their own lives, struggles over race, gender, labor rights, civil rights, and more. They focused not on shared identity, but on conflict, on those Americans left out and left behind by the larger (White, middle-class, male-dominated) society.

These historians took a more negative view of the New Deal, seeing in it, more than anything else, a missed opportunity, a failure to make the kinds of meaningful changes that would have truly tackled poverty and inequality. Like the consensus historians before them, they found fault with Roosevelt, but whereas the former view accepted FDR as a pragmatic politician, the New Left condemned him as a traitor to the reforming progressive tradition, a president who protected business interests at the expense of the "little man" (and woman). They admitted that he had been good for morale, but not much else, neither a visionary nor an intellectual giant.

Although liberal-leaning historians have had the most influence, we have also seen over the decades a conservative viewpoint that paints the New Deal as inhibiting economic growth. Some have gone so far as to claim that Roosevelt's policies actually made the Depression worse or prolonged it, creating a permanent welfare state that has crippled the United States ever since. For these scholars, the New Deal represents not a movement toward a more perfect democracy, not a unifying moment, but a tragic mistake.

The 1970s and beyond also saw a turning away from the older model of history that had emphasized presidents, politics, and wars in favor of what has been termed a "bottom-up" approach. No longer focused primarily on the long-held definition of history as the stories of great men, historians since the 1960s have been more open to looking at the past in tandem with other disciplines such as sociology. This has led to works that give a substantially more fleshed-out and nuanced picture of the 1930s and the lived experiences of ordinary Americans in this extraordinary era.

Recent decades have seen more studies that home in on specific topics. Many newer histories of the New Deal focus on labor, gender, class, race, identity, social shifts, politics, consumption, and culture, including popular culture. Some, including this one, examine one specific New Deal program and try to find larger historical relevance in this targeted focus.[39]

People outside the academic discipline of history sometimes ask why we continue to study things we already know all about. The answer is that we hope each new examination yields new ways of looking at the topic, new tidbits of information that shed additional light on a particular era or subject. We can never agree on all of the facts, and even less so on what they add up to.

This is not a political history, but FDR, the New Deal, and politics obviously play huge roles in the story of the Greenbelt towns. How one understands the man and his policies will unavoidably color one's assessment of the president's and the New Deal's success. Just as historians of the past saw the 1930s through the lens of their own times, so must everyone exploring history.

What makes the Greenbelt towns worthy of continued study is the fact that they represented something new and audacious—for many people, far too audacious. But as readers of today look around them, they see many of the same challenges: a huge wealth gap, unequal opportunities, deep concerns over the living environments of the most vulnerable Americans, to name just a few. And we continue to see sharp divides over whether the federal government should step in to fix these problems, and if so, how.

4

THE GREENBELT IDEA UNFOLDS

> I have been interested in not the mere planning of a single city but in the larger aspects of planning. It is the way of the future.
>
> —Franklin Delano Roosevelt, 1932

Franklin Delano Roosevelt believed in experimentation. The strength of his presidential candidacy and administration lay in his seemingly unending optimism, his belief that answers could be found by searching long enough and trying enough different solutions. He was a supremely skillful politician, knowing how to say something just vague enough for nearly everyone to think they had heard exactly what they wanted to hear.

Roosevelt also understood the potential power of planning. He knew that letting the free market and tradition rule the day had gotten the nation into an economic mess. As part of the upper class, FDR certainly held no animosity toward capitalism, but he did recognize that maintaining the economic status quo was, at least for the moment, untenable. He understood that it would take experts, working diligently, intentionally, and innovatively, to turn the economy around.

TUGWELL AND THE PLAN

During the 1932 presidential campaign, Samuel Rosenman, one of Roosevelt's speechwriters, had recommended looking to the universities for fresh perspectives on economic issues.[1] It certainly appeared that the financial expertise applied in the past had proven ill-equipped to predict or end the Depression. When the future president turned to one of his most trusted advisers, Columbia political science professor Raymond Moley, for thoughts on who might be a good choice, Moley suggested fellow Columbia professor Rexford Tugwell, known for his forward thinking—many would say unorthodox—ideas on economics and social issues. Tugwell was a prolific writer, having already completed two books—*The Economic Basis of Public Interest* in 1922 and *Industry's Coming of Age* in 1927—and nearly fifty articles, which included titles such as "Human Nature in Economic Theory" and "Economics and Ethics."[2] His expertise on the economics of agriculture and his emphasis on the practical benefits of planning made him a logical choice to advise Roosevelt during the presidential campaign.

When the two first met, Tugwell impressed FDR with his intellect and his eagerness to bring about needed change. Roosevelt brought him on board as a member of the so-called "Brain Trust," the group that proved integral in helping him win the presidency. The two men became friends, and remained so until FDR's death in spite of the president's well-known reluctance to allow any but a select few into his personal inner circle. After the election, the Brain Trust disintegrated, but Tugwell stayed on, serving first as assistant secretary of agriculture, and later as undersecretary of agriculture and head of the Resettlement Administration. He was for a short time one of Roosevelt's closest advisers, and the president eagerly sought his input on issues beyond economics and farm policy.

Yet many found Tugwell's influence with the president unsettling. Conservatives hinted that he harbored radical leanings. He had written passionately about the need to reassess and perhaps revise the way government interacted with the economy. He was openly critical of laissez-faire economics. He had traveled to the Soviet Union to see its system first-hand—certainly not the only curious American to do so, but his detractors later used his visit as allegedly incontrovertible evidence of his anti-Americanism and socialist sympathies. Although in truth he was never the dangerous radical his critics claimed him to be, many nonetheless saw him as a poor choice to be advising the president.

Tugwell believed that the root of the nation's problems lay in poverty sustained by exploitive economic practices. He was neither tied to a romantic conception of agrarian life nor to mindless, chaotic urbanization simply for the sake of growth. He recognized that both the countryside and the city had their entrenched areas of need, each had its own unique problems, and each posed almost overwhelming obstacles to upward mobility for those living at the lowest economic levels. But he believed those challenges could be overcome. "There can be no doubt that we live in a time when there is misery and suffering," he wrote in 1924, "but it is unnecessary to assume because of this that misery and suffering are the significant features of the future."[3] Tugwell knew that both the rural and urban poor desperately needed help, and he insisted that such help should properly come from the federal government.[4]

In Tugwell's estimation, the only hope for the United States, the solution to the problems that threatened to tear the nation apart, lay in a more unified, democratic spirit. But he also believed that such a cohesive spirit was nearly impossible given the inequalities of American society. He feared that the people were losing the cooperative outlook that had been, and continued to be, essential to the national identity. This was no naïve hope for brotherly love and mutual assistance—he understood that men of wealth and power would always resist relinquishing their privileged positions—nor was it radicalism in the Soviet mold, as his critics would claim.

Tugwell recognized that Americans needed opportunities, and he believed that, given those opportunities, they would naturally rally around a new civic-minded national identity, replacing the individualistic, self-absorbed character of the recent past. The every-man-for-himself attitude of uncontrolled capitalism had, he asserted, led the United States down the path to potential ruin. Now the crisis of the Depression opened the door to more forceful federal policies aimed at providing opportunities where they were so desperately needed. He wrote in 1935: "A consciousness of great events is stirring the nation. We feel ourselves caught up in the sweep of momentous changes. We would be dolts indeed if we remained intellectually unmoved and spiritually inert."[5] Tugwell saw the chance to achieve beneficial outcomes from the "good crisis" Walter Lippmann had spoken of. He hoped to effect positive change, to save Americans from their own worst inclinations.

In his capacity as adviser to the president, Tugwell called for governmental intervention, steps such as price controls and production quotas, meant to stabilize the economy and, as a result, to aid the poorer classes. He expressed disdain for traditional economic theory. He wrote in 1933: "The jig is up. The cat is out of the bag. There is no invisible hand. There never was. If the depression has not taught us that, we are incapable of education." Capitalism run wild, allowing men to follow their worst and most greedy instincts, had led to catastrophe. Once, "the anarchy of the competitive struggle was not too costly," he wrote. "Today it is tragically wasteful. It leads to disaster. We must now supply a real and visible guiding hand to do the task which that mythical, nonexistent invisible agency was supposed to perform, but never did."[6] He now had the ear of the president, and the president had a mandate from the people, at least for the moment. It seemed an ideal time for taking bold steps in a new direction.

While an expert in his field, Tugwell also looked beyond economics. He firmly believed that a flourishing democracy depended on Americans putting aside their own petty self-interests. Within this vision, he eventually came to embrace the idea that the best place for citizens to find common ground would be in communities where opportunities abounded, where squalor and isolation were banished, where a cooperative spirit replaced cut-throat competition.

Tugwell expressed his optimism in the power of New Deal programs and policies in 1935:

> They are an expression of the American faith. "The American faith," it seems to me, is preferable to the usual expression, 'the American dream.' A dream implies the unreal and the unrealizable. Faith is the substance of things actually hoped for; it has served to raise men by infinitely slow but certain stages into civilization. It will carry them further.[7]

He was overly optimistic. FDR's many new policies and agencies, in the end, did not provide the universal economic cure Tugwell had hoped; still, the countless individuals, families, and communities that personally benefitted saw the New Deal as a precious gift.

Franklin Roosevelt joined Tugwell in this optimism and enthusiasm for bold action. Exuding a cheerful confidence, FDR had a nearly childlike delight in the thrill of a challenge, the competition to find solutions. Like most presidents, he wished to be seen as a natural leader and national hero. How much his efforts reflected this wish and how much they reflected his genuine concern for his fellow Americans is impossible to say. Regardless of his inner motives, he tirelessly pursued the elusive formula for defeating the Depression. He knew all too well that history would judge his efforts; he had seen how Hoover bore national scorn for his mishandling of the crisis in its early stages. FDR understood that his legacy was on the line.

He also well understood the American people's deep emotional attachment to the concepts of family, home, and community. Roosevelt shared in many of the (sometimes simplistic) beliefs about these institutions, and how they worked to build the cornerstones of national identity. Like many others of the time, he worried about the effects of rapid urbanization, overcrowding, and alienation. He shared with much of the American public a firm belief in the benefits of living close to nature, and he harbored serious concerns about congested cities, especially slums.

Roosevelt had a role model when it came to the importance of civic planning. FDR's uncle, Frederic A. Delano (Franklin's mother's brother), was a successful businessman in the railroad industry who later turned his attention to planning. He contributed to the Chicago City Plan, served as chairman of the Regional Plan of New York and Its Environs, and helped in the effort to plan new parks for Washington, DC. Although not trained as a city planner, Delano was deeply involved in this new field and was well known and respected in urban and regional planning circles.[8]

When Tugwell took Roosevelt to the site near Berwyn, Maryland, just outside Washington, DC, in 1935, the plan he laid out appealed to both Roosevelt the politician and Roosevelt the believer in cozy American traditions.[9] The meeting set in motion an experiment in town building that Tugwell hoped would show the nation the benefits of rational planning and the potential for positive federal influence in aiding struggling Americans.

Yet this initial conversation also offers the first hint of potential troubles to come. Tugwell obtained the president's approval because he promoted the Greenbelts as means of tackling the problem of urban slums. Did he know at the time that substantial slum clearance was an impossible goal for this program? Was he simply manipulating FDR's well-known distaste for urban slums to get permission to try this new pet project? We cannot know, but we do know that this meeting introduced the first set of competing goals and visions for the Greenbelt towns. There would be more to come.

As the project progressed, Tugwell's name became literally synonymous with the Greenbelts, with some reporters referring to the communities as "Tugwelltowns."[10] Although he was undeniably the father of the Greenbelt program, he was from the start also a liability, the target of political opponents and the press, suspected by a wary public of harboring radical ideas. The negativity associated with him, and anything he touched, undoubtedly brought additional scrutiny to the project. He exited the RA, and the Roosevelt administration, well before the towns were completed, leaving others to oversee the details of bringing his vision to life.

REGIONAL PLANNING ASSOCIATION OF AMERICA

Although they were the work of a larger cohort of professionals, the physical designs of the Greenbelt towns can be traced most directly to a small group of respected architects and planners in the Regional Planning Association of America (RPAA). Founded in 1923 by a handful of city planners and others interested in the idea of promoting sensible, directed growth, this group took inspiration from Ebenezer Howard's garden city idea. Despite its impressive-sounding name, the RPAA was a fairly informal group, never more than twenty members strong. But the eminence of those who belonged made this an important organization. Key members included Lewis Mumford, Appalachian Trail founder Benton MacKaye, and respected architects and city planners Clarence Stein, Henry Wright, and Catherine Bauer.[11]

Mumford in particular advocated for more rational approaches to deal with what he termed "the fourth migration."[12] According to Mumford, the first three major American migrations had been the movement westward, the movement to early industrial and company towns aided by the railroads, and, by the end of the nineteenth century, the migration into major urban centers. The fourth migration, beginning around the turn of the twentieth century and still ongoing when he wrote an article by that name in 1925, would be a movement back out of those centers and toward the suburbs. Fellow RPAA member Clarence Stein similarly called for a better alternative to life in what he called "dinosaur cities."[13]

The RPAA was several things at once. It offered a forum for forward-thinking planners and other interested experts to gather and discuss the problems of modern American cities, and to imagine possible solutions for those problems. It was an organization devoted to regional planning, a term its members defined somewhat differently than others in the planning field. As Mumford saw it, most regional planning consisted of "the planning of big cities beyond their present areas." As the RPAA conceived of the term, however, it signified "the reinvigoration and rehabilitation of whole regions so that the products of culture and civilization, instead of being confined to a prosperous minority in the congested centers, shall be available to everyone at every point in a region where the physical basis for a cultivated life can be laid down."[14] Not a fully anti-urban outlook, it nonetheless recognized that large cities were likely to face competition from outlying regions and suburbs.

In 1933 RPAA members had written to FDR and encouraged him to create a program that would "design new communities in connection with industrial decentralization with the object of building a usable environment."[15] We will likely never know whether this notion had any influence over his eventual decision to pursue the Greenbelt towns program. Still, town and regional planning did in fact become public policy under the Roosevelt administration.

THE RADBURN INFLUENCE

Two RPAA members exerted a particularly strong influence on the actual design of the towns. Henry Wright took the lead in designing the ill-fated Greenbrook, New Jersey, and Clarence Stein served as a consultant to the overall Greenbelt program.

Wright had graduated with a degree in architecture from the University of Pennsylvania in 1901. His early career involved designing parks, and he was one of the planners for the 1904 St. Louis World's Fair. His work took him from St. Louis, where he also designed the Country Club subdivision, to the East Coast, where he served during World War I as town-planning assistant for the creation of wartime housing for the US Shipping Board.[16] In 1923 he moved to New York City and, with Stein, became a founding member of the RPAA.

Wright was recognized as a talented architect and planner in his day. He died relatively young, at just fifty-eight; in that time he had achieved an impressive record of professional accomplishments, and almost certainly would have achieved more had he lived longer.

Clarence Stein had absorbed the ideas of progressive reformers, had watched his nation become a modern industrial power, and felt disappointment in the fact that the combination of industrial innovation and reform spirit had failed to solve the problems of American society. He studied architecture briefly at Columbia University, and then spent a number of years studying at the École des Beaux Arts in Paris. While there, he traveled to see the latest European innovations in design and planning, which made a powerful impression on him. After a 1908 visit to Bourneville, a British model town just outside the industrial city of Birmingham, he wrote to his brother, "I felt it to be the most inspiring thing I had seen in England. Utopian dreams can be made realities, if we only go about it in a practical, sane way."[17] The desire to design and execute such "utopian" communities became a driving force of his career.

While in Britain, Stein also met Ebenezer Howard and visited Letchworth. Clearly impressed with the garden city idea, he went on to incorporate significant aspects of the concept into his own work in the coming years, causing him later to be called "the father of new towns in America."[18] During the war Stein served as a first lieutenant in the US Army Corps of Engineers, the post that eventually brought him into contact with Henry Wright, who would become his design partner and fellow RPAA founder.

Along with many of their colleagues following the war, both Stein and Wright expressed concern about the inadequacies of residential construction at the time, with Stein lamenting that most of the houses built were "little more than decorated wooden boxes crowded and shouldered by an army of other wooden boxes," and that "construction has been slovenly—poor materials badly put together."[19] The two saw innumerable problems inherent in the creation of working-class housing.

Among the most pressing of these problems was the fact that residential construction was largely carried out as a speculative, money-making venture, with the result, according to Stein, that the builder "is not interested in supplying a need; he wants to make a profit. He would rather employ a clever salesman than a competent plumber, an honest carpenter, or an efficient architect."[20] Sharing this view, Wright concluded that "it is highly improbable that we will make much real progress in housing improvement until the profit motive can be largely subordinated."[21]

Both men believed that much about the way housing had been provided in the past needed to be changed. They saw that the urban and industrial era had caused enormous shifts in American society and culture, but the way housing was provided had altered little. Their answer to this problem was to found the City Housing Corporation (CHC), with the close cooperation and support of fellow RPAA member Alexander M. Bing, partner in the Bing and Bing real estate development and management company. The CHC was a limited-dividend corporation (in other words, one specifically intended to make only a slight profit), and was to be the vehicle for funding the construction of workers' communities inspired by the English garden city concept.

Like Ebenezer Howard before him, Stein did not delude himself that industrialized nations could return to their rural past even if they had wanted to; rather, he recognized that urbanization was bound to continue, and that something must be done to rectify the problems of industrial living conditions before the situation became any worse than it already was. He contended that

> even if we patch the hole in the dam, the real damage will still exist, the flood will still beat against the wall. The flood is the rising tide of human beings seeking residences within their incomes. Each year... masses have been engulfed by it; they have been dragged down into the congested slums.[22]

Believing, along with many of his fellow architects and planners, that "the city is the mold in which we are formed," Stein contended that the creation of better urban and suburban environments was not a luxury, but a necessity. "The Garden City," he wrote, "is the solution."[23] He envisioned a community where a man's family would live in fresh air, where the factory would not "throw its shadow constantly over his home."[24] It would be a place where employment would be close at hand, making long, wasteful commutes unnecessary. It would offer peace and relaxation, a space for raising healthy children and building a vibrant, thriving society.

Another respected planner influenced Stein and Wright's designs as well as the plans for the Greenbelts, although he was neither a member of the RPAA nor a part of the Greenbelt program. City planner Clarence Perry advocated for redesigning cities rather than creating new suburbs. His interest focused on the community as both a physical and a social phenomenon, and his primary legacy is the promotion of the "neighborhood unit."[25] As Perry explained the neighborhood unit idea, it would be a community limited in size to the area serviced by a single elementary school. Major streets would serve as the neighborhood's boundaries so that children would not have to cross busy roads to get to school; an internal street system would facilitate circulation without adding the traffic, noise, and danger of main thoroughfares within. It would also include a local shopping district to serve the needs of residents.[26]

Before they became part of the Greenbelt planning teams, Stein and Wright had tried out many of the concepts that would find their way into the design of the towns. Their most notable collaboration, the community of Radburn, New Jersey, sixteen miles outside of New York City, would inspire many design elements in the Greenbelts. Along with the garden city, the neighborhood unit idea also found its way into the plans for Radburn.

Recognizing that the world had changed a great deal since Howard laid out his garden city vision, Stein wrote that Radburn would be "the first city that has been planned to meet the problems of the automobile age."[27] He understood the need to consider this new danger: in 1925 alone the United States had recorded 17,571 traffic fatalities.[28] Radburn, Stein wrote, would "answer the enigma 'How to live with the auto,' or, if you will, 'How to live in spite of it.'"[29] Radburn included several pedestrian underpasses, which took foot traffic under major roadways and safely to the other side.

Grafted loosely onto the concept of the garden city, the most important and innovative aspects of the Radburn Idea, or Radburn Plan, were superblocks and "houses turned around."[30] Stein readily admitted that "none of the elements of the [Radburn] plan was completely new"; his innovation was in bringing these ideas together.[31] A superblock design takes a large area for residential space and puts the major traffic arteries around the outer perimeter, as Perry advocated.[32] Ideally this would lead to substantially less traffic and slower speeds within the superblock, making the residential core quiet and safe. Dwellings are arranged primarily on truncated cul-de-sac streets. Believing that this concept would radically alter the way towns would be built in the future, Stein later wrote that "if the superblock had not existed logic would have forced us to invent it."[33] Henry Wright had found the inspiration for the idea of turning the houses around on a visit to Ireland, where he had noted that the orientation of many of the residences placed the kitchens and utility areas of the homes facing the road and the living spaces facing the quiet of the backyard, reversing the traditional American pattern. This would help ensure privacy and quiet for the families living in such homes.

The timing of the Radburn experiment proved unfortunate, with the Depression sweeping over the country before the town could be completed. The City Housing Corporation, which had financed the project, struggled to stay afloat, and eventually failed. As a result, the town fell far short of its intended size. Due to space limitations, it never had a greenbelt—a key aspect of the garden city model—and because of the importance Americans placed on private home ownership, Howard's idea of municipal ownership was never considered for Radburn. Still, despite these fairly significant deviations from Howard's vision, this community is seen by many to be, along with the later Greenbelt towns, the closest the United States ever came to building true garden cities.

Like other attempts at building quality working-class suburbs, Radburn ran up against the harsh reality that adequate homes in suburban surroundings could not be constructed inexpensively enough for their intended residents. Meanwhile, traditional suburbs remained beyond the financial means of anyone below the middle class, and working-class neighborhoods just outside cities failed to meet reformers' demands that all homes should be situated in areas close to nature and provide ample sunshine, fresh air, and safe places for children to play. Wright, Stein, and other planners, particularly those in the RPAA, held on to the hope that a way could be found to meet workers' needs at reasonable costs. The Depression, while cutting short the experiment at Radburn, provided another opportunity to do just that with the introduction of the New Deal.

THE GREENBELT PROGRAM

The goals laid out by Tugwell, Stein, and Wright would guide the plans for the Greenbelt towns, but for President Roosevelt, creating harmonious communities, while desirable, hardly took priority. The immediate official goal of both the RA and the Greenbelt program was to "make jobs, and quickly"; for FDR, at least, all other considerations remained secondary.[34] This meant that keeping men employed trumped efficiency and innovation in design, a fact that, in many ways, set the program up to fail from the outset. Tugwell especially wanted to see the plans executed as rapidly as possible specifically to demonstrate the power of well-planned towns to improve life for working-class Americans, but this clashed with the president's desire to employ as many as possible for as long as possible.

In March 1935, the first month of the project, Tugwell became rather testy with Roosevelt, writing in his diary:

> He [FDR] objected strenuously to my implied aspersion on his attempts to put men to work. He said he thought we ought to do a lot of this public work by hand methods... I told him that that reminded me of a story I had heard of two unemployed men who were watching a steam shovel. One said to the other, "If they did not have those damn machines, we would have a job." The other said, "Yes, and if they did it with spoons a lot more people would have jobs." The President said I was just trying to be clever and reduce the thing to an absurdity, but I had evidently made my point, because he was very much disturbed by it.[35]

Tugwell, too, wanted to create jobs, but he saw more at stake in this program than temporary employment and the disbursement of paychecks.

Roosevelt was right to see home-building as an important tool in fighting the Depression. Home construction, or the lack of it, carried huge implications for the American economy. Housing starts and sales have long been used to gauge the nation's economic health, and Depression-era statistics paint a grim picture. Urban housing starts fell from a high of 937,000 in 1925 to 330,000 in 1930 and to a scant 93,000 in 1933, or just one-tenth the 1925 rate.[36]

The downturn in this sector had a devastating effect on the economy overall. In normal times, the construction industry provided employment

4 | THE GREENBELT IDEA UNFOLDS

for a huge number of Americans; once the Depression hit with full force, so many workers in this sector lost their jobs that eventually about one third of the unemployed were those formerly in the building trades.[37] This had a dreadful ripple effect: construction workers thrown out of work could not buy consumer goods beyond absolute necessities (and sometimes not even those). Their forced frugality was felt throughout the economy as the retail sector saw its own profits dwindle. This provided a powerful incentive for the Roosevelt administration to create residential building projects as potentially one of the most effective ways to reverse the economic emergency.

Once Tugwell had approval to create the Greenbelt towns, he began building a team of administrators to aid in this enormous task. Among the throng, three stand out as having played vital roles: Warren Vinton, John Lansill, and Will Alexander.

Vinton began his working life as the director of the Vinton Company, a building contractor firm in Detroit. He went on to hold several government positions, including serving as assistant scientific attaché at the US Embassy in Paris during World War I. After studying to become an economist, he did research for the Federal Housing Administration, and would eventually become the head of the Research Division of Suburban Resettlement in the RA. In this role, he would oversee the selection of the sites for the towns. Vinton frequently met with the planners to discuss the designs of the communities.[38]

John Lansill and Tugwell had known each other when both were students at the Wharton School, but rather than going into academia following his education, Lansill had gone into finance, finding success on Wall Street.[39] After Tugwell had become part of the Roosevelt administration, Lansill visited him in Washington, at which time Tugwell offered him a post in the Federal Emergency Relief Administration (FERA) as director of its Land Utilization Program. Although Lansill had no administrative experience in dealing with land issues, and was a firm Republican, Tugwell apparently selected him based upon personal regard and trust rather than specific experience or political affiliation.[40] On the day that the RA was formed, Tugwell asked Lansill to move from FERA to head the RA's Suburban Division; he would take charge of the entire Greenbelt program. Although initially not enthusiastic about either Roosevelt or the New Deal, Lansill eventually became a supporter of both, as well as of the Greenbelt towns.

Will Alexander was even higher up in the chain, serving as Tugwell's deputy administrator in the RA. He would take over as the agency's head after Tugwell's resignation in November 1936. Alexander, though not one of the most influential characters in the Greenbelt experiment, is nonetheless interesting because he was both a southerner and an advocate for the rights of Black Americans, particularly in housing. His influence in this realm, however, would not extend to the Greenbelt towns themselves, which would begin as racially segregated communities.

When Tugwell had his administrative team in place, he instructed Vinton to study other possible locations in addition to the one he had already shown the president near Washington. Over one hundred cities were initially up for consideration. To whittle the list down, administrators weighed assorted factors. They ruled out some cities, such as Dayton, Ohio, because they were already slated to get housing developments through other New Deal programs. Selection criteria for the remaining contenders included the strength and diversity of local industries, a reasonably open attitude toward organized labor (to avoid creating a captive workforce that would be at the mercy of greedy business owners), a strong and growing population, and, of course, the availability of suitable land close by with good transportation routes into the city.[41] In choosing the Cincinnati area, they noted that the city's steady population growth made it a good choice. If a city relied too strongly on a single local industry, any disruption to that industry would doom the entire town to failure, so they found a huge asset in Cincinnati's "great diversity of industry" that would hopefully preclude any area-wide economic calamity. They also saw an advantage in the fact that Cincinnati's industrial employment was 21 percent higher than average for the one hundred largest cities in the nation.[42]

The list of potential sites for the Greenbelt towns was quickly pared down to the District of Columbia, Cincinnati, Milwaukee, St. Louis, and New Brunswick, New Jersey, near New York City. RA agents were unable to purchase land in St. Louis by the December 15, 1935, deadline, so that city was dropped from consideration. The plan now was to build four towns: Greenbelt, Maryland, near DC; Greenhills, a few miles from Cincinnati; Greendale, outside of Milwaukee; and Greenbrook, near New Brunswick, New Jersey. An official RA press release dated October 11, 1935, stated that establishment of four "greenbelt" suburban developments to provide low-cost housing for 5,000 low-income families and serve as models for future American communities, was announced today by W. W. [Will] Alexander, Assistant Administrator of the Resettlement Administration.[43]

Construction of Greenbrook, NJ, would later be blocked by a court order that declared the project unconstitutional, leaving just three towns to eventually be built.

THE DESIGN TEAMS: WHO AND WHY

Initially the task of designing the towns fell to engineers in the RA's Planning Section. The first drawings for Greenbelt, however, were apparently rather utilitarian and uninspired; for example, they had streets laid out in a traditional grid pattern that required some sixty miles of roadway.[44] As a result, John Lansill terminated the engineers' role and turned the job of designing the towns over to professional city planners.[45]

Lansill then consulted with the chief of town planning for the Tennessee Valley Authority, Tracy Augur, who was a member of the RPAA. Augur and fellow RPAA member Frederick Bigger discussed the challenge of designing the Greenbelt towns with three of the most well-known and respected American town planners at the time: John Nolen, Clarence Stein, and Henry Wright (Nolen had little further connection with the Greenbelt program once the design teams were chosen).

After Stein and Wright began considering the best way to proceed, they concluded that this project was far too large and complex to be placed in the hands of a single planner or architect, or even a single team of such professionals. They maintained that more diversity of input would result in better-designed towns and more innovation, and so suggested having a separate team for each community.[46]

The RA thus set up four teams, one for each proposed town. Each included one or two principal architects, town planners, and engineers (the engineers' functions related to the relatively unseen aspects of planning, such necessities as gas and sewer line placement, electrical service, and the construction of roads).[47] Much larger teams of design professionals and administrative staff worked under each of these four primary teams.

Stein and Wright helped spread the word, and soon many respected professionals had come on board. Some had previously collaborated with each other on other projects or had attended college together. A pamphlet to promote Greenbrook, New Jersey, proudly stated that "the community is being designed by some of the MOST FAMOUS TOWN PLANNERS AND ARCHITECTS in America. They are men who have PIONEERED in the field" (capitalization in the original).[48] This was particularly accurate for Greenbrook, as Henry Wright served as chief planner for that community. Many in the profession believed that he was one of the best in the nation.

In the hierarchy of the teams, the town planners generally had the greatest design responsibility, making decisions concerning the overall look of the communities, although all members of each individual team collaborated closely.

The autonomy afforded each team resulted in towns featuring different design elements, but driven by key central tenets. The planners wanted to try new ideas, and rejected the notion of copying old designs and plans simply out of habit; if they were to include traditional elements, they insisted that there be a clear and rational reason for doing so. They intended to offer up environments that would provide residents a better life—better communities, better leisure spaces, better homes—not just more of what had been done before.

Showing his propensity to turn to educated experts and weigh varying options, a trait he held in common with the president, Tugwell held a conference at the start of July 1935 in Buck Hill Falls, Pennsylvania, to bring together officials from the various agencies that would be involved in the Greenbelt program. Stein, who took part in the meeting—and was never particularly patient with outsiders meddling in his profession—wrote to his wife:

> There are about fifty or sixty experts in education, health, recreation, housing, community organization, home economics, and everything... They are shooting at this idea of how to build, manage, and create a new community, from every possible angle. It's hard to make any sense of it all: an orchestra of diversified prima donnas, all of them accustomed to having the whole show.[49]

At the end of the conference Tugwell made a sudden announcement in front of the entire group that Stein was "to design one of our towns." This revelation was made without Tugwell's having discussed it with Stein ahead of time, a demonstration of Tugwell's frequent lack of tact and diplomacy.[50]

The administration, however, decided to centralize the design staff in Washington, DC, a choice that clashed with Stein's desire to remain in New York. In the end, Stein's official role within the project was that of a consultant rather than one of the chief designers for any of the individual towns. Although he was not among the project leaders, Stein still played a pivotal role in the designs as the teams looked to this eminent planner for advice and suggestions throughout the project. Stein's influence shows most prominently in how strongly the Radburn concept made its way into the final design of each of the communities, especially Greenbelt. He later noted that the planning of Greenbelt married the ideas of Ebenezer Howard's garden city, Clarence Perry's neighborhood unit, and the Radburn plan he and Wright had created.[51]

The teams assembled in October and November of 1935 in offices set up in a vacant mansion in Washington. By all accounts they faced their task enthusiastically. Journalist Marquis Childs visited the offices filled with drafting tables and scale models, observing that the members of the planning staff were "as bright and fresh as paint," that this collection of economists, writers, artists, and sociologists represented "something brand new in government."[52] Yet the task before them would be complex, and they would face many difficulties.

Despite the challenges, the architects and planners expressed confidence that the program would prove successful, and that their work for the RA would long influence their professions. Henry Churchill, principal architect for Greenbrook, contended that the Greenbelts "constitute the most far-reaching and significant effort in housing today."[53] Greendale planner Elbert Peets predicted that "as one of the elements in the texture of urban regions, we expect the greenbelt town to appear, in varying forms and numbers, around all of our large cities."[54] These men anticipated that the communities would provide not just models for low-cost housing, but also a roadmap for the best overall town planning practices for the future.

Of course, some of these confident predictions may have been self-serving. Engaged in professions that generally depended on a strong economy, these experts sought to demonstrate that they could provide vital services even in times of economic hardship. A 1933 article in *Architectural Record* noted some dismal statistics: in 1928 some $3.6 million worth of building projects had been designed by professional architects; by 1932 just $500,000 had been spent on such architect-designed projects.[55] If those working on the Greenbelt towns could create truly groundbreaking communities, their own legacies—and their employment prospects—would be greatly enhanced.[56]

Unlike Tugwell, the architects and planners seem to have held fairly traditional social and political beliefs. Professional architects in fact tended to be rather conservative in their political views, and most architects who worked on the Greenbelts were Republicans.[57] Overall, they honored the sanctity of home and family, and they expected that residents would fit within the mainstream nuclear-family mold.

In spite of their generally conservative politics, apparently few felt their own views to be at odds with the New Deal. According to historian Joseph Arnold, several of the designers stated that although private practice would be more lucrative when the Depression ended, "they would remain in the Suburban Division [of the RA] forever if they could continue planning more greenbelt towns."[58]

Tugwell had cleared a path forward, selling the president on the Greenbelt idea, securing funding, land, and a circle of professionals eager to bring the plan to fruition. But the path was not without pitfalls and roadblocks. As administrators, planners, and workers combined forces to bring the towns to life, opponents of the New Deal, or of Roosevelt, or of Tugwell, or simply of anything new and innovative, sharpened their knives and set out to destroy this program that they saw as poised to undermine tradition and the American spirit of self-reliance.

SELLING THE IDEA

Understanding that government-built, federally subsidized housing would be seen by many as going against societal and cultural norms, the RA launched a public relations campaign to (hopefully) make people more open to this new model. They stressed the healthy, safe, suburban aspects of the plan. A pamphlet promoting Greenbrook made the case:

The town will be surrounded by a greenbelt of parks, gardens and farms. This means that THE NATURAL BEAUTY OF THIS SECTION of Somerset County will always be PRESERVED. It means that the people who live in the community can raise their children amidst SAFE, HEALTHY SURROUNDINGS. It means that the farmers who live in the greenbelt will only have to cross the fields in order to BRING THEIR PRODUCTS TO MARKET (capitalization in the original).[59]

For those living in overcrowded cities, this would have sounded like heaven on earth.

The promotional materials created for the program paid particular attention to the safety of the Greenbelt designs. A poster promoting the towns offers a prime example (Figure 4.1). The lower, larger portion depicts young boys playing in a city street, acting out gangster-type gunplay. A smaller picture shows boys beside a pristine lake, designed to recall such iconic images as Tom Sawyer and Huck Finn, or even just to evoke recollections of the viewer's own childhood. The text on the poster reads "Which Playground for your Child? Greenbelt or Gutter?"

Figure 4.1. RA poster promoting the Greenbelt towns as idyllic environments in which to raise children. John Scott Lansill Papers, University of Kentucky Special Collections and Digital Programs, Lexington, KY.

If the imagery seems heavy-handed, it is worth remembering that for many in the working class, city streets often really did offer the only convenient play space for urban children. Urban, suburban, or rural, most of the nation's youth spent much of their time, when not in school, at outdoor play. City youngsters were usually shooed out the door in the morning and expected to play outside and keep themselves amused whenever weather conditions allowed. But such play in the congested cities often involved dangerous proximity to traffic, dirt, and unsavory individuals. This was one of the issues reformers pointed to most as contributing to poor physical and mental health, as leading to juvenile delinquency, and as weakening the younger generation as the nation became increasingly urban. The Greenbelt towns, in contrast, provided abundant opportunities for safe and presumably wholesome activities intended to cultivate a healthy crop of children.

The dangers posed by cars also took center stage in promotional materials. The pamphlet created for Greenbrook, NJ, noted that "there have been MORE PEOPLE KILLED BY AUTOMOBILES IN THE PAST FIFTEEN YEARS THAN WERE KILLED BY BULLETS IN ALL THE WARS WE HAVE FOUGHT SINCE 1776" (capitalization in the original).[60] A poster similar to the one highlighting safe play spaces in the towns dramatized the potential dangers of cars on traditionally planned roads (Figure 4.2). The upper half of the image depicts the aftermath of a devastating traffic accident. The background to the crash scene shows a traditional grid street layout. The lower portion of the poster features the cocoon-like safety of a somewhat stylized Greenbelt plan, and declares that "no main highways pass thru" this community. Administrators and planners stressed the idea that traffic hazards could be avoided by the careful planning that produced the towns.[61]

Under the heading "The Penalty of Bad Planning," a booklet produced by the RA entitled *Greenbelt Towns* laid out the problem inherent in the previous, haphazard growth of cities: "Unfortunately, in the past almost no American city has had time for wise planning. Our towns have grown with feverish speed, and with virtually no forethought or control."[62] It went on to call this and the shortage of adequate affordable housing "a problem private industry has not solved"—and presumably never would be able to solve. The solution, as laid out in this booklet, would be carefully planned communities created by the federal government.

Yet this solution brought its own problems. FDR wanted to create the maximum possible number of jobs, which meant using hand labor and unskilled workers when possible. The planners wanted to show how to create superior communities, and naturally preferred the latest and most efficient techniques. These differing goals were in tension throughout the program. It simply was not possible for everyone to win.

Fig. 4.2. (left) RA poster on auto safety in Greenbelt towns. It is not clear where, or if, these posters were displayed to the public. John Scott Lansill Papers, University of Kentucky Special Collections and Digital Programs, Lexington, KY.

Fig. 4.3. (below) Image from Greenbelt Towns, a promotional booklet created by the RA, 1936.

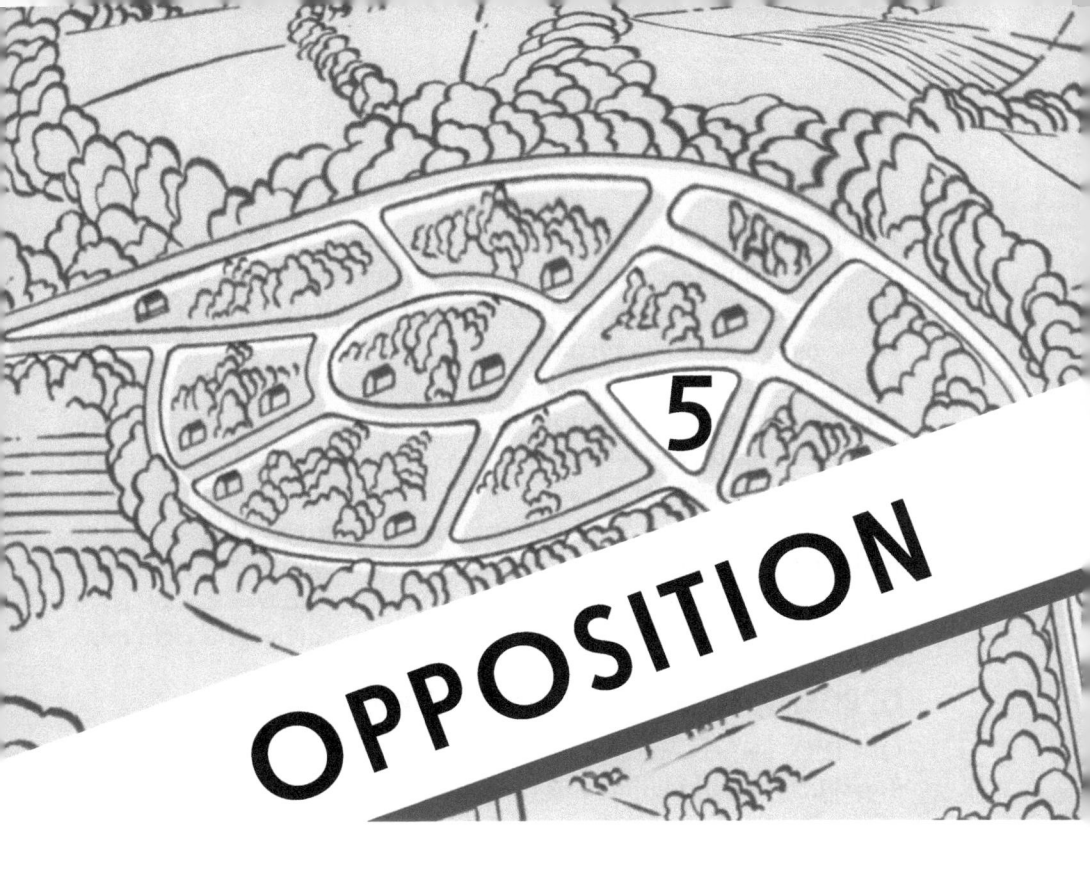

5

OPPOSITION

[The Greenbelt towns] were a part of Rexford Guy Tugwell's vision for the future that is still distant, a vision doubly damned because it was Tugwell's and Roosevelt's.

—Henry Churchill, 1945

Aside from the varying and sometimes competing goals for the Greenbelt program, other factors threw roadblocks in the way of complete success. FDR's New Deal, while heralded as a beacon of hope by many, also faced withering criticism by conservative politicians and media. To make matters worse, the RA at times lost opportunities to gain public support, instead allowing rumors and alarming conjecture about the nature of the project to circulate unchallenged. When officials finally stepped in to clear up misconceptions, it was often too late to fully reverse the negative attitudes. This is not to say that the Greenbelt program was widely unpopular. It seems that most Americans accepted it as yet another attempt, among a dizzying assortment, to right the economy and aid the suffering of the population. But occasional mishandling of public relations certainly gave ammunition to vocal opponents. That conservatives also targeted FDR and Tugwell for generally overstepping their authority only complicated things further.

The Greenbelt program represents only one of many New Deal efforts that provoked passionate disagreement over federal spending and overreach. But because of its particular mission of creating entire towns, government-built "utopias," as many labeled them, this project, more than most, used taxpayer money in a way that opened it up to higher scrutiny. It also triggered questions specific to the project's goals, such as how the government could mold its population to fit a preconceived idea of "good" democratic citizens and, more significantly, whether it had the right to try.

OPPOSITION TO TUGWELL AND THE RA

Of FDR's advisers, none seem to have so irked conservatives as Rexford Tugwell. Critics held him up as the prime example of the potential danger of allowing academics with alleged radical leanings into the upper echelon of American politics. His views made for sensational news stories, even if reporters often exaggerated the threat he posed. One newsman later admitted, "I know that Tugwell is no Communist," but also said that readers had to be given "labels which they can understand." Even at that, he acknowledged that the average reader did "not know what 'radical' means and what 'communist' means."[1] But such categorizations sounded menacing, whether or not those reading them truly understood the doctrines they stood for. These labels conjured fear, and fear sold newspapers.

Thus Tugwell became for many Americans the most recognizable symbol of radicalism within the New Deal. A January 1936 article in *Business Week* referred to him as "comely and cocksure," and noted that "Tugwell is rated as the New Dealer most devoutly hated by conservatives."[2] In spite of his stated intention to stabilize the economy and the democratic system, many felt that he had far too much influence, and believed he intended to push Roosevelt to the political left. Once he rose to national prominence he quickly became the public personality most linked to unconventional ideas and the dangerous potential of social and economic planning, concepts more often associated with the Soviet system than with the American.[3]

As the face of supposed radicalism, Tugwell's presence threatened the success of his most cherished experiments, including the Greenbelt towns. His vision brought him scorching criticism, forcing him to defend his motives and his character. It also sparked criticism of the RA and of the towns themselves, eventually causing him to walk away in order to distance the agency and the project from his reputation as a revolutionary.[4]

As Tugwell later wrote, "We were wrong about the probability of success... This caused countless difficulties in operation and encouraged those who viewed all the New Deal 'experiments' with chilly disapproval to regard this one with especial venom."[5] His influence on the New Deal, while powerful, was short-lived, lasting just from the 1932 presidential campaign until he submitted his resignation to FDR in November 1936.

A 1937 article in the *New York Times* summed up Tugwell's career: "He began, and he ended, disliked and distrusted by many."[6] Although some felt that he had been treated unfairly, his political opponents, many newsmen, and much of the public were relieved to see him go. Charges—whether true or not—that he harbored socialist sympathies were enough to tarnish him as, at best, a radical, and, at worst, a traitor to democracy and the capitalist ethos.

Whether due to Tugwell's involvement or not, many expressed grave doubts about the Resettlement Administration and the Greenbelt towns. Critics targeted the agency because of its large size and loose mandate. Many observers suspected—probably correctly—that Tugwell had purposely left the agency's mission broad and open to interpretation to justify the inclusion of pet projects such as the Greenbelts. Officially, the RA was intended to streamline the oversight of the many farm resettlement and slum clearance programs that had begun under separate agencies. But the wording of the executive order creating the RA allowed for building communities in suburban areas, wording that critics believed had been slipped in rather sneakily.

Felix Bruner, a regular contributor to the *Washington Post* and one of the RA's harshest critics, wrote a series of four commentaries appearing in that paper beginning in February 1936. Entitled "Utopia Unlimited," the pieces outlined what Bruner saw as the horrendous cost and inefficiency of the agency. In this series Bruner noted that the act creating the agency gave the RA, with Tugwell at its helm, the authority to "initiate and administer" projects including reforestation, work to stop soil erosion, and the resettlement of destitute farmers. But, he pointed out, the list of possible aims ended with "and other useful projects." Bruner charged that "those four words gave Tugwell the power to 'initiate and administer' anything!"[7] In the second article of the series, Bruner talked about the "Resettlement housing scheme"—not just the Greenbelt towns but all resettlement under the agency—noting that "like all things Tugwellian, it is far different from accepted ideas—at least, far from those accepted in America."[8]

Bruner called the RA "one of the most far-flung experiments in paternalistic government ever attempted in the United States." Their offices, he complained, occupied "all or parts of 19 Washington buildings—ranging from the palatial former home of a millionaire to temporary Government structures."[9] Such criticism may or may not have had merit—he never mentioned what rent was paid to use the mansion, for example, or whether there was a shortage of other usable office space in the capital—but the charges were, nonetheless, likely to spark the intended indignant response over alleged government waste and extravagance.[10]

It is little wonder that critics eventually challenged the legitimacy of the RA, citing its overly broad mission and the extreme latitude the president had in overseeing it. In the bureaucratic organization of the New Deal, Tugwell, in his RA role, answered only to the president, who in turn answered—at least initially—to no one. But congressional opposition to the agency grew over time. The fact that it had been created by executive order, that it operated with little congressional oversight, that it seemed to be nothing more than a whim of Roosevelt's and, worse, of Tugwell's, made this program a particularly tempting target for those who opposed, or feared, the New Deal.

MEDIA RESPONSE TO THE GREENBELT TOWNS

Any attempt to assess the level of opposition to the Greenbelt towns will result in, at best, only a partial picture. The most commonly expressed opinion by historians of the program seems to be that the towns sparked widespread criticism. For example, Joseph L. Arnold in his 1971 book *The New Deal in the Suburbs: A History of the Greenbelt Town Program 1935–1953*—

the most comprehensive twentieth-century book on the towns—states: "It is obvious that the majority of those who wrote and spoke about the towns reacted negatively." This assertion is nearly impossible to verify, and seems to be an exaggeration. The impossibility of studying every opinion from every newspaper, let alone more general, and largely unrecorded, public reactions, makes it unlikely that we will ever know exactly how popular or unpopular the program truly was. It appears that earlier historians often listened more to the loudest voices, and assumed that they spoke for the majority, but this may have been quite a flawed assumption.[11]

There was, to be sure, ample criticism. Anti-Roosevelt politicians formed a particularly angry chorus. Yet it would be a mistake to assume that much of the public was swayed when the most vocal critics of FDR and the New Deal made exaggerated, and often ludicrous, claims about the Greenbelt program specifically. At a time of such deep national crisis—and millions of individual crises—for most Americans the towns likely represented just another New Deal experiment among many. The public was, by the mid-1930s, accustomed to sharp debates over federal activities, and most opinions probably fell along predictable party lines. Those reading articles about the program likely took a skeptical view of any coverage that deviated from their own political leanings.

Some publications avoided the most vitriolic attacks, but still raised questions about the project. *Life* magazine, for instance, ran an article in 1937 that called the Greenbelt program Tugwell's "flossiest experiment." It followed one family as it moved from substandard DC housing into a new Greenbelt home. The piece noted that this tidy new house had been subsidized by "American taxpayers, the majority of whom can afford nowhere near such fine accommodations for themselves." And the article highlighted a larger problem. "Greenbelt is characteristic of New Deal housing ventures," according to the author. "For nearly five years the humanitarian Roosevelt Administration has stumbled & fumbled along with such expensive, uncoordinated 'demonstration projects,' [and] made scarcely a dent in the great and growing problem of providing adequate living quarters for the 'ill-housed' one-third of America."[12] It was a fair point, but failed to suggest a better alternative.

Some of the negative press that followed the Greenbelt program was riddled with inaccuracies and wild conjecture. The *Milwaukee Journal*, for example, ran an article in December 1935 that showed pictures of what the homes in Greendale would look like—but the pictures were of a Subsistence Homesteads project in West Virginia, which had no connection at all with the Greenbelts. The paper identified the image as showing a "Tugwelltown"—the inaccurate and derisive name often used in the critical press for the Greenbelts.[13] True, the Subsistence Homesteads were also part of the RA, so Tugwell officially oversaw both building ventures, but in claiming that the design of one project indicated the expected style of the other, the *Journal* was engaging in pure, and absolutely incorrect, speculation.

In March 1936 another article made a more blatant misstatement about the town's name, claiming that "with little ceremony the resettlement administration... dropped 'Tugwell town' as the name of the proposed suburban garden village to be built near Hales Corners and officially christened it Greendale."[14] The subheading further misrepresented the RA's previous intentions for naming the town, stating: "Administrator Drops His Own Name for Project." There is no evidence that either Tugwell or the RA ever suggested naming the towns for the agency's leader.[15] Whether inadvertent inaccuracies or intentional lies, such announcements further fueled negative attitudes toward Tugwell and his "vanity" project.

Targeting the overall Greenbelt program, a July 1936 article in the *New York Sun*, entitled "Dr. Tugwell's Satellite Towns Born of Chaos and Red Tape," cited as its source an architect who "after working loyally for months, finally quit the Utopian scheme in disgust." The aggravated former employee claimed to have witnessed immense waste and mismanagement in the program. He charged that there had been a total lack of coordination among the different directors, resulting in enormous inefficiency (though it is not clear whether he meant the different administrators, or the leaders of the different design teams, or just who these "directors" were). The article also made much of the fact that the designers were set up in an $800,000 mansion in the capital, and that the offices then had to be outfitted with drafting tables and other equipment. The situation was particularly absurd, according to the author, while "dust lay deep on drafting tables in architects' offices throughout the length and breadth of the land," and so the work "could very well have been let to private firms and have put men to work in their home cities." Failing to acknowledge that coordination between designers set up in different cities hundreds of miles apart would have been nightmarishly complicated, and almost certainly more inefficient, the article instead concluded that "Dr. Tugwell wanted the enterprise concentrated in Washington, where it could be under his thumb."[16] Of course, it made sense to consolidate the work near the offices of the agency and its head, but that fact apparently eluded the author of the article. As with Bruner's similar accusation, this article made no mention of what the use of this mansion was costing the federal government; just the fact that it was a mansion appears to have been enough to insinuate that administrators were engaged in wild extravagance.

Such attacks in the press must be viewed with caution, however. These few represent a handful of articles out of hundreds written on the program. The false idea that the RA ever officially used the name Tugwelltown and the fact that one alleged former employee in this enormous undertaking spoke out against the effort hardly constitute overwhelming evidence of egomaniacal mismanagement. In fact, like the assertion that the towns were to be named after the agency's head, the article about the alleged waste contained enough inaccuracies to spark deep skepticism about the source. For example, in describing the efforts to purchase land, the author made the agents in charge sound positively nefarious, saying that "to add further to the mystery of Dr. Tugwell's momentous undertaking, draftsmen and town planners employed on the projects were disguised as insurance agents, sent out to obtain factual data, and the surreptitious methods used to obtain options from land owners would have done credit to the worst land speculators."

In truth, when planners did visit the sites, it was to ensure that designs for the towns fit well with the actual topography of the land; yet the newspaper sneered at the idea that planning professionals should "obtain factual data" before drawing up their plans. It is also true that specialized researchers and purchasing agents were sent to the locations to study the areas and obtain land, and that they tried to keep the nature of their project quiet for as long as possible during this process. Some did pose as insurance agents, admittedly a less-than-candid practice. RA administrators knew, just as any private businessperson wanting to buy large tracts of land would have known, that a certain amount of secrecy was essential to keep land prices from skyrocketing. Such commonsense efforts to keep costs down, however, took on a sinister cast in the pages of the *Sun*.

The author also misstated basic facts about the Greenbelt program, beginning with getting Tugwell's name wrong in the very first sentence, calling him "Dr. Guy Rexford Tugwell," reversing his first and middle names. The tirade held up a construction project outside Hightstown, New Jersey, as proof of poor planning by the Greenbelt personnel. But this development, known as Jersey Homesteads (now Roosevelt), was a low-rent housing project for garment workers. It was not part of the Greenbelt program, and was not designed by the Greenbelt teams. The only connection between the two was that both were overseen by the RA. The author of the article had clearly not bothered to check this fundamental detail. Yet the general public would not have caught the mistake, so problems at Jersey Homesteads (and there were quite a few) could easily have been lumped together with the Greenbelts in the minds of many who read the *Sun*.

Reflecting alarmist concerns about potential radicalism in Tugwell's project, some of the most inflammatory articles appearing in the press openly accused the Greenbelt program of introducing full-fledged communism to America. One article, for instance, in the *Chicago American*, bore the title "U.S. Funds Building Communistic Town 90 Miles from City."[17] Author Charles E. Blake warned that "America's first COMMUNISTIC town is rapidly approaching completion and actually within ninety miles of Chicago—eight miles from the center of Milwaukee!" (capitalization in the original). The article supported its charge by quoting from the definition of communism given in the *New Century Dictionary*:

> A theory or system of social organization based on the holding of property in common, actual ownership being ascribed to the community as a whole OR TO THE STATE; A theory or system by which THE STATE CONTROLS THE MEANS OF PRODUCTION AND THE DISTRIBUTION and consumption of industrial products.

The federal government would indeed own the Greenbelt towns, but would in no way control the means of production or distribution of products.

Demonstrating a stunning lack of understanding of the US Constitution, the author offered further alleged evidence of the overt communism of the town by noting that the RA had supplied "everything, in fact, necessary to a town of approximately 3,000 inhabitants... EVERYTHING

EXCEPT CHURCHES" (ellipses and capitalization in the original). For the federal government to have built churches in the community would of course have violated the First Amendment. Such rhetoric, however, sought primarily to inflame public outrage—and to sell papers—not to offer a reasoned assessment.

An article in the *Pittsburgh Post-Gazette* serves as another example of some of the negative reporting, and misreporting, on the project. Like the Milwaukee claims about the original name for the towns, this article said of the Maryland project,

> Originally called Tugwelltown the Greenbelt model city has been stripped of the Tugwell title by Secretary of Agriculture [Henry] Wallace... Henceforth it will be known only as Greenbelt and will have no connection with the costly resettlement administration.[18]

This article appeared in September 1937, some nineteen months after the RA officially announced that the town would be called Greenbelt. Although reporters and politicians often rather sneeringly referred to the towns either individually or collectively as "Tugwelltown" or "Tugwelltowns," the RA never used those names. The Maryland town was known within the program simply as the Berwyn project (for the closest community) until given its official name. The article was correct in asserting that Greenbelt no longer had ties to the RA, but neither did any other program—the Resettlement Administration no longer existed by the time this article appeared, its programs having been absorbed by the Department of Agriculture in January 1937 under the new Farm Security Administration (FSA).

Some especially dubious "reporting" took place regarding Greenhills, Ohio. A very convincing-looking "newspaper"—with no masthead or affiliation in evidence—was distributed in the neighboring community of Mt. Healthy, warning of impending calamity.[19] Where a masthead should have been, it read "Tugwell's 'Experiment.'" Headlines in this sham newspaper included "Normal Real Estate Activity Already Slowing Down as Tugwell Promises to Move West End to the County" (the West End of Cincinnati was a notoriously low-income, poverty-ridden zone of the city). A small fill-in form in the paper exhorted:

> Mail or wire this protest direct to President Roosevelt. Honorable President: I respectfully ask that the Resettlement Housing Project be cancelled in Hamilton County because it is both unnecessary and undesirable.

Lines for the sender's name and address completed this brief, but hardly personalized or convincing, message.[20] Clearly this fear-mongering attempt to halt the construction of Greenhills failed, and the town was built. But it raises the question of who created it, and whether anyone was swayed by the frantic warning.

LOCAL OPPOSITION

It is impossible to know just how most locals responded to the news that a Greenbelt town would be built in their area; reporting on local reactions paints a confusing picture. It seems that most residents of the cities near the proposed Greenbelt towns worried less about the politics of the program and more about how their own lives and livelihoods, particularly local real estate values, might be impacted.

One such concern arose as construction got under way on Greenbelt and men from local transient camps were brought in as laborers.[21] Some newspapers pointed out the advantages of this situation, including an article appearing in the *Washington Daily News*, which announced: "Berwyn Jobs Partially Solve Transient Problem."[22] Yet many local residents expressed fears about large numbers of homeless men working nearby. The stigma of joblessness and homelessness clearly persisted even through the worst of the Depression.

In the Washington, DC, area, some newspapers reported widespread and fierce local opposition to the project overall, while others indicated popular support.[23] An article in the October 10, 1935, *Washington Post* carried the headline "Prince Georges Residents Mass to Fight 'Tugwelltown' Project" (Greenbelt is located in Prince George's County, Maryland). Yet another article from an unidentified newspaper reported just seven days later, "Disregarding reports of a revolt against 'Tugwelltown,' the Berwyn Heights town commissioners last night unanimously decided to cooperate with the Federal Government in making this low-income housing project a success."[24] The public was receiving immensely mixed messages—messages that leave historians at somewhat of a loss as to how to assess the feelings of nearby residents.

We have ample evidence, however, that some of the alleged opposition was more imagined than real. An article appearing in the *Washington Post* in 1947 shows that the plans were less controversial than often depicted:

> Just 3 days [after the October 1935 groundbreaking at Greenbelt] what had been advance-billed as a "mass protest" against the project was made to the Prince George's County commissioners. When all were inside and the doors closed, one solitary dissenter faced officials. He was Lansdale G. Sasscer, then president of the State senate.

Not only did the "mass protest" fail to materialize, but, as the article went on to explain, "Today Sasscer, a member of Congress whose district includes Prince George's, is one of Greenbelt's most stalwart supporters, [and] would like to forget that he once opposed the venture."[25]

The RA bore ample blame for much of the negative public reaction to the projects. When residents learned that the agency was planning construction in their area, officials often bungled the opportunity to get the local population on board.[26] In Cincinnati, for example, administrators initially kept the nature of the developments quiet; as a result, rumors flew. The *Cincinnati Enquirer* reported on November 26, 1935, that up to that point, "although persons have offered various theories as to the Government's intentions, and numerous groups and organizations have gone on record opposing the project, the Government has remained reticent as to its plans."[27] As a result, local residents had speculated that the project would bring in the poorest and most degraded portion of the population and the housing would be nothing more than newly constructed slums.[28]

The initial response of many people to news of the program coming to their area was one of fear and knee-jerk resistance, but it seems that this often gave way rather quickly to a more accepting stance. The day after the RA unveiled its plans, the *Cincinnati Enquirer* reported that "much of the unfavorable sentiment" expressed earlier by local realtors "appeared to subside" once they heard project details from an RA official, though some opposition lingered.[29]

In Cincinnati, some of the strongest criticism of the proposed town came from the Cincinnati Civic Club, which issued a report in January 1936 stating that there was no housing crisis in the area, so no such program was needed. They contended that the Mt. Healthy project, as it was sometimes known, was unwelcome because "the flooding of the local market with 1,500 homes [an overestimate on their part] will be a serious menace to the property owners and taxpayers of Greater Cincinnati." They further criticized the idea of federal ownership of the towns, saying, "Such tenantry is the outgrowth of the feudal system, of which the United States in its entire history has been completely free." The report concluded that "the Mt. Healthy satellite city project should be abandoned."[30]

Albert L. Miller, regional coordinator for Greenhills, answered the Civic Club's charges, contending that "conditions in Cincinnati refute the statement. The feudal system to which [the report] refers has existed in Cincinnati for generations, with the families of the low income group the serfs of the propertied barons whose concept of housing did not extend beyond collection of rents."[31] Information gathered by the RA also challenged the Civic Club's assertions that the region suffered from no housing crisis, noting that there had been "almost [a] complete stoppage in residential construction [in Cincinnati] since 1931," and that because vacancies stood at just 1 percent, rent was increasing sharply due to demand. The report noted particularly inadequate residential conditions for those with lower incomes. (The report, unfortunately, is not dated, but appears to have been compiled between mid-1935 and mid-1936.)[32]

On February 3, 1936, Tugwell himself, accompanied by John Lansill and Greenhills planner Justin Hartzog, attended the annual dinner of the Regional Planning Commission to address any remaining concerns about the project. Over six hundred Cincinnatians in attendance heard directly from the head of the RA as he tried to allay their fears. The *Enquirer* reported the following day that Hartzog had shown photos of some of the city's slum neighborhoods, as well as conceptual drawings of some designs for Greenhills. We have no record of how the information was received, but it seems likely that planners would have assessed the program more professionally, less emotionally, than others.

Hamilton County Regional Planning Commission member Alfred Bettman, later in 1936, dismissed remaining criticism, saying, "There seemed to have been a few people who, for reasons which they did not disclose, tried to stir up public opposition to the Greenhills project. But they utterly failed."[33] Although, as with the other proposed towns, locals expressed concerns that property values would decline due to the introduction of low-cost housing, some were more optimistic. One Cincinnati manufacturer stated that in his opinion Greenhills would "provide a stimulus to property values and to the business of building new homes."[34]

Many others in the Cincinnati region welcomed the RA's plans. An editorial in the *Cincinnati Post* in January 1936 supported the construction of Greenhills. The author noted,

> Better housing is needed for many hundreds of Cincinnati families, part of the great army of 10 million American families who are living in unsatisfactory homes and apartments at the present time. Aside from this general principle, there is the very practical consideration of the 10 million dollars for land, jobs, and building to be spent... It appears to us that an effort to stop this project would be a disservice to the community.[35]

THE GREENBROOK DREAM DIES

It is possible historians studying the Greenbelts have somewhat inflated the extent of local opposition to the towns because opponents of Greenbrook, New Jersey, actually managed to halt the project there. Yet even this example presents a rather skewed picture. Once again, the difficulty lies with trying to separate the few loud voices opposing the project from the quieter (probable majority) in favor.

In the case of Greenbrook, the noisy few were led primarily by John Mettler, a politically powerful, wealthy local Republican who owned a five-hundred-acre tract of land near Bound Brook, the closest community to the planned site. RA purchasing agents had hoped to obtain this tract; Mettler refused to sell. The preliminary site plan for the project shows that, had the construction gone ahead as intended, Mettler's property would have directly abutted the surrounding greenbelt for the town.[36] His wife later acknowledged that he was an ardent opponent of the New Deal.[37] Whether because of this proximity or his political conservatism, he worked ardently to stop the project. Some opponents charged that the whole project was a plot to undermine the firmly Republican nature of the district by offering houses to supporters of FDR.[38]

The initial announcement of the project in October 1935 said only that the RA would be building a "satellite" town for low-income families. Few further details were offered at first.[39] With little solid information to base their opinions on, local residents listened to rumors and let their imaginations conjure up any number of undesirable scenarios. Critics such as Mettler fueled these fears.[40] The Final Report on Greenbrook noted: "At Bound Brook . . . the [RA's Suburban] Division stumbled into a mare's nest of political opponents, who were able to capitalize on the original uneasiness of the neighborhood." The agency, in trying to maintain secrecy about its intentions, had allowed wild speculation to build to a dangerous level, which, once reached, was difficult to refute.

RA officials believed that this opposition was due to something more than just jittery residents. The report laid the responsibility for spreading misinformation squarely at the feet of political opponents of FDR and the New Deal, claiming, "The Republican Congressman for the District had informed [the] press and public that the Resettlement Administration planned to set up $500 shacks in the project area. Other officeholders and affiliates of the Republican machine had spread rumors to the effect that the Resettlement community would be a non-taxpaying colony inhabited by destitute individuals, who were to be transported from the New York slums."[41] By failing to get ahead of the rumors, the RA gave Mettler and others with a personal or political agenda the means to shape the narrative about the Greenbelt program and its aims.

Mettler also criticized the imagined architecture of the town, saying that the project would undoubtedly use prefabricated concrete construction for the houses. "No person," he contended, "would object to the right kind of houses which would bring a more desirable class of people than can be expected to occupy the pre-fabricated, flat roof, slab-type house."[42] The architectural drawings for Greenbrook were not yet complete, but opponents need only to have spoken with the planners or looked at Radburn, Wright's most famous accomplishment, to allay their fears. The designers fully intended for the community to be as attractive and well-built as possible within the budgetary constraints under which they worked.

It seems that Mettler and his fellow opponents were in the minority. The "Summarized History of Greenbrook" states that although there was apprehension before the whole plan for the community had been revealed, "it is now the opinion of local newspapermen and other expert observers that we are opposed only by a small but powerful group of Republican officeholders and wealthy individuals."[43] A local poll was prepared to gauge public opinion on the matter, but after the surveys were printed and ready to go, Mettler quashed the idea. The RA conducted its own poll, which found that 75 percent of local residents wanted Greenbrook. We cannot know how reliable their findings were, but it does seem that opposition was a minority view.[44] The "Summarized History" listed among those supporting the construction of the town "organized labor and building trades," and organizations including the West New Brunswick Improvement Society, the Second District Community Club of Franklin Township, and the Sports Club of Bound Brook. It listed just two organizations opposing the project.

Despite the apparent lack of public alarm over Greenbrook, Mettler and five other property owners who joined him in opposing the town took the issue to the Federal District Court in Newark, seeking an injunction to halt the project. They got their injunction, so while the case continued through the legal system the project was on hold. The suit was eventually heard by the US Court of Appeals for the District of Columbia.

A memo dated January 29, 1936, shows that the administration knew that the Greenbrook project was likely doomed, but also that it had powerful supporters. On White House letterhead, and addressed to one of FDR's secretaries, a handwritten note at the top reads, "Confidential," and "Show Tugwell." The memo says that

> Senator [A. Harry Moore of New Jersey] said there was no question of "us" carrying this county and the need for this project is very clear, but the Republicans have protested it and have taken it to court, and they have gone before the Supreme Courts to restrain Tugwell from going on. The Senator says he understands that Mr. Tugwell has been advised by his counsel that he will probably lose the case and that he has indicated he is not going through with it. He says it is very important that they have this housing project and very important that Tugwell go through

with it whether he is beaten or not, so that the people can see that they tried in every way to get it for them.[45]

Despite this urging not to give up, by this point Greenbrook was essentially dead. On May 18, 1936, the court handed down its ruling: the proposed project at Bound Brook was unconstitutional. Three of the justices declared that the Emergency Relief Appropriation Act, which had allowed for the creation of the RA, was unconstitutional because only Congress, and not the president, had the authority to fund such projects. The two dissenting justices agreed only as far as Greenbrook was concerned, feeling that a ruling on the entire act at this stage would be overly hasty. Initially RA officials hoped to appeal all the way to the Supreme Court, but they realized that if they did, and the Court found against them, all of their projects would be in jeopardy. The plan for Greenbrook was abandoned, but the RA lived on, although under a cloud of uncertainty about if or when the axe might fall on the rest of the program. At this point, the teams for the remaining three towns labored to finish as quickly as possible, hoping that they could complete their work before they, too, were ordered to stop.[46]

Greendale faced a similar legal threat, though with a different outcome. In August 1936, thirty-two Milwaukee building-and-loan businesses filed a suit against Rexford Tugwell and Treasury Department officials to halt the project. They filed a similar suit against Harold Ickes of the PWA to halt work on nearby Parklawn.[47] Charging that the government was interfering in private business by creating unfair competition and that there was no housing shortage in Milwaukee, they argued that there was no need for new housing, and that the program itself was unconstitutional.[48] Other local realtors, however, along with the Federated Trades' Council and the Building Trades' Council, fought for the projects to move forward, contending that their workers needed the jobs created by the two construction efforts.[49] A newspaper article (paper unknown) from May 1936 quotes the secretary of the Wisconsin State Federation of Labor as saying that his organization was taking steps to legally protect the Greendale project from "the attack on the low rent housing projects by selfish interests."[50] Plans to hold additional land for future expansion, however, were abandoned.[51] Meanwhile, work continued at both sites, and both Greendale and Parklawn were eventually completed.

The Greenhills project, too, sparked an attempt at court action aimed at halting construction. The *Cincinnati Post* reported in June 1936 that funds were being anonymously collected for this legal effort. The article, however, pointed out the benefits of a large federal expenditure in the area, and warned:

> The interests opposing such governmental projects have a perfect right to go into court, but we do not believe that keeping secret the names of the contributors will gain any sympathy for the movement. Apparently the promoters must realize how unpopular this attack will be in this community, hence the secrecy.[52]

Eventually word leaked that the Republican National Committee was behind the effort.

In September that same year the *Post* reported that "the local opposition to this federal project has not uttered a chirp for many months. Much of the original hostility faded as the scope and purpose of Greenhills became known." Standing firmly in support of the program, the paper stated, "You can't laugh off the fact that many hundreds of families cannot afford housing that measures up to the American standard of living. We cannot consider it a major crime of the Roosevelt administration that it has tried to do a little something (far from enough) to get rid of the slums and to give some fathers and mothers and their children a little better life."[53]

Alfred Segal, a columnist for the *Post* who wrote under the name "Cincinnatus," weighed in as well, writing,

> Cincinnatus is sad for the National Republican Committee which let itself get fooled by somebody in the matter of Greenhills. These simple-hearted politicians were misled to believe that in Cincinnati there is a sort of uprising against Greenhills and that Cincinnatians are almost on the point of burning the lovely village down; so angry are they about it. This was a great surprise to many Cincinnatians to hear.

Of the many visitors to the New Deal town, he wrote, "Their meditations turned gratefully to a government which cares so much about human beings."[54] Such sentiments, though not proof of unanimous support, clearly show that opposition to the town was not universal.

Even before the Greenbrook court decision, and much more so after, the Greenbelt planners understood that time was not their side. Congress applied pressure to move public works projects along quickly, while at the same time RA administrators employed construction techniques that purposely slowed down progress to keep the workers employed as long as possible. As congressional support waned, planners watched with alarm as their budgets were repeatedly slashed. They understood all too well that the financial resources needed to complete the towns were slipping away. They knew they had to work quickly; a finished town, after all, could not be stopped.

6
DESIGNING THE TOWNS

These towns... will be a demonstration of what new civic patterns can do towards making a better and more pleasant way of living. We have inherited smoke and stones and dirt, chaos and confusion: these experiments may help lead us back to air and grass and sunlight, order and harmony.

—Henry Churchill, 1936

O f the roughly one hundred housing projects produced under the New Deal, the Greenbelt towns program stands out for several reasons.[1] It was the largest of the efforts to provide homes, and the most expensive. It was also one of the few that went beyond mere housing to include the infrastructure of actual towns and to put such a heavy emphasis on the aesthetics and pleasantness of the communities. Although some building projects included infrastructure and others gave a nod toward good design, none combined all of these elements; none set out to accomplish as much as this single program did. As might be expected, such ambitious goals faced plentiful obstacles.

Had the original plans drawn up by Resettlement Administration engineers moved forward, the Greenbelt experiment still would have been huge, ambitious, and expensive. But it would not have been as lastingly significant as it is. These towns stand out because they were meticulously planned, carefully designed, and lovingly crafted to create something new—and yet also old. These were to be *real* communities, not just collections of buildings. They would bring people together and form bonds of neighborliness and friendship, and (hopefully) show the way to rekindle an old-fashioned unity of feeling and purpose.

Today this program still sparks interest in historians of the Depression era and scholars of town planning precisely because it aimed so much higher and did so much more than any of the other residential building projects of the New Deal. What began as a somewhat nebulous plan to create model towns with federal funds grew into something larger, more complex, and, in the end, more meaningful.

The mammoth task of building not just housing but entire towns complicated matters, but also inspired the planning teams to give the program their best efforts. Here they found a grand project where they could truly experiment, could show what they were capable of, could shine. Their directive was vague—"To create a community, protected by an encircling green belt... designed primarily for families of modest income, and arranged and managed so as to encourage a family and community life which will be better than they now enjoy."[2] The haziness of the directive left planners a good deal of room for individual interpretation and innovation.

One challenge the planners faced paralleled a basic problem of the New Deal: the public often saw experts and their ideas as being out of touch with the experiences of ordinary Americans, and not always incorrectly. When Marquis Childs observed the planning teams at work, he was initially impressed and enthusiastic. Yet the more time he spent with the Greenbelt staff, the more uneasy Childs became. He wrote afterward, "I remember being exhilarated and at the same time disturbed after a dinner or a lunch with these pioneers of a brave new world. I felt that somehow they didn't know the Middle West that I knew and the people in the Middle West. The whole process seemed far removed from the deeper currents of American life and no one was working to relate these exciting experiments to main currents."[3]

Yet Childs perhaps misplaced the blame; it was not that the planners and architects failed to know or understand much of the nation, but that, as experts, they brought to the project very different goals than average Americans might have. They could not help but be influenced by their own educations, experiences, and ideas about the usefulness of planning and design. This program offered a chance to do more than just demonstrate the superiority of curved streets over the traditional grid layout or the cost-effectiveness of rowhouses over detached single-family homes. It gave them a way to play with designs, to strategize, to solve the puzzle of how best to produce ideal communities—and all paid for from the (temporarily) deep pockets and largess of Uncle Sam. They must all have sensed that they would never again have such a magical opportunity. It would be understandable if they

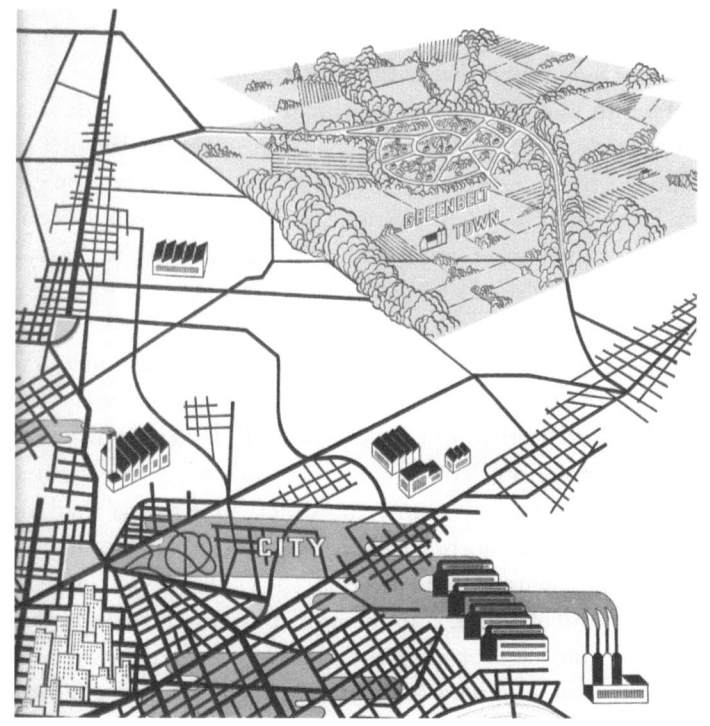

Figure 6.1. Illustration of the Greenbelt concept from the booklet Greenbelt Towns, RA, 1936. In the lower left corner the illustration shows the common grid pattern found in most American cities. The upper portion shows what a Greenbelt town could be, a flowing, neighborly community nestled among green space.

were nearly giddy with anticipation, but it would be equally understandable if the general population failed to share their excitement over experimentation on actual communities.

It is all too easy to forget that the design decisions for these towns did not spring up on their own. The design teams were made of men who were at the top of their fields, and who must therefore have had differing opinions. At one November 1935 meeting for the team working on Greenbrook, for example, "a general bicker about the town layout" arose among the members. In a rare glimpse of just how they hashed out their varying points of view, notes from a meeting of the Greenbrook team relayed that "[Henry] Wright stated that he was against glorifying the town center architecturally or in any other way. He would rather take the money saved on that and spend it on providing more open space. Mr. [Russell] Black said that Wright's scheme of open spaces was uneconomical to which Wright answered that he thought that with study it could be shown to be practical. [Ralph] Eberlin said that Wright's principle in theory was debatable, but said that in application might be O.K."[4] Where to locate the first cluster of homes and the town center, or as Wright called it, the "center of gravity for the town," also sparked debate. Wright specifically wanted to "concentrate a larger part of the main town together."[5] This fit with the general goal of the teams to create close-knit communities, but there was no clear, single answer as to how such a thing should be accomplished.

This core principle of creating neighborliness drove much of the planning process. The teams aimed to create true communities, places where residents knew each other and children could play safely, where the cares and stresses of modern urban life could be left behind. This desire was not unique to this program; Radburn and other "new towns" had aimed for the same kind of neighborly feel. But for the Greenbelts, more than for most other large town-building projects, the goal of unity among the residents, of calm, and of shared commitment to common goals, became a core concept, the foundation of what the towns were all about. This reflected Tugwell's intention to strengthen democracy by bringing a more egalitarian way of living to the working class. It meshed with FDR's hope to rescue people from the ill effects of life in the crowded cities. It fit the planners' desire to show that, when allowed to experiment widely and reach high, their profession could bring real change to people's daily lives. And more than anything else, it would demonstrate that the working class could be worthy of good housing if they had the chance, and that such an environment would lift them up and help make them into model citizens.

Some of the architects and planners working on the program left written accounts of their aims; most did not. Elbert Peets left the most detailed and prolific accounts of the thinking behind the designs. As a result, he appears prominently in the pages to come, not because he was the most important man on the teams, but because he left us the most comprehensive explanations for why his team made the choices it did. We can infer with some certainty the other teams' intentions by examining the towns they eventually created, but much of this comes down to logical deduction, not documentary evidence.

EBENEZER HOWARD

The first question the planners faced involved the type of town to be built, the basic arrangement of roads, public spaces, and homes. It has become common for scholars to stress the close ties between the Greenbelts and Ebenezer Howard's garden city idea.[6] This is in large part because those involved sometimes explicitly made this connection. Tugwell, for example, talked about Howard's concepts in a speech he gave on the Greenhills project in Cincinnati in February 1936.[7]

The planners also recognized this connection, but cited other influences as well. Henry Churchill, one of the lead architects for Greenbrook, wrote that "the prototypes of the towns are the 'garden cities' of Welwyn and Letchworth, England, [and] the industrial suburbs of Frankfort, Germany."[8] Elbert Peets wrote in his Final Report on Greendale about Howard and his garden cities, but went on to state that "the greenbelt town that was envisaged in the organization of the Division of Suburban Resettlement was not the thing Howard had in mind." Rather, the Greenbelts "were to be, not true satellite cities, substantially complete economically, but satellite dormitory suburbs for working people, a thing now for the first time thinkable since the universal use and cheapness of the automobile."[9]

Howard's ideas, then, had lent inspiration to the Greenbelt design teams, but these towns are not recognizable as true garden cities the way he envisioned the concept. His plan of deliberately building "satellite" communities on the periphery of large cities, of decentralizing industry, of incorporating parks and a sprawl-stopping greenbelt are evident in the original expectations for all three towns. Even his idea of corporate ownership was replicated in the program, although it was the federal government, and not the municipality, that retained ownership until after 1949, despite the RA's original intention that the towns would be turned over "to a nonprofit corporation or local housing authority" after completion.[10] But the Greenbelt towns resemble Howard's proposed garden cities more in theory than in fact.

The surrounding greenbelt itself formed the design element most closely borrowed from Howard. The swath of undeveloped land surrounding each town would, theoretically, keep the larger world out. Peets wrote of Greendale, "The reasons for placing the town out in the country, where it can be surrounded by a permanent belt of green, are not exclusively sanitary and esthetic. The open land around the town has the effect of throwing the town on its own resources."[11] Although it might seem that the introduction of the automobile into American life would have mitigated the isolating effects of the greenbelt, we must remember that most families that owned a car in the 1930s had only one. If the husband drove to work, the wife was left without personal transportation much of the time. And many families in the Greenbelt towns did not own cars initially, instead relying on carpools or public transportation to commute to and from the city.

The bands of preserved nature offered further benefits not shared by other suburban communities. Children could use the woods and streams as recreational wildernesses in which to play and explore.[12] The greenbelts provided a swath of insulation, of protection, of healthful contact with nature. As the name of the program itself reflects, they were integral to the design concept of the communities.

RADBURN

Stein and Wright's Radburn provided one of the other most obvious influences for the design of the towns. Especially in Greenbelt, Maryland, the designers fully embraced the superblock concept as a way to ensure the safety and coziness of the neighborhoods. Here, although a somewhat busy main street does go through the center of the town, key crossings feature underpasses to keep pedestrians safe. Most houses in the community sit within superblocks and are accessed by smaller, quieter streets. Residential units are primarily arranged in "courts," which sit just off the roadway.

The Radburn influence at Greenbelt is also quite pronounced because the homes' service spaces most often face the road and their living spaces face green interior courtyards.[13] O. Kline Fulmer, associate architect for Greenbelt, later explained the spatial arrangement: "Instead of facing only a barren street, the homes look out upon the grass and trees in the center. While each house has its own yard, much of the space is pooled for the common use. Sidewalks are not necessary along the streets because a network of paths runs through the safe and pleasant surroundings of the interior park. Kitchen doors usually open on small service courts indented from the street. These courts provide space for garages, laundry yards and delivery entries, and at the same time isolate dwellings from through traffic."[14] (The terminology that the planners used overlaps quite a bit: they referred to the service area, which included kitchen entrances, coal delivery, and laundry and parking spaces, as the "court," but also referred to the overall collection of buildings in each segment as a "court," and the interior green space as the courtyard.) To avoid replicating the overcrowding of the cities, each superblock spread out over fifteen to twenty acres and contained, at most, 120 homes.[15]

By facing the homes toward the inner courtyard (Fulmer calls it a "park"), by keeping these court groupings small, and by placing playgrounds for small children close to each group, the planners aimed to bring neighbors into contact with each other, to encourage shared space and shared experiences, and to foster a group identity within each small residential enclave as well as within the town overall. Unlike the traditional grid layout, or the postwar suburbs yet to come, the design of Greenbelt was specifically intended to force each neighborhood to look inward on itself, and to discourage isolation and unfamiliarity.

The planners of Greendale and Greenhills incorporated what might be termed a modified superblock design. Both towns to some extent use either the cul-de-sac or court idea; however, neither one uses true Radburn-style superblocks. Yet they also eschewed the traditional right-angle street grid,

Fig. 6.2. Drawing of a "typical superblock" for Greenbelt, MD. John Scott Lansill Papers, University of Kentucky Special Collections and Digital Programs, Lexington, KY.

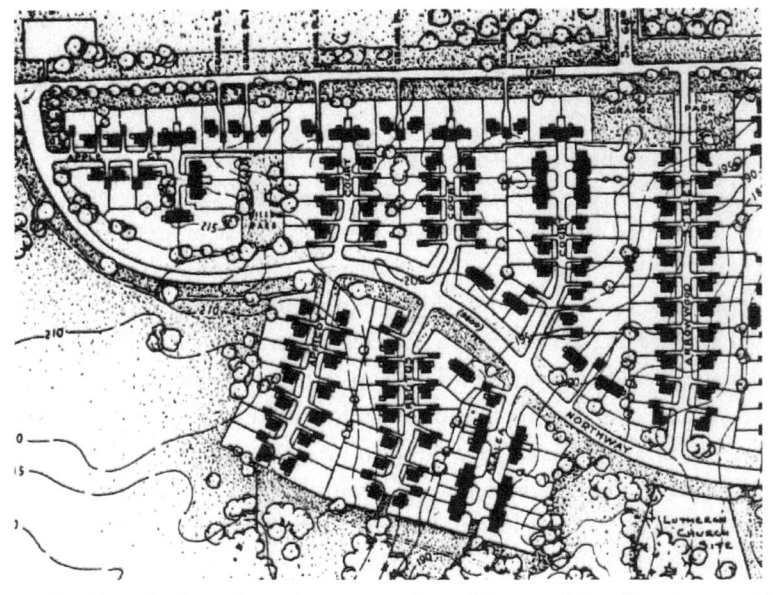

Figure 6.3. Detail plan of northwest section of Greendale, showing residential layout. Courtesy of the Greendale Historical Society, Greendale, WI.

choosing instead to arrange the homes into clusters, a cozy, neighborly orientation meant to encourage a sense of shared space and shared community. Greendale's Peets wrote, "We wanted to express repose and friendliness, order on an intimate personal scale. We wanted to make the streets clearly and emphatically town streets, the place where public ground comes into contact with private ground."[16]

Greenbrook, New Jersey, also would have included much Radburn-inspired design. This seems only natural, since Henry Wright, codesigner of Radburn, took a major role in planning Greenbrook. Drawings show that this community would have utilized the neighborly clusters of homes on cul-de-sacs evident in Radburn, but on an even cozier scale.

In terms of architecture and design, the interwar era saw two opposing design styles. Many people purchased Art Deco radios and admired the latest sleek, streamlined trains, celebrating the new and modern. At the same time, traditional styles also found great popularity in the 1930s. Decorating magazines often featured colonial-era antiques or, for those with more constricted budgets, reproductions.[17] Historian Lawrence Levine has

Figure 6.4. A portion of the preliminary plan for Greenbrook, New Jersey. John Scott Lansill Collection, University of Kentucky Special Collections and Digital Programs, Lexington, KY.

noted that "during the twenties Americans found it far easier to come to terms with the new if it could be surrounded somehow by the aura of the old."[18] They longed for what professor of architecture Edwin Park called "the enchanted past."[19] Even then some recognized this. Harlan Paul Douglass wrote in 1925, "It is not strange that a race moving forward with so doubtful a prospect should begin to look backward. This has always been man's resort when he dared not look forward."[20] Americans in the 1920s and 30s felt a strong sentimental connection to allegedly simpler times.

Greenbelt, with its fairly cohesive modern look, most demonstrates design with the machine age in mind. Its architecture exhibits elements of modernist styles recently in vogue throughout much of Europe. The commercial center and combination school/community building (generally referred to as the Central School by early residents) clearly feature the clean lines and minimal decoration of contemporary and Art Deco design. Some homes appear fairly traditional, with pitched roofs and brick facades, but more conspicuous to visitors in the 1930s would have been those in the new International Style, featuring the latest design aesthetic utilizing flat roofs, straight lines, and white-painted block facades with minimalist pastel accents.[21] Roughly half of the housing is cinderblock. The use of block

Figure 6.5. Greenbelt residential units: painted block with flat roofs in foreground, brick with pitched roofs in background. Interior court view. Library of Congress, Prints and Photographs Division, FSA-OWI Collection.

Figure 6.6. Greenbelt, view from the shopping center roof showing apartment houses on the hill, 1942. Library of Congress, Prints and Photographs Division, FSA-OWI Collection.

construction served two purposes: it lent itself to the modern aesthetic, and it could be used without the services of skilled carpenters or bricklayers, thus putting more unskilled or semiskilled laborers to work.[22]

Greenhills offers the most eclectic appearance of the three towns. The school/community facility and the swimming-pool building both show a strong Art Deco, modernist influence. Many of the homes reflect the modern International Style, but others are more traditional in design. As a broad generalization, the single-family detached and twin units tend toward traditional styles, while the row units and apartments are more often minimalist, even stark. The original exterior finishes were either cinderblock, brick veneer, asbestos siding that mimics wooden clapboards, stucco, or a combination of two of these treatments. These materials were chosen specifically to avoid the need for painting in the future.[23] The majority of roofs are flat, although some homes have pitched slate roofs and a few units received a topping of red clay tiles.[24]

Figure 6.7. Construction of street with differing housing styles in Green-hills, OH. Library of Congress, Prints and Photographs Division, FSA-OWI Collection.

It seems likely that the Greenhills designers felt that Midwest sensibilities would accept only so much of the modern aesthetic, a supposition that was likely correct. It is also possible that they purposely mixed styles to make the community seem less planned, less artificial, more like a normal town that simply grew "organically" over time.

Greendale offers a style at the opposite end of the spectrum from Greenbelt. Although, like the other two towns, this one features both modern and more traditional styles, historical design plays a much more prominent role at Greendale. Clearly the designers there felt more drawn to the past than the future.

On the national stage, one famous project illustrates this backward-looking tendency. The revitalization of Colonial Williamsburg in Virginia served as a temple to history—though a very selective and cleaned-up history—in the modern age. John D. Rockefeller, Jr. personally funded the restoration of Williamsburg beginning in the mid-1920s. He wanted to return the town, which had once served as colonial Virginia's capital, to its lost glory. The American public watched with great interest as the renovation, or more accurately, reimagination, of this village unfolded.[25]

The 1936 Colonial Williamsburg guidebook told visitors that the restoration had been undertaken so that "the future may learn from the past."[26] What visitors encountered, of course, was a sterilized, mythical version of the past. Rockefeller helped rewrite a colonial history that ignored the fact that half of the colonial population of Williamsburg was made up of slaves. And Williamsburg certainly did not replicate the odors that would have been encountered in eighteenth-century life—the smell of pigs, of horse droppings, of unwashed humans. In this sanitized version of the past, everyone apparently got along, shared a common vision for the future of the nation, and worked hand in hand with their neighbors.

Rockefeller presented a colonial town as historical theater. This was make-believe history, the past seen through a nostalgic haze. Williamsburg's image of the colonial era was intended to offer comfort in the very uncertain present.[27] Judging by the interest in the "restoration" and the popularity of Williamsburg as a destination through the decades, the formula appears to have worked.

Greendale planner Elbert Peets wrote extensively about the desire to replicate, or at least to pay tribute to, older styles such as those found in the colonial and small-town past. The community he helped create offers hints of modern design, but the overall flavor is much more traditional. Here both the commercial center and town hall were constructed of red brick, a material that echoes an eighteenth-century style and sensibility. The town hall, in fact, bears a striking resemblance to the buildings of Colonial Williamsburg. Peets explained that the layout of Greendale had actually been inspired by the look of the refurbished eighteenth-century town.[28] He pondered the popularity of Williamsburg, asking: "Is there a vein in us of nostalgic patriotism, a hungry love that we cannot feel for this harried present time but can freely give to that simple and beautiful and unworried golden age?"[29] (Peets, like Rockefeller and other fans of Williamsburg, conveniently ignored that the eighteenth century was hardly a golden age for everyone, with women, African Americans, and Native Americans all occupying decidedly inferior positions in society.)

Peets also wrote that "in its physical plan Greendale has greater resemblance to old European villages than it has to modern western towns."[30]

Figure 6.8. Greendale administration building. Courtesy of the Greendale Historical Society, Greendale, WI.

Thus, he contended, it had at its heart a concept that was "as old as history."[31] His town's design consciously aimed to elicit a particular response in its residents, to create a pleasant and cohesive look that stirred in the people a recognition of a common heritage.

Although in Greendale, as in Greenbelt, most of the dwellings were painted white, some feature a red-brick detail at the corners, giving them a more traditional, old-fashioned texture. The architects shunned flat roofs in favor of traditional peaked and hipped roofs, a choice that may have been dictated as much by the large snowfalls in Wisconsin as by aesthetic considerations.

Figure 6.9. Cluster of houses in Greendale. Library of Congress, Prints and Photographs Division, FSA-OWI Collection.

Peets also acknowledged an intentional effort to use a consistent style for the homes throughout the community, writing that

> most towns and landscapes that everyone calls beautiful have a conspicuous ingredient of uniformity. The Washington cherry blossoms are dramatic, almost overpowering, because they form such a large nearly uniform mass... Identity of material is the natural dress of rhythm in form.

Like so many others at the time, Peets and his team believed that the complexity of the modern world was wearing people down, and that a carefully designed, soothing physical environment could help overcome these negative effects. He noted that "even monotony may be sweet to senses wearied by the chaos of the world."[32]

Greenbrook, had it been built, would have been of great interest to planners and architects throughout the nation, possibly even more than Greenbelt, Maryland, primarily due to the reputation of Henry Wright. His Greenbrook design colleague Albert Mayer noted in a tribute upon Wright's death in 1936: "He was probably our most deeply American architect-town planner. He had an almost sensuous feeling for land and contour.

Figure 6.10. Greendale, September 1939. Library of Congress, Prints and Photographs Division, FSA-OWI Collection.

He was an artist in land; his mind often seemed to be a three-dimensional film on which the smallest nuance, the gentlest slope made its imprint, to be integrated later into the completed design.["]33 The plan for Greenbrook forms a crescent shape, much like that for Greenbelt, with the topography of the site determining the placement of the specific elements. Many within the professions of architecture and planning must have felt immense disappointment that the design for Greenbrook was never realized.

As for the housing style, Greenbrook homes would have featured clean lines, with houses neither particularly traditional nor startlingly modern. Mayer explained in a 1937 article on the town's design: the current "craze for individuality results in numerous hand-me-down styles, including the half-timbered 'Tudor,' the Spanish, the Norman, the Colonial, the Cape

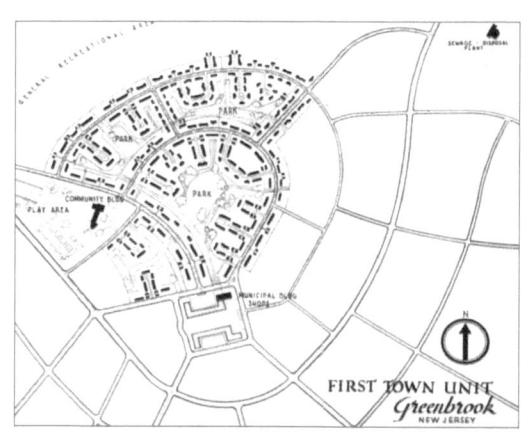

Figure 6.11. Greenbrook town plan, first town unit. Greenbrook Final Report I. John Scott Lansill Collection, University of Kentucky Special Collections and Digital Programs, Lexington, KY.

Figure 6.12. Drawing of proposed housing for Greenbrook, NJ. John Scott Lansill Papers, University of Kentucky Special Collections and Digital Programs, Lexington, KY.

Cod, and results in houses of stone-brick-wood-stucco, mixed in various proportions, and in multitudinous gables. There is no underlying principle but heterogeneity and diversity. In such work there can be no unity, no cumulative impression. It is precisely this unity, this continuity that we were seeking." To achieve this end, Mayer said, "We wanted to translate into architectural terms the community of interest to the people of our town. People are not independent of each other, nor independent of the community in which they live." He and his fellow designers saw Greenbrook as "an American town of the twentieth century."[34] It seems, then, that the architects for Greenbrook, like Peets for Greendale, saw repetition of design as a key element of the desired look of the towns they planned.

CARS

One aspect of modern life loomed large in the planners' thoughts: cars. In 1925, auto accidents killed 17,571 Americans; in 1930 traffic deaths totaled 29,080; in 1935, the number climbed to 34,183; and in 1937, the toll of traffic fatalities reached 37,205.[35] And these figures leave out the number of nonfatal accidents, many of which would have been devastatingly life-altering. In 1934 the number of traffic accidents, both fatal and nonfatal, totaled 882,000.[36]

Articles aiming to convince drivers to adopt more careful habits appeared in popular magazines, including, in 1931, "Our Delightful Man-Killer," and in 1935, "And Sudden Death."[37] The latter relied on shock value to convey its message, providing graphic descriptions of accident scenes and stating: "If ghosts could be put to a useful purpose, every bad stretch of road in the United States would greet the oncoming motorist with groans and screams and the educational spectacle of ten or a dozen corpses, all sizes, sexes and ages, lying horribly still on the bloody grass."[38] Other articles used less disturbing rhetoric, but repeated the warnings that cars could be dangerous weapons if not driven with appropriate caution.[39]

The possibility of death or injury to children seemed especially terrifying. Although during the early decades of the twentieth century deaths from preventable diseases and non-car-related accidents decreased among children, deaths from automobile accidents rose.[40] Throughout the twentieth century the fragility of children became less and less associated with dangerous contagions (polio being the most notable exception) and was instead increasingly associated with the ever-present possibility of deadly car accidents. An advertisement for a New Jersey highway safety campaign graphically illustrated these concerns (see Figure 6.13). The all-too-real possibility of fatal car accidents made this popular technology also something to be feared.

Figure 6.13. 1930s advertisement promoting highway safety. Reprinted with permission, New Jersey Motor Vehicle Commission.

Regardless of the dangers, people wanted cars. They seemed almost desperate for them. Robert and Helen Lynd noted in *Middletown* "the not uncommon practice of mortgaging a home to buy an automobile."[41] Some of those interviewed by the Lynds admitted that they would sooner skimp on clothing or food purchases than give up the family car.[42] This technology quickly became part of the fabric of daily life for people across the country, and once enmeshed in that daily routine, such conveniences were unlikely to be discarded, except, manufacturers hoped, in favor of newer models.

Americans, the planners recognized, would want cars, but in Greenbelt (and, to a lesser extent, in the other towns), they would not *need* cars. Notes from the early planning stages for Greenbrook relate that Henry Wright suggested that they should make it so that "it is as easy as possible for the inhabitants of the town to circulate within the town, and difficult for non-inhabitants."[43] He wanted to discourage those who might simply drive through the town, while making the community inviting for residents to stroll through on foot.

Clarence Stein had dubbed Radburn "the city for the motor age," and this idea was carried into the Greenbelt towns. The layout of the streets and, in Greenbelt, Maryland, the pedestrian underpasses, were specifically intended to minimize the dangers posed by increasing car use. As with many other desirable possibilities for the towns, however, such inclusions inevitably raised the cost of construction, which in turn increased opponents' claims of frivolous overspending. Greenbrook and Greenbelt were both intended to include underpasses. Greenbelt, in the end, was the only one of the towns to include this safety measure. The community also had interior walkways, rather than relying solely on traditional sidewalks running parallel to the streets as a way to further separate foot traffic from dangerous car traffic.

Greenhills primarily used the traditional pattern of placing sidewalks parallel to the road, but also included limited interior paths, and ordinary

Figure 6.14. Pedestrian underpass in Greenbelt, MD, 1942. Library of Congress, Prints and Photographs Division, FSA-OWI Collection.

Figure 6.15. Early rendition of planned pedestrian underpass for Green-brook, NJ. John Scott Lansill Collection, University of Kentucky Special Collections and Digital Programs, Lexington, KY.

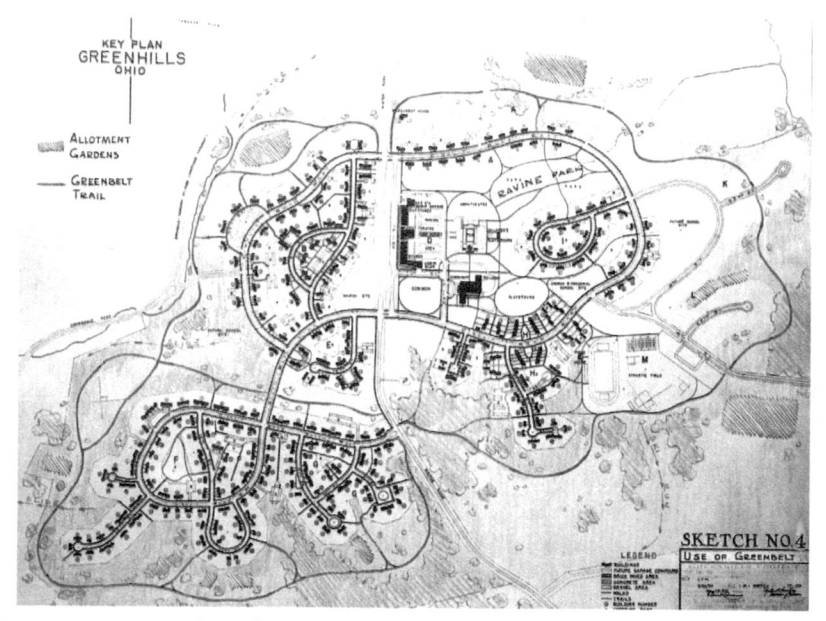

Figure 6.16. 1936 plan of Greenhills. Winton Road runs north–south through the town. Courtesy of the Village of Greenhills.

crosswalks at key spots. This site, however, differed substantially from the other two in that a major roadway bisected the community from the start. Underpasses apparently were not considered, and so this town dealt from the beginning with more hazardous travel for pedestrians as well as a much more pronounced physical separation of residents on opposite sides of Winton Road.[44]

The Greendale planners rejected directly copying the Radburn model of interior walkways because of the costs involved in constructing, lighting, policing, and maintaining them.[45] As a result Greendale used the same approach as Greenhills: traditional sidewalks parallel to streets along with paths connecting interior portions of the residential areas.

On the subject of pedestrian underpasses, in addition to cost, Peets wrote,

> We found ourselves unable to accept the premise on which this feature of Radburn is based... No matter what devices (such as limited highways and better lighting) may be employed to lessen traffic hazards, the principal protection of a pedestrian will lie in personal alertness and good judgment. These can best be learned in childhood... We believe that early training in adjustment to the automobile will save more lives than the provision of underpasses.[46] Instead, planners arranged Greendale so main roads ran along the edge of the town and houses were located on "almost private lanes."[47]

The system appears to have worked reasonably well; more than twenty years after the town was completed, it had yet to experience a pedestrian fatality.[48]

Sadly, Greenbelt, even with its heightened safety measures, could not escape the dangers of automobiles. Despite planners' best efforts to avoid such a tragedy, in 1939 a nine-year-old boy living in the community was killed when a hit-and-run driver struck his bicycle on the town's main road.[49] The designers may have hoped to keep the more hazardous elements of the modern world at bay, but in truth this was simply not possible. Still, the underpasses at Greenbelt continue in the twenty-first century to offer a safe method for crossing a relatively busy street, and provide a distinctive touch to the design of the town.

BEAUTY

The designers gave a great deal of thought to the visual impact of the towns. Reformers had argued that environment played a huge role in shaping personality and morality; it was among the chief reasons that they denounced slums. If superior neighborhoods were to be had, they would need to include open, green spaces, trees and flowers and shrubs, pleasing architecture, winding paths, soothing views. The design teams for each town defined beauty differently, but they all emphasized that visual appeal and plenty of green were keys to creating excellent environments.

In writing about the plans for the ill-fated Greenbrook, architect Albert Mayer explained the thinking behind the design for the town:

> The elements making for good architecture in our time, or any other time, include careful consideration of the relative placing of groups [of buildings] of different lengths and different masses; exploration of the possibilities of the best vistas; exploitation of the changing vistas of the curving streets; the study of the landscaping and the house architecture together; and maximum use of existing trees and natural features.[50]

Clarence Stein noted the emphasis on aesthetics, writing in 1947 of the people who helped design the towns, "they created... a finer background for living. Their part is like that of the scenic designer in the production of a play." (Acknowledging the purpose of the towns, though, he went on: "Ultimately, it is the actors who make the show. Here, in Greenbelt, it has been the people who have lived in it during the last ten years who have made Greenbelt.")[51]

Low-income housing designers often included landscaping as an afterthought, if at all. This was not the case with the Greenbelt towns, whose planners gave careful consideration to the sorts of plantings that would best complement the site and the buildings, and would provide pleasing views for residents.[52] The discipline of landscape architecture had in part provided the genesis for the field of town planning, so it is not surprising that the green backdrop took on a prime importance. The designers of the Greenbelt towns were eager to create a scene that echoed the verdant countryside surrounding the communities, and to avoid the kinds of sterile, concrete-laden vistas often associated with urban housing projects.

Natural elements already on the sites were left undisturbed if possible. Unlike later suburban developments, where bulldozers cleared the land for efficient construction, the planners tried, as much as possible, to leave larger trees in place, and they worked with the contours of the land rather than attempting to reshape it. The Final Report on Greenbelt noted that additional trees and shrubs would need to be brought in, since much of the land had been used for farming, and so lacked trees. They set up a plant nursery to ensure that landscape elements would be readily available at the site. Planners even determined where to place trees so they would provide shade for children playing outside.[53] A 1944 doctoral dissertation noted that "even the most casual observer notices the careful ecological planning that went into Greenbelt."[54]

In Maryland, Greenbelt's planners compiled lists of the trees to be used in the town. One area, for example, was slated for the planting of seven sugar maples, seventy-two flowering dogwoods, thirty-four apple trees, twenty white oaks, seventeen willow oaks, seventeen red oaks, twenty-five locusts—and the list goes on. In addition to the trees, planners enumerated quantities of shrubs (for instance, this same section was to receive sixty-three lilac and seventeen blueberry bushes).[55] It is safe to assume that each planning team gave equal thought to the landscaping of their projects. Since the Greenbelt towns were intended to bring together the best of country and city life, the teams saw the inclusion of greenery in the community as absolutely essential to providing a scenic, semi-rural environment. Such considerations also fit with popular notions of the healthful effects of fresh air and nature for body and spirit. This linkage between plant life and natural harmony also shows in the names of many of Greendale's streets, such as Apple, Azalea, Balsam, and Carnation.

Winding through the green landscape, the walking paths and sidewalks acted as integral components for bringing the residents together on a daily basis. Although planners recognized that car ownership would be a major factor in modern life, they also believed that convenient pedestrian walkways and pleasing vistas would invite citizens to meet and mingle as they strolled to their destinations. The designers of Greenbelt, Maryland, for example, recorded that they specifically included "pedestrian walks [that] lead from block to block, away from the main streets, following the pleasant, quiet interior parkway with houses facing from either side, and smaller lateral walks [that] lead into the houses."[56] They also used "strategically planned" planting barriers to encourage pedestrians to stay where they were supposed to be, well within the margins of these carefully laid-out walkways.

One resident of Greenbelt remembered decades later, "The town was a jewel set in a green forest."[57] The circle of undisturbed woods that surrounded the communities, the open expanses of grass and landscaping nestled among the homes reflected the belief that the stresses of modern life could be cured by intimate contact with the natural world. The fact that the towns were named specifically for the green that would surround and suffuse each community tells us that RA officials saw this element as integral to the overall vision.

The woodlands surrounding the towns had the additional function of providing a rural play space for children. One resident of Greenbelt recalled later in life how she and her friends had dug clay out of a streambed for art projects, how they had used a grapevine to swing out over a culvert, and how they played outside until the town's mothers whistled or rang a bell or called—a unique signal for each child to come home.[58]

COMMUNITY CENTERS

As another key feature, each of the towns included a combination school and community building. Along with providing space for educating children, these buildings also offered a place for adult education classes. In Greenbelt, for example, by January 1939, adults could take courses in drafting, metalworking, woodworking, typing, shorthand, and bookkeeping. Eventually college-credit classes were offered at the community center in conjunction with the University of Maryland; these included courses in history, sociology, and political science. Students of all ages could take art instruction offered through the WPA art project.[59]

Even more important for the broader goals of the program, though, the building hosted clubs and civic organizations. Tugwell's original vision for the Greenbelts saw these communities as fostering camaraderie and civic engagement, both as an antidote to the alienation of modern life and as a way to bolster the democratic spirit of the residents. Civic engagement in Greenbelt certainly met Tugwell's expectations; the August 24, 1938,

Figure 6.17. Greenbelt school/community building. Today the building is still used for community functions, and houses the Greenbelt Museum. It sits between the shopping center and the town's library; the three form the heart of the community. The swimming pool is also nearby. Library of Congress, Prints and Photographs Division, FSA-OWI Collection.

issue of the *Greenbelt Cooperator* listed thirty-one clubs and organizations in the town. More would be formed in the following months.[60] The community was not even at full occupancy until October of that year.[61] Until specific religious congregations could raise funds and build their places of worship on land set aside by the government for the purpose, the different religious meetings were also held in the community building.[62]

The Greenbelt planning teams wanted to prove that it was possible to create inviting and invigorating working-class communities. They wanted to offer something better than tightly packed, tenement-gorged city blocks and drab rows of workers' housing on the urban fringes. Their towns, they hoped, would uplift residents' spirits even as they lifted them out of the snare of poverty. The people of these communities would, in theory, form a tight bond. They all would have escaped inferior living conditions, all would have gratefully embraced this new middle-class-modeled lifestyle, all would see the benefits of a benevolent government and the democratic ideal. They would all be part of this grand experiment together.

On November 13, 1936, Franklin Roosevelt left the White House with Will Alexander and Rexford Tugwell to tour Greenbelt, Maryland. As the car pulled out of the White House gates, a throng of thousands of people watched him leave. Crowds lined the road all the way to the new town.[63]

Although construction was still under way, Greenbelt impressed FDR. A newspaper reporter described the event: "President Roosevelt drove into the autumn painted hills of Prince Georges County yesterday afternoon to see one of his dreams coming true—the building of a country township where families with little money may live in health and comfort... The President was visibly thrilled as he saw pleasant homes, schools and recreation centers springing to life, and was pleased as [a] small boy when he saw the newly made lake being stocked with prize fish."[64] As he stood "in front of one of the cheery homes where, in the near future, some family, now crowded in a squalid city street, will live," the president gave a short statement.[65] "Although I have seen the blueprints of Greenbelt," he said, "the sight of the project far exceeds anything I dreamed of. I wish everyone in the country could see it... The project is an achievement that ought to be copied in every city in the Nation."[66] As we know, that was not to be.

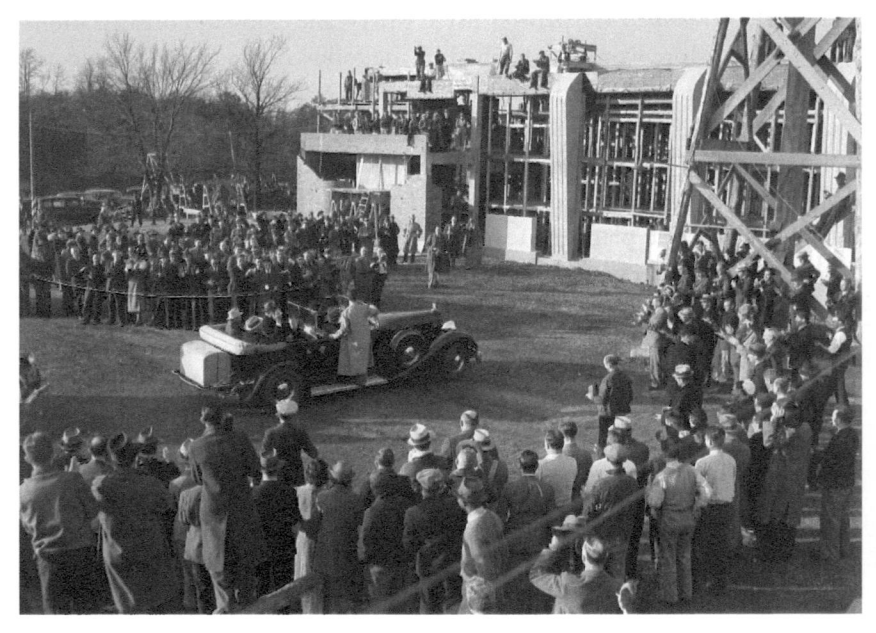

Fig. 6.18. Franklin Roosevelt visiting Greenbelt, November 13, 1936. Library of Congress, Prints and Photographs Division, FSA-OWI Collection.

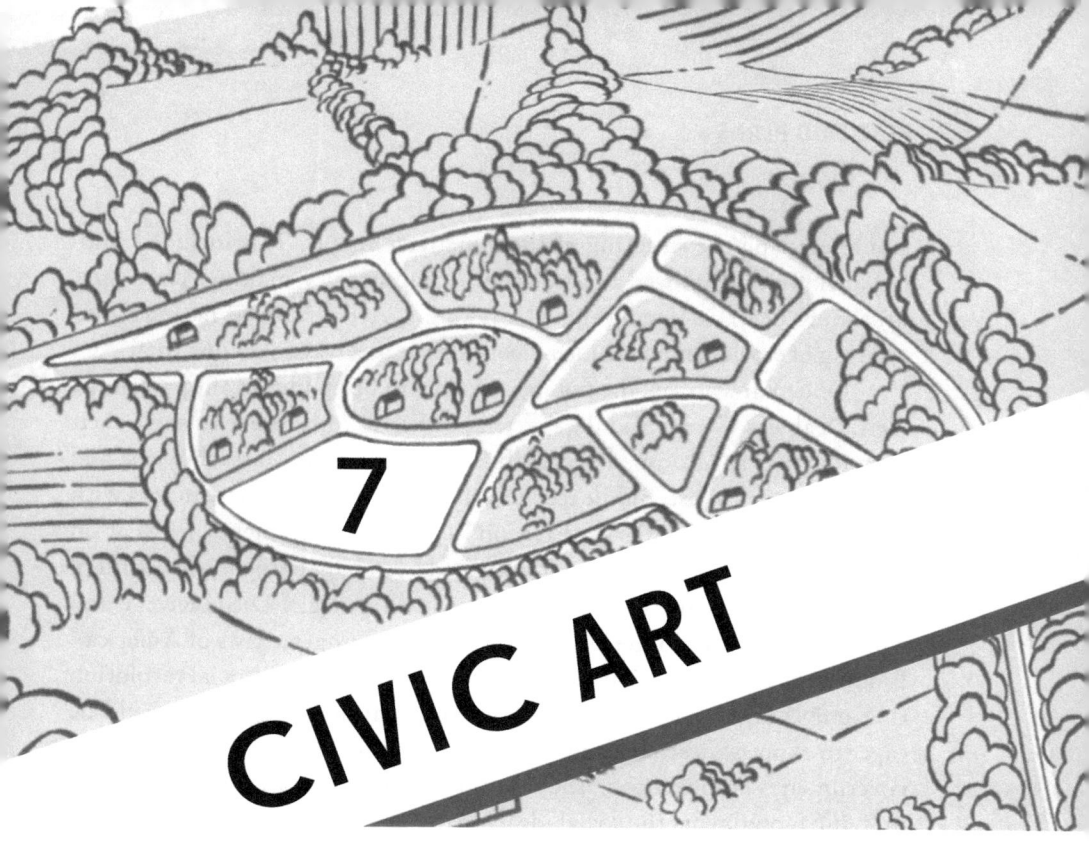

7
CIVIC ART

> Art is neither merely internal nor merely external; merely mental nor merely physical. Like every mode of action, it brings about changes in the world.
>
> –John Dewey, 1916

They say art feeds the soul, but during the Depression was this a compelling priority? Certainly vast numbers of Americans felt desolate, but was art the answer? Perhaps not. Nonetheless, the federal government set up arts programs across the country. Their goals were less to provide the public with art than to provide needy artists with a way to survive the crisis. Yet those leading such programs hoped that in filling the stomachs of unemployed painters, sculptors, photographers, musicians, and writers, they might also fill a cultural void as well.

Of the various features of the Greenbelt towns program, the inclusion of civic artwork may seem rather frivolous and unnecessary. Yet many of those charged with fulfilling the promise of the New Deal did not see it that way. They were tasked with providing solutions for specific problems and alleviating the suffering of the American people. This included finding work for unemployed artists, but also, importantly, making Americans' lives more bearable during this gloomy time. Art—a shared national outpouring of stories and emotions—could serve as a way to do just that.

One man who saw the potential for art to be an important part of the New Deal was George Biddle. A friend of Franklin Roosevelt's since their time together at Groton, a private boarding school in Massachusetts, and now a respected artist, Biddle reached out to his old schoolmate in 1933 with an idea. After congratulating FDR on his many achievements, he went on to briefly tell the president about what had been happening in the world of mural art, particularly in Mexico under the influence of Diego Rivera, and what it might mean to the United States. "The younger artists of America," Biddle wrote, "are conscious as they have never been of the social revolution that our country and civilization are going through; and they would be eager to express these ideals in a permanent art form if they were given the government's co-operation. They would be contributing to and expressing in living monuments the social ideals that you are struggling to achieve."[1]

Initially his old friend hesitated, but eventually Biddle was able to meet with several high-ranking New Dealers, including Rexford Tugwell and Secretary of the Interior Harold Ickes. Biddle recounted in a later memoir what he had said to Ickes: "Word has gone down, not a cent for art. Spend only on essentials. But cannot an artist expect as much in these lean years as a bricklayer?" Biddle, with the help of Edward Bruce, who would later head an art program run by the Treasury Department, obtained Ickes's assent to undertake a program aimed at employing artists on behalf of the federal government.[2] Through the remainder of the Depression civic art would become not just a means to keep needy artists working, but also an overt tool for unifying public opinion and sentiment and buoying a deflated national pride.

This was a new idea, that the US government would provide work for artists struggling to stay afloat through the emergency. Two agencies took the lead in the arts: the Section of Fine Arts (originally called the Section of Painting and Sculpture, and colloquially known simply as "the Section") within the Treasury Department and the WPA.

The Section of Fine Arts dealt only with newly constructed Treasury buildings, most prominently post offices and courthouses, with 1 percent of the budget for each new building set aside for decorative arts. Biddle wrote that the Section aimed "to obtain the finest quality of art—to produce a Michelangelo. That is what will justify it in the eyes of the taxpayers or of the none too sophisticated congressmen."³ No such artistic genius emerged, but a 1940 article in the *American Scholar* tallied the impressive accomplishments of the Section: over 950 murals or sculptures placed in public buildings in eight hundred cities, providing employment for six hundred artists.⁴

The other main agency involved in art was the WPA's Federal Art Project (FAP).⁵ Since the FAP's core mission was to keep artists working rather than to create great art, its production dwarfed that of the Section of Fine Arts, eventually employing over five thousand. These artists produced a much wider range of works: posters, murals, easel paintings, maps, diagrams, dioramas, models, ceramics, sculptures, and photographs. Other FAP employees worked at compiling an Index of American Design and giving art lessons in communities throughout the nation.⁶ The civic art for all three Greenbelt towns came out of the Federal Art Project.

Artists throughout history had depended on wealthy patrons who often dictated the subject and tone of the works created. The general populace, in turn, was expected to be suitably grateful for the art produced, and duly enlightened by it. The New Deal broke that tradition. With the federal government providing the funds, in the FAP at least, artists often had nearly total discretion in their choice of subject. This was democratic art—by the people and for the people, produced by professional artists but depicting scenes of everyday life past and present. Critics therefore found it easy to denounce the works created as pedestrian, not truly art in the traditional *artistic* sense. But more than the quality of the works produced, they also found it easy to target the overall concept. Taxpayer dollars going to pay for creations of contestable merit seemed the very definition of a boondoggle. Yet, as with the criticism of the Greenbelt towns, it seems that the public overall voiced little agitation over the program, seeing it as just another effort to bolster the economy by reducing unemployment rolls.

It certainly appears that this was how Franklin Roosevelt saw it. Most historians who have studied FDR have concluded that he had little interest in art or aesthetics. He was a pragmatic man. He saw some merit in art-centered relief programs once Biddle had broached the topic, but unlike his desire to get Americans out of slums or to save forests, he showed no particular passion for the arts.

One of the few who said otherwise was Holger Cahill, director of the Federal Arts Project. Cahill wrote in 1945, "Franklin Delano Roosevelt was more deeply interested in the arts than any other President since Thomas Jefferson. It is doubtful that any head of state since the Renaissance has equaled him as a patron of living art. No one has surpassed him in breadth and generosity of vision, in concern for the freedom of the artist, and the desire to bring the influence of the fine arts into every community and every home."[7] Cahill wrote these words the month after Roosevelt died, so he may have been burnishing FDR's cultural reputation out of respect and gratitude for the president's efforts to keep artists employed through the Depression. Cahill's certainly seems to be a minority opinion in the matter of Roosevelt's specifically artistic interests.

Indeed, for most New Dealers the art itself was secondary. WPA head Harry Hopkins reminded workers in his agency:

> Never forget that the objective of this whole project is... taking 3,500,000 off relief and putting them to work, and the secondary objective is to put them to work on the best possible projects we can, but we don't want to forget that first objective, and don't let me hear any of you apologizing for it because it is nothing to be ashamed of.[8]

As always, the New Deal came down, at its essence, to providing jobs, getting the economy moving again, and returning the nation to normal.

Edward Bruce saw these programs as doing more than just putting starving artists to work. He viewed the efforts as nothing less than a way to help the nation see beauty amid the gloom of the Depression. "What we need is not official and pompous art, but the fostering and cultivation throughout the country of the creative spirit which is ready to spring up everywhere," he wrote. "What we need is not relief dependent on a pauper's oath, but a friendly and helping hand to the men and women of this country who can create this new frontier of beauty and spiritual uplift."[9]

By sponsoring programs to employ artists, to enlighten and educate the public, or perhaps merely to distract them, the New Deal exerted an enormous influence on American art. A 1937 article in *Fortune* assessed the FAP's results: "Judged on public response alone... the government's adventure in the promotion of the arts would have to be rated successful."[10] People showed up for classes in painting and drawing and ceramics, and art began appearing in public places across the nation.

Yet the *Fortune* article also acknowledged the limitations of the program. The FAP could select just 10 percent of its employees without regard to financial need—in other words, on merit alone. Any person who could show that he or she had been employed as an artist and was now unemployed would be eligible for hire by the agency irrespective of any (admittedly subjective) assessment of talent. As a result, the author noted, "It was clear enough at the outset that the whole 5,500 relief painters and sculptors were not going to turn into Cézannes or Donatellos once they got a brush or a chisel in their hands and a hot plate of soup under their belts."[11] Biddle, too, understood the differences between the Section of Fine Arts and the FAP, noting that the latter

> rarely expects to obtain great art...The [Federal Art] Project often gets very bad pictures... *But it is the first time in history that many thousands of artists are working without censorship, without even the indirect censorship of the art dealer or of the collector. I believe this is the most quickening impulse in painting alive in the world today* (italics in the original).[12]

Director Cahill explained the limits and benefits of what the FAP was doing:

> The organization of the Project has proceeded on the principle that it is not the solitary genius but a sound general movement which maintains art as a vital functioning part of any cultural scheme. Art is not a matter of rare occasional masterpieces. The emphasis upon masterpieces is a nineteenth-century phenomenon. It is primarily a collector's idea and has little relation to an art movement.[13]

The works to come out of the FAP were in many ways "an art movement," though perhaps not in the sense or to the degree that Cahill meant.

Works produced through New Deal efforts also served as tools for public opinion. One recent historian has enumerated five key functions: art as grandeur (meant to inspire), art as enrichment, and art as an experience, but also art as a weapon and art as subversion.[14] Obviously, "subversion" is often in the eye of the beholder. Artists on the whole were less likely to be politically conservative, and those relying on federal contracts to stay afloat financially had every reason to promote the idea of government as savior.

Perhaps the most common theme running through New Deal artwork is unity among the American people in a shared enterprise. Whether depictions of hardy frontiersmen or industrial workers or families, the mutual needs and efforts of the people form a common refrain. This theme is particularly apparent in the works created for the Greenbelt towns, where the goals of cooperation and a more perfect democracy dominated so many design considerations.

CIVIC ART IN GREENBELT, MARYLAND

Greenbelt, Maryland, displays the most prominent artwork of the three towns in the form of public sculptures. Between 1935 and 1943 the FAP produced 17,744 sculptural works.[15] This artform is obviously much more expensive to create than paintings or drawings, and so seems an unlikely choice for relief projects, yet those who promoted the new public art endorsed sculpture as an essential inclusion. Sculptor Beniamino Bufano expressed it this way in 1936:

> We need artists who are interested in creating a universal culture. In being alive. In having something to say... Artists who will be the ambassadors of time into Time. Men who will ultimately be favorably judged on what they have created for the benefit of their fellowmen.

He also stated that New Deal art projects had "laid the foundation of a renaissance of art in America."[16] Perhaps he overstated their impact, but the artistic endeavors of those employed by the federal government make up a rich visual text for the Depression years. Historians have since applied the apt term "cultural democracy" to the Depression-era attempts to unite the nation in a shared cultural expression.

The FAP hired Lenore Thomas (later Lenore Thomas Straus) to produce a large free-standing piece for Greenbelt's commercial center and a series of bas-relief decorations for the exterior of the town's school/community building. A native of Chicago, Thomas had moved to the Washington area in hope of finding work. The FAP gave Thomas free rein in choosing the subjects for the sculptures. It is unclear whether she consulted with any planners or administrators in deciding on her topics, but her choices manage to represent precisely the sort of reverence for community cooperation and democratic spirit exhibited by the Greenbelt planners, and also reflect some of the more liberal attitudes of the New Deal in general.

Using a stylized, simplified realism that was extremely popular among artists during the Depression, Thomas created on the front of the town's school/community building a series of bas-reliefs that depict interpretations of the preamble to the US Constitution. She chose this subject because she felt "it better to use this vital and natively American material than to repeat the old clichés of Science, Industry, Education, etc., seated with rolls and scrolls and having no possible connection with the lives and interests of people living in a modern Greenbelt town."[17] The themes of science and industry in fact made up a substantial portion of New Deal art, but were generally transformed from the "rolls and scrolls" of which Thomas spoke to more ordinary, "everyman" workaday depictions. By highlighting the guarantees outlined in the preamble, she reinforced the notion that the government bore a responsibility to its citizens—a highly relevant but also highly charged topic in the New Deal era.

The theme begins over the building's entry doors with a frieze labeled "We the people." Here she depicts a cross-section of American life: a scientist, a farmer, a family, an office worker, and a miner, all with the US Capitol building centered in the background. She reminds viewers that the government is meant to serve Americans from all walks of life. The residents of Greenbelt would hardly have needed this reminder, living as they did in a town provided by a federal agency.

Thomas felt that the Constitution's preamble, though brief, embodied the spirit needed to face the current crisis. She noted of the phrase *to form a more perfect union*, "This idea finds its most contemporary realization in the co-operative enterprise, and in the co-operation between farm and industrial workers, between clerical workers, laborers and professionals" (see Figure 7.2).[18] In an era marked by intense social tensions, this seemed a particularly appropriate reminder that citizens needed to work together. The meeting of business (the city) and farmers (the country) represents the essence of the Greenbelt town idea.

The scene in the panel depicting *establish justice* shows an industrialist who, in Thomas's words, "sits fortified in his vested interests and property rights. Balanced against this is the consolidated strength of a group of unified workmen," signifying "the government... giving legal recognition

Figure 7.1. "We the people" bas-relief over the main entrance to the Greenbelt school/community building. Photo by the author.

Figure 7.2. Thomas's "To form a more perfect union" panel. Photo by the author.

to the right of labor to organize."[19] Although she wrote about her intention that this panel would represent organized labor, few seeing the piece would know this backstory. Instead, she appears to have consciously avoided making the image overtly political by depicting a scene ambiguous enough that each viewer could interpret it differently, for instance as citizens appealing to a judge or other government official (see Figure 7.3). At the time the image must also have called to mind the common scene during the Depres-

Figure 7.3. "Establish justice" panel. Photo by the author.

Figure 7.4. "Insure domestic tranquillity" panel. Photo by the author.

sion of Americans lining up to apply for relief, of breadlines and soup lines, of the need for those with more to help those who had nowhere else to turn.

For *insure the domestic tranquillity* Thomas provided an image of abundance, brought about by resilient American workers (Figure 7.4). A farmer holds sheaves of grain, and greets an industrial worker in a shared effort to supply the needs of the nation. Thomas's image again emphasizes

Figure 7.5. "Provide for the common defense" panel. Photo by the author.

Figure 7.6. "Promote the general welfare" panel. Library of Congress, Prints and Photographs Division, Historic American Buildings Survey.

cooperation between the city and the countryside. At a time when passions ran high about how and where federal aid was distributed, it was worth reminding the population of the need for goodwill between different social and economic groups.

The panel depicting *provide for the common defense* offers a much darker vision. It shows aggressive-looking soldiers marching in lockstep, spreading death (in the form of cemetery crosses) behind them, while being confronted by an American farmer defending his land and family, a pillar of unpretentious but self-assured strength (Figure 7.5). This scene, for most observers, would have brought to mind the recent Great War (as World War I was then called), but by this time events in Europe and Asia were causing many to recognize the very real possibility that another international conflict might lie ahead. The phalanx of soldiers seems to suggest the rise of fascism and militaristic fanaticism threatening continued peace in Europe.

In the *promote the general welfare* panel (Figure 7.6), Thomas depicted the clearest direct connection to the Greenbelt towns program, and to the spirit of the New Deal itself. Indebted to the federal government for her own employment, she was well aware that such projects were providing jobs and housing for others. Here Thomas illustrated the point with a scene of workers joining together to build and plant, to bring about a new community.

The Greenbelt panels were part of an artistic movement that had begun in the late 1920s and continued through the 1930s, which both portrayed and spoke to average Americans. Works in this genre depicted the quiet dignity of the American people. Thomas's Constitution-themed friezes represented a celebration of ordinary life in an extraordinary nation. These scenes also answered critics who often denounced the New Deal as decidedly un-American, showing that it was in fact legitimized by the Constitution itself. The Greenbelt school's artwork, displaying the most essential tenets of the republic on an Art Deco style building, provided physical evidence of the belief that old-fashioned democracy could be a vital part of modern America.

Greenbelt featured another, more visible piece of public art, a large statue of a mother nurturing a child. The RA's Special Skills Division initially commissioned Thomas to create the piece for the town. Just before Tugwell's resignation, one of his last acts as head of the RA was to order payment of $770 for the stone, plus $30 to mount it at her studio; Thomas believed that if the stone had not been paid for at this time, this commission likely would have been cancelled. As it was, the project moved forward, though her employment shifted from being under the RA to the WPA. To make this switch, Thomas had to be certified for public relief, which she later recalled as "a humiliating experience." The government paid her $5.40 per day for her work, plus $7 a day to rent an air compressor to aid her in cutting the large stone. It took Thomas over a year to create the mother and child statue at her studio in Accokeek, Maryland, even with the aid of an assistant carver. Once it was completed, the government paid an additional $195 to transport and mount the sculpture at Greenbelt.[20]

This piece quite literally illustrated the centrality of family to the Greenbelt idea. The mother kneels, giving the child food or drink, providing comfort and protection. In addition to emphasizing the importance of family bonds, this maternal image also embodied the role of the commu-

Figure 7.7. (above) Mother and child sculpture, Greenbelt, 1942. The commercial center sits to the right, out of frame. Apartment buildings can be seen in the background through the trees. Library of Congress, Prints and Photographs Division, FSA-OWI Collection.

Figure 7.8. (right) Greenbelt mother-and-child statue. Photo by the author.

146

nity in residents' lives—the promise of needs fulfilled, of acceptance and security and human belonging. This piece still serves as a focal point, sitting in a predominant location at the town's commercial center.

CIVIC ART AT GREENDALE, WISCONSIN

Greendale, Wisconsin, also featured public sculpture, though not to the same extent as Greenbelt. The most prominent piece stands at the base of the flagpole near the commercial center. Created by Alonzo Hauser, it depicts a group of men, a woman, and a child. A plaque placed at the site in 1991 explains that the sculpture "memorializes the mothers, youths, and working people who were to populate this uncharted urban–rural concept." The people depicted in this work were meant to represent a cross-section of American society: a laborer holding a shovel, a young girl embracing a woman who holds a book (her mother, possibly, or her teacher), a businessman (or, as he holds in his hand rolled-up papers that could easily be blueprints, perhaps an architect). They form a tight group, arranged as though

Figures 7.9 and 7.10. Flagpole sculpture by Alonzo Hauser, Greendale, WI. Photos by the author.

ready to defend the flag against any potential threat. Farmer, laborer, and professional, young and old, male and female, they stand united in strength and dignity.

Another Hauser piece adorned the end of the community building. This bas-relief, which was either twelve or fourteen feet tall (sources differ), was covered over by a 1971 addition to the building.[21] Smaller decorative bas-reliefs adorned the entry to the school/community center.

CIVIC ART AT GREENHILLS, OHIO

Figure 7.11. (above) Greendale school/community building. This piece was covered by an addition to the building in 1971. Photo used with the permission of the Greendale Historical Society.

Figure 7.12. (right) Small-scale reproduction of the bas-relief that was on the school. Photo by the author.

As George Biddle had hoped, murals provided some of the most accessible artwork to come out of the New Deal. A 1938 *Current History* article explained why this particular artform had suddenly become so important, calling it "perhaps… the most expressive of America." Such subjects as American folklore and history could be given ample scope in a large painting. These and other topics, the article noted, had begun

> appearing upon the walls of our public buildings where the present generation, and those who follow may possess it as a tradition as well as part of their daily lives. And it is this subtle pictorial pressure that will go a long way in moulding a citizenship as deep and as broad as the lands that sustain it.[22]

In Greenhills, several local artists created murals for the school/ community building under the FAP. Still on view today, one by Richard Zoellner graced the original library, filling the space between the tops of the bookshelves and the ceiling, with scenes depicting life along the Ohio River. Through Zoellner's art, library patrons saw the sweep of history from the arrival of settlers onto Native American land to the 1937 flood that devastated the Ohio Valley (though Zoellner's inclusion of a Spanish conquistador in the portion showing settlers building a fort with American Indians looking on is, frankly, baffling). A 1938 *Cincinnati Enquirer* article noted that Zoellner would be doing the work in a new and permanent kind of colored chalk.[23]

In the Ohio Valley, the river had from the start formed the lifeblood of settlement, both for Indigenous people and later for White residents. By choosing the river as his central theme, Zoellner found a unifying thread that ran through the history of the region. Regardless of background or purpose, all who struggled to survive in the area depended on this liquid lifeline. This shared dependence and common struggle brought home the mutual humanity of those who relied on, and were at the mercy of, this vital resource.

Like much history produced during the first half of the twentieth century, the story told in the mural highlighted progress, as those contending with the mighty Ohio River became, as most Americans then saw it, more civilized. But Zoellner also made sure to acknowledge that the river itself could not be civilized or tamed. Apparently he decided late in the painting

Figures 7.13 and 7.14. Murals in the Greenhills school/community building, original library. Photos by author.

stages to include a scene depicting the devasting 1937 flood, with a fire raging in the background, an admission that nature still wielded more power than humanity.[24]

Another mural, created in the Greenhills school's basement cafeteria, has been painted over, a particular shame since this work specifically depicted the expected life in the community. Created by Leo Murphy, its seven panels showed the relaxed life of Greenhills families. Murphy also gained local fame at the time for murals he painted for the Cincinnati Zoo's Reptile House. At Greenhills, he faced the challenge of painting on cinderblock walls, hardly an ideal surface, but he apparently used watercolors with great success. A short 1939 article in the *Cincinnati Enquirer* described the work, saying that the pieces showed "considerable poetic feeling and delicacy underlying their joyous... themes that give the spirit of community life in its happiest form."[25] The pieces served partially as celebration, partially as advertisement, depicting the community's commitment to family and shared ideals.

Figure 7.15. One of the panels created by Leo Murphy in the basement of the school, possibly unfinished. Library of Congress, Prints and Photographs Division, FSA-OWI Collection.

A third large mural graces what was once the school's band and music room. This work, created by Paul Chidlaw, explores the influence of music on American life. The artist depicted a conductor leading an orchestra, a mother and children listening to the radio, an elegant couple dancing, African Americans rejoicing. He captured some of the variety of musical life: a Spanish lady, a bluegrass band, a torch singer. The painting turns these smaller vignettes into a swirling, colorful mass celebrating music's centrality to the human experience.

Greenhills also has a decorative bas-relief in the gymnasium of the community building. It is still visible, but for many years has had the hanging structure for a basketball hoop in front of it, greatly diminishing the artistic impact.

Edward Bruce had written in 1935:

We need a better understanding of service and less selfishness. We need a new conception of the common good, and the happiness that comes from serving it. The time has gone by when the few can be happy living on the top of misery. Life, liberty, and the pursuit of happiness are being demanded as a right. The way is open, but to gain it we need a new valuation of life and the will to earn it.[26]

He had hoped that the New Deal arts programs might help bring this about.

Some Americans had their doubts. The April 1938 issue of *Current History* noted, "To most citizens the Federal Art Project, even after two successful years of work, is still a vague undefined agency contributing little or nothing to the life of the community in return for thousands of dollars of taxpayers [*sic*] money." The author went on to note that "this is an unfortunate situation and one that does injustice to a remarkable endeavor."[27] Many Americans actually did appreciate the projects; they took painting classes and enjoyed the artistic pieces that appeared in their communities. But artwork never shared the urgency of other needs, and when cuts seemed necessary, this appeared an obvious place to make them. Still, the Section of Fine Arts continued into 1938 and some aspects of the FAP lasted into 1942.

Lenore Thomas was likely correct in assuming that her sculpture for Greenbelt might have been cancelled had the stone not already been paid

Figure 7.16. Detail of Paul Chidlaw's musical mural, Greenhills community building. Photo by the author.

Figure 7.17. Detail of Paul Chidlaw's musical mural, Greenhills community building. Photo by the author.

for in Tugwell's final days with the RA. By this time FDR's political opponents were paring back some less-essential-seeming programs. In December 1938 Lewis Mumford wrote an open letter to Franklin Roosevelt in the *New Republic* making the case for continuing the New Deal's arts initiatives. Identifying himself as "a historical and critical interpreter of the arts in America," Mumford made an appeal to the president. "Through these efforts," Mumford wrote, "the salvage of individuals, undertaken through this relief agency, has unexpectedly become the salvation of the arts."[28]

Publishers' Weekly also weighed in, stating that

> there is danger... that many Congressmen might easily fail to recognize the enormous value of the arts projects to the country and might be inclined to curtail appropriations for these projects. If relief appropriations were cut down, the arts projects might, through lack of foresight, be the first to go (here are included not just the FAP and other visual arts, but also the Federal Writers' Project, Federal Theatre Project, and Federal Music Project).[29]

Despite these pleas, this was precisely what happened.

Additional works planned for Greenhills fell victim to such cuts, as well as to a combination of federal impatience and an artist's apparent leisurely pace. Four sculptures were commissioned for Greenhills, but the WPA fired the sculptor, Seth Velsey, in 1942 when he had completed just two. The pieces stood in the Dayton stone yard where they had been carved for years before Velsey donated them to the Dayton Art Institute, where they remain as of 2022. Greenhills residents have fought a long campaign to have them relocated to their town, but have thus far been unsuccessful.[30]

The fate of the public sculptures intended for Greenhills is somehow sadly emblematic of the Greenbelt program itself; noble intentions rarely won out over financial practicality and the need for rapid results. The arts programs, like the Greenbelt towns project, served to keep people employed and to remind Americans of their shared heritage and higher aspirations. Yet when the initial giddy enthusiasm for Roosevelt's experiments began to wear off, such wispy dreams fell before the hard reality of political partisanship and economic pragmatism.

Figure 7.18. Statue created for Greenhills, on display at the Dayton Art Institute. Photo by the author.

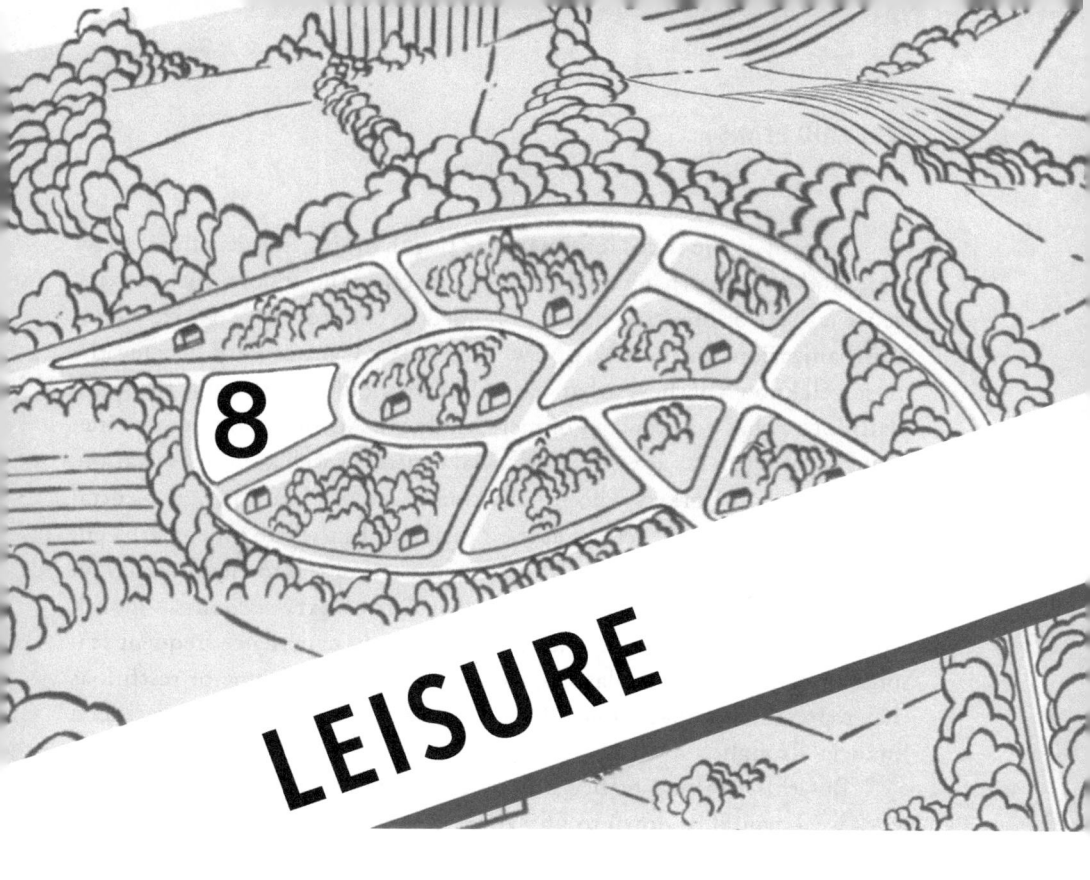

8

LEISURE

The proper use of leisure has created every civilization which has ever existed, the improper use has killed each one in turn.

—George Cutten, 1926

The issue of leisure is, to most Americans today, no issue at all. We take for granted that people will try to find a "work–life balance," to use one of the popular phrases of the early twenty-first century. We assume that even workers at the lowest-paying end of the economic spectrum will have ample time to relax, to unwind, to "recharge." Few question the ways their fellow citizens choose to fill their leisure time. But this has not always been true.

Americans in the interwar era expressed concerns about how and where workers might spend their fragments of free time. Those in the upper classes felt particularly acute anxiety over whether working-class urbanites would engage in wholesome rather than degrading and immoral activities.

As early as the 1840s reformers had begun urging municipalities to set aside land for parks that would allow city dwellers the opportunity to experience a sliver of uplifting nature intended to counter the negative effects of urbanization. In the 1850s New York City's Central Park became the most well known of these urban oases. But we should not imagine that park planning of that era grew out of mere kindness. Advocates often saw nineteenth-century parks as vehicles of social control as well as moral salvation.

The urban workers who initially made use of places such as Central Park had precious little leisure at their disposal. In the late nineteenth century an average factory operative's life consisted of ten to eleven hours on the job, six days a week—a working week of sixty to sixty-six hours—month after month, year after year.[1] Although they might experience frequent seasonal or other temporary layoffs, these were hardly welcome or restful, as they represented unpaid time off for those with little cushion to weather a financial drought.

But this working reality was about to change. By 1900, the average work week would be down to fifty-three hours.[2] The typical worker at that point enjoyed between seven and thirteen additional off-work hours each week, and could enjoy something his or her counterpart of a generation earlier could only dream of: true leisure.[3] This trend toward less time on the job and more time for oneself would continue in the coming decades, bringing shorter workdays and introducing the two-day weekend, developments welcomed by those who finally had time for themselves, time to do as they wished. One study estimated that from 1890 to 1926 the average industrial work week had decreased by twenty hours.[4] By the end of the 1930s, a typical working week for a large portion of Americans stood at forty hours. The age of ample leisure had arrived.[5]

For those reaping the benefits of shorter working hours, this transition was surely welcome, but experts began to warn of the dangers of *too much* leisure. In the 1920s and 30s especially, alarms about this supposed threat were being raised in magazine and journal articles with titles such as "The Menace of Leisure," "The Curse of Leisure," "The Bright and Perilous Face of Leisure," "Challenge of the New Leisure," "The New Leisure—A Curse or a Blessing?" and "The New Social Problem: Leisure Time." Books appeared, too, asking what should be done about the expansion of Americans' nonworking hours: in 1926 *The Threat of Leisure*; in 1933 *Time to*

Live: Adventures in the Use of Leisure; in 1934 *The Challenge of Leisure*; in 1938 *Using Leisure Time*; and in 1939 *Leisure—A National Issue: Planning for the Leisure of a Democratic People*, among others.[6] One commentator laid out the dire possibilities of increased free time:

> Breakdown of ambition, of health, of efficiency, and therefore of earning power; degrading of tastes and moral stamina; delinquency and crime, meaning the multiplication in the long run of subjects to be dealt with by doctor, nurse, hospital, social hygienist, psychiatrist, family welfare agency, juvenile and other courts, reformatory and prison. Waste of time, waste of money, waste of human substance![7]

Despite the enthusiasm workers felt for this recent turn of events, many experts and intellectuals clearly feared that too many people had too much time on their hands.[8]

The Depression only added to the amount of free time as employers laid off workers or cut their hours in an effort to keep businesses afloat. This obviously created serious economic strain, but some experts also worried about the effect of so much spare time on those not accustomed to it. The Puritan notion lingered that idle hands were the devil's playthings.

The fear that others had too much leisure (never, unsurprisingly, expressed as a fear that the actual commentator had too much free time) rode on a wave of class snobbery. The upper crust, experts seemed to assume, could manage their time well enough; they were called "the leisure class" for a reason. Those in the middle class apparently could also be trusted to find wholesome pursuits with which to fill the idle hours. But many feared that workers—those who labored in factories and warehouses, who were employed as meatpackers or construction workers or sales clerks—were ill equipped to find proper uses for their newfound leisure time.

Critics warned that the working class would spend their free time frivolously, gambling, drinking, dancing, and engaging in other forms of dissipation. The wealthy may have enjoyed precisely the same activities, but would not be held to the same standards. Moralizing observers pointed out that the affluent, after all, were not spending their time in seamy pool halls and burlesque houses. Presumably they were not squandering scarce family resources on questionable recreations (in truth, many in the more prosperous classes were doing exactly that, but their veneer of wealth and respectability made such situations seem merely pathetic rather than grossly irresponsible). The lower classes had long been kept more or less in line by the staggering amount of their time spent at work. The more well off wondered how these workers would amuse themselves now that they had time to do as they pleased.

PLAY

Many experts also worried that entertainment had become too passive and sedentary. They particularly expressed concern about the effects on the nation's youth, but by extension this put the physical vitality and mental health of the entire nation at risk. In the new hurried urban-industrial environment, time to simply play—for children and adults alike—seemed imperative.

A movement calling for playgrounds to serve urban youth had begun years earlier.[9] In 1917, for instance, Henry S. Curtis, a leading proponent of the playground movement, had made the case for keeping the nation's youth adequately entertained, arguing that delinquency arose from idleness. "If we could stop the production of juvenile delinquents," he argued, "we could probably stop at least ninety per cent of the crime of adults."[10] He wrote as the final thought in his book *The Play Movement and Its Significance*:

> An adequate system of public recreation would probably cost a hundred millions a year. It would very likely save a thousand millions from other expenses. But even if it effected no saving and gave no valuable training, if we can afford to spend three billions a year on drink and tobacco, we cannot well refuse a paltry hundred millions for the promotion of health and happiness and efficiency.[11]

His hopes proved rather too ambitious for his time, but the sentiments behind them remained alive in the coming decades.

By the 1920s it had become an article of faith that children denied the opportunity for innocent play were at increased risk of becoming a threat to society. In 1926 the director of the Chicago Crime Commission, Henry B. Chamberlain, observed that "in retracing the tortuous path of the youthful criminal it is seldom found that the trail leads back to the [baseball] diamond, the athletic field, or the community center."[12] Investment in such facilities, reformers argued, would yield huge dividends by reducing crime and creating a well-rounded population. Experts saw boredom as a significant problem, not just because it could lead to delinquency, but also because mental development required curiosity and stimulation.

Such ideas gained further ground during the Depression.[13] One of the reports from the President's Conference on Home Building and Home Ownership stated that "if [a child's] play activity is thwarted, it may stunt his talents as a worker as well as subvert his energy into undesirable channels."[14] Many New Dealers, with federal funds at their disposal, saw this as the perfect time to give the nation's children the kinds of recreational facilities reformers had long called for. Theories about the need for play could become more than just theories; they could be implemented, offering America's children the opportunity for carefree time spent outside, and building stronger minds and bodies, healthier citizens for a healthier nation.

The Greenbelt planners, who would have been well aware of this thinking, included ample spaces for outdoor play. They ensured that the communities' children could enjoy fresh air—an ever-present theme for the program—and good, clean, old-fashioned fun. Greendale featured five

Figure 8.1. Playground for small children in Greenbelt. Note the mothers watching and the father playing with a child. Library of Congress, Prints and Photographs Division, FSA-OWI Collection.

playgrounds located so that young children would not have to cross a street to get to one. The community building hosted a playground for older children. A baseball diamond, athletic field, tennis courts, and horseshoe pit rounded out the recreational facilities.[15]

The town of Greenbelt provided play spaces interspersed throughout the town. Three large playgrounds featuring a high slide, jungle gym, swings, and see-saws were provided for school-aged children. An additional thirteen smaller play spaces served younger residents and included a sandbox, slide, and/or see-saw, along with benches for parents.[16] The benches alongside each play space highlighted another key aspect of the program's vision: bringing together mothers (and, if scenes depicted in *The City* and Farm Security Administration photos are accurate, fathers as well) in chummy neighborliness.

Recreational facilities for older children and adults in Greenbelt took the familiar form of baseball diamonds, tennis courts, and other spaces for organized sports. By the mid-1930s such facilities were no longer particularly unusual or innovative in city planning, although the inclusion of so many in these low-income communities provides evidence that planners saw these recreational opportunities as being more than just pleasant little additions. The fact that so much thought, expense, and space was given over to outdoor leisure and play demonstrates that the RA and its employees believed that such facilities would be vital in cultivating a crop of model citizens.

Figure 8.2. Baseball game at Greenhills. Library of Congress, Prints and Photographs Division, FSA-OWI Collection.

One feature that was lacking in the original plans, however, was a space specifically for the towns' teens to meet. Although there were sports teams and organizations such as Little League, "Lassie League," Boy Scouts, and Girl Scouts in Greenbelt, there was no dedicated place for older youth to congregate. As a result, many gathered at the drugstore, which was apparently not seen as ideal. In 1944 the Greenbelt Athletic Club began allowing youth to use its facilities one night a week, and planning began on a youth center, with five parents and five teens serving on a committee to find a more permanent solution. The eventual youth center space, known as the Drop Inn, was housed in the basement of the firehouse and included a snack bar. It was dedicated to "wholesome fun for all and an opportunity for youth leadership," according to the town's twenty-fifth anniversary booklet.[17]

The large swaths of open space sprinkled throughout the residential portions of the towns offered additional opportunities for play, though a 1940s report on life in the towns noted, "These green areas are not supposed to be used for play but rather for beauty and open vistas. However, they adapt themselves nicely and are often used for such games as [badminton] and also for games by older children."[18] It seems naïve, even foolish, for the planners to have thought that open expanses of grassy space in a town deliberately intended to attract families with young children would not be put to use by the communities' youth as supplemental playgrounds. Many children in the towns' early years later recalled seeing their community as one large, sprawling play space, where they were free to roam in safety and relative freedom. An early resident of Greenhills later recalled, "We ran with wild abandon."[19] In the 1930s, it was not uncommon for children to have quite a bit of freedom to play, ride their bicycles, and be on their own for a large portion of the day on weekends and in the summer. But in the Greenbelt towns, parents could feel confident that their children were almost certainly safe.

It was not just children who needed recreation. If experts feared that youth without wholesome outlets for leisure would turn into delinquents, they feared, too, that adults without adequate and acceptable types of recreation would become little better than haggard robots at the mercy of the fast-paced modern workplace. Leisure expert Jesse Steiner made this connection in 1933: "For thousands recreation... opens the doors to a new world where during hours of pleasurable leisure the onerous drudgeries of life are forgotten."[20] Steiner felt that the importance of recreation could not be overstated, declaring that "it is an insurance of social health."[21]

Mass production, many experts feared, might be especially detrimental to the human spirit. Even as Americans celebrated the influx of less expensive factory-made goods, experts worried that the process of production brought unacceptable consequences for workers. Raymond Fosdick, who would later become president of the Rockefeller Foundation, asked in 1929, "What justification has the labour-saving machinery unless it saves the labourer?"[22] The following year the influential historian Charles Beard offered a disheartening assessment: "The machine chains man to his working process, deprives him of initiative, draws out his energies... When 'hands' are treated as quantities, the human spirit withers."[23] Sociologist Maurice Davie was more succinct, writing in 1932: "The city wage-earner is a mere cog in the industrial machine."[24] Many shared this opinion. When, in a 1932 poll, employed and unemployed engineers near New York City responded to the statement "Industry is making automatic machines out of human beings," 38 percent of employed and 55 percent of unemployed respondents either agreed or strongly agreed.[25] But Americans were not supposed to be cogs or robots; they were supposed to be independent, responsible citizens. The tension between enhanced productivity and the cultivation of competent citizens made a strong case for increasing leisure outlets for the nation's workers.

Even those working at office jobs seemed to have been negatively affected by the changing workplace. A 1913 article in *Collier's Weekly* conjured a particularly unflattering portrait of the white-collar urban worker: "In his work there is little to which he looks back with pride. A thousand weeks of filing cards, hammering typewriters, adding up columns of figures, have not left him with blithe memories of something accomplished, something done. One thing for him they have done; they have thoroughly tamed his spirit. There are no adventurous quests in him."[26] This was hardly the image of the rugged individualist upheld as the American ideal. (It is worth noting that as such clerical jobs became increasingly dominated by female rather than male workers, these concerns seem to have evaporated. Apparently women were not expected to seek "adventurous quests," and a career of filing and typing was expected to be enough to fill them with sufficient pride in "something accomplished.")

Outlets for escaping workaday cares had traditionally been provided by private enterprise. But many experts shared the views expressed in a 1935 article in the journal *School and Society*, which stated that "recreation and leisure time have not only been commercialized, but have fallen into the hands of the most commercial, the least social, the most unscrupulous and the least moral group in our modern society. The commercial group has turned the period of relaxation, the most fertile of all fields for culture and refinement, into a field of idle dissipation."[27] Just as children needed to be offered ways to engage in wholesome play, adults needed to be provided with options for wholesome and rejuvenating recreation and entertainment.

The New Deal addressed these concerns in a variety of ways. The Civilian Conservation Corps built recreational facilities in state and national parks and various federal agencies provided swimming pools in neighborhoods all across the nation. Among housing efforts, the Greenbelt program stands out for so comprehensively tackling the perceived need for everyday recreation.

To help the planning teams decide what leisure options potential residents of the towns would most want, RA researchers distributed questionnaires among the working class in the areas near the proposed sites. In Cincinnati, for instance, they distributed forms mainly through trade unions, industrial plants, social agencies, and churches.[28] The researchers then only tabulated responses from those who would theoretically qualify—and possibly be interested in living in—a home in Greenhills. They discarded replies from respondents who were not interested in the project, or who expressed interest but already owned their own homes, or who depended on boarders for part of their income. (The practice of taking in boarders had often been cited by housing experts as one of the chief causes of urban overcrowding, lack of family privacy, and other ills. As a result, it was prohibited in the Greenbelt towns.) Any forms received from families whose income disqualified them for a home in Greenhills—under $1,000 per year or over $2,000—were also discarded. Of the 24,000 questionnaires distributed in Cincinnati, just 852 were tabulated.[29]

Answers to the questionnaires distributed in each city helped shape the plans for recreational activities in the Greenbelts. The inclusion of a variety of entertainment and leisure options must surely have increased interest in the communities, both by would-be residents and by critics claiming that the plans were too grandiose for subsidized government housing. Regardless, the planners were intent on making the towns models for American life, meaning that they had to offer ways of allowing the people in the communities ample opportunities for play and relaxation.

They succeeded. The June 1, 1938, edition of the *Greenbelt Co-operator*, the local newspaper produced within the town, announced that a men's athletic club had been formed in February. They had, by June, already organized a basketball league, a volleyball league, and baseball and softball teams. The paper also stated that "150 Greenbelt women, on March 23, left husbands

Table 8.1. Community Facilities Desired by Town.

Community facilities desired	Percentage of families requesting		
	Greenbelt	Greendale	Greenhills
Library	89.0	86.1	82.2
Swimming pool	75.8	78.8	77.5
Playgrounds for small children	46.8	68.3	58.1
Community social hall	54.3	60.8	51.1
Baseball diamonds	34.0	57.0	63.0
Beauty parlor	43.4	45.8	44.7
Bowling alley	38.6	45.5	37.5
Tennis courts	50.9	41.2	35.1
Tavern	12.1	34.9	29.0
Football field	16.4	28.2	23.7
Basketball courts	21.0	24.3	20.8
Restaurant	23.3	21.8	20.5
Handball courts	20.8	20.6	18.5
Day nursery	13.5	12.7	7.5

Source: Questionnaire analyses, Final Reports on Greenbelt, Greendale, and Greenhills, John Scott Lansill Papers, University of Kentucky Special Collections and Digital Programs, Lexington, KY.

at home as nursemaids while they reported to the gymnasium for 'ladies' night.'" By June the women had formed softball teams and were looking into the possibility of such activities as badminton, darts, and tennis.[30]

In Greendale the WPA Recreational Department initially oversaw activities in the town, coordinating with a local Athletic Advisory Board. The objective was to "eliminate overlapping of activities and to provide adequate facilities for varying types of recreational programs."[31] The Thanksgiving issue of the *Greendale Review* noted that, sadly, the local softball team had "not had much success" thus far.[32]

Some recreational facilities were not completed until after residents had begun moving into the towns. In Greenbelt, where the first residents arrived in September 1937, the tennis courts, a handball court, and the swimming pool did not open until the spring and summer of 1939.[33]

AT THE MOVIES

The questionnaires did not ask about the desire for movie theaters; however, movies had become such an integral part of American life that both Greenbelt and Greendale would be given theaters. Greenhills did not include one, though at an early point in the planning stages designers had intended that it would. Instead, films were shown in the gymnasium at the school.[34]

Planners certainly expected that the theater at Greenbelt would play a vital role in the life of the town and its residents. Reportedly the first cooperatively run movie theater in the United States, the fully air-conditioned facility opened on September 21, 1938, showing the Shirley Temple film *Little Miss Broadway* as its inaugural feature. The entire town was invited to turn out for a community-wide grand opening celebration.[35]

In 1930, Americans purchased 100 million movie tickets each week—some estimates claimed as many as 115 million—out of a total population of just over 123 million.[36] In the era before TV, video games, and the myriad other amusements of later decades, children and teens attended motion pictures far more frequently in the 1920s and 30s than in any other era. According to the Reverend Fred Eastman, a frequent critic of the movies' influence on the nation's youth, in 1931, on average, each school-aged American child saw a movie once a week.[37] Journalist Henry James Forman, in his 1935 book *Our Movie Made Children*, cited a study conducted in Columbus, Ohio, finding that among boys aged eight to nineteen, 71 percent had attended a movie the week prior to being surveyed, and 27 percent had attended more than once (3 percent had gone to the movies four or more times). Girls were somewhat less likely to have gone to the movies the previous week, at just 64 percent; but 21 percent had gone more than once.[38] Children's attendance peaked on weekends, and by the mid-1930s about half of the nation's theaters were showing double features to entice customers, meaning that many children spent the better part of a Saturday or Sunday in a movie theater.[39]

The difficult economic times did not hit the motion picture industry as hard as they did most sectors of the economy. At the start of 1931 the nation boasted 22,731 movie theaters with a combined seating capacity of over 11 million. Movie ticket revenues in 1934 totaled over 1.5 billion dollars.[40] A 1934 study on people's leisure activities showed that going to the movies was topped only by listening to the radio and reading the newspaper as the most frequent pastimes.[41] As Jesse Steiner explained, "The motion picture... is apparently a necessary luxury, slow to feel cuts in the family budget. The important role it plays in the leisure time of the masses can hardly be exaggerated."[42] For those living in the two Greenbelt towns

Figure 8.3. Theater at Greenbelt, MD. Library of Congress, Prints and Photographs Division, FSA-OWI Collection.

graced with theaters, this seems to have exactly captured their sentiments. For families attending together or children meeting their friends for a day of cinematic fun, the movies provided a welcome escape during the grim days of the Depression.

The families—and particularly the children—of Greenbelt and Greendale enthusiastically made use of the theaters in their towns. Saturday matinee showings lasted all afternoon and included cartoons, a serial, short subjects, newsreels, and a feature film. This fairly economical way to spend a weekend afternoon kept a large portion of the communities' youth occupied, entertained, and—most important—out of trouble. And as the towns' planners had intended, the theaters also brought the larger community together. Movies provided a shared experience.

GOING FOR A SWIM

Another increasingly available and popular leisure venue in the interwar years was the municipal swimming pool. On a scorching summer day, the sparkling waters of a local pool beckoned young and old alike. Before residential air conditioning had become common, a swim offered one of the few ways to truly cool off. But beyond offering a refreshing respite from the heat, why did the construction of swimming pools in particular become such a frequent New Deal offering?

Progressives and urban reformers had by the early twentieth century begun to see pools as a way of keeping city youth out of trouble by filling free time and offering relief from aggravating city heat. When neighborhoods featured so much concrete and brick, and little grass or trees, summers could be brutally hot. Nerves frayed; tempers often flared. Civic leaders had long noted that soaring temperatures and crowds of idle, restless urban youth frequently made a volatile combination. A refreshing swim in the local pool offered the possibility of diffusing tempers and keeping youths occupied.[43] As a result, the New Deal as a whole provided almost 750 new public pools between 1933 and 1938, and oversaw the renovation of hundreds more.[44] A study of five thousand Americans and their leisure activities conducted by the National Recreation Association in 1934 showed that 60 percent of those surveyed considered themselves to be swimmers, and swimming was ranked the seventh most frequent, and second most desired, recreational pastime.[45]

When the RA surveyed residents of the cities near the coming Greenbelt towns, 75.8 percent of Washington respondents expressed a desire for a public swimming pool, as did 77.5 percent of those in Cincinnati and 78.8 percent in Milwaukee.[46] Public pools near the town center became a community focal point at Greenbelt and Greenhills. Greendale did not get a pool, in spite of potential residents' expressed desire for one; apparently the planners believed that relatively close proximity to Lake Michigan made a pool less necessary, but it's likely that the more northern climate also played a part in this decision.[47]

In addition to being a way to keep the towns' young people occupied in wholesome recreation, the pools also brought families and the community together in a way that, for example, attending movies could not. With many families' entertainment budgets stretched thin, a public pool offered a day's relaxation and fun at little cost. The community pool was a place where families could meet and relax, where they could engage in friendly chat and form neighborly bonds.

Figure 8.4. Swimming pool at Greenbelt, MD. Library of Congress, Prints and Photographs Division, FSA-OWI Collection.

The designers of Greenbelt, Maryland, also created a twenty-five-acre artificial lake in the town's large public park. A nearby picnic area offered a popular place for family outings. This park and lake replicated, perhaps more than any other feature of the town, the old-fashioned "good, clean fun" of days past, exactly the sort of recreation that seemed to have been lost as the nation became more industrialized and urban.

But it had problems. Although several scenes in the documentary *The City* show Greenbelt boys taking a dip in the lake, this enticing spot did not live up to the swimming potential depicted in the film. In June 1938 a boy from nearby Beltsville drowned in the lake after falling out of a boat; lifeguards were briefly added and swimming restricted to times when the guards were on duty.[48] Then, just the following month, lake swimming was halted altogether when tests of the water showed it to contain high bacteria levels.[49] The hazy, romantic image of "the old swimming hole," in the end, was no match for the clean, crystalline water of a chlorinated concrete pool.

AN AGE OF CONSUMPTION

The planners added one more element to their designs aimed at keeping residents in town and connected—the shopping center. Offering more merchandise and services than the old "mom-and-pop shops" common to most small towns, and much closer to home than the large department stores located in the big cities, shopping centers represented an important piece of the emerging suburban trend. The first such shopping centers consisted of multiple stores under separate ownership arranged side by side, allowing for a single-location choice not just of products, but of retailers as well. This new form of commercial space reflected the growing importance of consumption in American life.

Radburn provided commercial space with parking for cars; Stein had, after all, dubbed it "the city for the motor age." The accommodations for cars were relatively scant: just two rows of spaces in front of the shops.

During the 1930s, early "drive-in" strips began to be built in California. Mainly made up of open-fronted stalls for fresh produce and the like, these were nonetheless collections of independently owned, connected shops with parking in front so that customers could park, shop, and leave with ease and efficiency. In this period Washington, DC, also became an important center for the development of the modern shopping strip. One innovative and widely copied center, the Park and Shop, opened in the capital's Cleveland Park area in 1930. This commercial center had stores arranged in an L-shape, lining two adjacent sides of a parking lot that was much larger than had been common up to that time, a feature that became the model for many centers to follow.

The consumer impulse was growing stronger, though the coming importance of consumerism in American culture was not yet obvious. Robert Lynd, for example, badly underestimated the tidal wave of consumption to come, writing,

> While shopping is still a pleasure to some consumers, there is evidence that, with the multiplication of alternative activities, there is a mounting distaste on the part of both men and women for the labor of buying things, a desire to simplify and to expedite the process as much as possible.[50]

He could not have foreseen that within a few decades shopping and consumption would become significant avenues of leisure activity. One wonders what he would have thought of the large shopping malls that would dot the landscape by the 1980s. If sociologists such as Lynd could not predict this path, neither could town planners, including those who designed the Greenbelts. Rather than bracing for a coming age of consumption, they for the most part intended simply to offer convenient places for purchasing necessities. Shopping centers were, for planners, just the latest innovation aimed at making people's lives more pleasant and efficient.

Clarence Stein and Catherine Bauer did foresee that the commercial center would be an integral part of any community, even if they could not know how consumption-driven the nation would become through the remainder of the twentieth century. The two had collaborated in 1934 on a journal article on planning shopping centers, and their suggestions found their way into the plans for the Greenbelt towns.

Some of their ideas seem quaintly outmoded today. They wrote, for example, that "in the community of the future... most people will walk to the store because it will be convenient, safe and enjoyable." Their wildly incorrect prediction continued: "There will be facilities for parking automobiles, but in most built-up communities this will be of much less importance than a safe place to park the baby where the mother can watch it while she shops."[31] The idea of "parking" the baby outside while the mother shopped would strike later generations as grossly negligent, but in the relatively safe confines of the Greenbelts—and countless other small communities throughout the nation—it was an acceptable practice at the time.

Figure 8.5. Cooperative grocery store, Greendale, WI, 1939. Library of Congress, Prints and Photographs Division, FSA-OWI Collection.

Much as Lynd had underestimated the future allure of shopping as recreation, Stein and Bauer misjudged the true coming influence of the automobile, stating that

> if walking is made safe and attractive as it is in Radburn by completely separating pedestrian from vehicular traffic, and by paths passing through parks, there will be much less use of automobiles in local shopping. The wasteful use of the machine is likely to be more limited in the future.

This assumption led them to recommend that "no home should be more than half a mile from a neighborhood shopping center."[32] In Greenbelt,

Maryland, at least, walking did prove the more popular way to reach the stores in the town's early years, possibly because few housewives had a car at their disposal during the daytime. Many Greenbelt boys earned pocket money using their old toy wagons to deliver groceries so shoppers could walk home unburdened.

The Greenbelt planners felt that in addition to providing for daily needs, the commercial center in each town would be vital to the desired sense of community. They wanted to make these complete communities that met all of the needs of residents; to do so they had to provide adequate opportunities to obtain basic necessities without having to leave the towns. The commercial center would bring the population together, allowing them to meet and get to know each other.

Unlike later shopping centers and malls, these were not built specifically to encourage consumption. Because the goal was to offer necessities close to home, rather than to tempt buyers into making as many profit-generating purchases as possible, the planners had no accurate precedent for determining the best number and variety of shops.[53] They made use of available data on the day-to-day requirements of small communities for commercial activity and the results of research questionnaires distributed by the RA to try to assess the buying needs of the towns.

They finally decided that there should be no competition between stores; each town would have only one grocery store, for example, and just one drugstore. In keeping with the Greenbelt vision of community cooperation, and reflecting in part Tugwell's suspicion of laissez-faire economics, in all three communities the local businesses were initially expected to be run as cooperatives. Residents would become part-owners, and share in the stores' profits. Planners hoped that even though each type of establishment would have a local monopoly, the cooperative model would ensure that prices would be held in check. Membership in the co-op, in addition, would provide one more tie binding the residents together in a common interest.[54]

In terms of design, Greenhills and Greendale used the model of Washington's Park and Shop and other similar enterprises in a modified form. Elbert Peets, using the term generically, noted that Greendale's commercial center was based in part on careful study of "the 'park and shop' centers that are currently being built around Washington and other cities."[55] A drawing of an early conception of the Greenhills commercial center

Due to recent revisions of plans, this illustration is not accurate in detail. Replacements will be provided as soon as they are available. 5/16/36

Figure 8.6. Early conception of Greenhills shopping center. John Scott Lansill Papers, University of Kentucky Special Collections and Digital Programs, Lexington, KY.

(Figure 8.6) in fact shows a remarkable similarity to the L-shaped DC Park and Shop. When finally built, though, the stores in both Greendale and Greenhills formed a straight line, with parking spots in front.

The planners of Greenbelt, conversely, chose to locate shops in such a way as best to ensure that customers would have to stroll through the commercial area rather than park directly in front of the desired store (see Figure 8.7). Walkways from different directions converge in the center, which is made up of two parallel strips of shops with a one-hundred-foot-wide paved space between them.[56] The strips run perpendicular to the parking area, a layout that encourages residents to walk through the shopping center rather than dash into just one store and back to the car.

Although Greenbelt was the only one of the three towns to arrange the commercial space this way, all three communities placed the shopping center, along with the combination school/community building (and, in the case of Greendale, a separate administration building as well) in the center of town, to serve as a focal point and gathering place for neighbors.

The architectural styles of the centers differed from one town to the next. Greenbelt went the furthest in offering something new, boasting a shopping and entertainment area that was not just contemporary in design, but reflected the then-current trend of streamlining, a style strongly connected with Art Deco design. This look connoted modernity and speed. Trains and toasters, automobiles and office furniture—any object that designers wanted the American public to associate with rapid advancement—was likely to sport a streamlined look. In Greenbelt's shopping district, this meant long, low profiles, flat rooflines, and rounded corners. Greenhills' commercial strip also reflected modern design, with straight lines, a flat roof, ample plate glass, little ornamentation, and a bright white

Figure 8.7. Greenbelt shopping center under construction, 1937. Library of Congress, Prints and Photographs Division, FSA-OWI Collection.

Figure 8.8. Greendale commercial center. Courtesy of the Greendale Historical Society, Greendale, WI.

coating. Greendale's shopping center presents nearly the opposite look, its red brick outer shell giving it a much more traditional appearance.

Although not recreational spaces in the traditional sense, the shopping centers of the three towns played important roles in the social life of the communities. One Greenbelter recalled years later, for instance, that when they heard the news about the bombing of Pearl Harbor the "young men gathered as if by instinct at the Center."[57] Just as the design teams had intended, the commercial areas became hubs of community activity and offered the opportunity to obtain daily necessities, to socialize, and to stay connected to the pulse of the town.

For the Greenbelt towns, the inclusion of a swimming pool or movie theater, a park, or a shopping center offered visible proof that these were not ordinary low-income housing projects. They were not intended merely to house members of the working class, but to elevate them to the middle class, if not in economic reality, at least in lifestyle. At the same time, we must be careful not to make too much of this effort. The tenant selection process ensured to a certain extent that those who were chosen to live in the towns wanted such middle-class-style lives. This was not, in other words, an effort to impose a lifestyle on a reluctant populace, but to offer them what they apparently already desired.

9
THE HOMES

We moved to Greenbelt in July of 1938. I think that was the happiest day of my life. Everything was so new and beautiful. Just to have a home to call our own was exhilarating.

—Eva Howey, early Greenbelt resident

O n a Sunday afternoon in late February 1937, the New Deal's Resettlement Administration opened a small model home near Milwaukee to the public for the first time. Twenty-five thousand people lined up to see it.[1] Those sightseers eagerly anticipated the new town of Greendale, a community that when completed the following year would provide housing for 572 working- and lower-middle-class Milwaukee-area families.[2]

Like the rest of the nation, these visitors had witnessed more than seven years of crushing economic depression, the election of a patrician president who claimed to understand their suffering, and a procession of New Deal initiatives aimed at ending the crisis. One experiment after another had endeavored to stabilize businesses, or to assist farmers, or to put men to work, and while these programs undeniably helped countless individuals and families, none had managed to break the stranglehold of the Depression on the nation's economy or its spirits. Recovery remained elusive. Even among those who supported Franklin Roosevelt, countless Americans by this time had developed a degree of skepticism of federal plans and promises.

Yet these people stood outside for hours to see this one small home, to see what all the local fuss had been about, to see the latest the New Deal had to offer. Given the importance of home and family in American life, the actual residential spaces would be key elements in the potential success or failure of the Greenbelt experiment. Town planners had carefully crafted public spaces to promote a sense of community. The architects took equal pains in trying to design domestic spaces that were inviting and would be conducive to familial harmony. At the same time, they had to be ever aware that critical eyes were watching for evidence of frivolous waste. They had a fine line to walk.

The designers did not create entirely new home concepts out of thin air. They were not intent on presenting to the American people quixotic novelties. Unlike some architects and prognosticators, they had no desire to provide a vision for "the house of the future."[3] Rather, they built upon traditional and accepted social norms and expectations. Their goal was not to dazzle with unique innovations but to demonstrate that rational planning and careful execution could provide superior domestic environments and improved home life while staying within the limits of frugality and common sense.

As with other aspects of the designs, the planning teams saw the choice of what sorts of homes to provide as integral to the character of the towns. They carefully weighed such questions as whether to offer single- or multiple-family homes. They were constrained by both the budgetary limitations of the project and the extent to which the American public would be open to new innovations and ideas. In the choice of housing type, especially, planners were forced to make difficult compromises between what they knew many residents would prefer and what was economically feasible.

We should not assume, however, that financial considerations imposed from above were the only factors considered; for many of those who planned the Greenbelt towns, the project offered a chance to demonstrate not only that the tightly packed but socially isolated lifestyle of the city did not have to be the way of modern life, but also that the single-family detached home was not the only proper habitation for the American family. They wanted to show that low-cost housing for the working class could be economically built to be both sturdy and comfortable. Such homes, they believed, would make family and community stability possible for the working- and lower-middle class.

TYPES OF HOMES

The planning and design teams had to make choices about what types of homes to offer. The prevailing societal preference remained a detached home surrounded by a private yard. Even most American housing reformers, as Catherine Bauer pointed out in 1934, "believed that the ideal home was a small house with attached garden; anything else could be nothing more than an unfortunate compromise" (Bauer herself, it should be noted, did not share this view).[4] The popular imagination largely remained wedded to this vision, as well.

The questionnaires distributed by the RA, however, revealed regional variations in attitudes about single-family versus multiple-family homes. While nearly 68 percent of respondents in Cincinnati and 74 percent in Milwaukee expressed a desire for a single-family detached home, just under 32 percent of Washington residents indicated that this was their first choice.[5] Nearly half of Washington respondents showed a preference for group housing such as rowhouses, and nearly one quarter chose apartments, a much larger proportion than the 5.5 percent choosing the apartment option in Greenhills, for example. In crowded Washington, residents considered rowhouses and other group arrangements as decent, respectable homes, but the families in Cincinnati and Milwaukee showed a marked preference for detached, single-family houses.

Many of the Greenbelt planners relished the opportunity to demonstrate that something other than single detached homes could serve American families well. They may have been especially eager to embrace other forms because they faced the challenge of needing to keep costs down. Henry Wright in particular had made a name for himself within the profession for his studies of small house and apartment designs. Yet even Wright had once shared the established view that a detached home was preferable, writing in 1916:

> For health and to develop neighborhood sympathies and civic interest a dwelling which may be called a home is needed. A flat, one of twenty-four of similar character within the same walls, stimulates little home feeling and tends to estrangement from, rather than familiarity with, neighboring dwellers. Pride in the home and a sense of attachment can be developed only by dwellings which to some extent are set apart from other dwellings— a house with space about it.[6]

Over time, however, Wright changed his attitude. As he watched European housing efforts unfold, he caught glimpses of a possible solution to America's housing crisis. By 1925 he expressed his evolving thoughts on the matter, writing that perhaps someday the United States could match the housing achievements of European leaders such as Holland and Great Britain, but "in the meantime little is to be gained by excusing ourselves because of supposed American 'preferences' for foolish and wasteful types of houses."[7] He had not completely abandoned his earlier views, but rather had come to accept the reality of the situation: it was simply not reasonable to think that every American family could have a detached single-family home.

Other Greenbelt designers also saw the American affection for the single-family home as counterproductive. Henry Churchill, for example, wrote in his summary of the Greenbelt program that although "there was no doubt that the majority of people would prefer 'their own little home' on their own plot of land," this was in fact "a sentimental idea, without much else to recommend it."[8] (It should be noted, however, that Fred Naumer, regional coordinator for Greendale, disagreed, asserting, "We are not willing to concede the accuracy of this statement.")[9] The planners understood that for many who aspired to the middle-class lifestyle the quintessential home with a yard and picket fence might be the dream, but also that for those living in bleak and overcrowded urban districts a modest apartment or rowhouse in a Greenbelt town would represent a gigantic step toward the ideal American home.

Because residents of Washington's crowded neighborhoods were less tied to the single-family-house ideal, Greenbelt, Maryland, initially offered just five fully detached houses. Dubbed "experimental" houses, these were prefabricated units set somewhat apart from the center of town. The other 880 Greenbelt homes were either in multifamily apartment buildings or rowhouses, all but sixteen of the latter being two-story units, which today might be termed townhouses.[10] This likely reflected a preference among the town's planners for styles favored in Europe, where a detached home in an urban or suburban setting was the exception rather than the rule. It also indicates that the Greenbelt team largely rejected the common idea that such housing would be detrimental to inhabitants. They may have shared walls, but the homes were surrounded by open green space, and so felt entirely different from the overcrowded urban lodgings so denounced by experts.

Greendale's designers, on the other hand, bowed to the wishes of the majority of Milwaukee respondents, nearly three-quarters of whom stated a preference for a single-family detached house. Elbert Peets defended the team's decision to offer primarily these sorts of dwellings by stating that, having driven through nearby neighborhoods and noting the small detached "cottages" he saw there, the planners felt that they had to respect traditional American forms in order to offer housing that locals would find inviting. He wrote in Greendale's Final Report:

> If we should vary too much from this pattern the thing we built, though good of itself as one way to plan housing, might be so far from the deeply rooted folk-way that the two would have nothing in common and no bettering of the old way would come from the example of a new way.[11]

Peets felt that even though the town was to be populated by renters rather than owners, by building detached homes planners could re-create the beneficial influence of traditional homeownership. He wrote:

> We felt that the almost universal desire in America to hold a piece of land as part of the family home is not a mere relic of an outmoded culture of individualism, a relic that ought now to be forgotten. We believed, on the contrary, that personal use of and responsibility for a house and a piece of land around it served to facilitate family cooperation and the home training of children and to establish respect for the rights of other peo-

ple. We believed that it was not entirely romantic idealism to think that to be proprietor of a piece of land helped a man to be a better citizen.[12]

As a result, Greendale offered 274 single-family detached homes, 90 single-family side-by-side duplex units, 168 rowhouses, and just 40 apartments.[13]

While Greenbelt and Greendale offer the two extremes of the program's housing types, with Greenbelt favoring group housing and Greendale

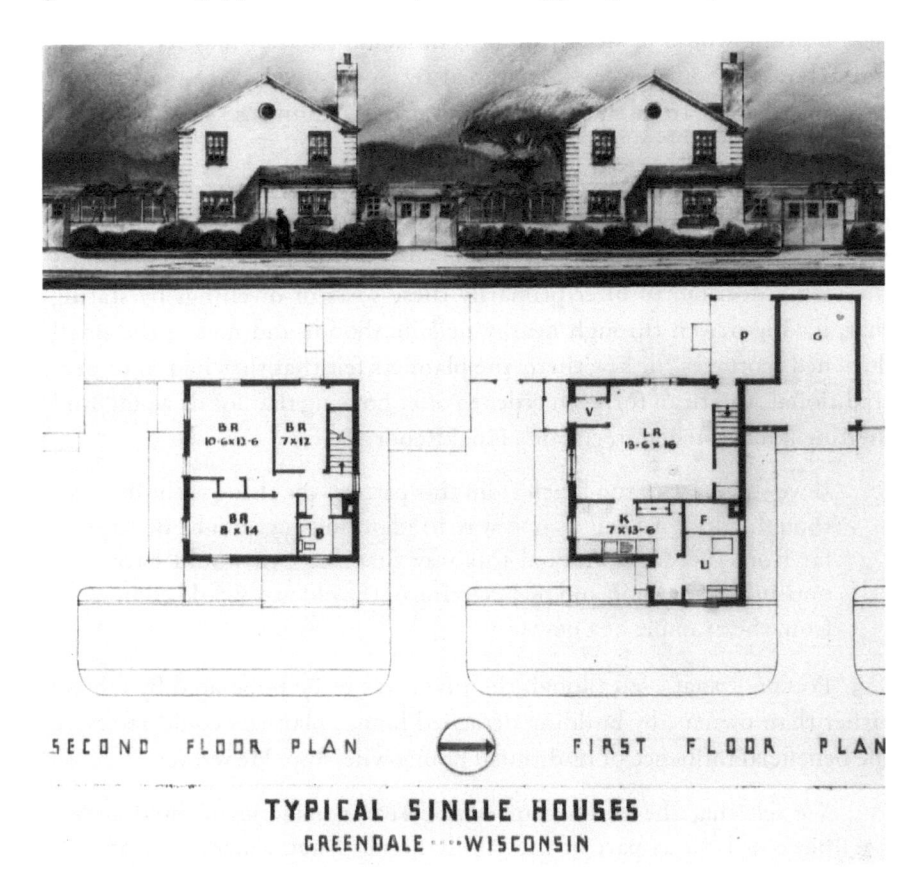

SECOND FLOOR PLAN FIRST FLOOR PLAN

TYPICAL SINGLE HOUSES
GREENDALE ···· WISCONSIN

Figure 9.1. Common style of Greendale single-family detached house (slight changes were made prior to actual construction; for example, the chimneys were placed on the front rather than the side and the arbors connecting house and garage were eliminated). This was the most-used style in Greendale, with 103 built. Courtesy of the Greendale Historical Society, Greendale, WI.

individual homes, Greenhills offered the widest variety of housing types. It featured just twenty-four single-family homes, far fewer than Greendale, but more than Greenbelt (some of these, however, were duplexes sharing only garage walls).[14] These were not prefabricated experimental homes, as Greenbelt's were, but carefully designed, traditional houses. It also contained rowhouses, with the number of units in individual rows varying from one group to the next and units staggered within rows in different patterns. According to Frank Cordner, principal architect for the town, the chief designers believed that "the local preference for detached houses, a preference not confined to this locality, arises largely through unfamiliarity with group houses of limited length and much architectural variety such as are employed on the projects, and that such prejudices as may exist will be overcome in the actual experience of tenants."[15]

The planners of Greenhills used a much more eclectic approach in their unit types and configuration. These seem not to have been random choices; planners appear to have intended to avoid the monotony offered in so many public housing projects, specifically choosing to go in the opposite direction of the architectural repetition that Peets so praised in Greendale.[16] The plans for Greenhills originally included four apartment buildings of two, three, and four stories. They would have provided 107 individual apartments ranging in size from studio (having no separate bedroom) to units with one or two bedrooms. These plans were discarded both because state building codes were stricter for such structures and because the budget was cut as work on the town progressed.[17]

Greenhills, in the early planning stages, was also slated to have what Cordner called a "community

Figure 9.2. Some early house plans for Greenhills, OH. Library of Congress, Prints and Photographs Division, FSA-OWI Collection.

boarding house." This building would have provided rooms for single residents working in the town. This, too, was eliminated as a cost-saving measure, but Cordner noted in a 1937 report that the land where this structure would have been built had been set aside "and will be available in the event that construction of a modest Inn or Restaurant may prove practicable at some future date." That date never arrived.[18]

Table 9.1. Number of Bedrooms and Unit Type by Town as Completed for All Three Towns

	Greenbelt, MD	Greendale, WI	Greenhills, OH
2-bedroom detached	0	44	0
3-bedroom detached	0	230	6
4-bedroom detached	0	0	18
1-bedroom duplex	0	12	–
2-bedroom duplex	0	60	–
4-bedroom duplex	0	18	–
1-bedroom rowhouse	16	0	–
2-bedroom rowhouse	411	126	–
3-bedroom rowhouse	152	42	–
Studio apartment	84	0	0
1-bedroom apartment	222	40	–
Total units	885	572	676

Sources: Farm Security Administration, "Greenbelt Communities," typed report, January 25, 1940, Greenbelt Museum, Greenbelt, MD; Greenbelt Final Report; "First Renters" file," Greendale Historical Society, Greendale, WI.

Notes: Because the design teams kept records differently for each town, it is not possible to make an exact comparison for Greenhills. Does not include experimental single-family homes in Greenbelt.

Table 9.2. House Types by Town as Completed for All Three Towns

	Greenbelt, MD	Greendale, WI	Greenhills, OH
Single-family detached	5	274	24
Duplexes	0	90	80
Rowhouses	574	168	420
Apartments	306	40	152
Total units	885	572	676

Sources: Farm Security Administration, "Greenbelt Communities," typed report, January 25, 1940, Greenbelt Museum, Greenbelt, MD; Greenhills Final Report.

And what of Greenbrook, the Greenbelt town that never was? Architect Albert Mayer noted in November 1935:

> The objective in house planning for speed and economy, as well as for ease in group relationships, is to arrive at a few satisfactory types eventually, to be combined in various interesting ways, rather than to seek a large number of varied individual plans. The cumulative effect of houses planned on the basis of similar considerations, properly spaced and grouped for rhythm and emphasis, is far more effective practically and esthetically than intentionally dissimilar houses which eventually produce an impression of restlessness and affectation.[19]

Early plans for Greenbrook called for accommodations for 750 families. These were to be provided in a variety of configurations: just 0.5 percent would be single-family detached homes, 9.5 percent flats and apartments, and 90 percent semi-detached or group houses.[20] Henry Wright's interest in designing better types of apartment buildings likely accounts for the inclusion of one building that would contain twenty-four units. The Final Report on Greenbrook noted that "it was felt that the existence of one exceptionally well planned apartment house will lend a certain amount of solidity to the Town."[21] The plans for some of the multiple-family buildings show the innovative spirit of the team; each unit included a designated yard, one side of the building being reserved for first-floor tenants and the other side for second-floor tenants.

INSIDE THE HOMES

The first impression upon stepping into one of the Greenbelt towns' homes in the early twenty-first century is that they are inarguably tiny by current standards. Yet they are also cozy and well-built. Reflecting their origins as part of a work-relief project meant to create low-income housing, the homes in the towns are efficient and utilitarian, intended to nurture families without opulence or frills.

Although working more or less independently, the separate planning teams shared some basic ideas in their overall housing designs. Families should have enough interior space for the needs of the occupants, with separate spaces for parents and children, and separate bedrooms for children of the opposite sex. If the occupants were careful and resourceful, even these small homes could provide adequate space for children to study and for parents to relax. The planners sought "to provide, within the frame of economical costs, quarters sufficiently spacious to foster a complete and happy family life."[22] This goal was not unique to the Greenbelts, but does seem to have been pursued with extra care in this highly scrutinized program.

Social critics and reformers had long seen overcrowding in urban slums as quite alarming; however, they generally meant crowding too many buildings into one block, too many families into one building, and the lack of space differentiation within a home. They worried, for example, about people eating, sleeping, and working all in the same room, as had long been common in tenements. They expressed concerns about families taking in boarders with no separation of space between family and non-family occupants.

In contrast, among New Deal housing efforts, as long as homes had separation between shared and private spaces and separate spaces for different household functions, the label of "overcrowded" was not applied, regardless of the often small interior area. The homes' designs and arrangements admitted abundant sunlight and fresh air, the two qualities experts most frequently cited as being essential for healthful and satisfying homes. Ample outdoor space also ensured that these communities would be nothing like the overcrowded slums so despised by reformers.

The designers expected conventional family structures, but they also allowed for a certain degree of flexibility in accommodations. Plans for family homes (as opposed to the few "bachelor apartments" intended for a single occupant) always included a separation between private bedroom space and shared spaces such as living and dining rooms. The designers understood, however, that circumstances in low-income families might force alternate arrangements and compromises. For example, the architects anticipated that, depending on a family's circumstances and needs, some might choose to use the dining area as an additional bedroom.[23] Cordner acknowledged that "in an era of economic pressure, an ideal house plan for families of modest income is one in which every element works to capacity all the time."[24] Many of the homes, for this reason, did not have a separate dining room, planners instead expecting that families would eat their meals at a table in the kitchen.

Rooms within the homes were generally small. In 1935 Clarence Stein conducted a study of minimum space requirements for different types of rooms. In his assessment, a room intended to hold a single twin-size bed, small dresser, and chest of drawers could be as small as 9'10" by 7'4" or 10'2" by 6'10".[25] Although the Greenbelt designers did not make their bedrooms quite this small, they did make many of the rooms in the homes as small as they felt they reasonably could. The "first bedroom" (meaning the largest) in the two most-used home plans in Greenbelt measured 11'2" by 11'8" and 11'4" by 11'8" respectively.[26]

Figure 9.3. Greendale bedroom, 1937. Library of Congress, Prints and Photographs Division, FSA-OWI Collection.

All of the towns' homes were similarly space-frugal, though less so than those in many other New Deal housing programs. A "first bedroom" in Greendale could range from 136 to 200 square feet, while the Federal Housing Administration (FHA) required just 100 square feet for such rooms, and the PWA 110.[27] The Greendale architects concluded that that theirs were "fairly generous bedroom sizes."[28] These would not have been considered terribly small bedrooms at the time, at least within that economic level. The smallest of the ready-to-build kit homes sold by Sears, Roebuck, and Company during the 1920s and 1930s, for instance, frequently offered bedrooms similar in size to those in the Greenbelt homes.[29]

The Special Skills Division of the RA offered custom-designed furniture to residents of the towns. Simple in appearance, the pieces featured clean lines, echoing the Scandinavian style, and were scaled to fit into the small rooms. *House Beautiful* included an article on the furniture in its April 1937 issue, praising the combination of affordability and good design. It argued that "beauty may seem a hypothetical item to some. But in creating a new environment for American families of modest income, it may turn out to be as practical as bricks and mortar."[30] Like the homes, the furniture was no-frills, not large, but sturdy. Residents could pay for their selections in installments. So many residents in Greenbelt, Maryland, ordered the specialized furniture that pieces were on back-order for a time and families had to wait to furnish their new homes.[31]

RA architects and administrators were undoubtedly aware that any sign of luxurious accommodation in this project would invite accusations of government waste. The Greenbelt planners and designers themselves, however, noted that although they worked to keep construction expenses down, they also wanted to experiment with how best to use cost-effective, efficient design in order to demonstrate the possibility of building decent housing, a desire that would likely require a bit more space than the bare minimum. Once again, differing aims within the program made total success difficult, if not impossible.

The same questionnaires that guided the choice of recreational facilities also helped determine home configurations. The analysis of the Washington area questionnaire, for example, told the teams that a two-person household among respondents averaged 1.1 bedrooms; three-person households averaged 1.4 bedrooms; four-person families averaged 1.8 bedrooms; families of five averaged 2.0; and of six 2.3.[32] Milwaukee and Cincinnati showed similar results. In other words, working-class families were used to a certain amount of space sharing, even crowding, in their current homes.

Rules for the Greenbelt towns ensured that the homes would not be filled beyond what experts considered a reasonable capacity. Families were assigned to a specific house size based on the number of occupants. For example, families made up of two parents and two children of the same sex qualified for a two-bedroom home, the assumption being that the siblings would share a room. Only those with two children not of the same sex, or with more than two children, were entitled to a home with three bedrooms.[33] The "spare bedroom" did not exist in these towns. Still, while insisting that there be no excess space, the planning teams ensured enough for privacy. Although it was not unheard of for brothers and sisters to share a bedroom in working-class and poor families, one of the architects working on the Greenbelt towns noted that "objectionable psychological and sociological consequences often result from such intermingling," certainly something to be avoided in these communities.[34] The largest homes in the towns boasted four bedrooms and were intended for families of up to seven.

These arrangements were often in stark contrast to what the families had experienced before their move to the new community. One early resident looked back on the place she had lived prior to the move to Greenbelt. Upon first arriving in Washington for her father's new government job, the family lived in the basement of a DC rowhouse. A bit later they moved to a pair of upstairs rooms in a house shared with others. The three children slept on army cots, which they folded away during the day, and the

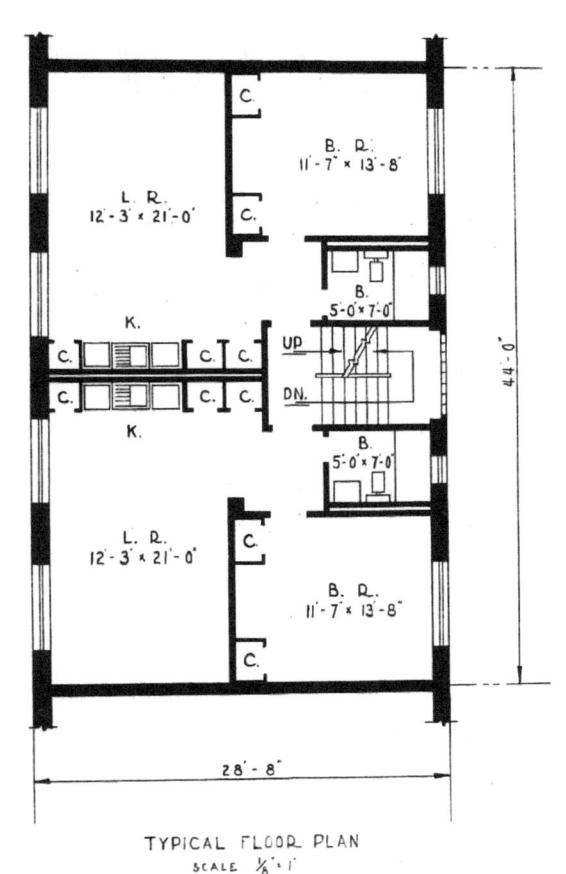

TYPICAL FLOOR PLAN
SCALE ⅛ ' : 1'

Figure 9.4. Floor plan of two mirror-image one-bedroom Greenbelt apartments. The kitchenette counted as one-half of a room; thus this was considered a two-and-a-half room unit, suitable for two-person occupancy. National Archives and Records Administration, College Park, MD.

family shared a bathroom with three or four other families in the home. When they moved to Greenbelt, the daughter got her own bedroom, and her brothers shared a room. It was quite a difference from their previous experience. She recalled also how clean and new everything was—a huge improvement over their earlier urban accommodations, which had been infested with roaches and mice.[35]

Limits on the number of bedrooms and residents also guaranteed that these would not be the sorts of multigenerational households associated in the American mind with poor immigrants, and that there would be no extra space for the taking in of boarders. Some families reimagined the expected sleeping arrangements, however. One early resident, the only daughter of four children, recalled that her parents for a time used the smaller bedroom so that her brothers could have the larger one. She slept in her parents' room with them. At another point, her parents slept on the sofa in the living room, and later still she slept on the sofa so that her parents could have their own bedroom again. Such shuffling around, she said, did not cause any friction within the family; this was simply "the way it was." They still felt privileged to have their Greenbelt home.[36]

Another common aspect of poor and immigrant households alarmed the planners. Researchers for Greenbrook visited nearby Bound Brook, New Jersey, to get a sense of how current residents of the area used their homes. They reported:

> The most prominent living tendency is the use of the kitchen for all purposes. This tendency is true among all nationalities. It is born of foreign conditions and perpetuated here by slum conditions. In the opinion of people familiar with these families if this tendency can be overcome families will be better off... It is felt that this strong tendency does not permit the standard of living which the house space offers.[37]

The architects for the Greenbelts ensured that each room had a designated use and that every space had a purpose, eliminating this multiuse approach. This designation of space was very much in keeping with the middle-class tradition, and represented a turning away from older folkways.

A WOMAN'S PLACE

The designers understood that much depended on the women of the Greenbelts. The experiment could only succeed with the approval and cooperation of the towns' wives and mothers. The plans for the homes' interiors show that the teams saw the need to provide the most up-to-date conveniences if these were truly to function as models for towns and homes for the future.

Although born of a government agency run by men, and being communities largely designed by men, the towns still managed to express a hint of the widening of women's horizons. Planners consulted professional female social workers and home economists, as well as female experts in architecture and housing reform; as a result, the Greenbelt towns illustrate the subtle shift taking place in expectations for and by American women. The designers did not just thoughtlessly repeat past forms, but instead tried to assess women's present needs and anticipate the changes that might lay ahead.

While understandably not foreseeing the enormous shifts to gender roles that would come before the end of the century, many of those engaged in the relatively new field of home economics understood that "the fairer sex" deserved—and possibly even *needed*—more than housework and family caretaking to create meaningful lives. This is not to say that they advocated the abandonment of defined gender roles, or that they asserted that women should have all the options open to them that their male counterparts had, but it did signal a tentative reassessment of previous beliefs that caring for the home and family could provide all the mental and social stimulation any woman could desire.

The most well-known home economist at the time, and the one most studied since, was Christine Frederick.[38] As early as 1914 Frederick asked, "Is the American housewife facing a great revolution? Is the efficiency idea, which has already revolutionized many industrial plants, now going to attack that last stronghold of tradition—the American Home?" She believed so. Noting that, in sharp contrast to earlier decades, just 8 percent of families in 1914 employed domestic help, she acknowledged that the vast majority of women now performed their own household chores. As a result, she stated, "If the home is to survive it must do so on a reorganized basis."[39] This would be her message over the coming years, as the use of domestic servants declined even further. Just as the reductions in immigration had disrupted upward mobility in low-income urban housing, it deprived middle-class housewives of a ready supply of inexpensive immigrant domestic help. As fewer immigrants arrived looking for even the lowest-paying work, the cost of household servants became prohibitive for all but the upper class. By 1932 just 2 percent of American housewives used paid help to do their chores; the other 98 percent were on their own.[40] If a woman hoped to manage the work previously done by servants, tasks must now be done more rationally and efficiently.

In her 1932 book *The Ignoramus Book of Housekeeping*, Frederick called on women to see their work in the home as a profession, and to approach it with the attentiveness and logic applied in business and industry.[41] Like other home economists, Frederick urged housewives to see their work as every bit as productive and necessary as any other labor, and claimed that it could also be as satisfying if approached with the right attitude and tools.

The streamlining of chores certainly seemed necessary. In 1929 economist Hildegarde Kneeland reported that the average housewife spent fifty-one hours per week performing her housework. The numbers dropped slightly, to an average of forty-eight hours, when looking only at housewives in large cities, where homes were presumably smaller and families had access to commercial laundries and other conveniences.[42]

Many assumed that the introduction of new electric gadgets and appliances would revolutionize how women managed the work on their own. A 1925 article on the wonders of vacuum cleaners, electric cookers, and other modern marvels, for instance, bore the title "The Abolition of Household Slavery."[43] In 1932 Frederick contended that

> American women as a mass have made up their minds that they wish to be freer from the crushing, age-old burdens of the home, which have been crushing precisely because they have not been sufficiently industrialized... They insist on the mechanization of the remaining tasks of the home, with the use of electricity and gas to keep pace with the rapid increase in the use of power per worker in the factory.[44]

Figure 9.5. Greendale living room with beamed ceiling, featuring furniture supplied by the Special Skills Division. Library of Congress, Prints and Photographs Division, FSA-OWI Collection.

Yet some technological innovations had actually added to the wife's burden of duties. The introduction of better cooking appliances led to higher expectations for turning out more creative and elaborate meals. The vacuum cleaner brought an increased pressure to keep a perfectly clean house.[45] The family car often turned the mother into the family chauffeur. As one female author noted in 1932, if one listened to some commentators, "One might think that the vacuum cleaners ran themselves and people subsisted on pills, not meals, that shops automatically delivered ready-mades in the very nick of a need."[46] A human—almost always the housewife—had to operate the appliances, buy the groceries, chop the vegetables, iron the clothes, and perform a seemingly never-ending list of other tasks.

Moreover, not all Americans were able to avail themselves of the latest innovations. In 1932, for instance, just 30.4 percent of families even owned a vacuum cleaner.[47] The architects for the Greenbelts took care to ensure that the homes in the towns would represent the latest thinking in household efficiency without lavishness, and of course the homes were fully wired for electricity. This was, by the 1930s, no longer a novelty, nor was it reserved only for the wealthy. For the most part, only those living in rural settings lacked this amenity; the 1930 Census showed that just 13.4 percent of farm homes had electric lights.[48] The fixtures in the Greenbelt homes were simple in design, but for those coming from dimly lit tenements or non-electrified rural homes, they represented the bright, clean, modern life.

Some design choices went beyond simple utility. In Greendale, for example, the living rooms in many of the homes featured wooden beams on the ceiling, recalling colonial designs and bringing a level of quaintness to the space (see Figure 9.5). Colonial styles and the use of antiques in interior design had become something of a fad among the middle class during the 1930s, and the designers of Greendale offered the town's residents this small nod to the past even as they provided what they hoped might be the home of the future.

BATHROOMS

By the early twentieth century medical experts and home economists well understood the importance of good hygiene, so the designers paid particular attention to providing the most up-to-date bath facilities. Although like most Greenbelt spaces the bathrooms were small, they provided precisely the sorts of superior facilities reformers called for.

Sanitary amenities for many Americans had been slowly improving through recent decades, but largely left behind those living in urban or rural poverty. The 1940 census reported that 69.9 percent of all households had running water inside the dwelling (the percentage for the North alone was even higher, at 79.1 percent).[49] Yet when it came to bathing facilities, just 56.2 percent of dwellings had exclusive use of a bathtub and 4.7 percent shared a bath with other tenants or residents; 39.1 percent had no bathtub or shower at all.[50] The statistics for toilet facilities were somewhat better, with 59.7 percent of all dwellings having exclusive use of a flush toilet within the unit and 5 percent having a shared toilet in the building—though many of these facilities were no better than the one shown in Figure 9.6. As late as 1940, 32.2 percent of Americans still relied on an outdoor toilet or privy (although again region made a huge difference; in the North, just 24.1 percent of households used an outdoor privy).[51]

Figure 9.6. (right) Toilet shared by three families in Hamilton County, OH, 1935. Library of Congress, Prints and Photographs Division, FSA-OWI Collection.

Figure 9.7. (below) Original bathroom fixtures in Greenbelt, MD, homes. Greenbelt Museum. Photo by the author.

The bathrooms in all three Greenbelt towns provided porcelain fixtures and chrome and glass hardware—towel bars, toilet paper dispensers, and soap dishes. It was all easy to clean, as was the ceramic tile used on floors and walls.

Although very few of the homes built through the program had more than one bathroom, even for families of up to six or seven people (some of the larger units had a bath and a half), those who lived in the homes did not see themselves as deprived. They had come from far worse living conditions. For them, the gleaming little bathrooms with the bright, clean fixtures were almost certainly an improvement over what they had known before, and in fact over what much of the population possessed. Like everything else about the Greenbelt homes, the bathrooms were certainly not large or opulent, but they still represented state-of-the-art modernity, a vast improvement over tenement or other low-income housing.

KITCHENS

Designers for the towns assumed that a great deal of the work performed by housewives would take place in the kitchen. Although fairly well equipped, the kitchens were, like the other rooms, small. This primarily resulted from efforts at keeping costs down, but it also fit experts' recommendations. A 1929 article in the *American Home*, for example, called large kitchens "a waste of time and energy."[52] One expert writing in *The Better Homes Manual*, which the Greenbrook team consulted in drawing up its plans, also advised that kitchens be kept small for the sake of convenience.[53] A compact but well-organized kitchen offered a modern alternative to the sprawling, inefficient farmhouse kitchen, or the pitifully equipped tenement kitchen then found in many working-class American homes.

Most of the homes in all three towns featured a modern electric refrigerator and range.[54] While electricity itself was common in cities and suburbs by this time, electric refrigeration was still something of a luxury, with just 11.5 percent of American homes having an electric refrigerator in 1932, and just 44.1 percent even by 1940.[55] Just 3.6 percent of homes had electric ranges in 1932, and although many of those who did not cook with electricity used gas, many others continued to rely on coal- or wood-burning stoves.[56]

Figure 9.8. Tenement kitchen, Hamilton County, OH, 1935. Library of Congress, Prints and Photographs Division, FSA-OWI Collection.

Figure 9.9. Kitchen in Greendale. Library of Congress, Prints and Photographs Division, FSA-OWI Collection.

Articles in women's magazines extolled the virtues of the electric range/oven combination, many offering tips for selecting and using it.[57] Because these were still relatively uncommon, in September 1938 experts from Westinghouse offered cooking demonstrations to show Greendale housewives how to use their new stoves.[58] We have no record of whether the wives in the Greenbelt towns agreed with the author of a 1932 *Better Homes and Gardens* article who stated, "When you own one of the new electric ranges cooking is a continuous pleasure," but the white enameled electric appliances in the Greenbelt homes certainly looked like a huge leap forward in cooking technology.[59] If authors of articles such as *Better Homes and Gardens'* "Your Silent Servants" oversold the idea that electric appliances would free the housewife of all drudgery, it still seems likely that the women of these low-income communities appreciated having conveniences previously only available to the upper and middle classes.

In addition to the latest appliances, the kitchens featured cabinets and sinks chosen specifically for both functionality and ease of cleaning. This was in keeping with typical advice of the era, such as a 1931 issue of *Good Housekeeping* promising that a "clean, orderly kitchen is a restful workshop."[60] Kitchens in the Greenbelt homes were no-frills spaces, but they supplied all that a housewife would need to prepare meals, and even if small, offered state-of-the-art conveniences.

As the paid working population had come to expect a certain amount of leisure time, Americans began to feel that housewives, too, should have some free time for other pursuits. Christine Frederick believed that women could find these leisure hours by sticking to strict schedules for the performance of household tasks, and she recommended that a woman have a set "cleaning plan" for each room, an order of operations that would make the work as efficient as possible.[61] If a woman wanted to have any time to spare, she would have to work long days, moving competently and quickly from task to task in a never-ending repetitive cycle. But if she planned well, that cycle would be punctuated with occasional bits of time away from housework.

Frederick suggested that, if possible, a housewife should allot two thirty-minute rest breaks in her daily routine; the remainder of the day would presumably be taken up by one household task or another. These rest breaks, however, hardly counted as leisure time; she recommended, among other possible "restful" activities, gardening and marketing. She noted that if women managed to be particularly well-organized and productive, "by good planning they may have one or more whole afternoons free for club, or other preferred activity."[62]

Eleanor Roosevelt also recognized that housework could be exhausting, though one wonders just how much housework this wife of a wealthy politician had ever performed. In *It's Up to the Women*, she suggested doing the heavy work in the morning; then "a couple of hours' rest should be allowed for before the regular afternoon work has to begin." However, she cautioned,

> Rest does not mean sitting with your hands folded. If you need extra sleep, perhaps you can get a nap, but if not, sewing or reading or doing some kind of work you enjoy may be your rest. It simply means that your regular routine work should be off your mind. [In this section she was specifically addressing farm wives; it is not fully clear whether she meant for this advice about rest to apply to all housewives.][63]

The Greenbelt planners tried to keep the communities' female inhabitants from undue drudgery. Although the small room sizes in the homes resulted mainly from the nature of the program as low-rent housing, it also translated to minimal space to keep clean. Designers chose surfaces for their ease of care and cleaning, with two notable exceptions. The first was the unfortunate choice of black linoleum tiles in many of Greenbelt's homes (ignoring Frederick's published advice that flooring should be "neither too dark nor too light").[64] Housewives in the town complained bitterly about the impossibility of keeping these black floors clean.[65] The task was made virtually impossible while construction on the town was still ongoing, with either red-clay dust or mud being continually tracked into the finished homes by anyone entering. Eleanor Roosevelt pointed out the second mistake when she toured Greendale: the placement of always-dirty coal bins too close to laundry tubs. The First Lady noted that it was obvious that the plans had been made by men; women would have known better.[66] Aside from these minor blunders, the planners clearly paid attention to home economists and other experts in designing the homes.

In choosing to lighten the household burdens of the towns' wives, the program's designers freed some of a housewife's time for socializing or civic activity. This was no accident. A large part of the vision for the Greenbelt towns centered around civic involvement. Women who had no free time could not take advantage of the various clubs and organizations that were to bring citizens together. Frazzled housewives spending every waking minute trying to maintain the home could not be engaged in the larger life of the community. In easing the workload of the towns' wives and mothers, the designers tried to guarantee that the homes would foster a neighborly and democratic spirit. One might also assume that a less-stressed housewife made for calmer family relations within the home.

Although they aimed to make wives' interactions with the homes as pleasant as possible, the designers appear not to have imagined any substantial shift in traditional family roles, and in fact appear to have designed the homes to reinforce middle-class gender status.[67] They assumed that women would largely stay home and run the household, so they designed homes that would be easy for wives to keep clean. They knew that having children outdoors in a safe and healthful environment, rather than underfoot, would aid family harmony. They recognized the need for women to have outlets other than just parenting and housework, but did not expect the women of the towns to work outside the home; in fact, initially families could be accepted as occupants only if the husband was the sole breadwinner.[68] Rather than being at all revolutionary, the changes designed into the towns simply brought traditional roles in line with the latest expert advice. In the end, the towns' architects provided remarkably traditional homes intended for thoroughly conventional families.

10

THE PEOPLE

It was like family. The whole city was almost like one big family.

—Larry Voight, early Greenbelt resident

A final, but absolutely vital, piece of the Greenbelt project remained to be put into place. After the plans had been drawn up and the public relations campaign had swung into action, after the favorable and unfavorable views of the program had been hashed out by politicians and the media, after the laborers had constructed the homes and shopping centers and swimming pools and schools, the towns needed residents. And in some ways, the success or failure of the experiment lay in this final piece as much as—or more than—any other feature of the Greenbelt towns project.

This program had been sold to the president, and eventually to the American people, as a way to ease urban overcrowding and erase urban blight. The three towns alone, of course, could make only the tiniest dent in these enormous problems, but if the experiment succeeded, they could show the way for future developments to carry the work forward and make a meaningful difference in Americans' lives.

In order to provide a proof of concept, the Greenbelts had to actually do what they set out to do. But that was, in truth, all but impossible. Because they were intended to provide the maximum amount of employment for as long as possible, the towns were constructed using inefficient methods. But because they were being paid for with taxpayer money, they needed to appear to be efficient and cost-effective. As they were to demonstrate the potential of new communities, they had to be first-rate, well-planned towns. But because they were to be outstanding communities, with modern facilities and conveniences, low rents could only be offered using federal subsidy, something that smacked of socialism to a huge number of citizens. They had initially garnered the enthusiastic support of the president, but eventually sparked hostile opposition from his detractors. The budget for the program had been squeezed and trimmed time and again, and yet the program was enormously expensive. Budget cuts had left the towns hollowed-out versions of their original concepts with an abundance of infrastructure for far fewer homes than had been anticipated. This seemed to offer up a prime example of federal waste, though in fact this "waste" had been created by the legislators who had slashed funding along the way.

By the time the Greenbelts were nearing completion, the sole aspect of the program over which the administrators still had full control lay in choosing who would occupy the towns. The perceived success of this huge, expensive experiment hinged on filling the communities with people who would show that, given the right living environment, Americans could improve their lives, could rise above the needy classes and become fully productive, respectable, civically engaged citizens.

Despite the expressed aims for the project, in the end the income limits put in place excluded the most needy in the working class. If the administrators had lowered these income requirements, it would have necessitated also lowering the rents, thus increasing the federal subsidy. It is also possible that the income requirements were specifically calculated to keep those in the lower tiers of the working class out of the towns, ensuring that residents would be more in the upper working class and lower middle class, in keeping with the social expectations laid out for the communities. Income requirements ranged from $800 to $1,600 per year for a single person, up to $1,300 to $2,200 for a family of six, with increments set for each family size in between. The income range for a family of four in the Greenbelt towns was $1,100–$2,000. Federal officials defined "low income" as $1,000 to $1,999 for a family of four, and above that as "middle income."[1] The minimum income requirement allowed officials to exclude the poorest workers, while still catering to "low-income" families. It appears that, in spite of their protestations to the contrary, they believed, like the American population overall, that those in the lowest income groups might not make ideal residents.

But could even those who met the requirements rise to administrators' expectations? The answer seemed to be a qualified yes, as long as careful measures were put into place to ensure that only the most promising applicants would be accepted.

RACE AND ETHNICITY

Among the criteria for acceptance into the towns, one in particular seems to have been established almost without question: race. It is safe to say that most White Americans at the time gave little thought to racial inequality on a daily basis. They saw the United States as a White nation built on a proud foundation of western civilization. Twenty-first-century notions of race as a fictional distinction, entirely invented by human societies, would have baffled most people in the 1930s. Race was seen at the time as clearly defined, literally black and white, with most Whites seeing themselves as "real," or at least normal, Americans, and people of color as "other." There was, of course, a wide range of attitudes regarding race, but we must oversimplify a bit to discuss this with any clarity.[2]

Existing norms, even in the North, generally dictated segregated living.[3] Except perhaps in the very poorest areas, Blacks and Whites occupied separate spaces.[4] In Washington, DC, more a southern city than a northern one in character, the idea of racially integrated housing would have been all but unthinkable to most of the local White population. Fourteen African Americans lived on the farms on the outer edge of Greenbelt, but were not considered to be residents and were not included in community activities.[5]

The 1930 census showed the District of Columbia as having a Black population of 132,068 out of the city's total 486,869 inhabitants, or just over

27 percent.[6] At this time the African American population of the nation as a whole was under 10 percent.[7] (A 2002 report by the National Archives points out just how inaccurate these counts may have been, however, noting that "instructions to census enumerators explained that a person who had both 'White and Negro blood was to be returned [counted] as a Negro, no matter how small the percentage of Negro blood.'" The report went on to say, "This categorization of interracial individuals as 'Negro' based on the existence of any Black ancestry reflected the bureau's continued reliance on nineteenth-century racial categories," a reference to the infamous "one-drop rule" that had long defined Black status in the United States.)[8]

The other two cities of the Greenbelt program, in theory, seem more likely candidates for integration, but that was not to be. Although it was more northern in nature than the nation's capital was, Cincinnati sat just across the river from Kentucky, and had always displayed a southern sensibility when it came to race. Discrimination was a prevalent characteristic of Cincinnati at this time, and strongly affected where African Americans could live and work. In 1930, the city had a total population of 451,160. Those identified as "Negro" totaled 47,818, or 10.6 percent of the total population, just barely higher than the national proportion.[9] Cincinnati native and later governor of Ohio John Gilligan recalled the city of his youth in the 1920s and the 1930s:

> Blacks were not allowed in theaters, nor even, as I remember, in Crosley Field [home of the Cincinnati Reds baseball team], or [local amusement park] Coney Island. There was virtually no social intercourse of any description between the races—it was absolute *apartheid* all the way. The racial attitudes which so shaped and influenced our own city seemed simply a part of the natural environment. That is just the way things were, had always been, and always would be.[10]

Coney Island would not be fully desegregated until 1961.[11] Clearly, being in a "northern" city gave no guarantee to Black Cincinnatians that they would be welcome everywhere.

Milwaukee had a much smaller Black population, at just 7,500 out of a total population of 578,249, or less than 1.3 percent.[12] This should not lead to the belief that racism was any less established there than in any other northern city, just that it would have been far less visible because African Americans themselves were far less visible. It is too easy to assume that racism existed only in the South, or only in places where the Black population was large enough to be seen by Whites as a "problem." Segregation and racism, almost without exception, existed everywhere in the United States at this time.

Yet some in the RA considered the possibility of helping African Americans. Several administrators believed that the New Deal should reach all citizens, regardless of race; perhaps the most notable of these was deputy RA administrator Will Alexander (a White southerner). In *Seeds of Southern Change: The Life of Will Alexander*, authors Wilma Dykeman and James Stokely explain Alexander's attitudes: "Negroes were not a Cause with him, although for twenty-five years after the First World War he was leader of the Interracial Commission in Atlanta, the principal agency working for justice and harmony in southern race relations." Instead, "Negroes were persons whom he cared for as individuals."[13] The fact that Alexander understood African Americans as individuals, and not as mere stereotypes, was rare enough at the time.[14]

Dykeman and Stokely also note the differences between Tugwell and his colleague, saying that Alexander

> had no academic background... [but] his patience with human frailty was remarkable... Tugwell had an intellectual range and agility and physical attractiveness that far exceeded Alexander's. But there was about [Alexander] a quality of solid goodness that perhaps drew him into easier friendships with a wider range of fellow Americans, permitting him to arrive, through sympathetic involvement, at many of the same conclusions Tugwell reached through cerebration.[15]

Both men seem to have been able, to an extent greater than most of their contemporaries, to see the humanity beneath the skin tone.

The inclusion of some African Americans was, in fact, briefly considered when the initial plans for the towns began to take shape. The original proposal for Greenbelt specified that nearly a third of the land purchased for the project would be set aside for Black residents, but in a separate section to be called Rossville. This would have been a "rural development," rather than part of the main suburban portion of the town. Exactly how serious these plans were is unclear. Will Alexander had stated in October 1935 that "there is little likelihood that any of the [Greenbelt] houses will be rented to colored tenants," but eight months later Rossville was added to the plans. Then, somewhere along the line, the Rossville idea disappeared from the project, quietly dropped, apparently without fanfare or comment.[16]

The attitudes of the wider population certainly would have been taken into account, and these attitudes were far from enlightened or inclusive. A report written by Milton Lowenthal of the RA's Suburban Division Research Section evaluated the racial and ethnic characteristics of the low-income inhabitants of the Cincinnati area, primarily the small village of Mt. Healthy, the nearest settlement to the Greenhills site. Dated February 1936, the assessment reads: "The inhabitants of this area are predominantly of German descent. There is a good proportion of negros [sic], and there are many 'hill-billy' Kentuckians, who have been brought in to work in the factories. From all indications, it will be impossible to consider negros for the project."

The report highlights the fact that prejudices of the era were not limited to race alone. Lowenthal continued: "The Kentuckians are shiftless and live on a very low standard (to which they are accustomed)." He concluded that this left for serious consideration only those of German descent. These, he noted, would make fine residents, being generally "good home-makers,... serious-minded, law-abiding, highly moral (church-goers), and somewhat conservative." Lowenthal admitted that the Germans did "not have too much imagination, but [were] not afraid of progress." It was hardly a glowing assessment, but far more favorable than the Kentuckians received.

He presented a progression of desirability: White residents whose ancestors had come from the more "civilized" regions of Europe—German immigrants in this case—then, much less desirable, the "hillbilly" Kentuckians, and last, the essentially unwanted African Americans. Here Lowenthal was showing his own biases, but he also undoubtedly mirrored the opinions of White society at large.

The New Deal overall, as has been noted by many historians, at times worked on behalf of Black Americans, but far more often left them out.[17] As historian Jefferson Cowie has noted, "There could be no whisper of black participation in the New Deal or there would be no political coalition"—

and so no New Deal at all.[18] There were some, however, who pushed for more inclusive policies. Dr. Robert C. Weaver, the first African American in the federal cabinet, held the title of "Advisor on Negro Affairs" in the US Department of the Interior.[19] In 1938 he wrote a clear-eyed account of the challenges facing Black Americans looking for better housing options. "When the incidences of race prejudice and racial attitudes are added to the national development of a slum," he wrote, "the problem becomes acute." The reason: "With a growth in the demand for housing for colored people, there is no corresponding supply."[20] The same mechanisms that worked to create a critical shortage of decent homes for lower-income White Americans affected minorities, but what was a serious problem for Whites was an almost insurmountable obstacle for Black citizens. In the rural South they faced discrimination in housing, employment, and education, along with a general societal hostility. In the urban North, they paid much higher prices for less desirable homes because landlords held all the power in determining who could live where, and at what price. For the few who had the means to purchase a home, the prospects were hardly better, as Blacks were routinely excluded from all but the poorest neighborhoods.

A report from 1949 titled "Public Housing Administration Racial Relations Policy," and labeled "Confidential," noted that in southern states, integrated housing was simply not an option, as the local White population would not tolerate it. However, the report also noted that even "in most Northern communities where there are no established patterns of enforced racial segregation in the use of public-aided facilities, varying degrees of racial segregation do exist in some residential neighborhoods."[21] Such a finding certainly would have come as no surprise to most Americans at the time.

One reason given for not integrating Greenbelt, Maryland, was the planned "Negro" housing at Langston Terrace Dwellings in Washington, DC.[22] This modern housing project promised to provide for African American families in the area, at least in part, what Greenbelt would offer to White residents. Langston Terrace, designed by respected Black architect Hilyard Robinson, opened in the spring of 1938. The first residents tended not to be from the very poorest and most blighted slums in DC, but did see Langston as a significant improvement, either due to lower rents or superior living conditions.[23] However, in spite of the clean and inviting environment, the careful planning, and the whimsical animal sculptures for children to play on, Langston Terrace was undeniably urban—no meandering paths through vast green spaces, no surrounding woodlands, no suburban dream come true. But its very existence allowed government officials to shrug off any insinuations that Greenbelt should perhaps be integrated. A scholar of Greenbelt wrote in 1944, "Even a self-styled 'liberal' said, 'Negroes wouldn't be happy here. They should have communities just like this, but it would do no one any good to mix them here.'"[24] White Americans for the most part wanted to keep the races separate, and convinced themselves that Black citizens felt the same way. Giving them their own housing project, away from Whites, could thus be rationalized as an act of kindness.

Many early Greenbelt residents were unaware that the towns were intentionally segregated. One resident of the Maryland town said later: "There were no blacks. Washington was rigidly segregated in those days, so it is not likely that blacks... would have applied."[25] Another speculated that Blacks did not want to live so far from the city.[26] At a time when few White Americans gave much thought to the plight of African Americans, it is perhaps unsurprising that many simply accepted the all-White community without questioning how it came to be that way. Residential segregation was so profoundly entrenched in American society that, for most Whites, it just seemed natural.

Cincinnati was not originally slated to have specific New Deal housing for the city's Black residents. A low-income housing project that was frequently compared to Greenhills, Laurel Homes, was, like the new Greenbelt town, initially to be for White residents only. The project was true slum clearance under the auspices of the PWA.[27] An artist's rendering in the *Cincinnati Enquirer* in March 1936 shows a sprawling complex of apartment buildings. The following month the *Enquirer* ran articles comparing the two plans. Laurel Homes, which was to be constructed in the crowded, impoverished West End of Cincinnati, would house four thousand residents on thirty acres. Greenhills was at that point projected to house roughly the same number of inhabitants, but on six thousand acres, including the greenbelt and surrounding farmland.[28]

Although African American families were among those displaced to make room for Laurel Homes—most of the city's Black population resided in the West End—they were not initially intended to be eligible for any of the units in the new development. In the spring of 1937, local Black leaders and residents began calling for some of the units in Laurel Homes to be "allotted to Negroes."[29] In the end, authorities agreed to set aside 30 percent of the units in the project for Black tenants; these units were themselves racially segregated and somewhat isolated from the remainder of the complex.[30] Cincinnati would see the construction of several new, Black-only housing projects beginning in 1940, including Lincoln Court, across the street from Laurel Homes.

When it came to the Greenbelt towns, RA administrators knew that they had to keep political fireworks to a minimum. They would have understood that pressing for racial integration would have generated a new opening for angry opposition to a program already under attack on several fronts. Given the racial attitudes among Whites of the day, the fact that little thought was given to even the possibility of integrating the Greenbelt towns should not come as a surprise, though many today see it as a lost opportunity.

Although African American families were not welcome as residents in the Greenbelt towns, many did nonetheless benefit from the program. Photos of the construction clearly show an integrated workforce, though how much the two races were actually working *together* is unclear.

Figure 10.1. Greenbelt workmen at lunch. Library of Congress, Prints and Photographs Division, FSA-OWI Collection.

After the town was settled, a small number of African Americans continued to be employed there. A doctoral dissertation from 1944 noted that these jobs were low-status positions such as janitors. The author, William Form, related that these Black workers "are at the bottom of the status hierarchy. They are not greeted by housewives like some of the White service workers. They have the worst jobs, the least pay, and no deference is paid to them."[31] Such was life in the 1930s for the majority of African Americans.

GETTING IN

Bill Shields needed a job. His family had come from Georgia and Florida; his wife had roots in Ohio and West Virginia. But during the Depression, like so many desperate others, they found their way to Washington, DC, as the federal government was among the few employers still hiring. Bill secured a position with the Interior Department and the family managed to rent space in a home that they shared with strangers. It was less than ideal for a couple with two young sons, but at least they now had money coming in.[32]

The family enjoyed another stroke of good luck when they applied for a home in a new planned community nearby. The selection process narrowed the flood of applicants down to a chosen few. To make the final list, they had to be deemed, among other criteria, to be a family with low income whose current residence was judged "least adequate."[33]

Mr. and Mrs. Shields's son Lee was just three months old when his family moved from the crowded city to the quiet suburban retreat of Greenbelt, Maryland, but he grew up understanding how fortunate his family had been. Instead of spending his childhood in a crowded city, he lived and played in a nearly idyllic community filled with friends and playmates, surrounded by nature. He reflected on his good fortune years later: "Compared with starting life in somebody else's house, it was magnificent. It was brand new and it was sumptuous."[34]

Because eligibility for specific house types depended on family size, it was not unusual for families to move from one house to another within the town as they had more children. After a younger sister came along, the Shields family moved to a slightly larger home in the town, a style known as a two-and-a-half-bedroom unit, the half bedroom—which Lee and his brother shared—being much smaller than the regular bedrooms.[35] From the children's point of view, their second Greenbelt home had something much better than large rooms; theirs was an end unit in a row of connected homes, which according to Lee boasted the largest yard in the community. He was "overjoyed" with this development.

As with many of the Greenbelt towns' early residents, this family found themselves in a remarkable situation, one in stark contrast to their recent experiences. Here Lee and his siblings could walk to school in safety, their mother could mingle with friends and neighbors as she did daily errands, their father could find calm at the end of the day, all for a rent of about $45 per month.[36]

The design of the town—the courtyards and walking paths, the movie theater and pool—Lee later recalled, added to the sense of community and neighborliness. Everyone helped everyone else. Greenbelt was perfect for children. He and his friends sometimes spent all day at the theater. They used the swimming pool nearly every day in the summer and skated on the lake in the winter. They played in the woods. Lee had, in short, a childhood utterly unlike anything he could have experienced had his family stayed in Washington. When he married his wife, Bonnie, who lived in nearby Berwyn Heights, they agreed that Greenbelt was their "first and only choice" for raising their own family.

Carl Jernberg, like Bill Shields, brought his young family to Greenbelt in its earliest days. He had once been on a path long recognized as the road to financial and social independence; as a south Texas farmer with a wife and children, he embodied the American character of determination and independence. Then the Depression changed everything. When the hard times came, it became increasingly difficult to support his family through farming, and by 1937 he had to seek other work. Reluctant to turn his back on agriculture completely, he took the civil service exam, hoping to obtain a job in nearby Brownsville. Such a position would enable him to earn a living while keeping his farm. But when he received notice that a position was available, he and his wife faced the difficult decision. The job would be in Washington, DC. The couple considered whether they should continue to try to survive in Texas or take their sons to a bustling city clear across the country. They eventually decided that they had to go where the work was;

jobs were simply too scarce to turn one down, no matter how wrenching such a move might be.[37]

But Washington was certainly nothing like south Texas. At this time housing experts recognized the nation's capital as one of the most congested and rundown urban residential areas in the United States. It must have seemed to the Jernbergs that they had gained a steady income at the expense of the sort of life they had envisioned for their boys. Carl was the kind of man Americans revered: hard-working, not asking anyone for a handout even in tough times. Yet the reward for his determination was an overcrowded city environment that seemed no fit place to raise children. Like the Shields family, the Jernbergs were fortunate; they had lived in Washington just nine months before they were able to move on, trading city life for the quiet suburban life in Greenbelt. It must have felt like a dream come true.

The chosen few families who moved into the new Greenbelt towns became part of a social experiment. They would be the vanguard, demonstrating that enlightened planning could pave the way for better housing and improved home life for families across the nation. To ensure the program's success, administrators chose the towns' first occupants with great care. Potential residents were expected to have the right attitude, to be willing to work toward the success of the community. In other words, the RA rigged the experiment's results.[38]

Among the guidelines for selecting residents for Greenbelt was the statement: "The family should desire to meet objectives of the community, namely to raise their standard of living by taking advantage of the improved living conditions offered; as well as to participate in a cooperative-minded community for the mutual advantage of the group both from the economic and social standpoints."[39] Administrators felt that the towns must be properly populated, must not confirm the worst fears of their critics. They must not devolve into slums, they must not become breeding grounds for delinquency and crime, and they must show that an improved environment would enhance not just the lives of the individual residents, but by extension, national stability and the civic strength of the American people.[40]

In September 1936 the RA began to accept initial inquiries for residency in Greenbelt; selection activities for the other towns would follow, with Greenhills not beginning this work until October 1937 and Greendale by February 1938.[41] The agency created criteria for choosing who would be able to obtain a home in the towns, with an overall set of standards for the program that would then be adjusted to fit each individual community.[42] Those wishing to be considered had to fill out a half-page registration form that asked such basic questions as name of head of household, current address, employer, and means of transportation to work. In addition, those registering were required to provide information about their current living conditions, including rent paid, salary, and the names of all household members.

These preliminary registration cards allowed the RA (after September 1937 the FSA) to weed out families who failed to meet the basic eligibility criteria. For Greenbelt, one of the most important factors, initially at least, was income.[43] The head of the household had to be employed and the family income had to fall within the specified range for a family of their size.

Based on their answers to these questions, potential residents received one of three replies from the RA. Many were rejected on the basis that they failed to meet the basic requirements. They were assured, however, that if the family's status changed the agency would be willing to review their registration. Some received instead a letter stating that there was "some doubt" as to the family's eligibility. These families would be asked for more information. The fortunate few received notice that they had been deemed eligible to apply for residency and were scheduled for an appointment to meet with tenant selection officials.[44] This by no means guaranteed them a home, but it was an important first step toward that goal.

Following this meeting, the interviewer filed a report summarizing the family's eligibility and potential as a good fit for the community.[45] While much of the information was strictly a matter of numbers and facts, some was subjective, such as the interviewer's sense of family cohesion and harmony, or personalities and attitudes that might pose problems in the town.[46]

Over 3,000 families submitted registration forms for the 572 homes in Greendale, and 2,700 for one of Greenhills' 676 homes. At Greenbelt, over 5,700 families returned the registration forms.[47] Presumably, the larger number of registrations for Greenbelt represents the much more desperate housing situation in and around the nation's capital, as men like Bill

Shields and Carl Jernberg found work with the government, but no acceptable housing in the city for their families.

If a family was judged a good possible addition after being assessed by the interviewer, and then being reviewed by a supervisor, they were asked to fill out a longer application form. Of the 5,700 registrations at Greenbelt, 2,300 families were invited to submit this more in-depth application.[48] This form again asked such basic questions as number of family members who would be moving to the town, residential and employment histories, and income, but it also inquired about indebtedness, education level, health, and car ownership.[49] Families also had to supply references from creditors, employers, and landlords. These references would be checked by a member of the selection team, and the family rated on a scale from being a "poor" prospect to "excellent."[50]

Next, the RA sent a representative from the Family Selection Committee to the prospective tenants' current home. In Greenbelt, at least, some families were visited multiple times. RA workers used a rating sheet to quantify such factors as physical need (current neighborhood; ventilation, heating, and sanitation in current dwelling), financial need, and social need.[51] One early resident recalled that when a representative visited the family's apartment to assess their desirability as residents, "he opened the drawers and went through everything."[52] Agents also noted how frequently the family had moved. They recorded current incomes and rent paid. And, as in the initial interview, the visiting RA representative noted family dynamics and the level of interest expressed in the Greenbelt project overall.

It is not clear how uniform the process was in the different towns, but for Greenhills, these rating sheets and summaries were reviewed by the division supervisor and then, if approved at that level, to a selection committee made up of the community manager and department supervisor, and the chairman of Cincinnati's Better Housing League.[53]

Failure to meet the income requirements, because the family earned either too much or too little, formed the primary reason applicants were turned away. At Greenhills, apparently in December 1938, 114 families had been rejected. Of these, forty-eight had too high an income and just one had too low (relying solely on a pension). Thirty-three were denied due to poor credit, four for "health factors," and two because they kept a boarder. Among the more subjective criteria, four failed to be accepted because of "poor adjustment in community," three due to poor family relationships, and two for their attitude toward the project.[54]

Much of the specific information on how tenants were selected has been lost over time, but we do have some selection criteria. For Greenbelt, the head of the household had to be at least twenty-one years old, and families with young children were preferred. Eighty percent were to be current residents of Washington, with the other 20 percent split evenly between those residing in Virginia and Maryland. There were also limits on how many residents could work for the federal government, and how many from each department.[55]

A publication titled *An Analysis of Methods and Criteria Used in Selecting Families for Colonization Projects*, written by J. B. Holt and published in 1937, offers some other potential clues for how families were selected. The author explains the way residents were chosen for rural "colonies," including those created by the Resettlement Administration. Because federal agencies tended to standardize procedures across programs, it seems likely that many of the same criteria that were applied for rural resettlement were also used for the suburban Greenbelt towns. Holt noted that the RA appeared to be "systematizing more and more completely its selection techniques,... emphasizing particular qualifications only with reference to the special requirements of individual projects."[56] Holt lists some of the criteria used across different federal agencies: education, health, age, and sex distribution of family members, all of which seem logical enough. But in keeping with the desire to ensure the potential for the success of resettlement projects, aspects such as "character, stability, and a sense of responsibility" were also considered. Holt specifically mentioned a social worker employed by the RA as stressing that "it is of primary importance that the family as a unit wish to own and establish a new home and have active participation in a growing community."[57] Other generally desirable characteristics for various projects included "cooperative ability," along with "religiosity, idealism, and emotional loyalty to a group."[58]

The fact that religiosity was included might seem strange for a government effort, where the separation of church and state would be expected. However, since this was included in the overarching category that listed idealism and loyalty, it was apparently not a make-or-break criterion on its own. These attributes, Holt observed, were "useful insofar as they foster...

cooperative and harmonious family life, good character,... and ability to cooperate in a common enterprise."[59] Not religion itself, but a desire to belong to a larger assemblage working for the common good, seemed particularly desirable.

Still, a box on the application forms for the towns did ask about religious affiliation.[60] Administrators said that they wanted Greenbelt, Maryland, to reflect the makeup of the greater DC population. The glaring exception to this plan was in excluding Black residents, and of course the income limits also kept the community from being a true mirror of the larger city. The guidelines stated that no more than 70 percent of the residents could be government workers. Officials also sought to have a variety of religious affiliations represented, with about 30 percent Catholics, 63 percent Protestant, and 7 percent Jewish.[61] Apparently administrators kept the inclusion of Jews quiet until just before residents began moving into the town.[62] It is unclear to what extent the selection committees for Greenhills and Greendale made use of the religious affiliation of residents in choosing who would and would not be welcomed into the towns.

It seems that Greenbelters accepted this somewhat limited "diversity." One early resident recalled Jewish families living next to Greeks, who lived next to those who had migrated from Appalachia.[63] This should perhaps not be surprising given that those with progressive views were favored in the selection process. As long as potential residents were considered by the larger population to be "white," they were apparently welcomed into the Greenbelt towns, and were seen as representative of the American populace.

In Greenbelt the Central School building served as the place for religious services in the early years, before the groups could build their own houses of worship. Such cooperation formed a hallmark of the community, from sharing worship space to the cooperative businesses in the commercial center, to the civic engagement of the residents.[64] The idea that the town was equally meant for all residents, and that all residents were equally part of the community, served as a central tenet.

Although Greenbelt administrators were adamant about the requirements for potential residents, screeners for the other two towns found that they could not be quite so stringent, as the demand for homes by qualified applicants was apparently lower than they had expected. In February 1939, ten months after the town opened to residents, 52 of Greendale's 572 homes remained unoccupied.[65] An article in the February 21, 1939, *Cincinnati Enquirer* quotes City Councilman Charles P. Taft, who had served on the Greenhills Advisory Board, as saying that "Greenhills is admitting families of incomes way above the United States Housing Authority maximum and it is not even requiring that they come from substandard housing."[66] Greenhills opened to its first residents in April 1938, but the town did not reach full occupancy until April 1940. Administrators in Greenhills and Greendale may have become more lenient about the acceptance guidelines as their towns sat partially empty.

One rule, however, was upheld in all three towns in the early years: wives were not permitted to be employed. This seems to have been primarily driven by the then-common belief that married women should devote themselves to home and family.[67] It also reflects the general definition of "middle class" in the early twentieth century; a family that needed more than one income to stay afloat would be seen as working class. Even though workers were originally slated to inhabit the towns, we see here a tension between the intent to aid the working class and the perceived desirability of having a largely middle-class, or at least middle-class-aspiring, population in the towns.

During the Depression a majority of Americans felt that women who worked for wages were taking jobs that rightfully belonged to men. A 1938 Gallup Poll asked, "Do you approve of a married woman earning money in business or industry if she has a husband capable of supporting her?" Seventy-eight percent of respondents said no; among men answering, 81 percent said no, but even among women, 75 percent disapproved of a wife working if she could be supported by her husband.[68] Still, as men lost their jobs or saw their hours cut, many families found that their survival depended on wages brought home by working wives, a situation that led to some apprehension about emasculated husbands. The issue of employment for married women, then, carried enormous social and cultural implications.

Some wives gave up their jobs in order to meet the Greenbelt program's eligibility requirements. Although this was most likely a purely pragmatic choice for the majority of those who did so—they saw a better home as being much more important than a larger income—it paradoxically set the family more firmly in middle-class standing even as their financial situation worsened.

The rule against working wives in the towns would be relaxed during World War II, when the federal government urged women—even married women—to do their part for the war effort by taking on jobs left vacant by servicemen. The rule would not be reinstated with the return of peace.

As people began applying for homes in the towns, supporters continued to make the case that this was a wonderful experiment. First Lady Eleanor Roosevelt made a point of painting a glowing picture of Greenbelt, Maryland. She had taken quite an interest in the program from the start, and maintained a greater curiosity than did her husband as the project unfolded.[69] In her syndicated newspaper column "My Day," she relayed in December 1937:

> This has been an interesting day. Dr. Will Alexander, the Administrator of the Farm Security Administration in the Department of Agriculture, and I went out to the Greenbelt, Maryland, project this morning to see what changes had come about since last spring.
>
> House after house is now occupied, a temporary cooperative store is open, a school is functioning and this place, which had only workmen when I was there before, is now a real community. I was amused to have the young mayor tell me that everyone wanted to hold meetings and start community activities, and that, though they had not grown up together, everybody wanted to know everybody else.[70]

The First Lady and Greenbelt's mayor, of course, were both motivated to play up the success of the town.

But we cannot ignore the fact that many early residents of the towns praised these as nearly ideal places to live. Some families remained in the towns for generations, or left but returned after discovering that they missed the community spirit. It seems that a great many of those who settled in one of these bright new towns felt themselves extremely fortunate.

One such resident was George A. Warner, an accountant who moved his family to Greenbelt in 1938. He would go on to serve on the city council and as mayor, as well as being editor of the local newspaper, the *Cooperator* (the title a nod to the cooperative businesses and general goals of the town). He later wrote a book about his experiences, *Greenbelt: The Cooperative Community*.[71] In it he described the reaction he and his wife had on deciding to move to the community:

> We realized that there would be many drawbacks. We would be leaving home and friends to be taking up residence in a new town among new people... We would be engaging in an untried experiment which gave no assurance of success.

And, as other residents later recalled, moving to a Greenbelt town meant "letting the whole world know that we were a so-called low-income family," which brought with it a degree of shame.[72]

The couple also saw the advantages. "We would be getting a fresh start under the best possible auspices," he wrote.

> We would have the satisfaction of exercising such talents as we possessed in a community dedicated to progress. We could engage in important and constructive work. We would become part of a classless society composed of persons of our own income status, where worth would be measured in terms of contribution to community welfare. We could grow in soil dedicated to democratic citizenship and derive those satisfactions which stem from working with others toward a common goal.[73]

Rexford Tugwell himself could not have stated a better case for making the move.

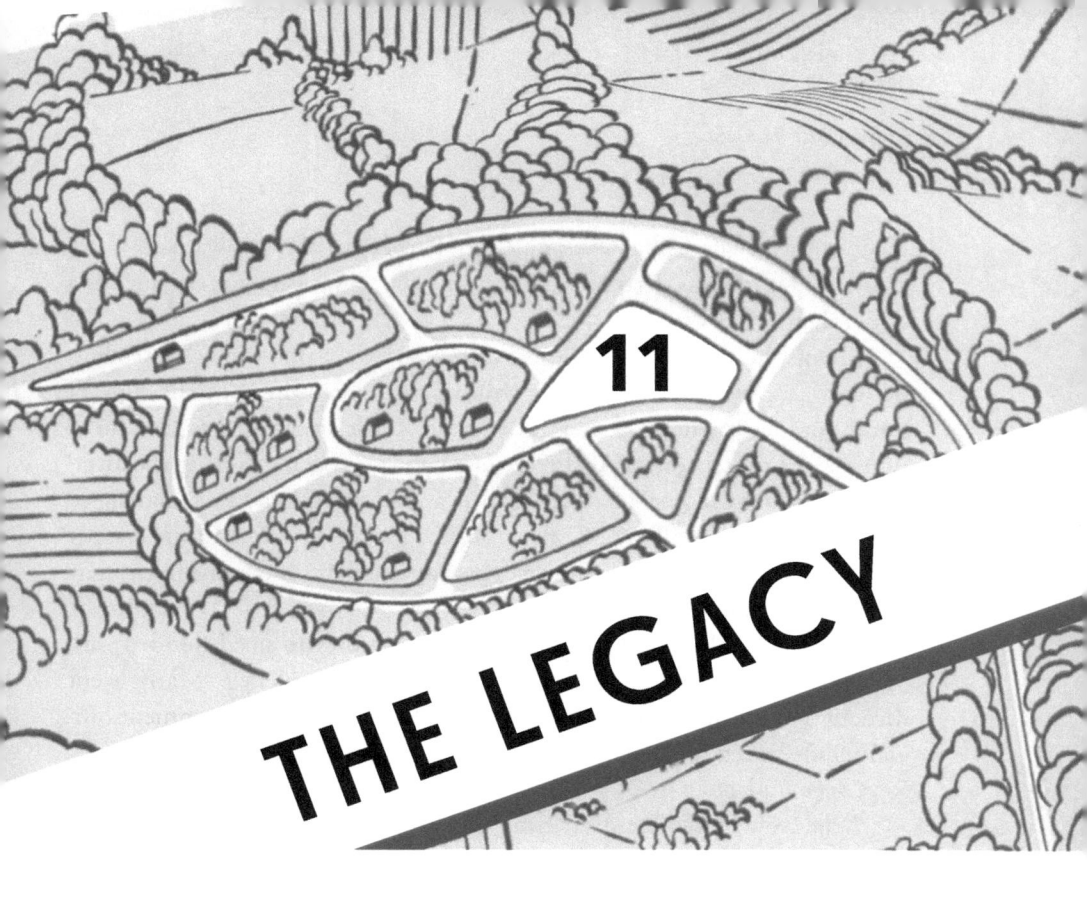

11

THE LEGACY

No apology, no explanation, no justification is needed. The project stands for all to see as a newer and better way to live. It is its own justification, well planned, well built, and serving those whose crying needs made this undertaking imperative.

—Justin Hartzog, 1938

I n February 1938 Marvin McIntyre, one of Franklin Roosevelt's secretaries, opened an envelope and found a handwritten letter accompanied by a somewhat grainy black-and-white snapshot. The photo showed a man with three young children; the letter was signed "Cassilda P. Berg." It described the Berg family's desperate search for a decent home. They had moved to Milwaukee when Mrs. Berg's husband found work there in 1936, but the job evaporated after just four months. They applied for a farmhouse offered by the Resettlement Administration, but that opportunity failed to pan out. They next appealed directly to Eleanor Roosevelt for help in finding somewhere better to live; she replied that they should try for a place in the new housing development of Parklawn, near Milwaukee. Once again the family was disappointed, finding that they were not eligible for a home there.

Now the parents and four children shared a one-room apartment, because, as the writer observed, "children are not wanted in the type of houses or apartments we can afford to rent." The situation was becoming urgent. The oldest son, aged three and a half, had been suffering the after-effects of a bout of encephalitis for over a year. The family was "having to struggle just to stay alive." Mr. Berg worked for the WPA, making $90 per month. Might they, Mrs. Berg asked, perhaps qualify for a home in the new town of Greendale?[1]

Such appeals to federal officials from families in need flooded into Washington throughout Franklin Roosevelt's presidency. Many went directly to FDR himself, many to the First Lady, many to government officials. Some asked for jobs, some for relief payments, and some, like this one, for a decent place to live.

The New Deal offered a lifeline to countless families across the nation, but it could not help everyone. McIntyre sent the letter on to an administrator at the FSA. From there the trail grows cold. Mr. and Mrs. Berg did not settle with their family in Greendale, and never told their children about the letter they had sent, perhaps because it represented one more disappointment for a family that had already faced many.[2]

The Bergs' story is less triumphant regarding the Greenbelt towns than those of the Shields and Jernberg and Warner families. This episode illustrates the limits of the program's success. In the end, slightly over two thousand families found homes in the newly completed Greenbelt communities. An article published in *Life* magazine in 1937 had been right: The greatest failing of such "demonstration projects" was that they had "made scarcely a dent in the great and growing problem of providing adequate living quarters for the 'ill-housed' one-third of America."[3] The Greenbelt towns, ambitious and expensive as they were, represented just a tiny drop in a vast ocean of desperate need.

Of course, nobody had expected this experiment to solve the nation's housing crisis single-handedly. It would be absurd to judge the success of the towns using such an unreasonable standard. Although we can acknowledge that the number of families directly aided by the program was quite small, we can still assess other aspects of this venture. The success of the Greenbelt project can be judged on several different levels: as low-cost housing, as a work-relief program, as a possible template for alternatives to crowded cities and expensive suburbs, and as actual communities.

The timing of the Greenbelt program undoubtedly worked against it. By the time the towns were being planned and constructed American enthusiasm for many of FDR's experiments had begun to wane. People saw more and more money being spent, but not the quick return to prosperity they had hoped for. By 1936 the New Deal was in an indefensible position. As historian William Leuchtenburg put it, "The more successful the New Deal was, the more it undid itself."[4] Expensive and experimental plans seemed no longer necessary once they began to work. On the other hand, if a program appeared not to be providing a speedy enough benefit it was labeled a failure.

THE GREENBELTS AS LOW-COST HOUSING

Homes in the Greenbelt towns were affordable, but only because the federal government had no expectation of recouping the costs of construction. Using Greenhills as an example, rents paid in the Cincinnati area, according to the surveys tabulated by the RA, had ranged from $10 to $35 per month, with the average being $20.54.[5] In Greenhills, base rents ranged from $18 for a one-bedroom apartment to $49 for a four-bedroom detached house.[6] Although the rents were slightly higher than those reflected in the Cincinnati surveys, the neighborhood, local facilities, and homes in Greenhills were far superior, at great government expense.

The program certainly failed to show how to produce low-cost housing for the enormous number of Americans in need. Much of this book has discussed the factors that made it nearly impossible for this program to fully succeed on this front. Although opposition from conservative politicians hampered the RA's efforts, and the outcome of the Greenbrook court case eventually curtailed the larger goals, money proved the most insurmountable hurdle. All told the project cost the federal government over $36 million.[7] The administration had to defend endlessly against charges that it was frittering away public funds and engaging in wasteful self-indulgence.

Those attempting to evaluate the cost-effectiveness of the program, both at the time and in the years since, have arrived at vastly differing figures depending on what criteria they have applied. A 1938 article in *Nation's Business* sneered at government efforts to whittle the cost per unit down to a palatable amount. Claiming that the cost came to $16,000 per home if dividing the total price tag by the number of homes, author George Morris stated that the FSA had arrived at lower numbers only by deducting the cost of intentional inefficiency aimed at employing more men, the cost of all public buildings, and the cost of infrastructure. Only by this "elastic" measurement, the author claimed, could the agency arrive at a final figure of just $5,423 per housing unit. Morris appears to have intentionally missed the point of the Greenbelt program, that the use of inefficient methods was indeed part of the plan from the start and that these towns were always intended to be something more than just low-cost housing projects.[8]

Construction of the towns was, by design, inefficient, and therefore costly. Although occasionally reporters took this into consideration, as an article in the *Washington Post* did when it acknowledged that "a certain percentage of this cost must be set down to unemployment relief," many papers ignored this fact.[9] Rexford Tugwell, as usual, put it bluntly: "No one in his senses would attempt to demonstrate the achieving of low costs on any job which uses relief labor."[10] He was correct; no program could

Figure 11.1. Work at Greenhills, 1936, using mules and hand labor, rather than modern machinery. Library of Congress, Prints and Photographs Division, FSA-OWI Collection.

have fully succeeded as both work-relief for unskilled workers and as an example of how to efficiently produce low-cost housing. The two were simply incompatible.

Other factors further complicate such calculations. For example, the designs for Greenbrook had largely been completed and paid for when construction was halted by court order, before building had even begun.[11] The planning costs for the town were thus wasted, not through mismanagement or error on the part of the staff, but because the court decision made the plans moot.

Another complicating factor: Budget cuts caused repeated reductions in the proposed number of dwelling units in each town. The number of planned units at Greenhills, as one example, had been cut on five separate occasions by the time the town was declared complete.[12] Initially the overall program called for a total of 3,500 dwelling units—1,000 each in Greenbelt and Greenhills, and 750 each in Greendale and Greenbrook. The finished towns provided 885 units in Greenbelt, 676 in Greenhills, and 572 in Greendale—a total of 2,133 units. Since the towns had been designed to support much higher populations than they ended up housing, all final infrastructure costs and expenses for public buildings were much higher on a per-home basis than if the original plans had remained in place.

As many previous attempts at building working-class housing had demonstrated, if the homes were to be well built and the neighborhoods inviting, the cost of construction would always push rents too high for the intended inhabitants.[13] Only government subsidies would make such ventures feasible, as had been the case throughout much of Europe. But the American appetite for subsidized housing diminished sharply once the early enthusiasm for New Deal spending began to dissipate. The nation eventually returned to the idea that individuals bore the responsibility to pull themselves up by their bootstraps. While subsidized housing for the poor continued, the idea that such environments should in any way mimic the suburban ideal vanished. Future low-rent housing would be utilitarian, even ugly, and more often than not devolved into inadequate, unsafe, unappealing environments in the decades that followed.

The Greenbelt program demonstrated, in case anyone in the planning field still harbored any illusions to the contrary, that without some sort of government subsidy housing for low-income groups could not be ideal communities, could not offer the modern amenities that might help inspire and lift the working class into the middle class. Low-cost housing was, by definition, limited in how good it could be. Excellent environments cost money. No amount of thoughtful planning could alter these facts. As a demonstration of how to economically produce environments that would elevate residents' lives, the project failed.

THE GREENBELTS AS WORK-RELIEF PROJECTS

From President Roosevelt's perspective, however, the Greenbelt program succeeded spectacularly. It put people to work. The planning and administrative staff alone employed more than four hundred men and women. Another twenty thousand to thirty thousand workers helped bring the towns to life.[14] The cost analysis for Greendale showed that for construction of the houses, for example, 52.2 percent of the costs went to workers' salaries. Another 28.8 percent went to materials and supplies, meaning that it also benefited those making the cinderblocks, bricks, pipes, electric

Figure 11.2. Workers arriving at Greenbelt, 1936. Library of Congress, Prints and Photographs Division, FSA-OWI Collection.

refrigerators, and everything else that went into the homes.[15] A pay rate list for constructing Greenbelt takes up several pages and includes metalworkers, bricklayers, carpenters, electricians, painters, plumbers, and more.[16] It is impossible to say how many families were saved from hunger or homelessness by the jobs created by the Greenbelt program. Those who looked solely at the per-unit cost of the homes, or even the overall price tag for the entire program, ignored this massively effective job creation.

Still, public works projects to create jobs generally aimed at producing something for the greater public benefit. The Tennessee Valley Authority produced electricity and controlled flooding for a huge region. The CCC engaged in reforestation and soil conservation, built structures for state and national parks, and more. True, other housing projects also produced only a limited number of homes, but none came with the enormous price tag of the Greenbelt towns. If few could deny that the program created jobs, many could question whether the end product was beneficial enough to the public at large to have been worthwhile.

THE GREENBELTS AS MODELS OF RATIONAL URBAN PLANNING

The professionals who helped bring the Greenbelt towns to life used their own distinct yardstick for measuring the success of the program. Many of these planners and architects expected the towns to demonstrate how to build better communities, to show the path forward, to prove that the problems of low incomes, urbanization, and housing shortages could be overcome through proper design. The towns were to usher in a new era in urban planning.

Jacob Crane made this case when he assessed the potential of the town he helped design:

> Greendale is based on the concept (we might say it is based on the American Dream) that for American families, not bleak, congested city housing, but an open green environment is demanded. This enterprise is one manifestation of the powerful American drive to achieve the ideals which tend to guide American life.[17]

Crane saw the physical attributes of the towns as integral to the project's success. Anyone could design new housing that would eventually deteriorate into new slums, but the Greenbelt towns would be different, bold, innovative, beautiful.

Albert Mayer, one of the architects for the ill-fated Greenbrook, also believed that the program marked a turning point in planning. He wrote just months before the court halted work on his town,

> The example of these four undertakings when completed should stir the building industry and the public as a whole into demanding developments more imaginative, more permanently pleasant, more permanently stable, with permanently controlled amenities and environment.[18]

Henry Churchill, the other lead architect for Greenbrook, wrote in 1945, "The greenbelt towns built by the Suburban Resettlement Administration were in many ways among the most significant experiments of the early Roosevelt administration."[19] Those involved with the creation of Social Security or the CCC or the TVA or any number of other New Deal endeavors would likely have challenged Churchill's assertion but, viewing this through his own professional lens, he saw the design of these towns, the plans to make them not just adequate environments but models for planning in the coming decades, as carrying enormous implications for the future of the nation.

This enthusiasm seems to have suffused the Greenbelt program. When journalist Marquis Childs visited the design staff offices in Washington, DC, he observed a group of professionals who were "exceptionally keen and intelligent. Earnest, hard-working, giving off ideas like showers of meteors, they stood on the threshold of the new era, a little tremulous." Childs seems to have absorbed their enthusiasm, writing that "Theirs was a cozy conspiracy of good will to remake America on a cleaner, truer, more secure pattern."[20] They saw their work as massively important for the eventual residents, but also for the prestige of their professions if they could prove that their work had the potential to be truly transformative.

Those who helped create the Greenbelt towns expressed great pride in the project that they believed marked a watershed in city planning. Crane forecast a lasting impact: "With some justification, we can assert that after these projects have been built and occupied, the future development of metropolitan districts will take a different turn from the course that has been followed during the last fifty years. Whoever carries out the development, and whenever it is carried out, the influence of these more rationally planned suburban projects is bound to be felt."[21]

The Greenbelt program certainly sparked great interest in the fields of planning and architecture. Articles about the towns appeared in magazines and journals in the United States and abroad in the years during and just after the towns' construction.[22] A 1942 article in the *South African Architectural Record* said that upon entering Greenbelt,

> the first reaction is one of sheer incredulity, for of all the things that one has come to associate with an American residential district, this has none of them. For it is quiet, peaceful and orderly. The neat buildings, unpretentious architecturally, group themselves in a formality that happily and unexpectedly avoids all mechanical rigidity... The ever-present greenery, and the background of the enveloping forest serve to emphasize the essential humanness of the scene.[23]

The towns were, and are, undeniably confident examples of innovative planning and design.

The professionals who made the towns were, however, overly optimistic about the lasting influence of their creations. Early public reaction to the completed towns was mixed. A 1937 piece in the *Washington Daily News* enthused about Greenbelt, Maryland: "For hundreds of years men will come and gaze and wonder and think maybe Uncle Sam stopped to do this as a great monument to decent living."[24] On the other hand, an article in the February 21, 1939, *Cincinnati Enquirer* judged Greenhills "at once lovely and hideous."[25]

Students of city planning still look to these towns as a bold effort, a once-in-a-lifetime opportunity for experts in urban design to experiment with a new suburban form meant to improve not just the surroundings of residents, but also their lives on a deep and personal level. But the model, while innovative, was far too costly to help the millions in need of decent, inexpensive homes.

THE GREENBELTS AS COMMUNITIES

This book has argued that the Greenbelt towns program was, in many ways, set up to fail. It could never meet the myriad competing goals heaped upon it. For those Americans looking on from a distance, counting the costs and tallying the returns, the experiment was simply that—an experiment, and not a terribly successful one. Enormous sums of money sunk into three small towns certainly did not measure up to more impactful New Deal programs.

But what of those assessing the towns not from a distance, but from within? Although the number of Americans who found a home in the towns was small, for those families it was life-changing. One early resident, recalling first moving into Greenbelt, said, "I shall never forget the gleaming beauty and wide open spaces of it all. I am sure my childhood sense of satisfaction about it reflected my parents' pleasure, too. There was a wonderful camaraderie among all the young parents at the time when economic survival itself was a difficult thing."[26] Another resident later declared, "If there is a heaven... there must be a place like Greenbelt up there. A place where neighbors share, and love one another."[27]

Planner Elbert Peets made the case for the larger importance of the program in his final report on Greendale, writing that the community he helped create must be "more than a housing project." He insisted, "It will not be merely another small town. It will not be just a pretty suburb...Greendale, to be a success, must be a productive social experiment. It must better its people as members of society, as citizens." Peets stressed that Greendale

> must be a model little piece of America, a democracy based on the dignity and good sense of the individual. It must do a thing that is probably more important than any other thing in this modern world—it must give its people the experience of working together in loyal, tolerant, and effective groups. The town should be as democratic as a pioneer community—which in fact it is.[28]

Implicit in the idea that each Greenbelt town was to be "a model little piece of America" was the notion that a specific, correct incarnation of "America" upon which to base this model existed. Tugwell expected that it would be something bold and new, while most of the administrators and planners envisioned communities where like-minded citizens could uphold fairly traditional—largely middle-class—values. In the end, it was a little bit of each: a relatively homogeneous population of traditional families in towns meant to reshape civic life.

The residents technically fell just below the middle class, but they clearly aspired to that lifestyle. And while many children who grew up in the towns later recalled feeling at least a twinge of shame at being in "low-income" housing, they also took comfort in the fact that everyone else in the town was on the same plane. There was no class conflict, no pressure to feign prosperity. One resident recollected that

> there were no first families, there were no rich people and there were no slum people. It was just a cross section of everybody who worked for a living and who was raising a family... You didn't bring in your ancestry and your D.A.R. [Daughters of the American Revolution] connections. You contributed and you were taken for what you were, at face value.[29]

A man who grew up in Greenhills put it more bluntly: "There weren't any highfalutin people or any... really down-and-out people."[30] This sense of commonality, with no preconceived hierarchy, everyone having an equal stake in making the town a success, undoubtedly engendered a community spirit that would be hard to replicate in most other settings.

Reminiscences of early residents generally paint the towns as nearly ideal places to live. But, of course, that had been the intention all along, and every effort had been made to ensure that the communities would be cohesive. Applicants who seemed critical of the concept, or who voiced a dislike of civic engagement, were far less likely to be offered homes. The families in the towns were all White, nearly all young, all in approximately the same economic situation.[31] They were specifically chosen to be similar. The religious diversity of the towns, though notable, was not the sort of true diversity that existed in the United States at the time. The Greenbelts may have been idyllic places for residents, but they were also largely artificial.

Peets had said that Greendale "must better its people as members of society, as citizens." And yet it seems just as likely that the careful selection of citizens improved the towns. Scientists know that the best experiments have only one variable, but the Greenbelts had two equally important ones: the overall design of the communities and the residents who were permitted to live in them. The careful selection process helped ensure the success of the towns, but also made the results of the experiment unreliable. Was it the design, the swimming pools and theaters, the play spaces, that made the towns such good places to live, or was it the meticulous selection of neighbors? We cannot know.

People of the same class, age range, and general outlook toward the program almost could not help but form a tightly knit community. Young wives found dozens of others like themselves within a few blocks. Fathers commuting into the larger cities had ample opportunities to ride along with their neighbors. The youngest residents had hundreds of other children in town, dozens on each block, and all the recreation they could want. And then, too, they all had the common bond of gratitude. These families had left behind the housing crisis, the slums, the crowding, and had landed in towns designed specifically for their needs. Many believed that their communities were nearly perfect.

The government worked to keep the towns that way, at least initially. Each resident received a manual upon moving in. New occupants of Greendale, for instance, were given "Helpful Suggestions for Greendale Residents." In it, readers were admonished, "Neglect in the observance of the suggestions herein set forth will result in increased management costs. If each one will do his part, we will all benefit."[32] The information primarily offered basic instructions—how to keep stoves, refrigerators, and floors clean; how to get a telephone; where to park.

An undated, but early, packet of information for Greenhills residents opened by saying, "This pamphlet is issued as a guide to pleasant relations and satisfactory living in Greenhills. It is not designed to be a code of restrictions." And yet, to some extent, that is what it was. In addition to containing instructions for maintaining the homes and appliances, the booklet told residents how high to set their lawnmower blades, what sorts of plants they could put in their yards, and how much to water the grass.[33] It was imperative that the town continue to look the way the designers had intended.

The question of pets caused particular problems. Greenhills residents were warned that the privilege of keeping pets is given at the specific request of the majority of residents of Greenhills. Continuation of this privilege depends upon the care of owners in eliminating nuisances which may result from presence of dogs and cats in the community... If owners do not respect property and rights of persons not owning pets, the Village Council may have to enact regulatory ordinances.[34]

It appears that they never had to act on that threat.

Greenbelt was another matter. The 1942 manual for the town laid out their rules: "Dogs, cats, chickens, ducks, etc., are not permitted. This regulation was adopted by a referendum of the citizenship of Greenbelt, as a protection for their children."[35] The rule had first been instituted by the FSA, with residents eventually permitted to vote on whether to retain it.[36] A short, indignant newspaper editorial on the issue read:

As far as I'm concerned you can take your damned Greenbelt utopia and throw it in the artificial lake out there, doubtless created for just that purpose. I'm not kicking about the cost, or the Government competing with private business, or the unfair subsidy to a handful of families. I'm griping about the FSA resolve to ban dogs in the supposedly ideal community. True, the prohibition is temporary, until the residents can vote on the subject, but what sort of a start is that for a New Jerusalem? Rather a slum hovel with Fido, than a Greenbelt house without him. Don't send those FSA officials around to pester me. I'll sic my dog on 'em![37]

When the vote came, the ban was upheld, but in spite of having been voted on by the population, the rule remained a source of sorrow and resentment for many families. We have evidence that the town was not a wholly unified utopia in the fact that officials had to remind residents of the ban over the years, as many chose to ignore the rule if they could get away with it.[38]

In June 1939 the Greenbelt Town Council also instituted a rule barring the wearing of shorts and swimsuits in the commercial center.[39] Given that the pool was close by, and summers in the area can be stiflingly hot, the regulation was apparently rarely enforced, but it was still officially on the books decades later. During that time exactly one ticket had been issued, resulting in a $5 fine.[40]

Greenbelt residents chafed at other rules, as well. Since it was located so near Washington, and was the subject of endless sightseeing and fact-finding tours in the early years, this community had more stringent regulations than the other two. The housewives of the town found one rule particularly irksome:

> All laundry, including bathing suits, must be removed from [laundry] lines, and the rope lines taken down, not later than 4:00 P.M. each afternoon, with the exception of Sundays, when no clothing or bedding of any kind is permitted on the lines from midnight Saturday to midnight Sunday... Wire lines may be left up permanently if they are drawn tightly, so as not to sag" (underlining in the original).[41]

If a housewife forgot to bring the items in, a policeman would knock on the door and remind her.[42] The homes did not have clothes dryers; laundry had to be hung to dry, and the weather did not always cooperate by being ideal during permitted drying times. Yet the visual messiness of this essential bit of housekeeping clashed with the contrived perfection of the town, at least during those times when outsiders were most likely to come and gawk.

Figure 11.3. Laundry on the line at Greenbelt, only permitted at certain times. Library of Congress, Prints and Photographs Division, FSA-OWI Collection.

And gawk they did. One early resident remembered that putting up curtains was the first order of business after moving in. "Hoards [*sic*] of people used to come out here, especially on weekends," she recalled. "We would be eating dinner and there would be the sound of voices. We'd look up and people would be walking up the hill in front of our house. Some would peer in the windows and say things like, 'They're eating their dinner,' just as if we were on display and were not real people. It happened often."[43] Another said that "it was just like you were in a fishbowl."[44] While it is easy to laugh at some of the rules, the image of the town was no laughing matter for FSA administrators and community leaders. For them, favorable public opinion of the program was vital. The town and its residents were the face of the Greenbelt program, and the world was watching.

Some of the perceived perfection was a facade. Residents who looked back on those early years in the town often mentioned that the towns had no crime.[45] Many commented on never feeling the need to lock their doors.[46] Neighbors might have disagreements; young men might occasionally get rowdy, but most believed that nothing more serious ever occurred.[47] But there was, in fact, "more crime than they let on," according to one early resident, although town officials felt it imperative to maintain the image of these as completely safe communities, so any criminal activity was kept fairly quiet.[48] Still, they were much safer places to live than almost any American city. But they were not cities; they were isolated little enclaves set out in the countryside. It should not be so surprising that the problems of the cities did not find their way to the little communities for many years.

Just as Ebenezer Howard had imagined for the garden city model, all three towns initially included farmland within the greenbelts surrounding the new communities. These were apparently all farms already present at the sites, not new construction, and the rural aspect of the program failed to live up to the original vision. The Greendale Final Report explains:

A brochure on greenbelt towns published by the Resettlement Administration in September 1936, contained, as the final statement of a "basic program," the following paragraph: "To develop a land-use plan for the entire tract; to devise a system of rural economy coordinated with the land-use plan for the rural portions of the tract surrounding the suburban community; and to integrate both the physical plans and the economies of the rural area and the suburban community." In February 1938, with the town practically built, there is little evidence at Greendale of progress toward the fine ideal thus so bravely stated.[49]

It went on to report, "As funds were allocated and budgets made and revised, the place of the town became dominant and the tendency was to leave it to the future to find money and ideas and plans for the rural work."[50]

The farms, though seldom mentioned in histories of the program, were no small part of the overall plan. Greendale, for example, included fifty small family farms of between one and ten acres, one large poultry farm, and fourteen dairy farms, some of which supplied fresh milk to the families in the town.[51]

One early farm resident at Greenhills recalled that her father raised chickens and sold eggs and produce at the farmers' market in the town. Her family moved to the farm in 1938; it is unclear whether the criteria for acceptance were similar to getting a home in the town. Their house was reported to be a hundred years old, and had no running water or central heat. The FSA added a filter for the cistern water and painted the house, but made no other improvements. She attended school in the town, and like many other early residents, she commented on the fact that there was no economic competition between families, as all were in similar financial

Figure. 11.4. A farm at Greenhills. Library of Congress, Prints and Photographs Division, FSA-OWI Collection.

situations. But she must have had a very different experience from her class-mates who lived within easy walking distance of everything the community had to offer.[52]

A doctoral dissertation on Greendale, written in 1943, noted that the farmers were "'the forgotten people.' They take no part in community affairs; they often voice the fact that they have no *interest* in the village."[53] Possibly it was easier for schoolchildren to feel integrated into the larger community, as they were frequently thrown into the company of the town's youth.

It is, unfortunately, immensely difficult to quantify just how satisfied residents were overall. Much of our information on this topic comes from reminiscences collected many years later. Those who were most likely to offer their recollections of the communities' early period were the ones who had fond memories to share. They were the ones who stayed.

We can get a somewhat broader view from scholarly studies.[54] William Form, a Greenbelt resident and doctoral student at the University of Maryland, wrote his 1944 dissertation on the sociology of his town. Unlike the portrait painted by the recollections of early residents, Form's work shows a community in search of an identity. He speaks of political apathy (just 11 percent of adults in the town voted in county and state elections in 1942), and of efforts made by many organizations to create "traditions" in a town that had none. Form cited the fact that all residents were renters, not owners, as a major cause of these problems.[55] Just as experts had long warned, it seems that home ownership strongly affected a person's feeling of having a stake in the community. Some families who moved in moved out again in a relatively short amount of time.[56] Some felt they did not fit in; some resented FSA rules; some had other reasons. We do not have their stories.

Other scholarly works from the first decade or so of the communities also offer somewhat less idealistic portraits than those of early residents looking back fondly from the distance of many years.[57] The towns' residents were much more educated, for instance, than the general population.[58] One study found that higher education correlated with greater success in Greendale; it ranked as more important than family size, religious affiliation, or income.[59] The occupation level of the head of household—educated professional or blue-collar—also served as a strong predictor of success, although this would have been closely tied to education, as well.

If we were to judge based solely on the recollections of early residents, the towns truly were wonderful places to grow up, to raise children, to find a sense of community. But again, they had been engineered that way. On the occasion of Greenbelt's fiftieth anniversary, one resident who had arrived in 1938 summed up the experience:

> We realized that we were an experiment, and I think that it encouraged us to put our best foot forward. I'm sure that most of us realized that we were specially chosen... I don't think anybody who lived in that community could have been more specially chosen than we were, all of us... The depression years were hard on people. Almost all of us were young people in Greenbelt, anxious to go forward. We all wanted a chance and we sure got it.[60]

Many of those who lived in the Greenbelts in the early years express an unmistakable affection for their towns. They smile when they speak of growing up in their close-knit communities. It is almost as if the towns themselves are beloved characters in residents' life stories. There were, to be sure, families who were dissatisfied, families who left. But a great many of those who have experienced life in Greenbelt, Greendale, or Greenhills express fondness, deep loyalty, and pride, a sense that they owed a debt of gratitude to the towns and the people who created them.

The Greenbelt towns offered residents exactly what had been promised: clean, safe, new communities where people could begin a new life, raise a family, find happiness. But the towns were an artificial reflection of an imagined ideal, a mythical "model little piece of America." They succeeded in offering well-priced homes, but only with the help of government subsidies. They created close-knit communities where civic engagement thrived, but largely because the tenant selection criteria had made that a priority. Like the towns themselves, life in them had been preplanned, designed by experts. Whether their success as communities could have been replicated under any other circumstances is, at best, doubtful.

EPILOGUE

THE BEST-LAID PLANS OF MICE AND MEN OFTEN GO AWRY

I have argued throughout this book that the Greenbelt program, in having such starkly competing goals, was set up to fail. But did it fail? It depends on how we define failure. It created jobs, created homes, created towns. Many past and current residents are fiercely protective of the history and reputation of their communities and might understandably chafe at the suggestion that the towns failed. But in its most central stated goals the program fell short. It did not provide a model for future residential development and did not provide a national path forward for improving civic engagement, unity, or democracy among citizens. As a test of the concept of using work-relief labor to create low-income housing, its only true success was in proving the idea unworkable.

The program aimed to make inexpensive homes, but not "cheap" housing. The towns were to be uplifting for residents, but not luxurious or wasteful of public funds. The conflicts were not unique to the Greenbelt towns, but this program demonstrates the seemingly eternal challenge of how to provide housing for the poorer classes that neither outrages the tax-paying population nor condemns the poor and working classes to substandard environments that virtually guarantee their continued social marginalization and degradation. Private enterprise will not take up the effort; there is no profit to be made in it. If government makes the attempt, the cost will be too high, or the outcome too disappointing, or both. In a nation devoted to the free market, the solution to housing inequality—to all social inequality—remains elusive.

Could it have gone differently? Could the program have made the lasting impact its creators dreamed of, given the right circumstances? While it is impossible to come to any definitive conclusions, we can speculate.

If Rexford Tugwell had not been so closely tied with the Greenbelt towns, it is possible that they would have attracted somewhat less scrutiny and opposition from conservative media and lawmakers. Of course, the idea was his from the start, so it would have taken great prescience and a fair bit of willpower to then step away so as not to spark resistance. But that alone would likely not have been enough to ensure smooth sailing for the program.

If funding had not been repeatedly slashed, would that have made a difference? It might have allowed the plans for the three towns to take their full shape, but shrinking budgets were not the only obstacle. Once the Greenbrook court case was decided, administrators knew that even the towns already under construction might be halted at any time by a similar ruling. Money alone, while crucial, did not, in the end, determine the fate of the towns. And a higher price tag would only have given additional ammunition to those who insisted that the program had provided just over two thousand families with homes paid for by millions of taxpayers who could never hope for such good fortune.

If RA messaging about the towns had been more effective, would the program's success have logically followed? Missteps along the way undeniably cost the agency some needed good will. In being as secretive as they sometimes were, RA officials allowed wild rumors to take hold among residents near each town. Although it appears that later efforts at convincing locals of the program's benefits improved the public's response, the initial fumbling of the message cost them time—time that opponents such as those who blocked the construction of Greenbrook used to full advantage.

If the court had decided the Greenbrook case differently, might that have made for a more broadly successful experiment? The program would have ended up providing four towns instead of three. The fourth, by the estimations of many involved, would have been consequential because Henry Wright was such a talented planner. The other towns, too, might have been allowed to implement their original plans for the wider provision of homes, assuming that funding also continued to flow. However, even though this would have come closer to the dream Tugwell had originally envisioned, the program as a whole still would have housed just a tiny fraction of the population so desperately in need, and at incredible cost.

What, then, could have permitted the full success of the vision? Most likely, nothing. If the RA had stuck with its original intention to use Planning Section engineers, rather than the talented and specialized teams that designed each town, they certainly would have saved money. If they had made the homes more utilitarian and less well-thought-out, if they had squeezed more homes onto the land, if they had given up on the vast green spaces and the theaters and the swimming pools and the playgrounds and the artwork, it might have allowed the completion of more homes or avoided charges of flagrant overspending. But perhaps not. In any case, such towns would not have lived up to the ideal of offering inspiring, uplifting communities that could raise needy citizens into respectable middle-class lives and spark an increased sense of civic responsibility. They would have been nearly indistinguishable from the other low-income housing that arose out of the New Deal and beyond—housing that often failed future residents miserably.

The goals of the Greenbelt program were simply too much at odds. Cost-effective housing and communities for the working class could not be built to the standards called for by experts. Unskilled and low-skilled workers using intentionally inefficient methods were certain to result in a high final cost. Political polarization guaranteed that those on opposite sides of the debate over federal responsibility to the nation's citizens would argue and attack each other and, eventually, grind the plans down to a shadow of those first lofty dreams.

There was still one path to success that might have worked—but not in the United States of the 1930s. European cities blossomed with public housing in that era because both national and local governments made such building projects a priority. Whether these efforts succeeded in the long term is well beyond the scope of this book, but regardless, such efforts could not have happened here. The United States, populated with people who believed that their nation was founded on individual hard work and tenacity, would not have approved of widespread federally funded housing programs. Although, for a time, they tolerated an experimental town here and there, subsidized housing on the European scale would have been virtually unthinkable.

AFTER

Together, the Greenbelt towns constituted the largest, most expensive, and one of the most controversial of the Resettlement Administration's projects. For some the towns illustrated the promise of the New Deal; for others they highlighted its folly.[1] Federal ownership of the towns, with the government acting as landlord, struck many as entirely inappropriate. At the start of the Greenbelt program, the plan had been that the government would construct the towns and act as owner and landlord only briefly until, it was hoped, a private corporation could be found to take over. Such a buyer never materialized. The towns were finally sold, in a patchwork of arrangements, in the early 1950s.[2]

The three towns have changed over the decades. Their greenbelts have been whittled away by new development, though each community retains remnants of this defining element, hints of the greenspace that once encircled the towns. Each community has undergone expansion, demographic transition, and challenging times. But the towns themselves remain.

Greenbelt was the first to grow. In 1941, on the eve of the Second World War, as workers flocked to the nation's capital for jobs in the ballooning federal government, the FSA constructed one thousand "defense homes" for war workers just outside the original residential area. Clarence Stein wrote that the design for this addition "was dumped into the factory-like office" of a federal agency, where "work was shot through the draftingroom efficiently and speedily, and was followed by economical and quick construction." Although he lamented the haste of the new project, he was pleased that the original plan for Greenbelt informed the placement of the newer homes, and he noted, "As you see them from the sky the two developments seem to be a single united design."[3] Few, however, saw them from the sky, and the newer construction was obviously different—frame homes with asbestos shingle siding, not the sleek, solid brick and block dwellings that had gone up just a few years before.

Many residents of the original community looked on in horror. One later recalled, "The building of the defense houses was a blow. We thought it was such a downgrading of the town that this would ruin it."[4] They were assured that the newer homes, which they felt were clearly being built to a lower standard, were temporary, and would be taken down after the war.[5] This did not happen. The defense homes are still in place, now considered a not-quite-original part of the community. In addition to more than doubling the size of the town, the war brought changes to the population as new families, no longer strictly screened by FSA officials, moved in and original families moved on. The bonds of the community did not break, but the people would never again be the same carefully selected, eager, experimental group.[6]

The war also ended any lingering hope that the Greenbelt towns might serve as models for future low-cost development. Unemployment plummeted as manufacturers set their sights on victory and men marched off to battle; this, not the New Deal, finally brought the Depression to an end. When the fighting stopped, the United States reverted to its long celebration of rugged individualism. Government subsidy was out; old-fashioned American self-reliance was in—never mind that this "self-reliance" was largely made possible by the GI Bill, federally funded interstate highway construction, and the growth of a government-fueled military-industrial complex.

It would not be the federal government, but profit-seeking developers such as William Levitt, builder of Levittowns in Pennsylvania, New Jersey, and New York, who would bring about the radical shift toward suburbanization for the masses in the postwar era. By the late 1940s, those below the middle class finally had a choice beyond substandard urban housing and equally substandard rural housing. There was now a third option.

Levittown and its many imitators put into practice the mass-production building techniques that the work-relief nature of the Greenbelt project had prohibited. To bring the masses to the suburbs Levitt and others employed the Greenbelt model of buying up inexpensive land just beyond the cities, but then erected houses like so many cars rolling off a Ford assembly line. By churning out homes as inexpensively as possible they had solved the problem of cost-effective construction. The poorest Americans were still left out, as were Blacks and other minorities, but the age of massive suburbanization for much of the working class had arrived.

The postwar American dream was not one of community cooperation, but was instead firmly anchored to a burgeoning consumer culture, inextricably linked to a vigorous economy, a baby boom, and rapidly multiplying suburbs. Post–World War II construction focused on individual families looking inward on themselves instead of outward to their communities. It unapologetically promoted personal liberty, as the members of each little kingdom gathered happily around the new TVs displayed proudly in their little suburban castles. The postwar mentality gloried in the triumph of the American dream (for the most part ignoring the unfortunate sorts who did not appear in commercials for Wonder Bread and Coca Cola).

WHAT WE CAN LEARN FROM THE GREENBELT IDEA

In the twenty-first century, many of the same problems that plagued the nation in the 1920s and 30s remain. Americans once again worry that economic inequality and partisan divides are tearing the nation apart. They fear that too much focus on soul-sapping work simply for the sake of ever-increasing consumption has led to mental stress and a loss of what were once seen as agreed-upon national values: thrift, independence, and the undeniable advantages, and obligations, of living in a democratic society. And there are new fears that people in the 1930s would not have imagined: the United States, and the world, must come to grips with the environmental toll and fossil-fuel dependence tied to the nation's wasteful suburban lifestyles and car culture.

Then on top of these concerns came a global pandemic. COVID-19 sparked a great deal of social change. It drove many Americans out of large cities and into smaller towns and suburbs. It reignited the fears of a century earlier over contagion and disease, demonstrating that we assume such dangers are ancient history at our peril. Huge numbers of white-collar workers began working from home as the internet made commuting into large cities far less necessary than we once believed. As I write this book, the question of whether traditional offices will soon cease to exist is widely debated. Possibly the nation will begin to reevaluate where and how we live as well as where and how we work. If so, the idea of smaller homes clustered together in walkable communities may once again seem wise.

The experts whose ideas inspired programs such as the Greenbelt towns believed in environmental determinism—the notion that quality of life is determined by one's home and neighborhood. Today most people would likely acknowledge that there is much truth in the idea, but also that it is absurdly simplistic. Poverty is far more complex than just the question of good or bad homes, arising also from factors including, but not limited to, a human tendency toward self-interest, centuries-old prejudices, and systemic inequality of opportunity in education and employment as well as housing. Simply providing new residential environments is clearly not a magical solution. It has also become clear that generational wealth builds up fastest through home ownership; marginalized groups who must rely on rental property face a much steeper climb to financial success.

This is not to say that better homes and neighborhoods can have no effect, but it leaves us with the same questions faced by housing reformers at the start of the twentieth century: How can a nation assist its neediest citizens? Should it even try? If so, what kinds of efforts would bring the most benefit? If homes and neighborhoods are part of the solution, who will build them? Who will pay for them? What, other than housing, would truly make a difference in the lives of low-income Americans?

It remains an incredibly difficult set of problems, not helped by the fact that today the political and ideological divide is every bit as wide as it was in the 1930s. Debate still rages between those who believe that the government has an obligation to aid its neediest citizens and those who believe that the only good government is small and hands-off. Resistance to being told what to do by federal authorities is, if anything, more entrenched now. Yet most Americans are well aware that growing income and residential inequality threaten national stability in the long run.

The Greenbelt project highlights an incongruous optimism in a dark and troubling era. It demonstrates a belief—a sadly naïve belief—that rational planning, and enough money, could fix the broken bits of society. But it also illuminates uglier realities: political hatreds, racism, an often stunning disregard for those less well off, and bitter hostility on the part of private enterprise when the government intrudes on its territory.

Marquis Childs showed great foresight when he observed: "As Doctor Tugwell found out, it is impossible to lay down a blueprint for even a small section of society in this vast, powerful, well-nigh ungovernable country. Under dictatorship, perhaps, at the cost of everything else, but in a democracy as diffuse as ours, hardly."[7] The Greenbelt program could never meet the sky-high expectations imposed on it because so many Americans' core beliefs stood, and still stand, in direct opposition to each other.

THE GREENBELT TOWNS TODAY

The Greenbelt towns no longer lie among farmland, having been swallowed up into the ever-widening rings of suburbanization that have encircled the larger cities nearby. They appear somewhat out of place in this modern landscape. The most striking visual component, their 1930s Art Deco and International Style architecture, once on the cutting edge of design, is now showing its age. But they still have charm, an echo of once-upon-a-time, when the American people united, briefly, and the federal government dared to take drastic steps on behalf of those in need.

The three communities have aged with varying degrees of grace, and have settled into being somewhat different types of communities. Greenbelt has perhaps retained its original appearance and character best, primarily through the efforts of the local housing co-op and inhabitants' dedication to the historic nature of the town. The Deco-style commercial center continues to exemplify its 1930s origins, as do the white block, minimalist rowhouses and apartment buildings that still sit along the town's walking paths.

Greenbelt is today a suburb of Washington, connected to the city by highways and the DC Metro (which unfortunately stops at a not-walkable distance outside of town). The greatly expanded city is multicultural, its residents reasonably prosperous.[8] The commercial center in the original town seems to be economically successful, or is at least holding on. The grocery co-op still serves the local population, though a newer shopping center with a larger chain grocery store and other retail establishments is a short drive away from the original core and must make survival of the old market more difficult.

I took my husband to see the town in the summer of 2019. It was a hot day, but residents milled around the commercial center and shopped the stalls of the weekly farmers' market. Small children chased each other around the mother-and-child statue while their parents looked on. Older residents sat on benches nearby. We wandered around town, taking the paths that weave through the residential area. The walkability and coziness of the original town, and the way these elements bring residents together, live up to the vision RA planners brought to their work.

Greendale, Wisconsin, has also aged well, though it is not quite as true to its original design. This has, however, in part been integral to its continued success. Within the past few decades private investment has contributed to updating the commercial center of the town, with the result that it has stayed more current than its sister communities. The fact that Greendale consists mostly of single-family homes lovingly maintained by their owners has likely also enabled it to continue to thrive.

It, too, has grown as newer development has spread out around the original town. Beginning in the 1950s new housing began to be constructed around the outer edges. The population doubled between 1950 and 1960, and then doubled again in the decade after that.[9] Yet the 1930s portion is clearly recognizable due to the distinct architecture and arrangement of its homes. Both the residential section and the commercial center have been well maintained and remain quaint and inviting. It is still largely a White, middle-class community.[10] It is difficult to say whether it continues to bring residents together in the way originally envisioned. Just outside of town, multilane roadways and a shopping mall make driving, rather than walking, a necessary way to get things done.

Greenhills, Ohio, has had the most difficulty retaining its original charm. This is partly because Greenhills is bisected by a major roadway that has only gotten wider and busier over time, and partly because some of its original housing stock is now owned by absentee landlords who many residents feel do not maintain the properties. The economic woes of the early twenty-first century left many of the stores in its shopping center vacant, and the shopping center itself no longer shows any trace of its original 1930s character.

Efforts by local authorities to revitalize the town have included encouraging new home construction within the community's original core. Much to the dismay of some residents, some of the 1930s housing has been demolished to make way for these new homes. The more recent construction does not fit the 1930s aesthetic; the newer homes have nearly a Victorian farmhouse look that, while attractive, is somewhat jarring set among the original International-Style dwellings. The population remains relatively small, at under four thousand, and overwhelmingly White.[11]

Greenhills still has some important assets. The swimming pool remains a popular attraction on hot summer days. And, more important, the adjacent Winton Woods, a Hamilton County park that was created from part of the original greenbelt, features a large lake, golf course, and other outdoor recreational opportunities. Although no longer part of the village, the park fulfills the expectations the planners had for the undeveloped land, with a forest and ample outdoor recreation surrounding the community.

The importance of the towns both as examples of New Deal experimentation and as models of innovative design is clear. Greenbelt's original portion was added to the National Register of Historic Places in 1980 and became a National Landmark in 1997. Greendale's Historic District was listed in the National Register in 2005 and was designated a National Historic Landmark in 2012. The original core of Greenhills was listed on the National Register of Historic Places in 1989, and in 2017 the Greenhills Historic District was named a National Historic Landmark.[12] These honors show that the Greenbelt idea was groundbreaking. Although it did not serve as a model for future development, as the planners hoped it would, the program has been held up by planning professionals in the United States and abroad as an innovative and intriguing effort.

THE LOW-INCOME HOUSING PROBLEM MORE RECENTLY

In the decades following World War II the United States tried, often feebly, to find more cost-effective solutions to low-income housing. Far too frequently the efforts only served up a different sort of substandard environment, new neighborhoods that functioned more as cages than as ladders. Often this came in the form of high-rise, low-income, urban housing, more in line with Cincinnati's Laurel Homes, but built to new heights for greater population density. This turned out to be a terrible mistake, and in the second half of the twentieth century it became obvious that these large complexes were certainly not the answer.[13] Many such projects were built after the Greenbelt towns, and many have already been demolished because they failed so spectacularly at improving the lives of their residents.

Urban housing authorities continue to seek solutions to the housing crisis for low-income city dwellers. Chicago provides a prime example of what did not work, and an example of new experiments. There high-rise complexes such as Cabrini-Green and the Robert Taylor Homes once promised good, safe, affordable housing, but proved that just new housing was not enough. The buildings were poorly maintained, and eventually became exactly what they had been intended to replace—substandard, unsafe, stigmatizing. When people in the 1970s talked about "the projects," meaning, essentially, new urban slum-like developments, these were exactly the sorts of places they had in mind.[14]

The demolition of Cabrini-Green and others like it was a clear admission that this idea had been a failure in the long run. Afterward, Chicago authorities tried a new model of more traditional housing, mainly apartments and townhouses rather than high-rises; a more mixed demographic; and a mixed level of resident incomes.[15] They recognized that placing so many impoverished people so tightly packed together in one place had been misguided. The newer developments would, they hoped, avoid this pitfall. Theoretically, including residents of different income groups would provide an opportunity for "role modeling" by the more well-off families.[16] In tiny echoes of the Greenbelt program, some of the new housing included "amenities" such as landscaping, playgrounds, and wading pools.[17] The other option that has been tried in Chicago and other cities is simply to give low-income residents Section 8 vouchers to use in whatever private rental properties they choose.[18] This, in fact, seems to be the direction low-income housing is increasingly heading.

It bears repeating, however, that the level of poverty experienced by the high-rise dwellers was much higher than that of Greenbelt town residents in the 1930s. It is also important to keep in mind that "the projects" were, to a large extent, places to virtually warehouse poor Blacks, much as Blacks had been relegated to segregated slums in the early twentieth century (and beyond). Residents had few opportunities to better their situations. The Greenbelt towns, on the other hand, were specifically intended to elevate residents to a middle-class lifestyle. They were provided with amenities and schools and a wide variety of means for personal self-improvement and civic engagement. Places such as Cabrini-Green were essentially the opposite of the Greenbelt towns in terms of expectations and opportunity. That one type was primarily built for Whites and the other for Blacks is no mere coincidence.

FINAL THOUGHTS

In the decades since the Depression, scholars have argued over whether the New Deal was a positive or negative force. They debate whether it really accomplished what it set out to do, and what collateral damage was inflicted along the way. Virtually all agree that it did not end the Depression, but other aspects fuel differing opinions. It clearly aided a huge number of Americans, but some contend that it did so at the expense of individual freedom and the unnecessary and undesirable expansion of the federal government. Was it at heart an effort to aid the neediest Americans, or to prop up capitalism at the expense of the working class? Were the policies purposely racist, accidentally or unthinkingly racist, or did they aim—however imperfectly—toward racial justice? Did FDR's patchwork of agencies create a more socially just and equal America, or simply maintain the status quo?

I plead a case for the middle ground. The New Deal and the Greenbelt program were good-faith efforts to bolster the economy and ease the suffering of as many citizens as possible. But too many ideas competed against each other. Too many deeply entrenched prejudices limited the vision and the results. Black people were largely left out, relegated to manual labor that helped put food on their tables, but denied them the larger benefits that White people enjoyed. Franklin Roosevelt was neither a saint nor a diabolical schemer; he was a politician with a strong urge to make his mark on history, to leave a legacy that would place him among the most revered leaders of the nation. Rexford Tugwell and the administrators and planners who helped bring the Greenbelt towns to life had good intentions, but good intentions were not enough to accomplish all that they hoped.

Those who look at the New Deal, or the Greenbelt program, and see only dollars spent, government expansion, and the birth of a welfare state ignore the very real distress, the fear that ate at very real human beings in desperate need of help. And those who see only that many efforts fell short, only see a missed opportunity to right the wrongs of American society, ignore the reality of economic constraints and immeasurable ideological divides in this nation.

I wish I could end this book with definitive answers to the still-pressing problems of improved housing, better neighborhoods, and the right way to help Americans in need. But I am just a humble historian; I have no answers. I can say this: The Greenbelt towns failed in many ways. They never could have been replicated at a cost that would aid enough of those in need. This must have been clear to RA staff and administrators long before the program came to its somewhat awkward end at the hands of budget-slashing politicians and the courts.

But by that time the program had taken on a life of its own and represented other dreams beside just creating low-cost housing. The Greenbelts represented a particular vision of the American dream: community life in small towns filled with like-minded neighbors. It is, of course, a flawed vision, relying too heavily on a mythical image of what America had once been. The nation had never been this way. It is, and has always been, messy and complex and filled with people of differing backgrounds and competing ideas. FDR enjoyed a temporary political unity that eventually, inevitably, crumbled. RA officials saw the need to carefully select residents because they understood the fractious nature of the American people.

My old school still stands in Greenhills, though it is mainly empty. A branch location of the Cincinnati and Hamilton County Public Library occupies part of the building, and the Greenhills Historical Society maintains exhibit space to keep the story alive. But the classrooms and hallways I once walked sit silent. The town around it stands, not quite the bright, shining new town it once was, a reminder of the Depression era, a time of desperation and of dreams.

Figure. Epilogue 1. Schoolchildren at the Greenhills School, 1939. Library of Congress, Prints and Photographs Division, FSA-OWI Collection.

APPENDIX

ARCHITECTS AND PLANNERS ON THE TEAMS

Director's Staff

John S. Lansill	Director
Frederick Bigger	Chief of Planning
Warren Jay Vinton	Chief of Research

Greenbelt, Maryland

Hale Walker	Town Planner
Reginald J. Wadsworth	Principal Architect
Douglas D. Ellington	Principal Architect

Greenhills, Ohio

Justin A. Hartzog	Town Planner
William A. Strong	Town Planner
Roland A. Wank	Principal Architect
G. Frank Cordner	Principal Architect

Greendale, Wisconsin

Jacob Crane	Town Planner
Elbert Peets	Town Planner
Harry H. Bentley	Principal Architect
Walter G. Thomas	Principal Architect

Greenbrook, New Jersey (never built)

Henry Wright	Town Planner
Allan F. Kamstra	Town Planner
Albert Mayer	Principal Architect
Henry S. Churchill	Principal Architect

In addition, the final report on Greenbelt lists Tracy Augur, Catherine Bauer, Russell Black, Earle Draper, Robert Davison, J. Andre Fouilhoux, Louis Grandgent, and Clarence Stein as consultants for the program. The entire staff structure (including regional coordinators and engineers, excluded here) appears in a letter from Lansill to Will Alexander attached to the Greenbelt Final Report.

ACKNOWLEDGMENTS

I can't begin to express how much my family's support and encouragement helped during the very long process of researching and writing this book. My husband, who says he "didn't really do anything" to help, has in fact been particularly helpful. I also thank both of my sons for always assuming that what I was doing was important, and for cheering me on. Jeff, Ben, and Nic, thank you so much for never expecting much from me in the way of domesticity, and for never expressing the slightest doubt that I could do this.

Many former professors also played a part in getting me to this point, even if not all directly weighed in on this book. I had so many inspiring models at the University of Cincinnati and Miami University that I won't try to list them all. Two, however, deserve to be specifically named. In my undergraduate and MA days at UC, Zane Miller always expected much of me and undoubtedly made me a better scholar. He encouraged me in writing this book; I wish he had lived to see its completion. And from Miami University, Allan Winkler showed me, and countless other graduate students, how to engage with historians and their work. He also provided advice on forging ahead with this book when I needed it, along with just being a genuinely nice person who is generous with his time and knowledge. I have also benefitted from the encouragement of student and teaching colleagues over the years. Thank you all.

Too many who helped along the way remain semi-anonymous to me. The research librarians at Cornell University's Carl A. Kroch Library were so kind and helpful on my very first research trip many years ago. In fact, at every archive and library I visited along the way, everyone I encountered clearly desired to be of assistance. I sincerely thank the kind souls who labor quietly at the Franklin D. Roosevelt Presidential Library and Museum, University of Kentucky's Special Collections and Digital Programs Library, the Prince George's County Memorial Library in Greenbelt, the National Archives in College Park, and the Library of Congress. You are truly unsung heroes.

I also received a warm welcome and much assistance from the historical societies of each of the Greenbelt towns. Whether it was allowing me access to records or sending a speedy reply to a sudden email asking for clarification, the workers at Greenbelt, Greendale, and Greenhills—all dedicated volunteers—helped in innumerable ways. Although I can't list the names of all who aided me, Jill St. John was particularly helpful in the early days of my research, even going so far as to secure the Greenbelt visitors' apartment for my first visit (sadly, the town no longer offers this accommodation). The opportunity to live for a week in an original Greenbelt home gave me an appreciation for the towns that I couldn't have found from simply reading the sources.

It was a delight to speak with two of the children of Cassilda Berg about the letter their mother (or father) sent to FDR's secretary asking for help obtaining a home in Greendale. The letter sat in a file in the FDR Presidential Library for decades, and the Bergs' children knew nothing about it. I was pleased to be able to fill in this small bit of their family history for them, and I thank them for allowing me to share the story.

The Greenbelt residents who sat down with me for interviews also gave me insights I could never have gotten elsewhere. Thank you to Shirley Bailey, James Walsh Barcus, Rena Hull, Dale Jernberg, Lee and Bonnie Shields, Bob Sommers, and Larry Voigt for sharing your memories of Greenbelt, Maryland. The affection of early and long-time residents for their town was a delight to see and a huge help in discovering the intimate, lived legacy of the program.

FOR FURTHER READING

Historiography

Auerbach, Jerold S. "New Deal, Old Deal, or Raw Deal: Some Thoughts on New Left Historiography." *Journal of Southern History* 35, no. 1 (February 1969): 18–30.

Brinkley, Alan. "Prosperity, Depression, and War, 1920–1945." In *The New American History*, edited by Eric Foner, 119–41. Philadelphia: Temple University Press, 1997.

Hamby, Alonzo L. "The New Deal: Avenues for Reconsideration." *Polity* 31, no. 4 (Summer 1999): 665–81.

Keller, Morton. "The New Deal: A New Look." *Polity* 31, no. 4 (Summer 1999): 657–63.

Kidd, Stuart. "Redefining the New Deal: Some Thoughts on the Political and Cultural Perspectives of Revisionism." *Journal of American Studies* 22, no. 3 (December 1988): 389–415.

McGirr, Lisa. "The Interwar Years." In *American History Now*, edited by Eric Foner and Lisa McGirr, 125–50. Philadelphia: Temple University Press, 2011.

Parrish, Michael E. "1929–1941." In *A Companion to 20th-Century America*, edited by Stephen J. Whitfield, 36–53. Malden, MA: Blackwell Publishing, 2004.

Podair, Jerald, and Darren Dochuk, eds. "The Great Depression and New Deal—A Historiographical Survey." In *The Routledge History of the Twentieth-Century United States*, 25–36. New York: Routledge, 2018.

Purcell, Aaron D. "Historical Interpretations of the New Deal and the Great Depression." In *The New Deal and the Great* Depression, edited by Aaron D. Purcell, 4–39. Kent, OH: Kent State University Press, 2014.

On the Great Depression and the New Deal

Cowie, Jefferson. *The Great Exception: The New Deal and the Limits of American Politics*. Princeton, NJ: Princeton University Press, 2016.

Leuchtenburg, William Edward. *Franklin D. Roosevelt and the New Deal, 1932–1940*. New York: Harper & Row, 1963.

"The Living New Deal." https://livingnewdeal.org/.

McElvaine, Robert S. *The Great Depression: America, 1929–1941*. New York: Times Books, 1984.

Rauchway, Eric. *The Great Depression and the New Deal: A Very Short Introduction*. New York: Oxford University Press, 2008.

Rauchway, Eric. *Why the New Deal Matters*. New Haven, CT: Yale University Press, 2021.

Schlesinger, Arthur M., Jr. *The Coming of the New Deal*. Boston: Houghton Mifflin, 1958.

Watkins, T. H. *The Great Depression: America in the 1930s*. Boston: Little, Brown, 1993.

On the Greenbelt Towns/Program

Alanen, Arnold R., and Joseph A. Eden. *Main Street Ready-Made: The New Deal Community of Greendale, Wisconsin*. Madison: State Historical Society of Wisconsin, 1987.

Arnold, Joseph. *The New Deal in the Suburbs: A History of the Greenbelt Town Program, 1935–1954*. Columbus: Ohio State University Press, 1971.

Christensen, Carol A. *The American Garden City and the New Towns Movement*. Ann Arbor, MI: UMI Research Press, 1986.

Conkin, Paul K. *Tomorrow a New World: The New Deal Community Program*. Ithaca, NY: Cornell University Press, 1959.

Gournay, Isabelle, and Mary Corbin Sies. "Greenbelt, Maryland: Beyond the Iconic Legacy." In *Housing Washington: Two Centuries of Residential Development and Planning in the National Capital Area*, edited by Richard Longstreth, 203–28. Chicago: Center for American Places at Columbia College Chicago, 2010.

Knepper, Cathy Dee. *Greenbelt, Maryland: A Living Legacy of the New Deal*. Baltimore: Johns Hopkins University Press, 2001.

Leighninger, Robert D., Jr. *Long-Range Public Investment: The Forgotten Legacy of the New Deal*. Columbia: University of South Carolina Press, 2007.

"New Deal Neighbors: Oral Histories of Greenhills, Ohio." https://www.newdealneighbors.com/.

Reblando, Jason. *New Deal Utopias*. Heidelberg, Ger.: Kehrer Verlag, 2017.

Warner, George A. *Greenbelt: The Cooperative Community: An Experience in Democratic Living*. New York: Exposition Press, 1954.

On New Deal Agencies

Ickes, Harold. *Back to Work: The Story of the PWA*. New York: Macmillan, 1935.

Leighninger, Robert D., Jr. *Long-Range Public Investment: The Forgotten Legacy of the New Deal*. Columbia: University of South Carolina Press, 2007.

Maher, Neil M. *Nature's New Deal: The Civilian Conservation Corps and the Roots of the American Environmental Movement*. New York: Oxford University Press, 2008.

Smith, Jason Scott. *Building New Deal Liberalism: The Political Economy of Public Works, 1933–1956*. New York: Cambridge University Press, 2006.

White, Ann Folino. *Plowed Under: Food Policy Protests and Performance in New Deal America*. Bloomington: Indiana University Press, 2015.

On Roosevelt

Brinkley, Douglas. *Rightful Heritage: Franklin D. Roosevelt and the Land of America*. New York: Harper, 2016.

Daniels, Roger. *Franklin D. Roosevelt: Road to the New Deal, 1882–1939*. Urbana: University of Illinois Press, 2015.

Hamby, Alonzo L. *For the Survival of Democracy: Franklin Roosevelt and the World Crisis of the 1930s*. New York: Free Press, 2004.

On Cities, Suburbs, and Communities

Conn, Steven. *Americans Against the City: Anti-Urbanism in the Twentieth Century*. New York: Oxford University Press, 2014.

Orvell, Miles. *The Death and Life of Main Street: Small Towns in American Memory, Space, and Community*. Chapel Hill: University of North Carolina Press, 2012.

NOTES

INTRODUCTION

1   Not her real name.

2   The Resettlement Administration (RA), later the Farm Security Administration (FSA), employed photographers to document the experience of the American people in this difficult time. In all, they would produce some 150,000 images under the RA's Historical Section. Scholars of the Greenbelt towns have benefited tremendously from the vast number of photographs created of the towns and their construction, including most of the images in this book. The originals are housed at the Library of Congress, but many have also been digitized and placed on the Library of Congress website.

3   Walter Lippmann, *Interpretations 1933–1935* (New York: Macmillan, 1936), 18; from a newspaper column originally published March 7, 1933, specifically addressing the banking crisis.

4   Many historians of the New Deal tend to see FDR as having focused on what to actually do only after he had been elected, and that even then he flailed about for

strategies. Eric Rauchway counters this contention in "The New Deal Was on the Ballot," *Modern American History* 2, no. 2 (July 2019): 201–13. FDR quotes are from "The Philosophy of Social Justice through Social Action," campaign address at Detroit, MI, October 2, 1932, https://www.presidency.ucsb.edu/documents/campaign-address-detroit-michigan.

5   For a thorough background of the RA, and of the Farm Security Administration (FSA), which replaced it, see Sidney Baldwin, *Poverty and Politics: The Rise and Decline of the Farm Security Administration* (Chapel Hill: University of North Carolina Press, 1968).

6   Rexford Tugwell, personal diary, March 14, 1935, Tugwell Papers Collection, Franklin D. Roosevelt Presidential Library, Hyde Park, NY.

7   Tugwell diary, March 14, 1935.

8   Greenbelt, Maryland, was the most visible to Washington's powerful politicians. Planners were well aware that the powerful elite of the nation's capital were watching every step in the planning and construction of the town, and that if Greenbelt failed to impress, the entire program would be in peril.

9   Paul Conkin, *Tomorrow a New World: The New Deal Community Program* (Ithaca, NY: Cornell University Press, 1959); Conkin includes just a single chapter on the Greenbelt towns, but this brief examination is still quite useful. Conkin, it should be noted, was part of the New Left history movement. See also Joseph Arnold, *The New Deal in the Suburbs: A History of the Greenbelt Town Program, 1935–1954* (Columbus: Ohio State University Press, 1971).

Several works have focused on single Greenbelt towns, with Greenbelt, Maryland, receiving the greatest amount of scholarly attention. *Greenbelt: The Cooperative Community: An Experience in Democratic Living* (New York: Exposition Press, 1954), written by George A. Warner, provides an illustration of the life of early Greenbelt residents. Warner was among the earliest occupants of the town and served on the community newspaper staff, and so offers an insider's perspective on the early years of residence. Kathy Dee Knepper, in *Greenbelt, Maryland: A Living Legacy of the New Deal* (Baltimore: Johns Hopkins University Press, 2001), examines the intentional cultivation of a spirit of camaraderie and cooperation in the town through its cooperative retail establishments and community groups. Although she does provide some overview of the early planning of the town, this portion is relatively brief, with the majority of her work focusing on the postwar period.

Greendale, Wisconsin, has also been the subject of several scholarly works. The most comprehensive is *Main Street Ready-Made: The New Deal Community of Greendale, Wisconsin*, by Arnold R. Alanen and Joseph A. Eden (Madison: University of Wisconsin Press, 1987). Much like Arnold's *The New Deal in the Suburbs*, this book offers up a plethora of information on the RA, the Greenbelt program, and its planning and construction, but in this case only for the town of Greendale. Just a fraction of the book deals with these early concerns, as the authors examine the community into the 1980s. In her book *The American Garden City and the New Towns Movement* (Ann Arbor, MI: UMI Research Press, 1986), Carol A. Christensen devotes a chapter to discussing Greendale, supplying information on such issues as the selection of the first residents, cooperative activities of the community, and the general design of the town.

Greenhills, Ohio, has received the least attention from scholars, and has no monographs devoted to its study.

More recently, Jason Reblando's *New Deal Utopias* (Heidelberg, Ger.: Kehrer Verlag, 2017) offers a beautiful photographic essay on the towns as they currently exist. In 2016 the Public Broadcasting System (PBS) aired a special called *Ten Towns That Changed America*. Greenbelt, Maryland was one of the featured towns.

1 | THE NEED

Epigraph: Edith Elmer Wood, *Slums and Blighted Areas in the United States* (Washington, DC: Federal Emergency Administration of Public Works, 1935), 15.

1   Charles Harris Whitaker, "What Is a House?" in *The Housing Problem in War and in Peace* (Washington, DC: Journal of the American Institute of Architects Press, 1918), 6.

2   Edith Elmer Wood, *The Housing of the Unskilled Wage Earner: America's Next Problem* (New York: Macmillan, 1919), 1, 28.

3   Henry Wright, *The American City: An Outline of Its Development and Functions* (Chicago: A. C. McClurg, 1916), 161.

4   Catherine Bauer, *Modern Housing* (Boston: Houghton Mifflin, 1934), 106.

5   Meighen Katz, *Narratives of Vulnerability in Museums: American Interpretations of the Great Depression* (New York: Routledge, 2020), 73. Katz uses the Greenbelt House Museum as a case study in her book.

6   Many works have examined the housing conditions of the urban poor, and the efforts to address those problems, among them Christine M. Boyer, *Dreaming the Rational City: The Myth of American City Planning* (Cambridge, MA: MIT Press, 1983); Paul Boyer, *Urban Masses and Moral Order in America, 1820–1920* (Cambridge, MA: Harvard University Press, 1978); Gordon E. Cherry, ed., *Shaping an Urban World* (New York: St. Martin's Press, 1980); Kenneth T. Jackson and Stanley K. Schultz, eds., *Cities in American History* (New York: Alfred A. Knopf, 1972); and Gail Radford, *Modern Housing for America: Policy Struggles in the New Deal* (Chicago: University of Chicago Press, 1996).

7   Warren S. Thompson, "Movements of Population," *American Journal of Sociology* 40, no. 6 (May 1935): 718; US Census Bureau, *Selected Historical Decennial Census Population and Housing Counts*, Urban and Rural Populations, 1990, http://www.census.gov/population/www/censusdata/files/table-4.pdf.

8   R. D. McKenzie, "The Rise of Metropolitan Communities," in *Recent Social Trends in the United States: Report of the President's Research Committee on Social Trends*, vol. 1 (New York: McGraw-Hill, 1933), 443.

9   Robert G. Barrows, "Beyond the Tenement: Patterns of American Urban Housing, 1870–1930," *Journal of Urban History* 9, no. 4 (August 1983): 399.

10 The Census Bureau in the 1920s and 1930s did not distinguish between large urban areas, smaller towns, and suburbs; they simply categorized based on population—and the relatively small count of 2,500 residents was enough to classify a settlement as a "city." Whether in the city center or on the outer edges, however, decent housing for the working class was almost always in short supply, overpriced, and inadequate.

11 Lewis Mumford, *Sticks and Stones: A Study of American Architecture and Civilization* (New York: Boni and Liveright, 1924), 163; Radford, *Modern Housing for America*, 11.

12 Edith Elmer Wood, *Recent Trends in American Housing* (New York: Macmillan, 1931), 100. Wood provides a nice overview of the World War I housing crisis, 66–82.

13 Wood, *Recent Trends in American Housing*, 83.

14 Jacob Riis, *How the Other Half Lives* (New York: Charles Scribner's Sons, 1890).

15 Bleecker Marquette, "The Human Side of Housing: Are We Losing the Battle for Better Homes?" *Proceedings of the National Conference of Social Work, 1923* (Chicago: National Conference of Social Work, 1923), 344; Wood, *Slums and Blighted Areas in the United States*, 19; Wood, *Recent Trends in American Housing*, 294.

16 Edith Elmer Wood, *Introduction to Housing: Facts and Principles* (Washington, DC: Federal Works Agency, United States Housing Authority, 1940), 59.

17 Niles Carpenter and Clarence Quinn Berger, "Social Adjustments in Cities," *American Journal of Sociology* 40, no. 6 (May 1935): 735.

18 Carpenter and Berger, "Social Adjustments in Cities," 735.

19 Clarence Stein, "Housing and Common Sense," *Nation*, May 11, 1932, 541.

20 Radford, *Modern Housing for America*, 20.

21 Leo Wolman and Gustav Peck, "Labor Groups in the Social Structure," in *Recent Social Trends in the United States*, vol. 2 (New York: McGraw-Hill, 1933), 817.

22 David E. Kyvig, *Daily Life in the United States, 1920–1940: How Americans Lived through the "Roaring Twenties" and the Great Depression* (Chicago: Ivan R. Dee, 2002), 210–11. This figure leaves out the roughly 2.5 million single-person households, which were not counted as "families." The Brookings Institution estimated incomes in 1929: 7.6 percent of families at $500 or less per year; 13.8 percent at $500–1,000; 20.9 percent at $1,000–1,500; 17.1 percent at $1,500–2,000; 11 percent at $2,000–2,500; 7.2 percent at $2,500–3,000; 5.2 percent at 3,000–3,500; 3.6 percent at $3,500–$4,000; 2.6 percent at $4,000–4,500; 1.8 percent at $4,500–5,000; and 8.2 percent at $5,000 or more. Carol Aronovici and Elizabeth McCalmont, *Catching Up with Housing* (Newark, NJ: Beneficial Management Corp., 1936), 21.

23 Kyvig, *Daily Life in the United States*, 211.

24 Herbert Hoover, *Address of President Hoover at the Opening Meeting of the President's Conference on Home Building and Home Ownership* (Washington, DC: US Government Printing Office, December 1931), 1.

25 Herbert Hoover, "Statement Announcing the White House Conference on Home Building and Home Ownership, Sept. 15, 1931," *Public Papers of the Presidents of the United States, Herbert Hoover, Containing the Public Messages, Speeches, and Statements of the President January 1 to December 31, 1931* (Washington, DC: US Government Printing Office, 1976), 423–24. The conference was later more commonly referred to as simply the President's Conference.

26 John M. Gries and James Ford, eds., *The President's Conference on Home Building and Home Ownership*, vol. 11, *Housing Objectives and Programs* (Washington, DC: National Capital Press, 1932), 150.

27 Wood provides a nice summary of some of the housing studies conducted prior to the 1930s in *Recent Trends in American Housing*, 19–29.

28 Robert S. Lynd and Helen Merrell Lynd, *Middletown: A Study in Modern American Culture* (1929; rpt. San Diego: Harvest/Harcourt Brace 1957), 97.

29 US Census Bureau, "Historical Census Statistics on the Foreign-Born Population of the United States: 1850 to 1990," Table 8, "Race and Hispanic Origin of the Population by Nativity: 1850 to 1990."

30 Wood, *Slums and Blighted Areas in the United States*, 6.

31 Editors of *Fortune*, *Housing America* (New York: Harcourt, Brace, 1932), 12.

32 Editors of *Fortune*, *Housing America*, 11. One-fourth population statistic from "A Study of the Characteristics, Customs and Living Habits of Potential Tenants of the Resettlement Project in Cincinnati," February 1936, Justin Hartzog Papers, Cornell University, Ithaca, NY.

33 Editors of *Fortune*, *Housing America*, 12.

34 Editors of *Fortune*, *Housing America*, 10–11.

35 Peyton Stapp, *Urban Housing: A Summary of Real Property Inventories Conducted as Work Projects, 1934–1936* (Washington, DC: US Government Printing Office, 1938), 4–5.

36 Lewis Mumford, "New Homes for a New Deal III: The Shortage of Dwellings and Direction," *New Republic*, February 28, 1934, 70.

37 Barrows, "Beyond the Tenement," 402–4; Radford, *Modern Housing for America*, 8.

38 Editors of *Fortune*, *Housing America*, 13–14.

39 Editors of *Fortune*, *Housing America*, 20.

40 Elizabeth Longan, "Evolving Standards in American Housing." *Journal of Home Economics* 27 (April 1935): 207. Longan was the assistant director of the National Association of Housing Officials.

41 Editors of *Fortune*, *Housing America*, 10–11.

42 John Nolen, "Meeting the Housing Needs of the Modern Family." *Journal of Home Economics* 22, no. 10 (October 1930): 820.

43 For a nice summary of Nolen and Mariemont, see Bradley D. Cross, "'On a Business Basis': An American Garden City," *Planning Perspectives* 19, no. 1 (2004): 57–77.

For Nolen's own take on his planning philosophy, with an extensive discussion of Mariemont, see John Nolen, *New Towns for Old: Achievements in Civic Improvement in Some American Small Towns and Neighborhoods* (1927; rpt. Amherst: University of Massachusetts Press, 2005). For a later perspective, see Millard F. Rogers, Jr., *John Nolen and Mariemont: Building a New Town in Ohio* (Baltimore: Johns Hopkins University Press, 2001).

44　See, for instance, Albert Farwell Bemis, *The Evolving House*, vol. 2, *The Economics of Shelter* (Cambridge, MA: Technology Press, Massachusetts Institute of Technology, 1934); Wood, *Recent Trends in American Housing*. "Single-family" did not always mean detached. A single-family home could share one or more walls with neighbors, such as in the case of a rowhouse. Many sources make the distinction between detached, semi-detached, or group (or row) homes, but sometimes these distinctions were not made fully clear. In this work, I will observe the definitions used in the President's Conference on Home Building and Home Ownership: A detached home refers to one that shares no walls with neighbors. Such a building need not be single-family, as in the case of a multifamily dwelling where each family occupies one or more entire levels. Semi-detached means a side-by-side pairing where just one wall is shared; each side of the building may house one or multiple families, again, occupying one or more levels each. In a group or rowhouse arrangement, only the end units share just one wall; central units share walls on either side. These may be multiple stories high, as in large apartment buildings housing many families. Buildings constructed on the lot line, with no space between it and its neighbor, are also considered either semi-detached or row. John M. Gries and James Ford, eds., *The President's Conference on Home Building and Home Ownership*, vol. 4, *Home Ownership, Income and Types of Dwellings* (Washington, DC: National Capital Press, 1932), 149.

45　Gries and Ford, *The President's Conference on Home Building and Home Ownership*, vol. 4, 171.

46　Gries and Ford, *The President's Conference on Home Building and Home Ownership*, vol. 4, 163.

47　Wood, *Introduction to Housing*, 4. Bear in mind that "single-family" did not necessarily mean detached.

48　John M. Gries and James Ford, eds., *The President's Conference on Home Building and Home Ownership*, vol. 5, *House Design Construction and Equipment* (Washington, DC: National Capital Press, 1932), 26.

49　Henry Wright, "Housing—When, Where, and How?" *Architecture* 68, no. 1 (July 1933): 21.

50　Lewis Mumford, "The Chance for Civilized Housing," *New Republic*, September 17, 1930, 116.

51　Wood, *The Housing of the Unskilled Wage Earner*, 14. The 20 percent figure is also given by the editors of *Fortune* in *Housing America*, 23.

21　Radford, *Modern Housing for America*, 21, 25. Families in this lowest range earned, on average, $1,160 per year, or $97 per month. Although an expenditure of 20 percent of this income should have meant rents of just $19 per month, average rents were actually $35 per month.

53 "Washington Housing: A National Example," US Department of Agriculture, "Final Report of the Greenbelt Project of the Greenbelt Town Program" (Washington, DC, 1938), John Scott Lansill Papers, University of Kentucky Special Collections and Digital Programs, University of Kentucky, Lexington, KY. Hereafter cited as Greenbelt Final Report.

54 "Washington Housing: A National Example," Greenbelt Final Report.

55 Ernest R. Groves, *Social Problems of the Family* (Philadelphia: J. B. Lippincott, 1927), 231–32.

56 National Association of Housing Officials, *A Housing Program for the United States* (Chicago: National Association of Housing Officials, 1934), 5–6.

57 See Colin G. Pooley, ed., *Housing Strategies in Europe 1880–1930* (New York: St. Martin's Press, 1992).

58 Editors of *Fortune, Housing America*, 135.

59 Sir Raymond Unwin, "The Problem of Housing," in *America Can't Have Housing*, ed. Carol Aronovici (New York: Committee on the Housing Exhibition by the Museum of Modern Art, 1934), 9.

60 Stein, "Housing and Common Sense," 544.

61 Federal Emergency Administration of Public Works (FEAPW), *Homes for Workers* (Washington, DC: US Government Printing Office, 1937), 15.

62 Wood, *Introduction to Housing*, 131.

2 | CITIES AND ANTI-URBAN BACKLASH

Epigraph: Niles Carpenter, *The Sociology of City Life* (New York: Longmans, Green, 1931), 275.

1 Robert Wojtowicz, *Lewis Mumford and American Modernism: Eutopian Theories for Architecture and Urban Planning* (New York: Cambridge University Press, 1996), 143.

2 Ralph Steiner and Willard Van Dyke, dirs., *The City* (American Institute of Planners, 1939).

3 *The City* was first conceived when respected city planner Clarence Stein—just recently a consultant on the planning of the Greenbelt towns—after seeing the 1937 documentary *The River*, decided to create a similar film project extolling the virtues of planned communities. He convinced fellow members of both the Regional Planning Association of America (RPAA) and the American Institute of Planners (AIP) that the New York World's Fair would be the perfect showcase for their profession's latest ideas. To that end, a subset of the AIP's members formed Civic Films, Inc., obtained $50,000 from the Carnegie Foundation, and hired two of the most respected documentary filmmakers of the 1930s to oversee the project: Ralph Steiner, cinematographer for *The Plow That Broke the Plains*, and Willard Van Dyke, cinematographer for *The River*. The board of directors for Civic Films included the AIP's president, Tracy Augur, who also had only recently been a planning consultant

for the Greenbelt program. The RPAA was integral to the making of the film; three of the six members of Civic Films' board of directors were members of the organization, as was Stein. Lewis Mumford, also an RPAA member, wrote the narration. *The Plow That Broke the Plains*, one of the most important of the Depression-era documentaries, was produced by the Resettlement Administration. Steiner served as producer, codirector, and cinematographer on *The City*; Van Dyke was co-director and cinematographer. Richard M. Barsam, *Nonfiction Film: A Critical History* (Bloomington: Indiana University Press, 1973), 153, 166; William Alexander, *Film on the Left: American Documentary Film from 1931 to 1942* (Princeton, NJ: Princeton University Press, 1981), 247; Howard Gillette, Jr., "Film as Artifact: *The City* (1939)," *American Studies* (Fall 1977): 72–73; *Official Guide Book New York World's Fair 1939* (New York: Exposition Publications, 1939), 204; Kermit C. Parsons, ed., *The Writings of Clarence S. Stein: Architect of the Planned Community* (Baltimore: Johns Hopkins University Press, 1998), 362–63; Archer Winsten, "*The City* Goes to the Fair," in *The Documentary Tradition*, ed. Lewis Jacobs (New York: W. W. Norton, 1979), 126; "Wonder City Seen in Film at Fair," *New York Times*, May 28, 1939. The fair was open from April 30, 1939, through October 31, 1939, and again from May 11, 1940, through October 27, 1940.

4   Steiner and Van Dyke, *The City*. The village of the past was actually Shirley Center, Massachusetts, home of RPAA member Benton MacKaye. Gillette, "Film as Artifact: *The City* (1939)," 85n27.

5   Winsten, "*The City* Goes to the Fair," 126, 128.

6   Although most of the "better community" scenes were filmed in Greenbelt, some were also shot in Radburn, New Jersey, another planned community with ties to the Greenbelt towns. It is perhaps worth noting that filmmaker Ralph Steiner was himself no fan of either town, later referring to both Radburn and Greenbelt as "modern slums." Gillette, "Film as Artifact: *The City* (1939)," 75.

7   Bob Sommers, interview with the author, Greenbelt, MD, February 14, 2008. Mr. Sommers played the part of a boy whose bicycle tire goes flat in the film.

8   Margaret Marsh argues that this image was largely upheld by men, and that women were more favorably inclined toward city life than their male counterparts. Margaret Marsh, *Suburban Lives* (New Brunswick, NJ: Rutgers University Press, 1990).

9   Warren Simpson Thompson, "On Living in Cities," *American Mercury* 20 (June 1930): 192.

10   Steven Conn, *Americans Against the City: Anti-Urbanism in the Twentieth Century* (New York: Oxford University Press, 2014), 7.

11   Theodore Roosevelt, Special Message to the Two Houses of Congress (speech, Washington, DC, February 9, 1909), *American Presidency Project*, https://www.presidency.ucsb.edu/documents/special-message-366.

12   Benjamin Clarke Marsh, *An Introduction to City Planning: Democracy's Challenge to the American City* (New York, 1909), 6.

13   Franklin Roosevelt, "Address before the American Country Life Conference on the Better Distribution of Population Away from Cities, Ithaca, New York, August 19,

1931," in *The Public Papers and Addresses of Franklin D. Roosevelt*, Volume 1: *The Genesis of the New Deal 1928–1932* (New York: Random House, 1938), 511.

14 Ernest R. Groves, "The Urban Complex," *Sociological Review* 12, no. 2 (Autumn 1920): 79. Cosmopolitan humor, at the same time, often portrayed those living in the countryside as hicks and rubes. As with much human thought, the depiction of the "ideal" American environment was complicated.

15 William F. Ogburn, *You and Machines* (Chicago: University of Chicago Press, 1934), 33–34. Ogburn served as president of the American Sociological Society in 1929. Planner Clarence Arthur Perry quoted parts of this same passage in his *Housing for the Machine Age* (New York: Russell Sage Foundation, 1939), 22–23.

16 Lawrence K. Frank, "Childhood and Youth," in *Recent Social Trends in the United States: Report of the President's Research Committee on Social Trends*, vol. 2 (New York: McGraw-Hill, 1933), 772.

17 Charles Horton Cooley, *Social Organization: A Study of the Larger Mind* (New York: Charles Scribner's Sons, 1909), 5, 11, 26–27; Clarence Arthur Perry, "The Neighborhood Unit," in *Regional Survey of New York and Its Environs*, vol. 7 (New York: Committee on Regional Plan of New York and Its Environs, 1929), 126–27.

18 Robert E. Park, Ernest W. Burgess, and Roderick D. McKenzie, *The City* (Chicago: University of Chicago Press, 1925), 111. This chapter was written by Park.

19 Wood, *Recent Trends in American Housing*, 294.

20 Wood, *Introduction to Housing*, 55. It should be noted that, in the terms used at that time, "race" referred to ethnicity as well as what people generally mean by "race" today.

21 Wood, *Introduction to Housing*, 57.

22 Wood, *Slums and Blighted Areas in the United States*, 8–9.

23 Harry M. Schulman, "A Study of Crime and the Community," quoted in John M. Gries and James Ford, eds., *The President's Conference on Home Building and Home Ownership*, Vol. 8, *Housing and the Community—Home Repair and Remodeling* (Washington, DC: National Capital Press, 1932), 130, 140.

24 Perry, "The Neighborhood Unit," 124–25.

25 Louis Wirth, "Urbanism as a Way of Life," *American Journal of Sociology* 44, no. 1 (July 1938): 12.

26 Wirth, "Urbanism as a Way of Life," 17.

27 John Giffen Thompson offers many quotations from a variety of commentators in *Urbanization: Its Effects on Government and Society* (New York: E. P. Dutton, 1927), 14–18.

28 Charles Downing Lay, "The Freedom of the City," *North American Review* 222 (September 1925): 123.

29 Ebenezer Howard, *Garden Cities of To-morrow* (originally published as *To-morrow: A Peaceful Path to Real Reform*, London, 1898) (Cambridge, MA: MIT Press, 1965), 102.

30   Howard, *Garden Cities of To-morrow*, 111.

31   Howard, *Garden Cities of To-morrow*, 128.

32   Mumford, *Sticks and Stones*, 232.

33   See, for example, McKenzie, "The Rise of Metropolitan Communities," 1; and James Dahir, *Communities for Better Living: Citizen Achievement in Organization, Design, and Development* (New York: Harper, 1950), 107.

34   Harlan Paul Douglass, *The Suburban Trend* (New York: Century, 1925), 3–4. Douglass was a Congregationalist minister with a keen interest in sociology. Although he had no formal degree in sociology, he did take graduate courses in the discipline at Chicago and Columbia. Douglass wrote books on the sociology of religion as well as on rural life, small towns, and cities.

35   Jon Teaford, *City and Suburb: The Political Fragmentation of Metropolitan America, 1850–1970* (Baltimore: Johns Hopkins University Press, 1979), 77–81. Mary Corbin Sies has argued, however, that the attraction of suburbs for the upper and middle classes has been overstated in many histories. She notes that cities retained a preferred and elevated status in some locations until the 1940s. Mary Corbin Sies, "North American Suburbs, 1880–1950: Cultural and Social Reconsiderations," *Journal of Urban History* 27, no. 3 (March 2001): 313–14.

36   Douglass, *The Suburban Trend*, 123–29.

37   Benjamin Clarke Marsh, *An Introduction to City Planning*, 129.

38   Douglass, *The Suburban Trend*, 327.

39   Douglass, *The Suburban Trend*, 36.

40   Ray E. Baber, *Marriage and the Family* (New York: McGraw-Hill, 1939), 10.

41   Carol Aronovici, *Housing the Masses* (New York: John Wiley and Sons, 1939), 185.

42   Two such efforts of the 1920s were Mariemont, Ohio, designed by John Nolen, and Radburn, New Jersey, designed by Clarence Stein and Henry Wright.l

3 | THE NEW DEAL

Epigraph: Franklin D. Roosevelt, Nomination Acceptance Speech, Chicago, July 2, 1932, in *The Public Papers and Addresses of Franklin D. Roosevelt*, Volume 1, *The Genesis of the New Deal 1928–1932* (New York: Random House, 1938), 648.

1   Roosevelt, Nomination Acceptance Speech, 659.

2   Franklin D. Roosevelt, Inaugural Address, March 4, 1933, in *The Public Papers and Addresses of Franklin D. Roosevelt*, Volume 2, *The Year of Crisis 1933* (New York: Random House, 1938), 12–13.

3   Rexford G. Tugwell, *FDR: Architect of an Era* (New York: Macmillan, 1967), 11.

4   Joseph P. Lash, *Dealers and Dreamers: A New Look at the New Deal* (New York: Doubleday, 1988), 1.

5   Frederick Lewis Allen, *Only Yesterday: An Informal History of the 1920s*. (1931; rpt. New York: Harper Perennial Modern Classics, 2010), 38.

6   For example, Lawrence Dennis, *The Coming American Fascism* (New York: Harper, 1936); Lewis Corey, *The Crisis of the Middle Class* (New York: Covici, Friede, 1935).

7   For example, "Semi-Dictator?" *Barron's* 13, no. 7 (February 13, 1933): 12; Lippmann, *Interpretations 1933–1935*), a compilation of Lippmann's syndicated columns; Raoul E. Desvernine, *Democratic Despotism* (New York: Dodd, Mead, 1936).

8   Lewis Mumford, *Technics and Civilization* (New York: Harcourt, Brace, 1934), 405.

9   *Annals of the American Academy of Political and Social Science* 180 (July 1935).

10 Rexford Guy Tugwell, speech delivered in Olympic Auditorium, Los Angeles, October 28, 1935, Tugwell Papers Collection, Franklin D. Roosevelt Presidential Library, Hyde Park, NY.

11 Milton O. Hall, "Attitudes and Unemployment: A Comparison of the Opinions and Attitudes of Employed and Unemployed Men," *Archives of Psychology* 165 (March 1934): 26.

12 Hall, "Attitudes and Unemployment," 26.

13 Hall, "Attitudes and Unemployment," 27.

14 Hall, "Attitudes and Unemployment," 28.

15 Spencer Miller, Jr., "Labor and the Challenge of the New Leisure," *Harvard Business Review* 11 (June 1933): 463.

16 See Neil M. Maher, *Nature's New Deal: The Civilian Conservation Corps and the Roots of the American Environmental Movement* (New York: Oxford University Press, 2008). Also Douglas Brinkley, *Rightful Heritage: Franklin D. Roosevelt and the Land of America* (New York: Harper, 2016), especially 170–86; and Robert D. Leighninger, Jr., *Long-Range Public Investment: The Forgotten Legacy of the New Deal* (Columbia: University of South Carolina Press, 2007), 11–34.

17 See Paul K. Conkin, *A Revolution Down on the Farm: The Transformation of American Agriculture since 1929* (Lexington: University Press of Kentucky, 2008), 63–68; Paul K. Conkin, *The New Deal* (Wheeling, IL: Harlan, Davidson, 1992), 40–42; Gilbert C. Fite, "Farmer Opinion and the Agricultural Adjustment Act, 1933," *Mississippi Valley Historical Review* 48, no. 4 (March 1962): 656–73; Ann Folino White, *Plowed Under: Food Policy Protests and Performance in New Deal America* (Bloomington: Indiana University Press, 2015); Arthur M. Schlesinger, Jr., *The Coming of the New Deal* (Boston: Houghton, Mifflin, 1958), 60–63.

18 For more on the PWA, see Harold Ickes, *Back to Work: The Story of the PWA* (New York: Macmillan, 1935); Leighninger, *Long-Range Public Investment*, 35–42, 80–101, and 131; Jason Scott Smith, *Building New Deal Liberalism: The Political Economy of Public Works, 1933–1956* (New York: Cambridge University Press, 2006).

19 Smith, *Building New Deal Liberalism*, 3.

20 Smith, *Building New Deal Liberalism*, 3.

21 See Benjamin L. Alpers, *Dictators, Democracy, and American Public Culture: Envisioning the Totalitarian Enemy 1920s–1950s* (Chapel Hill: University of North Carolina Press, 2003).

22 "Semi-Dictator?" 12.

23 "Semi-Dictator?" 12.

24 "Roosevelt—Dictator?" editorial, *Catholic World* (April 1934): 1–8. The same argument was made by William Henry Chamberlin in *Collectivism: A False Utopia* (New York: Macmillan, 1937), 118.

25 Commentators differed in their definitions of what constituted fascism. One of the briefest was offered by UCLA political science professor H. Arthur Steiner. He wrote that true fascism must have all of these characteristics ("when one or more are lacking, we have something similar, but not identical"): "(1) the rejection of democracy; (2) a dictatorial technique; (3) repression of individual freedom; (4) repression of organized labor; (5) intense nationalism; and (6) a reactionary perspective." "Fascism in America?" *American Political Science Review* 29, no. 5 (October 1935): 823.

26 E. Francis Brown, "The American Road to Fascism," *Current History* (July 1933): 392–98.

27 Hugh Stevenson Tigner, "Will America Go Fascist?" *Christian Century*, May 2, 1934, 592.

28 J. B. Matthews and R. E. Shallcross, "Must America Go Fascist?" *Harper's* (June 1934): 1–15.

29 George Soule, *The Coming American Revolution* (New York: Macmillan, 1934), 293.

30 Lawrence Dennis, "Fascism for America," *Annals of the American Academy of Political and Social Science* 180 (July 1935): 65.

31 Dennis, *The Coming American Fascism*, 7.

32 See V. F. Calverton, "Is America Ripe for Fascism?" *Current History* 38 (September 1933): 701–4; Pendleton Herring, "A Prescription for Modern Democracy," *Annals of the American Academy of Political and Social Science* 180 (July 1935): 138–48; and the Editors of *The Economist* (London), *The New Deal: An Analysis and Appraisal* (New York: Alfred A. Knopf, 1937), 144–49.

33 Raymond Gram Swing, *Forerunners of American Fascism* (New York: J. Messner, 1935), 17.

34 See for instance George Boas, "A Defense of Democracy," *Harper's* 169 (September 1934): 418–46; Will Durant, "Is Democracy Doomed?" *Saturday Evening Post*, September 15, 1934, 23, 78, 80–82, 84.

35 For a thorough examination of both Long and Coughlin, see Alan Brinkley, *Voices of Protest: Huey Long, Father Coughlin, and the Great Depression* (New York: Vintage Books/Random House, 1982). See also Robert S. McElvaine, *The Great Depression: America, 1929–1941* (New York: Times Books, 1993), 238–40 and 243–48.

36 Edwin Amenta and Yvonne Zylan, "It Happened Here: Political Opportunity, the New Institutionalism, and the Townsend Movement," *American Sociological Review* 56, no. 2 (April 1991): 250–65; McElvaine, *The Great Depression*, 241–42.

37 For suggested readings on the historiography—the history of the history—concerning the New Deal, see the list of works for further reading.

38 Aaron D. Purcell, "Historical Interpretations of the New Deal and the Great Depression," in *The New Deal and the Great Depression*, ed. Aaron D. Purcell (Kent, OH: Kent State University Press, 2014), 6.

39 Among recent works addressing specific aspects of the New Deal are Scott Borchert, *Republic of Detours: How the New Deal Paid Broke Writers to Rediscover America* (New York: Farrar, Straus, and Giroux, 2021); Lizabeth Cohen, *Making a New Deal: Industrial Workers in Chicago, 1919–1939* (New York: Cambridge University Press, 2003); Lionel Kimble, Jr., *A New Deal for Bronzeville: Housing, Employment, and Civil Rights in Black Chicago, 1935–1955* (Carbondale: Southern Illinois University Press, 2015); Cory Pillen, *WPA Posters in an Aesthetic, Social, and Political Context: A New Deal for Design* (New York: Routledge, 2020); Eric Rauchway, *Winter War: Hoover, Roosevelt, and the First Clash Over the New Deal* (New York: Basic Books, 2018); Eric Rauchway, *Why the New Deal Matters* (New Haven, CT: Yale University Press, 2021); Lauren Rebecca Sklaroff, *Black Culture and the New Deal: The Quest for Civil Rights in the Roosevelt Era* (Chapel Hill: University of North Carolina Press, 2009); Jill Watts, *The Black Cabinet: The Untold Story of African Americans and Politics during the Age of Roosevelt* (New York: Grove Press, 2020).

4 | THE GREENBELT IDEA UNFOLDS

Epigraph: Franklin D. Roosevelt, "Growing Up by Plan," *The Survey* 67 (February 1932): 483.

1 Lash, *Dealers and Dreamers*, 1.

2 He eventually authored fifteen books, as well as serving as coauthor or editor of six more, and wrote over 150 articles. A complete list of Tugwell's writings can be found in Bernard Sternsher, *Rexford Tugwell and the New Deal* (New Brunswick, NJ: Rutgers University Press, 1964), 413–24.

3 Rexford Guy Tugwell, "Our Philosophy of Despair," *University Journal of Business* 2, no. 4 (September 1924): 431.

4 Like the majority of reformers of his era, Tugwell was largely silent on the problems that specifically faced African Americans and other racial minorities, though it seems that he expected that federal help for the poor would aid everyone, that a rising tide would lift all boats.

5 Rexford G. Tugwell, *The Battle for Democracy* (New York: Columbia University Press, 1935), 69.

6 Rexford G. Tugwell, "Design for Government," *Political Science Quarterly* 48, no. 3 (September 1933): 330. The same excerpt also appears in Tugwell, "Government in a Changing World," *Review of Reviews and World's Work* (May 16, 1933): 56; and Tugwell, *The Battle for Democracy*, 14.

7 Rexford G. Tugwell, "The Progressive Tradition," *Atlantic Monthly* (April 1935): 409–10.

8 Patrick D. Reagan, *Designing a New America: The Origins of New Deal Planning, 1890–1943* (Amherst: University of Massachusetts Press, 1999), 28–52.

9   Tugwell had actually communicated with Eleanor Roosevelt about possible uses for this stretch of land as early as 1933. Jennifer Karen Kerns, "A Social Experiment in Greenbelt, Maryland: Class, Gender, and Public Housing" (PhD diss., University of Arizona, 2002), 60. Tugwell had also expressed his desire to build the first of what eventually became the Greenbelt towns to John S. Lansill, the director of the Federal Emergency Relief Administration's Land Program, on February 24, 1935. At that time he took Lansill to the Berwyn site to show him where he believed the town should be built. Wallace Richards, Greenbelt Final Report, section 8, "Summary Chronology of Greenbelt Project," 1.

10   For example: "Traffic Safety in Tugwelltown Is Assured by Highways System," *Washington Post*, October 21, 1935; "Tugwelltown for New Jersey Meets with Local Resistance," *Baltimore Sun*, November 19, 1935; "Bound Brook's 'Tugwelltown' Will Be Taxable," *New York Herald Tribune*, March 4, 1936; "Million Allotted to Tugwelltown," *Washington Star*, October 11, 1936. The name "Greenbelt" was announced on January 28, 1936.

11   Bauer and Stein would later serve as consultants for the Greenbelt towns program, and Wright would be a principal planner for the never-built Greenbelt town of Greenbrook, New Jersey. Other RPAA members would also work on the Greenbelts.

12   Lewis Mumford, "The Fourth Migration," *Survey Graphic* 7 (May 1925): 130–33.

13   Clarence Stein, "Dinosaur Cities," in *Planning the Fourth Migration: The Neglected Vision of the Regional Planning Association of America*, ed. Carl Sussman (Cambridge, MA: MIT Press, 1976), 67. Originally published in *Survey Graphic* 7 (May 1925): 134–38.

14   Lewis Mumford, "Regions—To Live In," in *Planning the Fourth Migration*, ed. Sussman, 92. Originally published in *Survey Graphic* 7 (May 1925): 151–52.

15   Sussman, ed., *Planning the Fourth Migration*, 38–39.

16   Obituary of Henry Wright, *Architectural Record* 80 (August 1936): 83.

17   Clarence Stein to Herbert Stein, August 13, 1908, in Parsons, ed., *The Writings of Clarence S. Stein*, 53.

18   Martin Filler, "Planning for a Better World: The Lasting Legacy of Clarence Stein," *Architectural Record* 170, no. 10 (August 1982): 122.

19   Stein, "Housing and Common Sense," 541.

20   Stein, "Housing and Common Sense," 542.

21   Henry Wright, "Community Planning, 'Lo!' the Poor One-Family House," *Journal of the American Institute of Architects* 14, no. 3 (March 1925): 120.

22   Clarence Stein, address to members of the Advisory Council of the Commission of Housing and Regional Planning, December 27, 1923, in Parsons, ed., *The Writings of Clarence S. Stein*, 120.

23   Clarence Stein, essay written for class, May 13, 1917, in Parsons, ed., *The Writings of Clarence S. Stein*, 86, 89.

24 Stein, essay written for class, May 13, 1917, in Parsons, ed., *The Writings of Clarence S. Stein*, 87.

25 Although F. J. Osborn, in the introduction to *Garden Cities of To-morrow*, stated that this idea originated with Ebenezer Howard, and architectural historian Donald Leslie Johnson has claimed that architect William E. Drummond proposed the neighborhood unit around 1912 or 1913, the concept is most closely associated with Perry, especially in the United States. Osborn, introduction to *Garden Cities of To-morrow*, 18; Donald Leslie Johnson, "Origins of the Neighborhood Unit," *Planning Perspectives* 17, no. 3 (July 2002): 227–45.

26 Perry, "The Neighborhood Unit," 34–35.

27 Clarence Stein, "Notes on the New Town Planned for the City Housing Corporation," January 13, 1928, in Parsons, ed., *The Writings of Clarence S. Stein*, 150.

28 US Census Bureau, *Statistical Abstract of the United States 1939*, Table 450, "Motor-Vehicle Fatalities in Continental United States 1914–1937," (Washington, DC: US Government Printing Office, 1940), 397.

29 Clarence Stein, *Toward New Towns for America* (Liverpool: University Press of Liverpool, 1951), 41.

30 For more on Radburn, see Robert B. Hudson, *Radburn, a Plan of Living* (New York: American Association for Adult Education, 1934); Stein, *Toward New Towns for America*; Daniel Schaffer, *Garden Cities for America: The Radburn Experience* (Philadelphia: Temple University Press, 1982); Parsons, ed., *The Writings of Clarence S. Stein*.

31 Stein, *Toward New Towns for America*, 44.

32 Stein, *Toward New Towns for America*, 44.

33 Stein, *Toward New Towns for America*, 44.

34 John Lansill to W. W. Alexander, attached to Greenbelt Final Report.

35 Tugwell diary, March 14, 1935.

36 Barrows, "Beyond the Tenement," 399.

37 Mark I. Gelfand, *A Nation of Cities: The Federal Government and Urban America, 1933–1965* (New York: Oxford University Press, 1975), 59.

38 Biographical information primarily from the Warren Vinton Papers, Cornell University, Ithaca, NY. On meeting with the planners: Alanon and Eden, *Main Street Ready Made*, 7.

39 Clarence Stein, initially at least, seemed none too impressed with the reliance upon non-experts, writing to his wife that "Tugwell seems to have surrounded himself with a group of the sons of wealthy dads [apparently a reference to Lansill, though not accurate, as Lansill had amassed his wealth himself], who know about as little about the subject with which they are dealing as he does." Clarence Stein to Aline Stein, June 19, 1935, in Parsons, ed., *The Writings of Clarence S. Stein*, 308–9.

40 Arnold, *The New Deal in the Suburbs*, 29–30.

41 Henry Churchill, "America's Town Planning Begins," *New Republic*, June 3, 1936, 96.

42 Resettlement Administration, "Summary of Information, Greenhills, Hamilton County, Ohio," n.d., but compiled before the town was completed. The date can be estimated based on the fact that the report states that Greenhills will contain 1,000 housing units, meaning that it was written prior to budget cuts that forced the plan to be reduced. One such cut (though apparently not the first) took place in September 1936. John Scott Lansill Papers, University of Kentucky Special Collections and Digital Programs, University of Kentucky, Lexington, KY.

43 Resettlement Administration press release, dated October 11, 1935, Official file, OF 1568, box 1, "September–November 1935," Franklin D. Roosevelt Presidential Library, Hyde Park, NY.

44 Arnold, *The New Deal in the Suburbs*, 47. In contrast, the final design, which relied heavily on the use of the superblock and cul-de-sac, resulted in just six miles of interior streets, curving to fit the site's topography. Conkin, *Tomorrow a New World*, 311.

45 Arnold, *The New Deal in the Suburbs*, 47.

46 Henry S. Churchill, "Greenbelt Towns: A Study of the Background and Planning of Four Communities for the Division of Suburban Resettlement of the Resettlement Administration, John S. Lansill, Director," n.d., typed manuscript, chapter 3, "Organization," 2, John Scott Lansill Papers, University of Kentucky Special Collections and Digital Programs, University of Kentucky, Lexington, KY. Hereafter cited as Churchill manuscript.

47 For more on the design teams, see Arnold, *The New Deal in the Suburbs*, 46–50.

48 Resettlement Administration, "Homes for Workingmen," n.d., Greenbrook file, John Scott Lansill Papers, University of Kentucky Special Collections and Digital Programs, University of Kentucky, Lexington, KY.

49 Clarence Stein to Aline Stein, July 2, 1935, in Parsons, ed., *The Writings of Clarence S. Stein*, 312–13.

50 Clarence Stein to Aline Stein, July 4, 1935, in Parsons, ed., *The Writings of Clarence S. Stein*, 313.

51 Stein, *Toward New Towns for America*, 122.

52 Marquis W. Childs, *I Write from Washington* (New York: Harper, 1942), 12. In addition to the architects, town planners, and engineers, a host of professionals from a wide variety of fields took part in the Greenbelt program, conducting surveys, helping to establish good housing guidelines, determining optimal dwelling size, setting up tenant eligibility criteria, and managing public relations.

53 Churchill, "America's Town Planning Begins," 96.

54 Elbert Peets, US Department of Agriculture, "Final Report of the Greendale Project of the Greenbelt Town Program" (Washington, DC, 1938), 2:15, John Scott Lansill Papers, University of Kentucky Special Collections and Digital Programs, University of Kentucky, Lexington, KY. Hereafter cited as Greendale Final Report.

55 T. S. Holden, "How Many Architects Are Carrying On?" *Architectural Record* 74 (July 1933): 57.

56 See Albert Mayer, "The Architect and the World," *Nation*, January 8, 1936, 43–45. Mayer served as one of the lead architects on the Greenbrook project. See also Charles S. Ascher, "What the Depression Has Done to Planning," *Public Management* 17 (February 1935): 35–37.

57 Arnold, *The New Deal in the Suburbs*, 50.

58 Arnold, *The New Deal in the Suburbs*, 50. Among the planners, Clarence Stein and Henry Wright, at least, seem to have held more progressive beliefs.

59 Resettlement Administration, "Homes for Workingmen."

60 Resettlement Administration, "Homes for Workingmen."

61 Produced by the RA to promote the Greenbelt towns.

62 Resettlement Administration, *Greenbelt Towns* (Washington, DC: US Government Printing Office, September 1936).

5 | OPPOSITION

Epigraph: Henry Churchill, *The City Is the People* (New York, Reynal & Hitchcock, 1945), 80.

1 Quoted in Leo C. Rosten, *The Washington Correspondents* (New York: Harcourt, Brace, 1937), 268.

2 "'Tugwelltown' Tussle," *Business Week*, January 25, 1936, 36–37.

3 See, for example, Alva Johnston, "Tugwell, the President's Idea Man," *Saturday Evening Post*, August 1, 1936, 8. This publication consistently expressed a conservative viewpoint.

4 Baldwin, *Poverty and Politics*, 88. Tugwell's resignation was also likely due at least in part to his impending divorce from his wife of over twenty years in order to marry his administrative assistant, Grace Falke, a move that further harmed his public reputation. Ibid., 119–20.

5 Rexford Tugwell, "The Resettlement Idea," *Agricultural History* 33, no. 4 (October 1959): 159.

6 "Departing Pair Afford Brain Trust Contrast," *New York Times*, January 17, 1937.

7 Felix Bruner, "Utopia Unlimited," *Washington Post*, February 10, 1936.

8 Felix Bruner, "Utopia Unlimited," *Washington Post*, February 11, 1936.

9 Felix Bruner, "Utopia Unlimited," *Washington Post*, February 10, 1936.

10 An article in *Literary Digest* about the offices in the mansion explains that the reason for using this building was a shortage of office space in Washington. "'Alphabet Soup' in Washington Mansion," *Literary Digest*, August 31, 1935), 10.

11 Robert B. Fairbanks is one of the few earlier historians to acknowledge that "no systematic study has been done to verify these observations." Fairbanks, "Cincinnati and Greenhills: The Response to a Federal Community, 1935–1939," *Cincinnati Historical Society Bulletin* 36, no. 4 (Winter 1978): 223.

12 "American Housing: A Failure, a Problem, a Potential Boon and Boom," *Life*, November 15, 1937, 45.

13 "Competition Is Looming among 'Federal' Homes," *Milwaukee Journal*, December 5, 1935.

14 "Greendale Is Chosen as Name of 'Tugwell Town,'" newspaper unknown, March 24, 1936, scrapbook, Greendale Historical Society, Greendale, WI.

15 However, in the reminiscences of some early residents, they mention Greenbelt as having been initially called Tugwell Town (see *Looking Back: Greenbelt Is 50, 1937–1987*, an anniversary booklet produced by the city in 1987). This seems to be a case of residents absorbing the misconception that this was the actual name of the town at some point solely because this incorrect information had been repeated over the years.

16 Patrick Lee, "Dr. Tugwell's Satellite Towns Born of Chaos and Red Tape," *New York Sun*, July 11, 1936.

17 Charles E. Blake, "U.S. Funds Building Communistic Town 90 Miles from City," labeled as *Chicago American*, October 26, 1936, scrapbook, Greendale Historical Society.

18 "'Tugwell's Folly' Opens Soon," *Pittsburgh Post-Gazette*, labeled as September 1937 (no specific date given on label), newspaper clipping file, Tugwell Room, Greenbelt Library, Greenbelt, MD.

19 This imitation newspaper does not identify who created it or when, but the Summary Chronological History of [the] Greenhills Project in the Final Report on Greenhills notes that on November 18, 1935, "Circulars designed to crystalize sentiments against Project are circulated in Cincinnati and Hamilton County." It is possible that this is referring to this "newspaper." US Department of Agriculture, "Final Report of the Greenhills Project of the Greenbelt Town Program" (Washington, DC, 1938), Analysis of Questionnaire Results, 1, John Scott Lansill Papers, University of Kentucky Special Collections and Digital Programs, University of Kentucky, Lexington, KY. Hereafter cited as Greenhills Final Report.

20 The bogus newspaper is in the collection of the Mt. Healthy Historical Society, Mt. Healthy, OH. It includes no indication of who created it, when, how, or where it was distributed, or any other information. In researching this book, this author has never seen another copy of this paper, or any other reference to it.

21 "Transient Use Protested Hotly," unidentified newspaper, n.d., Falls scrapbook, Greenbelt Museum, Greenbelt, MD; "'Tugwell-Town' Laborers Called Menace," *Washington Times*, October 15, 1935.

22 "Berwyn Jobs Partially Solve Transient Problem," *Washington Daily News*, November 13, 1935.

23 "Berwyn Housing Plans Opposed," appears to be labeled as *Washington Herald*, October 1935 (exact date obscured), Falls scrapbook, Greenbelt Museum; "Prince Georges Residents Mass to Fight 'Tugwelltown' Project," labeled as (Washington?) *Post*, October 1935 (exact date obscured), Falls scrapbook, Greenbelt Museum;

"Berwyn Backs Tugwelltown," labeled as (Washington?) *Herald*, October 17, 1935, Falls scrapbook, Greenbelt Museum; "Industrialists Clamoring for RA Projects," labeled as *Baltimore Sun*, October 17, 1935, Falls scrapbook, Greenbelt Museum.

24 "Board at Berwyn Unanimous in Accepting 'Tugwelltown,'" unidentified newspaper clipping labeled October 17, 1935, Tugwell scrapbook, Tugwell Room, Greenbelt Library.

25 "Greenbelt—The Boondoggle That Made Good," *Washington Post*, June 8, 1947.

26 For a much more thorough discussion of how resistance and acceptance unfolded in the Cincinnati area, see Fairbanks, "Cincinnati and Greenhills: The Response to a Federal Community, 1935–1939."

27 "Plans Bared for Housing Site," *Cincinnati Enquirer*, November 26, 1935.

28 For example, Greenhills planner Justin Hartzog wrote about this in an apparently unpublished paper housed in the John Scott Lansill Collection at the University of Kentucky.

29 "Realtors Table Disapproval of Mt. Healthy Settlement; Sentiment Changed by Talk," *Cincinnati Enquirer*, November 27, 1935.

30 "Report Criticizes U.S. Resettlement Plan at Mt. Healthy," *Cincinnati Times-Star*, January 13, 1936.

31 "U.S. Official Hits Civic Club Housing Report," *Cincinnati Post*, January 20, 1936.

32 Resettlement Administration, "Summary of Information, Greenhills."

33 "Greenhills Project Is Defended against National G.O.P. Blast," *Cincinnati Post*, September 24, 1936.

34 "Crabbs Defends Resettlement," *Cincinnati Post*, November 26, 1935.

35 "Attack on Tugwell," *Cincinnati Post*, January 13, 1936.

36 Preliminary Plan Book, Bound Brook Suburban Resettlement, n.d., John Scott Lansill Papers, University of Kentucky Special Collections and Digital Programs, University of Kentucky, Lexington, KY.

37 Arnold, *The New Deal in the Suburbs*, 65.

38 Arnold, *The New Deal in the Suburbs*, 65.

39 "Tugwell to Spend $6,000,000 on 'City,'" *New York Times*, November 3, 1935.

40 Arnold, *The New Deal in the Suburbs*, 63–64.

41 US Department of Agriculture, "Public Relations," "Final Report of the Greenbrook Project of the Greenbelt Town Program" (Washington, DC, 1938), John Scott Lansill Papers, University of Kentucky Special Collections and Digital Programs, University of Kentucky, Lexington, KY. Hereafter cited as Greenbrook Final Report.

42 Quoted in Arnold, *The New Deal in the Suburbs*, 65.

43 "Summarized History of Greenbrook," Tugwell Room, Greenbelt Library, Greenbelt, MD.

44 Arnold, *The New Deal in the Suburbs*, 71.

45 Memo in Greenbrook file, John Scott Lansill Papers, University of Kentucky Special Collections and Digital Programs, University of Kentucky, Lexington, KY. The memo is signed simply "R.B."

46 For a more detailed discussion of the Greenbrook opposition and court case, see Arnold, *The New Deal in the Suburbs*, 61–77; and Daniel Schaffer, "Resettling Industrial America: The Controversy Over FDR's Greenbelt Town Program," *Urbanism Past & Present* 8, no. 1 (Winter/Spring 1983): 18–32, though Schaffer relies heavily on Arnold. For historians wishing to do more research on the rise and fall of Greenbrook's possibility, see the nice, detailed chronology in "Greenbrook, NJ, Project History," John Scott Lansill Papers, University of Kentucky Special Collections and Digital Programs, University of Kentucky, Lexington, KY.

47 "Parklawn and Greendale Are Targets of Lawsuit," *Milwaukee Journal*, August 31, 1936; "Act to Halt U.S. Housing Projects Here," newspaper clipping in scrapbook at Greendale Historical Society, labeled "*Sentinal* [*sic*], 8–31–1936"; "Ban Is Sought on Milwaukee New Deal Jobs," same scrapbook, labeled "*Wash. Post*, Sept. 1st, 1936."

48 "Parklawn and Greendale Are Targets of Lawsuit."

49 "Labor to Fight Housing Suits," unnamed newspaper, n.d., scrapbook at Greendale Historical Society.

50 "Labor Backs Housing Jobs," *Milwaukee Journal*, May 20, 1936.

51 "Change Plan for Greendale; No Expansion," newspaper clipping in scrapbook at Greendale Historical Society. Alanen and Eden, *Main Street Ready-Made*, 23.

52 "Attack on Greenhills," *Cincinnati Post*, June 23, 1936.

53 "Who Done It?" *Cincinnati Post*, September 25, 1936.

54 Alfred Segal, "Cincinnatus," *Cincinnati Post*, September 25, 1936.

6 | DESIGNING THE TOWNS

Epigraph: Churchill, "America's Town Planning Begins," 98.

1 The figure of one hundred projects appears in Conkin, *Tomorrow a New World*, 6. Leighninger's *Long-Range Public Investment* offers a very nice accounting of various New Deal building projects, not just housing.

2 John S. Lansill, Foreword to the Greenbelt Final Report.

3 Childs, *I Write from Washington*, 13.

4 Preliminary Plan Book, Bound Brook Suburban Resettlement, Site Planning Conference, November 15, 1935, handwritten pages 41–42.

5 Preliminary Plan Book, Bound Brook Suburban Resettlement, Bound Brook Project meeting summary by Kenneth Kassler, November 8, 1935, handwritten page number 36.

6 Conkin perhaps goes the furthest in drawing this parallel, writing that "the three completed greenbelt cities represented the culmination of the garden city movement in America. They remain the nearest American approximation of Ebenezer Howard's garden city idea." Conkin, *Tomorrow a New World*, 305. Others merely mention the

garden city idea as one of the progenitors of the Greenbelt concept; see for example Arnold, *The New Deal in the Suburbs*, 5–8; "Brave New Towns That Aged Awkwardly," *Business Week*, January 9, 1971, 22–24; Christensen, *The American Garden* City, 71; James Dahir, "Greendale Comes of Age" (manuscript prepared for the Milwaukee Community Development Corporation, 1958), 4–5, Greendale Historical Society, Greendale, WI; Flora C. Stephenson, "Greenbelt Towns in the United States," *Town and Country Planning* 10, no. 40 (Winter 1942–43): 121.

7   Rexford Tugwell, Address to the Regional Planning Association of Hamilton County, Ohio, February 5, 1936, Tugwell Papers Collection, Franklin D. Roosevelt Presidential Library, Hyde Park, NY.

8   Churchill, "America's Town Planning Begins," 96. In general the Greenbelt planners did not publicly acknowledge any debt to German housing projects, perhaps because the Greenbelt towns were already frequently depicted in the press as being of foreign, possibly "radical" origin.

9   Peets, Greendale Final Report, 2:1.

10   Arnold, *The New Deal in the Suburbs*, 124.

11   Peets, Greendale Final Report, 2:62.

12   It is possible to get a sense of just how important this was to the children of Greenhills by reading through the oral interviews posted on "New Deal Neighbors, Oral Histories of Greenhills, Ohio," https://www.newdealneighbors.com/. The swimming pool and the woods are routinely cited as the most loved places for the town's children. See interviews with Oscar Hoffman, Dan Rolfes, Glory Green Southwind, Louis Steinert, and Jane Steinway.

13   This same orientation is common in the homes in Greenhills as well.

14   Otis Kline Fulmer, *Greenbelt* (Washington, DC: American Council on Public Affairs, n.d.), 7. This booklet notes that Fulmer was an associate architect on Greenbelt's planning team. Upon completion of the town he moved there and became assistant resident manager. He lived in the town for at least four years.

15   Leslie Gene Hunter, "Greenbelt, Maryland: A City on a Hill," *Maryland Historical Magazine* (June 1968): 117

16   Peets, Greendale Final Report, 2:19.

17   Barbara Haskell, *The American Century: Art and Culture 1900–1950* (New York: Whitney Museum of American Art, 1999), 240.

18   Lawrence Levine, *The Unpredictable Past: Explorations in American Cultural History* (New York: Oxford University Press, 1993), 204.

19   Edwin Avery Park, *New Backgrounds for a New Age* (New York: Harcourt, Brace, 1927), 51.

20   Douglass, *The Suburban Trend*, 310.

21   Janet M. James, *Looking Back*, reminiscence section, 41.

22   O[tis]. Kline Fulmer, "Why Some Greenbelt Houses Have Flat Roofs," *Greenbelt Cooperator*, January 5, 1938.

23   Frank Cordner, "Architectural Planning, Greenhills, Ohio," Greenhills Final Report, 14. Cordner was the principal architect for Greenhills.

24   Some of the flat roofs apparently leaked early on and so were replaced by pitched roofs. "Description of Houses, Greenhills Project," n.d., Record Group 96: Farmers Home Administration file, National Archives and Records Administration, College Park, MD.

25   For analyses of the Williamsburg restoration, see, for example, Anders Greenspan, "How Philanthropy Can Alter Our View of the Past: A Look at Colonial Williamsburg," *Voluntas* 5 (June 1, 1994): 193–203; Jihong Kim and Bong Hee Jeon, "Restoration of a Historic Town to Commemorate National Identity: Colonial Williamsburg in the Early Twentieth Century," *Journal of Asian Architecture and Building Engineering* 11, no. 2 (2012): 245–51; Miles Orvell, *The Death and Life of Main Street: Small Towns in American Memory, Space, and Community* (Chapel Hill: University of North Carolina Press, 2012), 32–35.

26   *A Guide Book for Williamsburg, Virginia* (Williamsburg, VA: Colonial Williamsburg, Inc., 1936), 23.

27   For more on reverential attitudes about the past during this period, see Alan Brinkley, *Culture and Politics in the Great Depression* (Waco, TX: Markham Press Fund, 1998); Harvey Green, *The Uncertainty of Everyday Life: 1915–1945* (New York: Harper Perennial, 1993); Haskell, *The American Century*; Levine, *The Unpredictable Past*; Roderick Nash, *The Nervous Generation: American Thought, 1917–1930* (Chicago: Ivan R. Dee/Elephant Paperback, 1990).

28   Peets, Greendale Final Report, 2:149–50; and "Greendale," in *On the Art of Designing Cities: Selected Essays of Elbert Peets*, ed. Paul D. Spreiregen (Cambridge, MA: MIT Press, 1968), 222.

29   Elbert Peets, "Washington, Williamsburg, the Century of Progress, and Greendale," in *City Planning, Housing*, vol. 2, ed. Werner Hegemann, William W. Forster, and Robert C. Weinburg (New York: Architectural Book Publishing, 1936), 398.

30   Peets, Greendale Final Report, 2:149–50.

31   Peets, Greendale Final Report, 2:148.

32   Peets, Greendale Final Report, 2:149–50.

33   Albert Mayer, "Henry Wright: Creative Planner," *Survey Graphic* 25 (September 1936): 530.

34   Albert Mayer, "A Technique for Planning Complete Communities," *Architectural Forum* 66 (January–February 1937): 135–36.

35   US Census Bureau, *Statistical Abstract of the United States 1939*, Table 450, "Motor-vehicle Fatalities in Continental United States 1914–1937" (Washington, DC: US Government Printing Office, 1940). These figures include all automobile-accident deaths except those involving collisions with trains or streetcars, or motorcycle accidents.

36   "The Hazard of Driving and Walking: Analysis of Motor-Vehicle Accidents and Fatalities." *American City* 50 (May 1935): 99. This article provides a breakdown of accidents by type.

37   Seth K. Humphrey, "Our Delightful Man-Killer," *Atlantic Monthly* 148 (December 1931): 724–30; J. C. Furnas, "And Sudden Death," *Reader's Digest* (August 1935): 21–26. Furnas's article was reprinted in several other magazines.

38   Furnas, "And Sudden Death," 22.

39   For example: "Another Bad Year of Motor Vehicle Deaths," *American City* 44 (February 1931): 85; "Child Victims of the Auto," *Literary Digest*, February 2, 1929, 34; William Junkin Cox, "Accidents Can Be Stopped," *Woman's Home Companion* 64 (May 1937): 106, 108; W[illiam] J[unkin] Cox, "Why Automobile Accidents?" *Harper's* 171 (June 1935): 54–66; "Death All Day," *New Republic*, March 4, 1936, 98–99 [in answer to "And Sudden Death"]; Paul L. Green, "Accidents Can Be Reduced," *American City* 50 (October 1935): 71, 73, 75, 77; Paul L. Green, "Accidents Can Be Reduced," *American City* 50 (December 1935): 69, 71; "Hazard of Driving and Walking," 99, 101; Boyden Sparkes, "The Reckless Other Fellow," *Saturday Evening Post*, September 26, 1936), 33, 100–102; James A. Tobey, "The Hazard of the Automobile," *Scientific Monthly* 32, no. 6 (June 1931): 519–21.

40   Frank, "Childhood and Youth," 759.

41   Lynd and Lynd, *Middletown*, 254.

42   Lynd and Lynd, *Middletown*, 255–56.

43   Preliminary Plan Book, Bound Brook Suburban Resettlement, Site Planning Conference, November 15, 1935, handwritten page number 41.

44   The most thorough study of the planning of Greenhills to date is Charles Bradley Leach, "Greenhills, Ohio: The Evolution of an American New Town" (PhD diss., Case Western Reserve University, 1978). Leach covers such aspects as land acquisition, development of the town plan, budget, and public opinion.

45   Peets, Greendale Final Report, 2:36–37.

46   Peets, Greendale Final Report, 2:36–37.

47   Jacob Crane, "Safety Town," *Public Safety* (August 1937): 29.

48   K. W. Bauer, "A Greenbelt Town Grows Up," *The American City* 74 (October 1959): 144.

49   "Cyclist Killed by Hit-Runner in Greenbelt," *Washington Post*, August 25, 1939.

50   Mayer, "A Technique for Planning Complete Communities," 136. This article provides a trove of information on the design decisions for Greenbrook.

51   Clarence Stein, "The Conception of Greenbelt," typewritten paper, July 24, 1947, Tugwell Room, Greenbelt Library, Greenbelt, MD.

52   Assistant Chief Town Planner W. A. Strong to Justin Hartzog, August 10, 1936, Justin Hartzog Papers, Cornell University, Ithaca, NY.

53   Greendale Final Report, Section III, Town and Site Planning, III-16.

54 William Form, "The Sociology of a White Collar Suburb" (PhD diss., University of Maryland, 1944), 4.

55 Greenbelt Plant Field List, October 22, 1936. Courtesy of Greenbelt Homes, Inc.

56 Hale Walker and Magnus Thompson, Greenbelt Final Report, section 3, 12.

57 Timothy Evans, "Emerald City," letter to *Historic Preservation* 46, no. 6 (November 1994): 8.

58 Marion Benson Hastings, "Notes on Early Greenbelt Memories," January 1997, Greenbelt Museum, Greenbelt, MD.

59 Warner, *Greenbelt*, 88–89.

60 Warner, *Greenbelt*, 84.

61 Warner, *Greenbelt*, 91.

62 The religious groups initially meeting in the community building included the Catholic Church, the Mormon Church (Church of Jesus Christ of the Latter-Day Saints), and the Greenbelt Community Church (a nondenominational Protestant church). "Directory of Greenbelt Organizations," mimeographed, October 1, 1938, Greenbelt Museum. In 1939 a Jewish congregation also began meeting in the building. Ethel Rosenweig, "The Way It Was," Mishkan Torah file, Greenbelt Museum.

63 Wilma Dykeman and James Stokely, *Seeds of Southern Change: The Life of Will Alexander* (Chicago: University of Chicago Press, 1962), 222.

64 "Rural Housing Area Viewed by President," n.d., newspaper clipping in Falls scrapbook, Greenbelt Museum.

65 "Rural Housing Area Viewed by President."

66 Sidney Olson, "President Likes 'Tugwelltown,' Fishes and All," *Washington Post*, November 14, 1936.

7 | CIVIC ART

Epigraph: John Dewey, *Democracy and Education: An Introduction to the Philosophy of Education* (New York: Macmillan, 1916), 159.

1 George Biddle, *An American Artist's Story* (Boston: Little, Brown, 1939), 268.

2 Biddle, *An American Artist's Story*, 274.

3 Biddle, *An American Artist's Story*, 278.

4 George Biddle, "The Government and the Arts." *Harper's*, October 1, 1943, 428. The Section of Fine Arts closed down in 1943.

5 It is not unusual to see documents that simply refer to the one as the Section and the other as the Project. The National Youth Administration also produced art as a byproduct of the lessons given to its young members, but this was not a primary goal of the program.

6 Biddle, "The Government and the Arts." 428. For more on the WPA/FAP, see also George Biddle, "Five Years of Federal Patronage," *American Scholar* 9, no. 3 (Summer 1940): 327–38; "Incalculable Record," *Magazine of Art* 32 (August 1949): 460–71,

494–95; and Francis V. O'Conner, ed., *Art for the Millions: Essays from the 1930s by Artists and Administrators of the WPA Federal Art Project* (Greenwich, CT: New York Graphic Society, 1973). Sharon Ann Musher gives more attention to other programs, but does devote some of her discussion to the WPA/FAP in *Democratic Art: The New Deal's Influence on American Culture* (Chicago: University of Chicago Press, 2015).

7   Holger Cahill, "Franklin Delano Roosevelt," *Magazine of Art* 38 (May 1945): 163.

8   Quoted in Richard D. McKinzie, *The New Deal for Artists* (Princeton, NJ: Princeton University Press, 1973), 80.

9   Edward Bruce, "Art and Democracy," *Atlantic* 156 (August 1935): 152.

10   "Unemployed Arts," *Fortune* 15 (May 1937): 113.

11   "Unemployed Arts," 113.

12   Biddle, *An American Artist's Story*, 279.

13   "Unemployed Arts," 113–14.

14   Musher, *Democratic Art*, 5.

15   O'Conner, *Art for the Millions*, 305.

16   Beniamino Bufano, "For the Present We Are Busy," in O'Connor, ed., *Art for the Millions*, 109.

17   Lenore Thomas file, undated summary of Thomas's work for Greenbelt, Greenbelt Museum, Greenbelt, MD.

18   Lenore Thomas file.

19   Lenore Thomas file.

20   Lenore Thomas file.

21   According to the Greendale Historical Society, it was fourteen feet, but an article from a (presumably local) newspaper stated that it would be twelve feet. Unnamed article, unnamed newspaper, n.d., scrapbook at Greendale Historical Society, Greendale, WI.

22   "WPA Federal Art Project," *Current History* 48, no. 4 (April 1, 1938): 71.

23   "The Week in Art Circles," *Cincinnati Enquirer*, August 21, 1938.

24   Zoellner also created a smaller piece for the library, depicting a family with the school in the background. This piece was lost after being removed for renovations.

25   "The Week in Art Circles." The article lists the subjects of the panels: "a group of women and children in front of the Community store"; "young people in the street dancing to the music of the accordion and the banjo under swaying Japanese lanterns"; a "baseball game, played in a field surrounded by trees, under which picnickers are eating their lunch"; "a family working happily in their community garden"; and two panels that show children "digging in their sand piles or dressed in Indian costume, playing games in a sunny park."

26   Bruce, "Art and Democracy," 149.

27   "WPA Federal Art Project," 68.

28 Lewis Mumford, "Letter to the President," *New Republic*, December 30, 1936, 263.

29 "Maintain the Arts Projects," *Publishers' Weekly*, January 22, 1938, 22.

30 The case is complicated by the fact that no documentation appears to exist showing that Velsey was ever paid for his work. If the WPA had paid him, the sculptures should have gone to Greenhills, but if not, they were his to do with as he wished. Lew Moores, "Dispute Over Art Is Carved in Stone," *Cincinnati Enquirer*, March 8, 2001.

8 | LEISURE

Epigraph: George Cutten, *The Threat of Leisure* (New Haven, CT: Yale University Press, 1926), 87.

1 Jeremy Atack and Fred Bateman, "How Long Was the Workday in 1880?" *Journal of Economic History* 52, no. 1 (March 1992): 137.

2 Donald M. Fisk, "American Labor in the 20th Century," in *Compensation and Working Conditions* (Washington, DC: US Bureau of Labor Statistics, Fall 2001), 2.

3 In this book, "leisure" will be used as most Americans would have understood it in the interwar era: as time free of other duties such as paid employment, commuting to and from work, household chores, required child-tending tasks, necessary errands such as shopping for food, and personal maintenance (including eating and sleeping, except when done as leisure activities).

4 Wolman and Peck, "Labor Groups in the Social Structure," 828.

5 Many publications of the era noted the general increase in leisure time, including Cutten, *The Threat of Leisure*, 31–33; Maurice R. Davie, *Problems of City Life: A Study in Urban Sociology* (New York: John Wiley and Sons, 1932), 565–66; "Extent of 5-Day Week in American Industry, 1931," *Monthly Labor Review* 33, no. 3 (September 1933): 487–92; and Maurice Leven, Harold G. Moulton, and Clark Warburton, *America's Capacity to Consume* (Washington, DC: Brookings Institution, 1934), 18.

6 Helen McAfee, "The Menace of Leisure," *Century* 114 (1927): 67–76; Walter Henderson Grimes, "The Curse of Leisure," *Atlantic Monthly* (September 1928): 355–60; John Adams, "The Menace of Leisure," *School and Society* 33 (1931): 651–56; D. C. Fisher, "The Bright and Perilous Face of Leisure," *Journal of Adult Education* 5 (June 1933): 237–43; Jesse Frederick Steiner, "Challenge of the New Leisure," *Recreation* 27 (February 1934): 517–22; E. E. Calkins, "The New Leisure—A Curse or a Blessing?" *Recreation* 28 (April 1934): 23–27; George Gardner, Mabel Z. Smith, and Helen Gardner, "The New Social Problem: Leisure Time," *School and Society* 42 (August 31, 1935): 294–96; Cutten, *The Threat of Leisure*; Gove Hambidge, *Time to Live: Adventures in the Use of Leisure* (New York: McGraw-Hill, 1933); Arthur Newton Pack, *The Challenge of Leisure* (New York: Macmillan, 1934); Mabel C. Hermans and Margaret M. Hannon, *Using Leisure Time* (New York: Harcourt, Brace, 1938); Eduard Lindeman, *Leisure—A National Issue: Planning for the Leisure of a Democratic People* (New York: Association Press, 1939).

7   Eugene T. Lies, "The Community's Responsibility toward the Leisure Time Problem," *National Conference on Social Welfare, Proceedings 1928*, 311.

8   For a more thorough examination of the worry about leisure and its consequences than is possible here, see Susan Currell's *The March of Spare Time: The Problem and Promise of Leisure in the Great Depression* (Philadelphia: University of Pennsylvania Press, 2005). Currell argues convincingly that many New Deal programs arose specifically in response to these concerns. David George Surdam also discusses these concerns in *Century of the Leisured Masses: Entertainment and the Transformation of Twentieth-Century America* (New York: Oxford University Press, 2015), 23–25.

9   See, for example, Henry S. Curtis, *The Play Movement and Its Significance* (New York: Macmillan, 1917); Clarence E. Rainwater, *The Play Movement in the United States: A Study of Community Recreation* (Chicago: University of Chicago Press, 1922); Rhea Foster Dulles, *America Learns to Play: A History of Popular Recreation, 1607–1940* (New York: D. Appleton-Century, 1940); and Howard P. Chudacoff, *Children at Play: An American History* (New York: New York University Press, 2007).

10 Curtis, *The Play Movement and Its Significance,* 324.

11 Curtis, *The Play Movement and Its Significance,* 339.

12 Quoted in Cutten, *The Threat of Leisure*, 93–94.

13 See, for example, Jesse Frederick Steiner, *Americans at Play: Recent Trends in Recreation and Leisure-Time* (New York: McGraw-Hill, 1933); and Austen Fox Riggs, *Play: Recreation in a Balanced Life* (Garden City, NY: Doubleday, Doran, 1935).

14 John M. Gries and James Ford, eds., *The President's Conference on Home Building and Home Ownership*, vol. 10, *Homemaking, Home Furnishing, and Information Services* (Washington, DC: National Capital Press, 1932), 26.

15 *This Is Greendale*, tenth anniversary booklet (Greendale, WI: Greendale Historical Society, ca. 1947 or 1948).

16 "Greenbelt 25th Anniversary, 1937–1962," Greenbelt Museum, Greenbelt, MD; "Life in the Communities of Sunnyside, Radburn, Hillside, Greenbelt, Greenhills," ca. 1947–48, typed report, Clarence Stein Papers, box 2, file 13, Division of Rare and Manuscript Collections, Cornell University Library, Ithaca, NY.

17 "Greenbelt 25th Anniversary."

18 "Life in the Communities of Sunnyside, Radburn, Hillside, Greenbelt, Greenhills."

19 Glory Green Southwind, oral history, "New Deal Neighbors."

20 J. F. Steiner, "Recreation and Leisure Time Activities," in *Recent Social Trends in the United States: Report of the President's Research Committee on Social Trends*, vol. 2 (New York: McGraw-Hill, 1933), 913.

21 J. F. Steiner, "Recreation and Leisure Time Activities," 913.

22 Raymond Fosdick, *The Old Savage in the New Civilization* (New York: Doubleday, Doran, 1929), 104–5.

23 Charles A. Beard, ed., "Introduction," *Toward Civilization* (London: Longmans, Green, 1930), 6.

24   Davie, *Problems of City Life*, 30.

25   Hall, "Attitudes and Unemployment," 26. The fact that unemployed men responded in the affirmative in substantially higher numbers, however, suggests a certain amount of bitterness toward unemployment, rather than toward machines.

26   "Buried Alive," *Collier's* 50, no. 19, January 25, 1913.

27   Gardner, Smith, and Gardner, "The New Social Problem: Leisure Time," 295.

28   Samuel Ratensky to Warren Vinton, Report of the Second Week's Activity in Cincinnati, Cincinnati, OH, February 6, 1936, Justin Hartzog Papers, Cornell University, Ithaca, NY. Similar distribution methods were also used in the other locations.

29   There seems to have been some discrepancy in the final number of eligible Greenhills questionnaires, with 522 actually eligible, but only 427 counted. This appears to have been an error, as the report says that "it was felt that the additional 95, which made a total of 522 . . . did not justify a second complete tabulation." Greenhills Final Report, Analysis of Questionnaire Results, 1. Greenbelt and Greendale had the same culling process, resulting in similarly small final totals: 438 for Greenbelt and 1,000 for Greendale (Greendale had the highest number of forms returned, 2,231).

30   "Women's Athletics," *Greenbelt Co-operator*, June 1, 1938.

31   "Athletic Advisory Board," *Greendale Review*, September 10, 1938.

32   "Sports," *Greendale Review*, November 17, 1938.

33   "Greenbelt 25th Anniversary."

34   Ann Brooks, oral history, "New Deal Neighbors."

35   "Greenbelt Opens Theater Tonight," unidentified clipping in the Falls scrapbook, Greenbelt Museum, Greenbelt, MD. For a thorough examination of the importance of the introduction of air conditioning, see Salvatore Basile's *Cool: How Air Conditioning Changed Everything* (New York: Fordham University Press, 2016).

36   J. F. Steiner, "Recreation and Leisure Time Activities," 940; US Census Bureau, *Fifteenth Census of the United States: 1930*, Population, Table 1 (Washington, DC: US Government Printing Office, 1932).

37   Fred Eastman, "Are Movies Fit for Children?" *Parents* 6 (October 1931): 20.

38   Henry James Forman, *Our Movie Made Children* (New York: Macmillan, 1935), 16.

39   Forman, *Our Movie Made Children*, 19; Loren Baritz, *The Good Life: The Meaning of Success for the American Middle Class* (New York: Alfred A. Knopf, 1989), 160.

40   J. F. Steiner, "Recreation and Leisure Time Activities," 940.

41   National Recreation Association, *The Leisure Hours of 5,000 People* (New York: National Recreation Association, 1934), 10.

42   J. F. Steiner, "Recreation and Leisure Time Activities," 941.

43   For a thorough exploration of the history of municipal swimming pools, see Jeff Wiltse, *Contested Waters: A Social History of Swimming Pools in America* (Chapel Hill: University of North Carolina Press, 2007).

44   Wiltse, *Contested Waters*, 93.

45 *Leisure Hours of 5,000 People*, 10, 21. Playing tennis, somewhat surprisingly, came in as the most desired activity.

46 Final Reports on Greenbelt, Greenhills, and Greendale.

47 Leach, "Greenhills, Ohio: The Evolution of an American New Town," 128.

48 "2 Boys Drowned as Capital's Thermometers Hit 1938 High," *Washington Post*, June 12, 1938; "Swimming in Lake Restricted," unidentified newspaper clipping, Falls scrapbook, Greenbelt Museum.

49 "Bacteria Abound in Greenbelt Lake So Now It's Closed," *Washington Post*, July 11, 1938.

50 Robert S. Lynd, "The People as Consumers," in *Recent Social Trends in the United States 2* (New York: McGraw-Hill, 1933), 910.

51 Clarence Stein and Catherine Bauer, "Store Buildings and Neighborhood Shopping Centers," *Architectural Record* 75 (February 1934): 185.

52 Stein and Bauer, "Store Buildings and Neighborhood Shopping Centers," 183.

53 Hale J. Walker, "Some Major Technical Problems Encountered in the Planning of Greenbelt, Maryland," *Planners' Journal* 4, no. 2 (March–April 1938): 37.

54 The hope was that all businesses would be run as co-ops; however, if there was not enough interest, the government would lease the spaces to business owners. In Greenbelt, at least one half of the resident families had to join, or the business in question would be leased out. Initially the grocery store, drugstore, gas station, movie theater, barbershop, variety store, and beauty shop were run by the co-op Greenbelt Consumer Services. "Greenbelt 25th Anniversary"; Warner, *Greenbelt: The Cooperative Community*, 60. In Greendale, some businesses were co-ops, but the drugstore, for instance, was leased to a proprietor. Reminiscences of Ken and Jeanette De Jardin, Greendale Historical Society, Greendale, WI; *This Is Greendale*.

55 Peets, Greendale Final Report, 2:65.

56 Hale Walker and Magnus Thompson, Greenbelt Final Report, section 3, "Town and Site Planning," 17.

57 Richard G. Benson, *Looking Back*, reminiscence section, 4.

9 | THE HOMES

Epigraph: Eva Howey, *Looking Back*, reminiscence section, 39.

1 Greendale Final Report. The model home opened for tours February 21, 1937.

2 John O. Walker, "Greenbelt Towns," *Shelter* 3 (January 1939): 21.

3 A very nice overview of such visions for the home of the future appears in Joseph J. Corn and Brian Horrigan, *Yesterday's Tomorrows: Past Visions of the American Future* (New York: Summit Books, 1984), 61–85; also in Brian Horrigan, "The Home of Tomorrow, 1927–1945," in *Imagining Tomorrow: History, Technology, and the American Future*, ed. Joseph Corn (Cambridge, MA: MIT Press, 1986).

4 Bauer, *Modern Housing*, 188.

5   Final Reports on Greenbelt, Greendale, and Greenhills.

6   Wright, *The American City*, 160–61.

7   Wright, "Community Planning, 'Lo!' the Poor One-Family House," 120–21.

8   Churchill manuscript, chapter 4, "Planning the Town," 36.

9   Memorandum by Fred Naumer to John Lansill, March 9, 1937, copy attached to Churchill manuscript.

10   RJ Wadsworth, Greenbelt Final Report, vol. II, section V, "Architectural Planning Greenbelt, Maryland," 6; "Greenbelt Communities," typed report, January 25, 1940, 12, Greenbelt Museum, Greenbelt, MD; Fulmer, *Greenbelt*, 43.

11   Peets, Greendale Final Report, 2:41.

12   Peets, Greendale Final Report, 2:41–42.

13   Farm Security Administration, "Greenbelt Communities," 11–12.

14   John O. Walker, "A Demonstration in Community Planning," *Shelter* 3 (February 1939): 30.

15   Cordner, "Architectural Planning, Greenhills, Ohio," 14.

16   For more on the housing designs of the three completed towns, see "Comparative Architectural Details in the Greenbelt Housing," *American Architect and Architecture* (October 1936): 21–36.

17   Cordner, "Architectural Planning, Greenhills, Ohio," 11.

18   Cordner, "Architectural Planning, Greenhills, Ohio," 11–12. This boardinghouse was to have been built in the E block of the town, west of Winton Road.

19   Albert Mayer, notes on architecture and house planning for Greenbrook, Preliminary Plan Book, Bound Brook Suburban Resettlement, November 19, 1935, handwritten page number 77.

20   Greenbrook Final Report.

21   Greenbrook Final Report II.

22   Bentley, Greendale Final Report, 3:7. For Greendale's expected occupancy, see Appendix I.

23   "Comparative Architectural Details in the Greenbelt Housing," 22. The article notes that "the dining room can be used for sleeping, study, or play."

24   Cordner, "Architectural Planning, Greenhills, Ohio," 22.

25   Minimum Space Requirements of Bedroom, prepared by Clarence Stein, November 18, 1935, Justin Hartzog Papers, Cornell University, Ithaca, NY.

26   Greenbelt blueprints, records relating to the Greentown projects, file 196.5.9, Records of the Public Housing Administration, Record Group 196.5, National Archives at College Park, MD. The C2-1 was used 131 times in Greenbelt, and the C2-7 was used 106 times.

27   Harry H. Bentley, Greendale Final Report, "Report on Residential and Non-residential Construction," 3:5. The most-used style was number 3SE, which was used

for 103 single-family detached homes. The bedrooms in this three-bedroom model were 135.6 square feet, 113.1 square feet, and 85.8 square feet. List of first renters and floor plans, Greendale Historical Society, Greendale, WI.

28 Bentley, Greendale Final Report, 3:9.

29 As an example, the Sears model known as "The Fairy," which was offered in 1925, 1926, 1928, 1929, 1932, and 1933, had two bedrooms, sized 9'2" by 10'8" and 9'2" by 9'8". Somewhat larger models tended to offer bedrooms that measured just under 11' by 11'. Katherine Cole Stevenson and H. Ward Jandl, *Houses by Mail: A Guide to Houses from Sears, Roebuck, and Company* (Washington, DC: Preservation Press, 1986), 50, 68, 74, 81.

30 "Low-Cost Furniture," *House Beautiful* 79 (April 1937): 131–33.

31 "Greenbelt Furniture," *Greenbelt Co-operator*, June 1, 1938; Warner, *Greenbelt: The Cooperative Community*, 120–21.

32 Greenbelt Final Report, "Analysis of Questionnaire Results," Present Home Composition, 33.

33 Dorothy and George Eshbaugh, *Looking Back*, reminiscence section, 22.

34 Cordner, "Architectural Planning, Greenhills, Ohio," 18.

35 Louise Steinle Winker, *Looking Back*, reminiscence section, 73.

36 Rena Hull, interview with the author, Greenbelt, MD, March 11, 2008.

37 Preliminary Plan Book, Bound Brook Suburban Resettlement, handwritten page number 41.

38 See, for example, Barbara Ehrenreich and Deirdre English, *For Her Own Good: Two Centuries of the Experts' Advice to Women* (New York: Doubleday, 1978); Glenna Matthews, *Just a Housewife: The Rise and Fall of Domesticity in America* (New York: Oxford University Press, 1987); Susan Strasser, *Never Done: A History of American Housework* (New York: Henry Holt, 2000); and Carolyn M. Goldstein, *Creating Consumers: Home Economists in Twentieth-Century America* (Chapel Hill: University of North Carolina Press, 2012). The most thorough treatment of Frederick can be found in Janice Williams Rutherford, *Selling Mrs. Consumer: Christine Frederick and the Rise of Household Efficiency* (Athens: University of Georgia Press, 2003).

39 Christine Frederick, "Putting the American Woman and Her Home on a Business Basis," *Review of Reviews* 49 (February 1914): 199, 200.

40 Christine Frederick, *The Ignoramus Book of Housekeeping* (New York: Sears Publishing, 1932), 47.

41 Frederick, *The Ignoramus Book of Housekeeping*, 3.

42 Hildegarde Kneeland, "Is the Modern Housewife a Lady of Leisure?" *Survey* (June 1929): 302.

43 Mary Pattison, "The Abolition of Household Slavery," *Annals of the American Academy of Political and Social Science* 118 (March 1925): 124–27.

44 Frederick, *The Ignoramus Book of Housekeeping*, 30.

45 For a very nice examination of this topic, see Ruth Schwartz Cowan, *More Work for Mother: The Ironies of Household Technology from the Open Hearth to the Microwave* (New York: Basic Books, 1983).

46 Frances Drewry McMullen, "New Jobs for Women," *North American Review* 234, no. 2 (August 1932): 133.

47 Bemis, *The Evolving House*, 2:67.

48 John M. Gries and James Ford, eds., *The President's Conference on Home Building and Home Ownership*, vol. 7, *Committee on Farm and Village Housing* (Washington, DC: National Capital Press, 1932), 12.

49 US Census Bureau, *Sixteenth Census of the United States, 1940, Housing*: vol. 2, part 1, 1943 United States Summary, Table 7, "Water Supply for All Dwelling Units, by Occupancy and Tenure, for the United States, by Region, Urban and Rural, 1940." A further 4.8 percent had a hand pump in the dwelling unit, 4.2 percent had running water within fifty feet, 16.5 percent had some "other water supply within fifty feet," and 5.1 percent had no water supply within fifty feet.

50 Ibid., Table 7b, "Bathing Equipment for All Dwelling Units, by Occupancy and Tenure, for the United States, by Regions, Urban and Rural, 1940."

51 Ibid., Table 7a, "Toilet Facilities for All Dwelling Units, by Occupancy and Tenure, for the United States, by Regions, Urban and Rural, 1940."

52 Virginia Nixon, "Outfitting the Kitchen for Convenience," *American Home* 1 (February 1929): 398.

53 "Preliminary Plan Book, Bound Brook Suburban Resettlement," 87; Greta Grey, "Kitchen Planning," in *The Better Homes Manual*, ed. Blanche Halbert (Chicago: University of Chicago Press, 1931), 455.

54 It appears that all homes in the three towns were equipped with electric stoves, the size of the appliance varying with the size of the kitchen. In Greenhills, at least, not every unit came with an electric refrigerator. Frank Cordner reported that "a very large portion of the dwellings [in Greenhills] will be equipped with electric [ice] boxes," and that 37 percent of families returning questionnaires already owned an electric refrigerator. The architects recommended that the town forbid the use of old-fashioned iceboxes because they were prone to leaking, which could cause water damage to the home. Cordner, "Architectural Planning, Greenhills, Ohio," 35.

55 Bemis, *The Evolving House*, 2:67; US Census Bureau, *Sixteenth Census of the United States, 1940, Housing*: vol. 2, part 1, United States Summary, Table 9b, "Refrigeration Equipment for Occupied Units, by Tenure and Color of Occupants, for the United States, by Region, Urban and Rural, 1940."

56 Bemis, *The Evolving House*, 2:67.

57 For example, Helen Whitson Kendall, "Your First Electric Range," *Good Housekeeping* 90 (April 1930): 96–97; Ethel R. Peyser, "The Robot of the Kitchen," *House Beautiful* 69 (May 1931): 518–19; Katherine Fisher, "A Turn of the Switch," *Good Housekeeping* 94 (March 1932): 80–81, 198; and Nell B. Nichols, "No More Pot-Watching," *Woman's Home Companion* 59 (May 1932): 58–62.

58 *Greendale Review* 1, no. 2 (September 10, 1938): 4.

59 Mabel J. Stegner, "Cooking Is a Continuous Pleasure," *Better Homes and Gardens* 10 (May 1932): 36.

60 "Clean, Orderly Kitchen Is a Restful Workshop," *Good Housekeeping* 93 (October 1931): 86–87.

61 Frederick, *The Ignoramus Book of Housekeeping*, 85–92.

62 Frederick, *The Ignoramus Book of Housekeeping*, 81.

63 Eleanor Roosevelt, *It's Up to the Women* (New York: Frederick A. Stokes, 1933), 55–56.

64 Frederick, *The Ignoramus Book of Housekeeping*, 67.

65 See, for example, Dorothy Harris, *Looking Back*, reminiscence section, 33.

66 Dorothy Harris, *Looking Back*, reminiscence section, 34; Alanen and Eden, *Main Street Ready-Made*, 50; Arnold, *The New Deal in the Suburbs*, 86–87.

67 The argument that the Greenbelt towns were specifically intended to shore up middle-class gender norms among those rising from the working class forms a core thesis of Jennifer Karen Kerns's doctoral dissertation, "A Social Experiment in Greenbelt, Maryland: Class, Gender, and Public Housing."

68 A 1936 Gallup poll found that 82 percent of the population believed a wife should not work if her husband was employed. The overwhelming opinion in the nation held that more jobs given to women meant fewer jobs for men; the assumption was that wives who chose to enter the workforce even though their husbands were employed were simply taking food out of the mouths of someone else's family.

10 | THE PEOPLE

Epigraph: Larry Voight, interview by the author, Greenbelt, MD, 2008.

1 Arnold, *The New Deal in the Suburbs*, 138–39. The full requirements: for one occupant, $800–$1,600; for two, $900–$1,650; for three, $1,000–$1,800; for four, $1,100–$2,000; for five, $1,200–$2,100; and for six, $1,300–$2,200.

2 In truth, most Americans would have listed Asians as another distinct race, but the Asian population, outside of the West Coast, was small enough to be virtually ignored by most of those in the eastern United States.

3 For details on segregation and integration in New Deal housing, see Leighninger, *Long-Range Public Investment*, 126–27, 129–30, 145–46.

4 A note on phrasing throughout this section: as of this writing, in 2022, the preferred terminology is in flux. The older label of "black," having fallen out of favor by the end of the twentieth century, has had a resurgence, with the addition of capitalization: *Black*. The phrase that replaced "black" as the favored term by the turn of the twenty-first century, "African American," has been rejected by many as being overly broad and often inaccurate. Currently, the phrase "people of color" seems to be most acceptable, but since it includes those of Asian or Indigenous descent, it is not quite

specific enough here. Although race is a fuzzy and complex concept, the way Americans in the 1930s would have understood it is necessary for this discussion. For that reason, for the sake of clarity, I will be using both African American and Black, interchangeably, to denote the stark distinctions between Black and White that would have existed at the time.

5   Arnold, *The New Deal in the* Suburbs, 142–43.

6   Campbell Gibson and Kay Jung, *Historical Census Statistics on Population Totals by Race, 1790 to 1990, and by Hispanic Origin, 1970 to 1990, for the United States, Regions, Divisions, and States*, Working Paper No. 56, Table 23, "District of Columbia—Race and Hispanic Origin: 1800 to 1990" (Washington, DC: US Census Bureau, Population Division, 2002.

7   US Census Bureau, *Historical Statistics of the United States, 1789–1945: A Supplement to the Statistical Abstract of the United States* (Washington, DC: United States Department of Commerce, 1949), chapter B, Population Characteristics and Migration, Series B 13–23, "Population, Decennial Summary—Sex, Urban-Rural Residence, and Race: 1790 to 1940." More specifically, 9.685 percent of the population was identified as "Negro."

8   David Hendricks and Amy Patterson, "The 1930 Census in Perspective," *Prologue Magazine* 34, no. 2 (Summer 2002). This publication was produced by the National Archives and Records Administration. https://www.archives.gov/publications/prologue/2002/summer/1930-census-perspective.html.

9   US Census Bureau, *Fifteenth Census of the United States: 1930*, Volume 3, *Population, Reports by States* (Washington, DC: US Government Printing Office, 1932), Ohio, Table 12, "Population by Age, Color, Nativity, and Sex, for Cities and Villages of 10,000 or More, 1930."

10 John J. Gilligan, "Learning about Race in Cincinnati," *Queen City Heritage* 52, no. 3 (Fall 1994): 4. Gilligan was born in 1921.

11 Roger C. Hansen, "Pioneers in Nonviolent Action: The Congress of Racial Equality in Cincinnati, 1946–1955," *Queen City Heritage* 52, no. 3 (Fall 1994): 30.

12 US Census Bureau, *Fifteenth Census of the United States: 1930*, Volume 3, *Population, Reports by States*, Wisconsin, Table 12, "Population by Age, Color, Nativity, and Sex, for Cities and Villages of 10,000 or More, 1930."

13 Dykeman and Stokely, *Seeds of Southern Change*, viii.

14 For additional information on race and the RA, see "The Negro in the New Deal Resettlement Program," by Donald Holley, *Agricultural History* 45, no. 3 (July 1971): 179–93, as well as a response to that article, "The Negro in the New Deal Resettlement Program: A Comment," by Robert E. Nipp, *Agricultural History* 45, no. 3 (July 1971): 195–200.

15 Dykeman and Stokely, *Seeds of Southern Change*, 217.

16 Arnold, *The New Deal in the Suburbs*, 143.

17 See, for example, Cheryl Lynn Greenberg, *To Ask for an Equal Chance: African Americans in the Great Depression* (Lanham, MD: Rowman & Littlefield, 2009);

Rauchway, *Why the New Deal Matters*, 103–32; and Harvard Sitkoff, *A New Deal for Blacks: The Emergence of Civil Rights as a National Issue: The Depression Decade* (New York: Oxford University Press, 2008).

18   Jefferson Cowie, *The Great Exception: The New Deal and the Limits of American Politics* (Princeton, NJ: Princeton University Press, 2016), 124.

19   For more on Weaver, see Dykeman and Stokely, *Seeds of Southern Change*, 196, 250, 254–58. See also Walter B. Hill, Jr., "Finding Place for the Negro: Robert C. Weaver and the Groundwork for the Civil Rights Movement," *Prologue Magazine* 37, no. 1 (Spring 2005), https://www.archives.gov/publications/prologue/2005/spring/weaver.html.

20   Robert C. Weaver, "The Negro in a Program of Public Housing," *Opportunity* (July 1938). I have been unable to find the original article in *Opportunity*, but a reprint is housed at Cornell University in the Warren Vinton Papers.

21   "Public Housing Administration Racial Relations Policy," labeled CONFIDENTIAL, Warren Vinton Papers, Cornell University, Ithaca, NY.

22   Arnold, *The New Deal in the Suburbs*, 143.

23   Kelly Ann Quinn, "Making Modern Homes: A History of Langston Terrace Dwellings, a New Deal Housing Program in Washington, DC" (PhD diss., University of Maryland, College Park, 2007), 29.

24   Form, "The Sociology of a White Collar Suburb," 218.

25   Mary Clare Bonham England, *Looking Back*, interview section, 20.

26   Joseph Comproni, *Looking Back*, interview section, 16.

27   "How Laurel Homes Will Look When Completed," *Cincinnati Enquirer*, March 22, 1936, 12.

28   "Government Is Launched on Building Projects; 'Laurel Homes' Is Compared with 'Greenhills,'" *Cincinnati Enquirer*, April 1, 1936, 8.

29   "Negro Housing Sought," *Cincinnati Enquirer*, May 29, 1937, 19. For a thorough discussion of the issue of integration at Laurel Homes, and of later appeals for housing for Black citizens, see Robert B. Fairbanks, *Making Better Citizens: Housing Reform and the Community Development Strategy in Cincinnati, 1890–1960* (Urbana: University of Illinois Press, 1988), 124–45.

30   Fairbanks, *Making Better Citizens*, 131.

31   Form, "The Sociology of a White Collar Suburb," 217.

32   Lee Shields, interview with the author, Greenbelt, MD, March 12, 2008.

33   "Life in the Communities of Sunnyside, Radburn, Hillside, Greenbelt, Greenhills."

34   Lee Shields, interview.

35   The half bedrooms in Greenbelt's C-9 style, which is likely what the Shields family moved to, were just under eight feet by just over four feet, or about thirty-two square feet, according to the blueprints. US Department of Agriculture, Resettlement Administration, Division of Suburban Resettlement, National Archives and Records Administration, College Park, MD.

36 "Report on the Rental Market in Relation to Project #000–0040, Farm Security Administration at Greenbelt, Maryland," Federal Housing Administration Division of Economics and Statistics, July 12, 1938. Marked "Confidential—not for publication." Federal Housing Administration records, National Archives and Records Administration, College Park, MD.

37 Dale Jernberg, interview with the author, Greenbelt, MD, February 13, 2008.

38 On September 30, 1937, the Resettlement Administration was succeeded by a new agency, the Farm Security Administration (FSA). In terms of the Greenbelt program this shift had little impact, but the reader should be aware of the alternating use of RA and FSA. The two agencies were, for this program at least, virtually the same.

39 Quoted in Form, "The Sociology of a White Collar Suburb," 58.

40 Early Greenbelt resident George Warner noted that it was also imperative that the first residents be capable of forming a town government and performing other necessary tasks to get the community running smoothly. Warner, *Greenbelt: The Cooperative Community*, 61.

41 Cedric Arthur Larson, "Educational Activities of the Federally Planned Community of Greenbelt, Maryland" (Master's thesis, George Washington University, 1939), 28; Mary W. Feldman, "A Study of Greenhills Project, Cincinnati, Ohio, A Public Housing Project Sponsored by the Farm Security Administration" (MA thesis, University of Chicago, 1939), 36. Although master's theses may not always be the most authoritative sources, I am using these two because they were written so soon after the towns were completed and many of the original sources used by these authors are no longer available. Feldman offers the most detailed explanation of the selection process on pages 48–79. Additional information on tenant selection can be found in Form, "The Sociology of a White Collar Suburb," 55–60. The date for Greendale is a bit uncertain. A newspaper article from February 1938 states that the initial process to register for possible application was already under way, and that official applications, the next step in the process, would be accepted beginning March 1. "Greendale to Sign Up Tenants," newspaper clipping in scrapbook, unknown newspaper, labeled February 1, 1938, Greendale Historical Society, Greendale, WI.

42 Feldman, "A Study of Greenhills Project," 48.

43 History of Greenbelt Eligibility, typewritten document, Tugwell Room, Greenbelt Public Library, Greenbelt, MD. Rents for those first families ranged from $18 per month for a single-person efficiency apartment to $40 for the largest units.

44 Copies of these letters for potential Greenhills residents were included in the appendix to Leach's dissertation, "Greenhills, Ohio: The Evolution of an American New Town." The registration form was the same for all three towns.

45 Feldman, "A Study of Greenhills Project," 57.

46 Feldman, "A Study of Greenhills Project," 58.

47 Arnold, *The New Deal in the Suburbs*, 137.

48 Larson, "Educational Activities of the Federally Planned Community of Greenbelt, Maryland," 28.

49 The information in this and the following few paragraphs is derived from Larson's and Feldman's theses. I have never come across any other copies of the application or rating forms, or any information on who served on the selection committee. It appears that these materials, still available in 1939, have disappeared since, or at least that they are not in any expected archives or collections.

50 Feldman, "A Study of Greenhills Project," 62.

51 Though original copies are apparently long since lost, the rating worksheet was re-produced in Feldman's and Larson's appendices.

52 Elsie Steinle, *Looking Back*, reminiscence section, 70.

53 Feldman, "A Study of Greenhills Project," 80.

54 Feldman, "A Study of Greenhills Project," 88.

55 Form, "The Sociology of a White Collar Suburb," 56.

56 J. B. Holt, *An Analysis of Methods and Criteria Used in Selecting Families for Colonization Projects* (Washington, DC: Farm Security Administration, 1937), 31.

57 Holt, *An Analysis of Methods and Criteria Used in Selecting Families for Colonization Projects*, 7.

58 Holt, *An Analysis of Methods and Criteria Used in Selecting Families for Colonization Projects*, 13.

59 Holt, *An Analysis of Methods and Criteria Used in Selecting Families for Colonization Projects*, 13.

60 Unless otherwise noted, all information on the religious makeup of Greenbelt, Maryland, comes from Sally Sims Stokes, "God, Government, and Greenbelt: Lived Religion and the Cultural Politics of (In)Tolerance in the Social Engineering of a Cooperative New Deal Resettlement Town, 1937–1940," in *Lived Religion and the Politics of (In)Tolerance*, ed. R. Ruard Ganzevoort and Srdjan Sremac, Palgrave Studies in Lived Religion and Societal Challenges (Cham, Switzerland: Palgrave Macmillan, 2017), 135–70.

61 Hunter, "Greenbelt, Maryland: A City on a Hill," 125.

62 Stokes, "God, Government, and Greenbelt," 136. Stokes does not give a citation, but says the fact "that Jews were not excluded was suppressed until just before the pioneers moved in." Stokes offers the most comprehensive analysis to date of the subject of religion in Greenbelt.

63 Lee Shields interview.

64 For more on the cooperative businesses and organization in Greenbelt, see Form, "The Sociology of a White Collar Suburb," 326–36 and 425–31.

65 "There's Room at Greendale," newspaper clipping in scrapbook at Greendale Historical Society, Greendale, WI, labeled *Journal* [presumably the *Milwaukee Journal*], February 5, 1939. The reason given in the article for the unoccupied homes is that these were the larger and more expensive units, and the rents were simply too high. The smaller and less expensive units had rented much more quickly. A rent decrease for these larger homes was announced March 11, 1939. "Adjust Rents to Meet Large

Family Needs," newspaper clipping in scrapbook at Greendale Historical Society, labeled "*Greendale Review*," March 11, 1939.

66 Joseph Garretson, Jr., "Greenhills Draws on Hilltop Areas for Tenants," *Cincinnati Enquirer*, February 21, 1939.

67 Kerns argues that Greenbelt was specifically set up as "a reaffirmation of the mythical ideal of separate spheres." "A Social Experiment in Greenbelt, Maryland," 39. Although I agree with Kerns's argument that the program aimed to shore up middle-class values, I do not necessarily agree with the assertion that the towns were designed and populated to maintain rigid gender roles. I see the program as reflecting the prevailing middle-class gender ideals of the time, but not necessarily trying to strengthen those ideals.

68 *The Gallup Poll*, CD-ROM (N.p.: Scholarly Resources, 2000), December 25, 1938 poll, 129.

69 A letter dated November 6, 1937, to Mrs. Roosevelt from Wallace Richards, who had been the project coordinator at Greenbelt, asked that the First Lady use her influence to ensure that Greenbelt be completed. She apparently passed the letter along to her husband, with a handwritten note in the margin saying, "FDR—This seems to me most important. There is a new experiment being involved which curtailment may seriously hurt. Won't you look into it? E.R." The original letter with the note and a summary with Mrs. Roosevelt's plea typewritten are housed at the Franklin Roosevelt D. Presidential Library, Hyde Park, NY. Eleanor Roosevelt visited Greenbelt several times, and visited Greendale once. I have found no evidence that she ever visited Greenhills.

70 Eleanor Roosevelt, "My Day," December 10, 1937.

71 Warner, *Greenbelt: The Cooperative Community*. This book offers the fullest account of the early formation of the town's cooperative businesses and government. Knepper's *Greenbelt, Maryland: A Living Legacy of the New Deal* devotes all of chapter 2 to the formation of the community's cooperative spirit.

72 Warner, *Greenbelt: The Cooperative Community*, 33. Dale Jernberg later recalled that although Greenbelt was a nearly ideal place to grow up, he was aware that living in the town meant "We were poor people and shouldn't have to live here. I didn't want to be poor." Dale Jernberg, interview with author, Greenbelt, MD, February 13, 2008.

73 Warner, *Greenbelt: The Cooperative Community*, 33.

11 | THE LEGACY

Epigraph: Justin Hartzog, typewritten paper, 1938, John Scott Lansill Papers, Greenhills files, 15, University of Kentucky Special Collections and Digital Programs, Lexington, KY.

1 Cassilda Berg to Marvin H. McIntyre, Official File, OF 1568, Farm Security Administration, Franklin D. Roosevelt Presidential Library, Hyde Park, NY. Interestingly, although American citizens reached out directly to the President and First Lady in

letters throughout Roosevelt's time in office, this particular letter was not addressed to FDR but to McIntyre, possibly because it was widely known that the president received so many pleas for assistance. According to Mrs. Berg's daughter, the letter is in fact in her father's handwriting, not her mother's; it is unclear whether he simply served as the scribe or actually conceived of the letter himself but believed that it would have more impact if seeming to come from a distraught mother.

2　McIntyre forwarded the letter, along with a brief memo, to Will Alexander of the Farm Security Administration, who replied that he would forward it to the community manager at Greendale. Whether the effort on behalf of the Bergs continued within the Greendale administration is unclear.

3　"American Housing: A Failure, a Problem, a Potential Boon and Boom," 45.

4　William Edward Leuchtenburg, *Franklin D. Roosevelt and the New Deal, 1932–1940* (New York: Harper & Row, 1963), 273.

5　Greenhills Final Report, Analysis of Questionnaire Results, 13.

6　Carol A. Lippmeier, *Act of Congress, Greenhills, Ohio, 1938–1976* (Greenhills, OH: Greenhills Civic Foundation, 1976), 10.

7　Arnold, *The New Deal in the Suburbs*, 49, 117–18.

8　George Morris, "$16,000 Homes for $2,000 Incomes," *Nation's Business* 26 (January 1938): 22. These same figures are presented by Hunter, "Greenbelt, Maryland: A City on a Hill," 105–36, but with a far less negative assessment overall. See also Conkin, *Tomorrow a New World*, 320. For Greendale, see "Greendale: Final Report of Project Costs Including Analysis of Actual Construction Costs from Inception of the Project to June 30, 1938," US Department of Agriculture, Farm Security Administration, National Archives and Records Administration, College Park, MD. For Greenhills, see Feldman, "A Study of Greenhills Project, Cincinnati, Ohio," 44–46. This is by no means a comprehensive list of attempts to analyze the costs.

9　"Costly Greenbelt," *Washington Post*, July 8, 1937. *Time* magazine did acknowledge the work-relief nature of the program and how this affected costs, although the article overall presented the program fairly negatively: "Greenbelt," *Time*, September 13, 1937, 10.

10　Rexford Tugwell, "The Meaning of the Greenbelt Towns," *New Republic*, February 17, 1937, 42.

11　See, for example, Ira S. Robbins, "Resettlement Administration Only Partially Unsettled: Greenbelt Project Held Invalid," *American City* 51 (June 1936): 5. For a more detailed discussion of the Greenbrook opposition and court case, see Arnold, *The New Deal in the Suburbs*, 61–77.

12　Arnold, *The New Deal in the Suburbs*, 89, 117–18; Justin Hartzog (apparently unpublished paper), Lansill Papers, University of Kentucky. Some of these cuts were detailed in a report by Frank Cordner, principal architect for Greenhills, in a typed report, "Architectural Planning, Greenhills, Ohio," US Department of Agriculture, Farm Security Administration, Division of Suburban Resettlement, November 1937, 10. This report is held by the Village of Greenhills.

13 For example, construction on Forest Hills Gardens, in Queens, New York, began in 1908 to provide decent homes for the working class. When costs made prices too high for this income group, it became instead a middle-class community. Orvell, *The Death and Life of Main Street*, 155–62. Later efforts that ended up creating more expensive communities than initially conceived included Radburn, New Jersey, and Mariemont, Ohio.

14 Arnold, *The New Deal in the Suburbs*, 49, 117–18.

15 "Greendale: Final Report of Project Costs."

16 Pay rate list for Greenbelt workers, offices of Greenbelt Homes, Inc. Greenbelt, MD.

17 Jacob Crane, "Greendale—The General Plan," *Planners Journal* 3, no. 4 (July–August 1937): 89.

18 Albert Mayer, "Green-belt Towns for the Machine Age," *New York Times Magazine*, February 2, 1936, 18.

19 Churchill, *The City Is the People*, 80.

20 Childs, *I Write from Washington*, 12.

21 Crane, "Greendale—The General Plan," 90.

22 For example, in the United States (not including the many written by those directly involved with the Greenbelt program): "Site Plans of 'Greenbelt' Towns," *American City* (August 1936): 56–59; John Dreier, "Greenbelt Planning: Resettlement Administration Builds Three Model Towns," *Pencil Points* (August 1936): 441–60; M. E. Gilfond, "Introducing: 'Greenbelt, Md.,'" *Christian Science Monitor Magazine*, August 11, 1937, 5; "Greenbelt Towns," *Architectural Record* (September 1936): 215–34; Hugh A. Bone, "Greenbelt Faces 1939," *American City* 54 (February 1939): 59–61; "A Planned Community Appraised," *Architectural Forum* 72 (January 1940): 62–64. International: R. Kantorowich, "A Report on the Greenbelt Towns in the United States of America," *South African Architectural Record* 27 (December 1942): 385–92; Stephenson, "Greenbelt Towns in the United States," 121–22; "Los Pueblos Greenbelt en Estados Unidos," *Arquitecto Peruano* 8 (May 1944): 4–6.

23 Kantorowich, "A Report on the Greenbelt Towns in the United States of America," 387.

24 Abe Lincoln Mahony, "Reporter Goes to Greenbelt and Sees Monument to Life," *Washington Daily News*, April 15, 1937.

25 Joseph Garretson, Jr., "Greenhills Draws on Hilltop Areas for Tenants," *Cincinnati Enquirer*, February 21, 1939.

26 Martha (Likens) Spudis, *Looking Back*, reminiscences section, 46.

27 Charles T. Howey, *Looking Back*, reminiscences section, 38.

28 Peets, Greendale Final Report, Report of the Town Planning Section of the Greendale Planning Staff, 2:124. Original residents in all three towns did in fact refer to themselves as "pioneers."

29 Ben Rosenweig, *Looking Back*, section 3, 57.

30 Al Dilz, oral history, "New Deal Neighbors."

31 For example, the median age in Greenbelt in 1940 was 24.7 years, as opposed to the median age in Washington, DC, which was 33.2 years. Form, "Sociology of a White Collar Suburb," 60. On economic similarity, see Greenbelt, see *Looking Back*, reminiscence section, William E. Colliver, Ethel Rosenweig. For Greenhills, see interviews with Oscar Hoffman, Roger Petering, "New Deal Neighbors."

32 "Helpful Suggestions for Greendale Residents," Elbert Peets Papers, Cornell University, Ithaca, NY.

33 "Greenhills Manual," Greenbelt Museum, Greenbelt, MD.

34 "Greenhills Manual."

35 "Greenbelt Maryland Manual" (Washington, DC: Farm Security Administration, 1942), 9.

36 The Falls scrapbook includes "Greenbelt Dog Problem Worries Our Columnist," *Wash. Daily News*, November 15, 1937; "Greenbelt Heads Given Demand for Dog Ballot," December 1937; Greenbelt Dog Ban Splits Community," December 19, 1937; "Dogs Come Out in Tail End of Greenbelt Vote," February 24, 1938; "Greenbelt Poll Shows Dogs in Disfavor," February 24, 1938; "Greenbelt Council to Set Dog Vote Date," February 24, 1938; "No Canine Capers for Greenbelt," February 24, 1938; and "Greenbelt Moves to Enforce Regulation against Pets," March 1, 1938. Falls scrapbook, Greenbelt Museum.

37 Signed "Cave Cane," and listed only as "Editor, The News," this clipping appears in the Falls scrapbook, Greenbelt Museum. The date is handwritten as 11–15–37.

38 In May 1951 the *Baltimore Sun* reported that all pets in Greenbelt must be removed. The issue flared again in 1957, when the town threatened to evict residents who refused to give up their pets. In 1959 the matter was finally settled when a judge from Maryland's Seventh Judicial Circuit ruled that the town could regulate pet ownership, but not forbid it. "Residents of Greenbelt Given a Week to Remove Their Pets," *Baltimore Sun*, May 30, 1941; "Greenbelt's Pet Owners Can Stay," *Baltimore Sun*, April 11, 1959.

39 Pearl Ellerin, *Looking Back*, reminiscence section, 21; Shirley Morrison Clute, *Looking Back*, reminiscence section, 55; Pauline St. Martin Bordas, *Looking Back*, reminiscence section, 81; Mary Clare Bonham England, *Looking Back*, interview section, 23; Kathleen Scott McFarland, *Looking Back*, interview section, 125.

40 "Greenbelt 25th Anniversary," 30.

41 "Greenbelt Maryland Manual," 6.

42 Stanley Edwards, *Looking Back*, reminiscence section, 21; Pearl Ellerin, *Looking Back*, reminiscence section, 21; Dorothy Harris, *Looking Back*, reminiscence section, 34; Evelyn Barcus, *Looking Back*, interview section, 1; Mary Clare Bonham England, *Looking Back*, interview section, 23; Kathleen Scott McFarland, *Looking Back*, interview section, 125.

43   Dorothy Harris, *Looking Back*, reminiscence section, 33; Pauline St. Martin Bordas, *Looking Back*, reminiscence section, 81; Mary Clare Bonham England, *Looking Back*, interview section, 23.

44   Bernice Brautigam, *Looking Back*, interview section, 47b.

45   James and Margaret Gallagher, *Looking Back*, reminiscence section, 29; Ruth Bowman, *Looking Back*, interview section, 39.

46   June Hammersla Franklin, *Looking Back*, reminiscence section, 31; Ben Goldfaden, *Looking Back*, section 3, 21; Eleanor Hauswirth and D. Kapocius, 1995 interview transcript, 2, Greendale Historical Society, Greendale, OH; Jane Steinway, oral history, "New Deal Neighbors."

47   Larry Voight said in an interview with the author that one time a young man had too much to drink and got into an altercation with a neighbor. Someone tried to break up the fight and was injured. Larry Voight, interview with author, Greenbelt, MD, March 11, 2008.

48   Lee Shields interview.

49   Greendale Final Report, Agriculture and the Greenbelt Town, 79.

50   Greendale Final Report, Agriculture and the Greenbelt Town, 79–80.

51   *Greendale: 50 Years, 1938–1988* (N.p.: N.p., n.d.), 21.

52   Marian Lampl, oral history, "New Deal Neighbors."

53   Douglas George Marshall, "Greendale: A Study of a Resettlement Community" (PhD diss., University of Wisconsin, 1943), 67.

54   See Marshall, "Greendale: A Study of a Resettlement Community"; Sally Scott Rogers, "Community Planning and Residential Satisfaction: Case Analysis of Greenbelt, Maryland" (PhD diss., University of Maryland, 1975).

55   Form, "The Sociology of a White Collar Suburb," 47–54.

56   On families moving out of the towns, see Feldman, "A Study of Greenhills Project," 104.

57   See, for example, Marshall, "Greendale: A Study of a Resettlement Community"; Form, "The Sociology of a White Collar Suburb," especially pages 84–87. Both Marshall and Form acknowledge that the towns were, in 1943 and 1944 respectively, still quite new, which may have affected the lack of cohesive community feeling among residents.

58   Form, "The Sociology of a White Collar Suburb," 65, 67.

59   Marshall, "Greendale: A Study of a Resettlement Community," 52.

60   Bernice Brautigam, *Looking Back*, interview section, 48.

EPILOGUE

1   Conkin, *Tomorrow a New World*, 305, 336–37.

2   The story of the sale of the three towns is rather convoluted. For a more detailed

discussion, see Arnold, *The New Deal in the Suburbs*, 229–38; Joseph A. Eden and Arnold R. Alanen, "Looking Backward at a New Deal Town: Greendale, Wisconsin, 1935–1980," *Journal of the American Planning Association* 49, no. 1 (Winter 1983): 49–51; Alanen and Eden, *Main Street Ready-Made*, 79–88; Kristin Szylvian, *The Mutual Housing Experiment: New Deal Communities for the Urban Middle Class* (Philadelphia: Temple University Press, 2015), 134–36.

3   Stein, *Toward New Towns for America*, 137.

4   Mary Clare Bonham England, *Looking Back*, interview section, 27.

5   Mary Clare Bonham England, *Looking Back*, interview section, 27; Clayton McCarl, *Looking Back*, interview section, 106; Ben Goldfaden, *Looking Back*, section 3, 19.

6   For more on the defense housing and the war years, see Arnold, *The New Deal in the Suburbs*, 220–26; Knepper, *Greenbelt, Maryland*, 62–78; Mary Lou Williamson, ed., *Greenbelt, History of a New Town, 1937–1987* (Norfolk, VA: Donning, 1987), 117–22.

7   Childs, *I Write from Washington*, 14.

8   A July 2010 Census *QuickFacts* page puts the population of the city (not just the original 1930s and 1940s portions of the town) at 23,224. Just under half of the residents are Black, about one quarter are White, and the rest primarily Hispanic or Latino (16.5 percent), Asian (9.5 percent), mixed race (3.1 percent) or American Indian/ Alaskan Native (0.5 percent). Nearly 27 percent are foreign-born. Just 10 percent live in poverty. US Census Bureau, *QuickFacts*, Greenbelt city, Maryland, https:// www.census.gov/quickfacts/fact/table/greenbeltcitymaryland/PST045219.

9   *Greendale: 50 Years, 1938–1988*, 33.

10   The population of the village in 2010 was 14,143, of which nearly 83 percent were non-Hispanic/Latino Whites. Under 5 percent of the population lives in poverty. US Census Bureau, *QuickFacts*, Greendale village, Wisconsin, https://www.census. gov/quickfacts/fact/table/greendalevillagewisconsin/POP060210.

11   US Census Bureau, *Ohio: 2010: Summary Population and Housing Characteristics*, Table 3, Race and Hispanic or Latino Origin: 2010, https://www.census.gov/prod/ cen2010/cph-1-37.pdf, 148. As of 2010, 88 percent of the residents were White.

12   National Register of Historic Places records for Greenbelt, https://catalog.archives. gov/id/106777962; for Greendale, https://catalog.archives.gov/id/106781660; and for Greenhills, https://catalog.archives.gov/id/71989203.

13   The book *High-Risers: Cabrini-Green and the Fate of American Public Housing*, by Ben Austen and Robert Philip Gordon (New York: Harper, 2018) does an excellent job of exploring just how disastrous such projects turned out to be.

14   In fact, the 1970s TV show *Good Times* was set in Cabrini-Green and centered on life in "the projects" for poor Blacks.

15   For more on Cabrini-Green and later Chicago efforts, see the video *70 Acres in Chicago: Cabrini Green, the Demolition of Public Housing in Chicago*, dir. by Ronit Bezalel (New Day Films, 2015).

16   James E. Rosenbaum, Linda K. Stroh, and Cathy A. Flynn, "Lake Parc Place: A Study of Mixed-Income Housing," *Housing Policy Debate* 9, no. 4 (January 1998): 711.

17   Rosenbaum, Stroh, and Flynn, "Lake Parc Place: A Study of Mixed-Income Housing," 705.

18   For example, see Devereux Bowly, Jr., *The Poorhouse: Subsidized Housing in Chicago*, 2nd ed. (Carbondale: Southern Illinois University Press, 2012), especially 221–54; Anne Gunderson, "The Affordable Housing Gap Leaves Low-Income Renters without Options," *Chicago Policy Review* (June 30, 2017); Emily Rosenbaum and Laura E. Harris, "Low-Income Families in Their New Neighborhoods," *Journal of Family Issues* 22, no. 2 (March 2001): 183–210.

BIBLIOGRAPHY

Adams, John. "The Menace of Leisure." *School and Society* 33 (1931): 651–56.

Alanen, Arnold R., and Joseph A. Eden. *Main Street Ready-Made: The New Deal Community of Greendale, Wisconsin*. Madison: State Historical Society of Wisconsin, 1987.

Alexander, William. *Film on the Left: American Documentary Film from 1931 to 1942*. Princeton, NJ: Princeton University Press, 1981.

Allen, Frederick Lewis. *Only Yesterday: An Informal History of the 1920s*. 1931. Reprint. New York: Harper Perennial Modern Classics, 2010.

Alpers, Benjamin. *Dictators, Democracy, and American Public Culture: Envisioning the Totalitarian Enemy 1920s–1950s*. Chapel Hill: University of North Carolina Press, 2003.

"Alphabet Soup in a Washington Mansion." *Literary Digest*, August 31, 1935, 10–11.

Amenta, Edwin, and Yvonne Zylan. "It Happened Here: Political Opportunity, the New Institutionalism, and the Townsend Movement." *American Sociological Review* 56, no. 2 (April 1991): 250–65.

"American Housing: A Failure, a Problem, a Potential Boon and Boom." *Life*, November 15, 1937, 45–52.

Annals of the American Academy of Political and Social Science 180 (July 1935).

"Another Bad Year of Motor Vehicle Deaths." *American City* 44 (February 1931): 85.

Arnold, Joseph. *The New Deal in the Suburbs: A History of the Greenbelt Town Program, 1935–1954*. Columbus: Ohio State University Press, 1971.

Aronovici, Carol. *Housing the Masses*. New York: John Wiley and Sons, 1939.

Aronovici, Carol, and Elizabeth McCalmont. *Catching Up with Housing*. Newark, NJ: Beneficial Management Corp., 1936.

Ascher, Charles S. "What the Depression Has Done to Planning." *Public Management* 17 (February 1935): 35–37.

Atack, Jeremy, and Fred Bateman. "How Long Was the Workday in 1880?" *Journal of Economic History* 52, no. 1 (March 1992): 129–60.

Austen, Ben, and Robert Philip Gordon. *High-Risers: Cabrini-Green and the Fate of American Public Housing*. New York: Harper, 2018.

Baber, Ray E. *Marriage and the Family*. New York: McGraw-Hill, 1939.

Baldwin, Sidney. *Poverty and Politics: The Rise and Decline of the Farm Security Administration*. Chapel Hill: University of North Carolina Press, 1968.

Baritz, Loren. *The Good Life: The Meaning of Success for the American Middle Class*. New York: Alfred A. Knopf, 1988.

Barrows, Robert G. "Beyond the Tenement: Patterns of American Urban Housing, 1870–1930." *Journal of Urban History* 9, no. 4 (August 1983): 395–420.

Barsam, Richard M. *Nonfiction Film: A Critical History*. Bloomington: Indiana University Press, 1973.

Basile, Salvatore. *Cool: How Air Conditioning Changed Everything*. New York: Fordham University Press, 2016.

Bauer, Catherine. *Modern Housing*. Boston: Houghton Mifflin, 1934.

Bauer, K. W. "A Greenbelt Town Grows Up." *American City* 74 (October 1959): 143–44.

Beard, Charles, ed. *Toward Civilization*. London: Longmans, Green, 1930.

Bezalel, Ronit, dir. *70 Acres in Chicago: Cabrini Green*. New Day Films, 2015.

Bemis, Albert Farwell. *The Evolving House*. Vol. 2, *The Economics of Shelter*. Cambridge, MA: Technology Press, Massachusetts Institute of Technology, 1934.

Biddle, George. *An American Artist's Story*. Boston: Little, Brown, 1939.

Biddle, George. "Five Years of Federal Patronage." *American Scholar* 9, no. 3 (Summer 1940): 327–38.

Biddle, George. "The Government and the Arts." *Harper's*, October 1, 1943, 427–34.

Boas, George. "A Defense of Democracy." *Harper's* 169 (September 1934): 418–26.

Bone, Hugh A. "Greenbelt Faces 1939." *American City* (February 1939): 59–61.

Borchert, Scott. *Republic of Detours: How the New Deal Paid Broke Writers to Rediscover America*. New York: Farrar, Straus, and Giroux, 2021.

Bowly, Devereux Jr. *The Poorhouse: Subsidized Housing in Chicago*. 2nd ed. Carbondale: Southern Illinois University Press, 2012.

Boyer, Christine. *Dreaming the Rational City: The Myth of American City Planning*. Cambridge, MA: MIT Press, 1983.

Boyer, Paul. *Urban Masses and Moral Order in America, 1820–1920*. Cambridge, MA: Harvard University Press, 1978.

"Brave New Towns That Aged Awkwardly." *Business Week,* January 9, 1971, 22–24.

Brinkley, Alan. *Culture and Politics in the Great Depression*. Waco, TX: Markham Press Fund, 1998.

Brinkley, Alan. *Voices of Protest: Huey Long, Father Coughlin, and the Great Depression*. New York: Vintage Books/Random House, 1982.

Brinkley, Douglas. *Rightful Heritage: Franklin D. Roosevelt and the Land of America*. New York: Harper, 2016.

Brown, Francis. "The American Road to Fascism." *Current History* (July 1933): 392–98.

Bruce, Edward. "Art and Democracy." *Atlantic* 156 (August 1935): 149–52.

Cahill, Holger. "Franklin Delano Roosevelt." *Magazine of Art* 38 (May 1945): 163.

Calkins, E. E. "The New Leisure—A Curse or a Blessing?" *Recreation* 28 (April 1934): 23–27.

Calverton, V. F. "Is America Ripe for Fascism?" *Current History* 38 (September 1933): 701–4.

Carpenter, Niles. *The Sociology of City Life*. New York: Longmans, Green, 1931.

Carpenter, Niles, and Clarence Quinn Berger. "Social Adjustments in Cities." *American Journal of Sociology* 40, no. 6 (May 1935): 729–36.

Chamberlin, William Henry. *Collectivism: A False Utopia*. New York: Macmillan, 1937.

Cherry, Gordon E., ed. *Shaping an Urban World*. New York: St. Martin's Press, 1980.

"Child Victims of the Auto." *Literary Digest*, February 2, 1929, 34.

Childs, Marquis W. *I Write from Washington*. New York: Harper, 1942.

Christensen, Carol A. *The American Garden City and the New Towns Movement*. Ann Arbor, MI: UMI Research Press, 1986.

Chudacoff, Howard P. *Children at Play: An American History*. New York: New York University Press, 2007.

Churchill, Henry S. "America's Town Planning Begins." *New Republic,* June 3, 1936, 96–98.

Churchill, Henry S. *The City Is the People*. New York: Reynal and Hitchcock, 1945.

Churchill, Henry S. "Greenbelt Towns: A Study of the Background and Planning of Four Communities for the Division of Suburban Resettlement of the Resettlement Administration, John S. Lansill, Director." Typed manuscript, n.d. John Scott Lansill Papers, University of Kentucky Special Collections and Digital Programs, University of Kentucky, Lexington, KY.

"Clean, Orderly Kitchen Is a Restful Workshop." *Good Housekeeping* 93 (October 1931): 86–87.

Cohen, Lizabeth. *Making a New Deal: Industrial Workers in Chicago, 1919–1939*. New York: Cambridge University Press, 2003.

"Comparative Architectural Details in the Greenbelt Housing." *American Architect and Architecture* (October 1936): 21–36.

Conkin, Paul K. *The New Deal*. Arlington Heights, IL: Harlan Davidson, 1975.

Conkin, Paul K. *A Revolution Down on the Farm: The Transformation of American Agriculture Since 1929*. Lexington: University Press of Kentucky, 2008.

Conkin, Paul K. *Tomorrow a New World: The New Deal Community Program*. Ithaca, NY: Cornell University Press, 1959.

Conn, Steven. *Americans against the City: Anti-Urbanism in the Twentieth Century*. New York: Oxford University Press, 2014.

Cooley, Charles Horton. *Social Organization: A Study of the Larger Mind*. New York: Charles Scribner's Sons, 1909.

Corey, Lewis. *The Crisis of the Middle Class*. New York: Covici, Friede, 1935.

Corn, Joseph J., and Brian Horrigan. *Yesterday's Tomorrows: Past Visions of the American Future*. New York: Summit Books, 1984.

Cowan, Ruth Schwartz. *More Work for Mother: The Ironies of Household Technology from the Open Hearth to the Microwave*. New York: Basic Books, 1983.

Cowie, Jefferson. *The Great Exception: The New Deal and the Limits of American Politics*. Princeton, NJ: Princeton University Press, 2016.

Cox, William Junkin. "Accidents Can Be Stopped." *Woman's Home Companion* 64 (May 1937): 106, 108.

Cox, W[illiam]. J[unkin]. "Why Automobile Accidents?" *Harper's* 171 (June 1935): 54–66.

Crane, Jacob. "Greendale—The General Plan." *Planners Journal* 3 (July–August 1937): 89–90.

Crane, Jacob. "Safety Town." *Public Safety* (August 1937): 28–29.

Cross, Bradley D. "'On a Business Basis': An American Garden City." *Planning Perspectives* 19, no. 1 (2004): 57–77.

Currell, Susan. *The March of Spare Time: The Problem and Promise of Leisure in the Great Depression*. Philadelphia: University of Pennsylvania Press, 2005.

Curtis, Henry S. *The Play Movement and Its Significance*. New York: Macmillan, 1917.

Cutten, George. *The Threat of Leisure*. New Haven, CT: Yale University Press, 1926.

Dahir, James. *Communities for Better Living: Citizen Achievement in Organization, Design, and Development*. New York: Harper, 1950.

Dahir, James. "Greendale Comes of Age." Manuscript prepared for the Milwaukee Community Development Corporation, 1958. Greendale Historical Society, Greendale, WI.

Davie, Maurice R. *Problems of City Life: A Study in Urban Sociology*. New York: John Wiley and Sons, 1932.

"Death All Day." *New Republic,* March 4, 1936, 98–99.

Dennis, Lawrence. *The Coming American Fascism*. New York: Harper, 1936.

"Description of Houses, Greenhills Project," n.d. Record Group 96: Farmers Home Administration file. National Archives and Records Administration, College Park, MD.

Desvernine, Raoul E. *Democratic Despotism*. New York: Dodd, Mead, 1936.

Dewey, John. *Democracy and Education: An Introduction to the Philosophy of Education*. New York: Macmillan, 1916.

Douglass, Harlan Paul. *The Suburban Trend*. New York: Century, 1925.

Dreier, John. "Greenbelt Planning: Resettlement Administration Builds Three Model Towns." *Pencil Points* (August 1936): 441–60.

Dulles, Rhea Foster, *America Learns to Play: A History of Popular Recreation, 1607–1940*. New York: D. Appleton-Century, 1940.

Durant, Will. "Is Democracy Doomed?" *Saturday Evening Post*, September 15, 1934, 23, 78, 80–82, 84.

Dykeman, Wilma, and James Stokely. *Seeds of Southern Change: The Life of Will Alexander*. Chicago: University of Chicago Press, 1962.

Eastman, Fred. "Are Movies Fit for Children?" *Parents* 6 (October 1931): 20–21, 52.

The Editors of *The Economist* (London), editors of. *The New Deal: An Analysis and Appraisal*. New York: Alfred A. Knopf, 1937.

Eden, Joseph A., and Arnold R. Alanen. "Looking Backward at a New Deal Town: Greendale, Wisconsin, 1935–1980." *Journal of the American Planning Association* 49, no. 1 (Winter 1983): 40–58.

Ehrenreich, Barbara, and Deidre English. *For Her Own Good: 150 Years of the Experts' Advice to Women*. Garden City, NY: Doubleday, 1978.

Evans, Timothy. "Emerald City." *Historic Preservation* 46, no. 6 (November 1994): 8.

"Extent of 5-Day Week in American Industry, 1931." *Monthly Labor Review* 33, no. 3 (September 1933): 487–92.

Fairbanks, Robert B. "Cincinnati and Greenhills: The Response to a Federal Community, 1935–1939." *Cincinnati Historical Society Bulletin* 36, no. 4 (Winter 1978): 222–41.

Fairbanks, Robert B. *Making Better Citizens: Housing Reform and the Community Development Strategy in Cincinnati, 1890–1960*. Urbana: University of Illinois Press, 1988.

Federal Emergency Administration of Public Works. *Homes for Workers*. Washington, DC: US Government Printing Office, 1937.

Feldman, Mary W. "A Study of Greenhills Project, Cincinnati, Ohio, a Public Housing Project Sponsored by the Farm Security Administration." MA thesis, University of Chicago, 1939.

Filler, Martin. "Planning for a Better World: The Lasting Legacy of Clarence Stein." *Architectural Record* 170, no. 10 (August 1982): 122–27.

Fisher, D. C. "The Bright and Perilous Face of Leisure." *Journal of Adult Education* 5 (June 1933): 237–43.

Fisher, Katherine. "A Turn of the Switch." *Good Housekeeping* 94 (March 1932): 80–81, 198.

Fisk, Donald M. "American Labor in the 20th Century." In *Compensation and Working Conditions*. Washington, DC: US Bureau of Labor Statistics, Fall 2001.

Fite, Gilbert C. "Farmer Opinion and the Agricultural Adjustment Act, 1933." *Mississippi Valley Historical Review* 48, no. 4 (March 1962): 656–73.

Form, William Humbert. "The Sociology of a White Collar Suburb." PhD diss., University of Maryland, 1944.

Forman, Henry James. *Our Movie Made Children*. New York: Macmillan, 1935.

The Editors of *Fortune*. *Housing America*. New York: Harcourt, Brace, 1932.

Fosdick, Raymond. *The Old Savage in the New Civilization*. New York: Doubleday, Doran, 1929.

Frank, Lawrence K. "Childhood and Youth." In *Recent Social Trends in the United States: Report of the President's Research Committee on Social Trends*, vol. 2, 751–800. New York: McGraw-Hill, 1933.

Frederick, Christine. *The Ignoramus Book of Housekeeping*. New York: Sears Publishing

Frederick, Christine. "Putting the American Woman and Her Home on a Business Basis." *Review of Reviews* 49 (February 1914): 199–208.

Fulmer, Otis Kline. *Greenbelt*. Washington, DC: American Council on Public Affairs, 1942.

Furnas, J. C. "And Sudden Death," *Reader's Digest* (August 1935): 21–26.

Gallup Poll. CD-ROM. N.p.: Scholarly Resources, 2000.

Gardner, George, Mabel Z. Smith, and Helen Gardner. "The New Social Problem: Leisure Time." *School and Society* 42 (August 31, 1935): 294–96.

Gelfand, Mark I. *A Nation of Cities: The Federal Government and Urban America, 1933–1965*. New York: Oxford University Press, 1975.

Gibson, Campbell, and Kay Jung. *Historical Census Statistics on Population Totals by Race, 1790 to 1990, and by Hispanic Origin, 1970 to 1990, for the United States, Regions, Divisions, and States*. Working Paper No. 56. Washington, DC: US Census Bureau, Population Division, 2002.

Gilfond, M. E. "Introducing: Greenbelt, Md." *Christian Science Monitor Magazine*, August 11, 1937, 5.

Gillette, Howard Jr. "Film as Artifact: *The City* (1939)." *American Studies* 18, no. 2 (Fall 1977): 71–85.

Gilligan, John J. "Learning about Race in Cincinnati." *Queen City Heritage* 52, no. 3 (Fall 1994): 3–8.

Goldstein, Carolyn M. *Creating Consumers: Home Economists in Twentieth-Century America*. Chapel Hill: University of North Carolina Press, 2012.

Green, Harvey. *The Uncertainty of Everyday Life: 1915–1945*. New York: Harper Perennial, 1993.

Green, Paul L. "Accidents Can Be Reduced." *American City* 50 (October 1935): 71, 73, 75, 77.

Green, Paul L. "Accidents Can Be Reduced." *American City* 50 (December 1935): 69, 71.

"Greenbelt." *Time*, September 13, 1937, 10.

"Greenbelt 25th Anniversary, 1937–1962." Greenbelt Museum, Greenbelt, MD.

Greenbelt blueprints. Records relating to the Greentown projects, file 196.5.9. Records of the Public Housing Administration, Record Group 196.5. National Archives at College Park, MD.

"Greenbelt Maryland Manual." Washington, DC: Farm Security Administration, 1942.

Greenbelt Plant Field List, October 22, 1936. Offices of Greenbelt Homes, Inc., Greenbelt, MD.

"Greenbelt Towns." *Architectural Record* (September 1936): 215–34.

Greenberg, Cheryl Lynn. *To Ask for an Equal Chance: African Americans in the Great Depression*. Lanham, MD: Rowman & Littlefield, 2009.

Greendale: 50 Years, 1938–1988. N.p.: N.p., n.d. Tugwell Room, Greenbelt Public Library.

"Greenhills Manual." Greenbelt Museum, Greenbelt, MD.

Greenspan, Anders. "How Philanthropy Can Alter Our View of the Past: A Look at Colonial Williamsburg." *Voluntas* 5, no. 2 (June 1, 1994): 193–203.

Grey, Greta. "Kitchen Planning." In *The Better Homes Manual,* edited by Blanche Halbert, 455–57. Chicago: University of Chicago Press, 1931.

Gries, John M., and James Ford, eds. *The President's Conference on Home Building and Home Ownership.* Vol. 4, *Home Ownership, Income and Types of Dwellings.* Washington, DC: National Capital Press, 1932.

Gries, John M., and James Ford, eds. *The President's Conference on Home Building and Home Ownership.* Vol. 5, *House Design Construction and Equipment.* Washington, DC: National Capital Press, 1932.

Gries, John M., and James Ford, eds. *The President's Conference on Home Building and Home Ownership.* Vol. 7, *Committee on Farm and Village Housing.* Washington, DC: National Capital Press, 1932.

Gries, John M., and James T. Ford, eds. *The President's Conference on Home Building and Home Ownership.* Vol. 11, *Housing Objectives and Programs.* Washington, DC: National Capital Press, 1932.

Grimes, Walter Henderson. "The Curse of Leisure." *Atlantic Monthly* (September 1928): 355–60.

Groves, Ernest R. *Social Problems of the Family.* Philadelphia: J. B. Lippincott, 1927.

Groves, Ernest R. "The Urban Complex." *Sociological Review* 12, no. 2 (Autumn 1920): 73–81.

A Guide Book for Williamsburg, Virginia. Williamsburg, VA: Colonial Williamsburg, Inc., 1936.

Gunderson, Anne. "The Affordable Housing Gap Leaves Low-Income Renters without Options." *Chicago Policy Review* (June 30, 2017).

Hall, O. Milton. "Attitudes and Unemployment: A Comparison of the Opinions and Attitudes of Employed and Unemployed Men." *Archives of Psychology* 165 (March 1934): 1–66.

Hambidge, Gove. *Time to Live: Adventures in the Use of Leisure.* New York: McGraw-Hill, 1933.

Hansen, Roger C. "Pioneers in Nonviolent Action: The Congress of Racial Equality in Cincinnati, 1946–1955." *Queen City Heritage* 52, no. 3 (Fall 1994): 23–55.

Haskell, Barbara. *The American Century: Art and Culture 1900–1950.* New York: Whitney Museum of American Art, 1999.

"The Hazard of Driving and Walking: Analysis of Motor-Vehicle Accidents and Fatalities." *American City* 50 (May 1935): 99, 101.

"Helpful Suggestions for Greendale Residents." Elbert Peets Papers, Cornell University, Ithaca, NY.

Hendricks, David, and Amy Patterson. "The 1930 Census in Perspective." *Prologue Magazine* 34, no. 2 (Summer 2002). https://www.archives.gov/publications/prologue/2002/summer/1930-census-perspective.html.

Hermans, Mabel C., and Margaret M. Hannon. *Using Leisure Time*. New York: Harcourt, Brace, 1938.

Herring, Pendleton. "A Prescription for Modern Democracy." *Annals of the American Academy of Political and Social Science* 180 (July 1935): 138–48.

Hill, Walter B. Jr. "Finding Place for the Negro: Robert C. Weaver and the Groundwork for the Civil Rights Movement." *Prologue Magazine* 37, no. 1 (Spring 2005). https://www.archives.gov/publications/prologue/2005/spring/weaver.html.

History of Greenbelt Eligibility, typewritten document, Tugwell Room, Greenbelt Public Library, Greenbelt, MD.

Holden, T. S. "How Many Architects Are Carrying On?" *Architectural Record* 74 (July 1933): 57–58.

Holley, Donald. "The Negro in the New Deal Resettlement Program." *Agricultural History* 45, no. 3 (July 1971): 179–93.

Holt, J. B. *An Analysis of Methods and Criteria Used in Selecting Families for Colonization Projects*. Washington, DC: Farm Security Administration, 1937.

Hoover, Herbert. *Address of President Hoover at the Opening Meeting of the President's Conference on Home Building and Home Ownership*. Washington, DC: US Government Printing Office, December 1931.

Hoover, Herbert. "Statement Announcing the White House Conference on Home Building and Home Ownership, Sept. 15, 1931." *Public Papers of the Presidents of the United States, Herbert Hoover, Containing the Public Messages, Speeches, and Statements of the President January 1 to December 31, 1931*. Washington, DC: US Government Printing Office, 1976.

Horrigan, Brian. "The Home of Tomorrow, 1927–1945." In *Imagining Tomorrow: History, Technology, and the American Future*, edited by Joseph J. Corn, 137–63. Cambridge, MA: MIT Press, 1986.

A Housing Program for the United States. Chicago: National Association of Housing Officials, 1934.

Howard, Ebenezer. *Garden Cities of To-morrow*. Originally published as *To-morrow: A Peaceful Path to Real Reform*, 1898. Reprint. Cambridge, MA: MIT Press, 1965.

Hudson, Robert B. *Radburn, a Plan of Living*. New York: American Association for Adult Education, 1934.

Humphrey, Seth K. "Our Delightful Man-Killer." *Atlantic Monthly* 148 (December 1931): 724–30.

Hunter, Leslie Gene. "Greenbelt, Maryland: A City on a Hill." *Maryland Historical Magazine* (June 1968): 105–36.

Ickes, Harold. *Back to Work: The Story of the PWA*. New York: Macmillan, 1935.

"Incalculable Record." *Magazine of Art* 32 (August 1949): 460–71, 494–95.

Jackson, Kenneth T., and Stanley K. Schultz. *Cities in American History*. New York: Alfred A. Knopf, 1972.

Johnson, Donald Leslie. "Origins of the Neighborhood Unit." *Planning Perspectives* 17, no. 3 (July 2002): 227–45.

Johnston, Alva. "Tugwell, the President's Idea Man." *Saturday Evening Post*, August 1, 1936, 8–9, 73–74.

Kantorowich, R. "A Report on the Greenbelt Towns in the United States of America." *South African Architectural Record* 27 (December 1942): 385–92.

Katz, Meighen. *Narratives of Vulnerability in Museums: American Interpretations of the Great Depression.* New York: Routledge, 2020.

Kendall, Helen Whitson. "Your First Electric Range." *Good Housekeeping* 90 (April 1930): 96–97.

Kerns, Jennifer Karen. "A Social Experiment in Greenbelt, Maryland: Class, Gender, and Public Housing." PhD diss., University of Arizona, 2002.

Kim, Jihong, and Bong Hee Jeon. "Restoration of a Historic Town to Commemorate National Identity: Colonial Williamsburg in the Early Twentieth Century." *Journal of Asian Architecture and Building Engineering* 11, no. 2 (2012): 245–51.

Kimble, Lionel Jr. *A New Deal for Bronzeville: Housing, Employment, and Civil Rights in Black Chicago, 1935–1955.* Carbondale: Southern Illinois University Press, 2015.

Kneeland, Hildegarde. "Is the Modern Housewife a Lady of Leisure?" *Survey* 62 (June 1929): 301–2, 331, 333, 336.

Knepper, Cathy Dee. *Greenbelt, Maryland: A Living Legacy of the New Deal.* Baltimore: Johns Hopkins University Press, 2001.

Kyvig, David. *Daily Life in the United States, 1920–1940: How Americans Lived through the "Roaring Twenties" and the Great Depression.* Chicago: Ivan R. Dee, 2002.

Larson, Cedric Arthur. "Educational Activities of the Federally Planned Community of Greenbelt, Maryland." Master's thesis, George Washington University, 1939.

Lash, Joseph P. *Dealers and Dreamers: A New Look at the New Deal.* New York: Doubleday, 1988.

Lay, Charles Downing. "The Freedom of the City." *North American Review* 222 (September 1925): 123–134.

Leach, Charles Bradley. "Greenhills, Ohio: The Evolution of an American New Town." PhD diss., Case Western Reserve University, 1978.

Leighninger, Robert D. Jr. *Long-Range Public Investment: The Forgotten Legacy of the New Deal.* Columbia: University of South Carolina Press, 2007.

Leuchtenburg, William E. *Franklin D. Roosevelt and the New Deal, 1932–1940.* New York: Harper & Row, 1963.

Leven, Maurice, Harold G. Moulton, and Clark Warburton. *America's Capacity to Consume.* Washington, DC: Brookings Institution, 1934.

Levine, Lawrence. *The Unpredictable Past: Explorations in American Cultural History.* New York: Oxford University Press, 1993.

Lies, Eugene T. "The Community's Responsibility toward the Leisure Time Problem." *National Conference on Social Welfare, Proceedings 1928,* 310–13.

"Life in the Communities of Sunnyside, Radburn, Hillside, Greenbelt, Greenhills." ca. 1947–48. Typed report, Clarence Stein Papers, box 2, file 13, Division of Rare and Manuscript Collections, Cornell University Library, Ithaca, NY.

Lindeman, Eduard. *Leisure—A National Issue: Planning for the Leisure of a Democratic People.* New York: Association Press, 1939.

Lippmann, Walter. *Interpretations 1933–1935.* Edited by Allan Nevins. New York: Macmillan, 1936.

Lippmeier, Carol A. *Act of Congress, Greenhills, Ohio, 1938–1976*. Greenhills, OH: Greenhills Civic Foundation History, 1976.

Longan, Elizabeth. "Evolving Standards in American Housing." *Journal of Home Economics* 27 (April 1935): 207–10.

Looking Back: Greenbelt Is 50, 1937–1987. Greenbelt, MD: City of Greenbelt, 1987.

"Los Pueblos Greenbelt en Estados Unidos." *Arquitecto Peruano* 8 (May 1944): 4–6.

"Low-Cost Furniture." *House Beautiful* 79 (April 1937): 131–33.

Lynd, Robert S. "The People as Consumers." In *Recent Social Trends in the United States: Report of the President's Research Committee on Social Trends*, vol. 2, 857–911. New York: McGraw-Hill, 1933.

Lynd, Robert S., and Helen Merrell Lynd. *Middletown: A Study in Modern American Culture*. 1929. Reprint. San Diego: Harvest/Harcourt Brace, 1957.

Maher, Neil M. *Nature's New Deal: The Civilian Conservation Corps and the Roots of the American Environmental Movement*. New York: Oxford University Press, 2008.

"Maintain the Arts Projects." *Publishers' Weekly*, January 22, 1938, 301.

Marquette, Bleecker. "The Human Side of Housing: Are We Losing the Battle for Better Homes?" *Proceedings of the National Conference of Social Work, 1923*, 344–49. Chicago: National Conference of Social Work, 1923.

Marsh, Benjamin Clarke. *An Introduction to City Planning: Democracy's Challenge to the American City*. New York, 1909.

Marsh, Margaret. *Suburban Lives*. New Brunswick, NJ: Rutgers University Press, 1990.

Marshall, Douglas George. "Greendale: A Study of a Resettlement Community." PhD diss., University of Wisconsin, 1943.

Matthews, Glenna. *Just a Housewife: The Rise and Fall of Domesticity in America*. New York: Oxford University Press, 1987.

Matthews, Joseph Brown, and R. E. Shallcross, "Must America Go Fascist?" *Harper's* (June 1934): 1–15.

Mayer, Albert. "The Architect and the World." *Nation*, January 8, 1936, 43–45.

Mayer, Albert. "Green-belt Towns for the Machine Age." *New York Times Magazine*, February 2, 1936, 8–9, 18.

Mayer, Albert. "Henry Wright: Creative Planner." *Survey Graphic* 25 (September 1936): 530.

Mayer, Albert. "A Technique for Planning Complete Communities." *Architectural Forum* 66 (January–February 1937): 126–46.

McAfee, Helen. "The Menace of Leisure." *Century* 114 (1927): 67–76.

McElvaine, Robert S. *The Great Depression: America, 1929–1941*. New York: Times Books, 1993.

McKenzie, Richard D. *The New Deal for Artists*. Princeton, NJ: Princeton University Press, 1973.

McKenzie, R[ichard]. D. "The Rise of Metropolitan Communities." In *Recent Social Trends in the United States: Report of the President's Research Committee on Social Trends*, vol. 1, 443–96. New York: McGraw-Hill, 1933.

McMullen, Frances Drewry. "New Jobs for Women." *North American Review* 234, no. 2 (August 1932): 132–38.

Miller, Spencer Jr. "Labor and the Challenge of the New Leisure." *Harvard Business Review* 11 (June 1933): 462–67.

Morris, George. "$16,000 Homes for $2,000 Incomes." *Nation's Business* 26 (January 1938): 21–23, 109.

Mumford, Lewis. "The Chance for Civilized Housing." *New Republic*, September 17, 1930, 115–17.

Mumford, Lewis. "The Fourth Migration." In *Planning the Fourth Migration: The Neglected Vision of the Regional Planning Association of America*, edited by Carl Sussman, 55–64. Cambridge, MA: MIT Press, 1976. Originally published in *Survey Graphic* 7 (May 1925): 130–33.

Mumford, Lewis. "Letter to the President." *New Republic,* December 30, 1936, 263.

Mumford, Lewis. "New Homes for a New Deal III: The Shortage of Dwellings and Direction." *New Republic*, February 28, 1934, 69–72.

Mumford, Lewis. "Regions—To Live In." In *Planning the Fourth Migration: The Neglected Vision of the Regional Planning Association of America*, edited by Carl Sussman, 89–93. Cambridge, MA: MIT Press, 1976. Originally published in *Survey Graphic* 7 (May 1925): 151–52.

Mumford, Lewis. *Sticks and Stones: A Study of American Architecture and Civilization.* New York: Boni and Liveright, 1924.

Mumford, Lewis. *Technics and Civilization.* New York: Harcourt, Brace, 1934.

Musher, Sharon Ann. *Democratic Art: The New Deal's Influence on American Culture.* Chicago: University of Chicago Press, 2015.

Nash, Roderick. *The Nervous Generation: American Thought, 1917–1930.* Chicago: Ivan R. Dee/Elephant Paperback, 1970.

National Association of Housing Officials. *A Housing Program for the United States.* Chicago: National Association of Housing Officials, 1934.

National Recreation Association. *The Leisure Hours of 5,000 People.* New York: National Recreation Association, 1934.

National Register of Historic Places. Records for Greenbelt, Greendale, and Greenhills. https://www.nps.gov/subjects/nationalregister/database-research.htm.

"New Deal Neighbors, Oral Histories of Greenhills, Ohio." https://www.newdealneighbors.com/.

Nichols, Nell B. "No More Pot-Watching." *Woman's Home Companion* 59 (May 1932): 58–62.

Nipp, Robert E. "The Negro in the New Deal Resettlement Program: A Comment." *Agricultural History* 45, no. 3 (July 1971): 195–200.

Nixon, Virginia. "Outfitting the Kitchen for Convenience." *American Home* 1 (February 1929): 398, 428.

Nolen, John. "Meeting the Housing Needs of the Modern Family." *Journal of Home Economics* 22, no. 10 (October 1930): 819–24.

Nolen, John. *New Towns for Old: Achievements in Civic Improvement in Some American Small Towns and Neighborhoods.* 1927. Reprint. Amherst: University of Massachusetts Press, 2005.

Obituary of Henry Wright. *Architectural Record* 80 (August 1936): 83.

O'Conner, Francis V., ed. *Art for the Millions: Essays from the 1930s by Artists and Administrators of the WPA Federal Art Project*. Greenwich, CT: New York Graphic Society, 1973.

Official Guide Book New York World's Fair 1939. New York: Exposition Publications, 1939.

Ogburn, William F. *You and Machines*. Chicago: University of Chicago Press, 1934.

Orvell, Miles. *The Death and Life of Main Street: Small Towns in American Memory, Space, and Community*. Chapel Hill: University of North Carolina Press, 2012.

Pack, Arthur Newton. *The Challenge of Leisure*. New York: Macmillan, 1934.

Park, Edwin Avery. *New Backgrounds for a New Age*. New York: Harcourt, Brace, 1927.

Park, Robert E., Ernest W. Burgess, and Roderick D. McKenzie. *The City*. Chicago: University of Chicago Press, 1925.

Parsons, Kermit C., ed. *The Writings of Clarence S. Stein: Architect of the Planned Community*. Baltimore: Johns Hopkins University Press, 1998.

Pattison, Mary. "The Abolition of Household Slavery." *Annals of the American Academy of Political and Social Science* 118 (March 1925): 124–27.

Pay rate list for Greenbelt workers. Offices of Greenbelt Homes, Inc., Greenbelt, MD.

Peets, Elbert. "Greendale." In *On the Art of Designing Cities: Selected Essays of Elbert Peets*, edited by Paul D. Spreiregen, 216–22. Cambridge, MA: MIT Press, 1968.

Peets, Elbert. "Washington, Williamsburg, the Century of Progress, and Greendale." In *City Planning, Housing*, vol. 2, edited by Werner Hegemann, William W. Forster, and Robert C. Weinburg, 407–16. New York: Architectural Book Publishing Co., 1936.

Perry, Clarence Arthur. "The Neighborhood Unit." In *Regional Survey of New York and Its Environs*, vol. 7. New York: Committee on Regional Plan of New York and Its Environs, 1929.

Peyser, Ethel R. "The Robot of the Kitchen." *House Beautiful* 69 (May 1931): 518–19.

Pillen, Cory. *WPA Posters in an Aesthetic, Social, and Political Context: A New Deal for Design*. New York: Routledge, 2020.

"A Planned Community Appraised." *Architectural Forum* 72 (January 1940): 62–64.

Pollard, James E. *The Presidents and the Press*. New York: Macmillan, 1947.

Pooley, Colin G., ed. *Housing Strategies in Europe 1880–1930*. New York: St. Martin's Press, 1992.

Preliminary Plan Book, Bound Brook Suburban Resettlement, n.d. John Scott Lansill Papers, University of Kentucky Special Collections and Digital Programs, University of Kentucky, Lexington, KY.

"Public Housing Administration Racial Relations Policy." Labeled "CONFIDENTIAL." Warren Vinton Papers, Cornell University, Ithaca, NY.

Purcell, Aaron D. "Historical Interpretations of the New Deal and the Great Depression." In *The New Deal and the Great* Depression, edited by Aaron D. Purcell, 4–39. Kent, OH: Kent State University Press, 2014.

Quinn, Kelly Ann. "Making Modern Homes: A History of Langston Terrace Dwellings, a New Deal Housing Program in Washington, DC." PhD diss., University of Maryland, College Park, 2007.

Radford, Gail. *Modern Housing for America: Policy Struggles in the New Deal Era*. Chicago: University of Chicago Press, 1996.

Rainwater, Clarence E. *The Play Movement in the United States: A Study of Community Recreation*. Chicago: University of Chicago Press, 1922.

Ratensky, Samuel, to Warren Vinton. Report of the Second Week's Activity in Cincinnati, Cincinnati, OH, February 6, 1936. Justin Hartzog Papers, Cornell University, Ithaca, NY.

Rauchway, Eric. "The New Deal Was on the Ballot." *Modern American History* 2, no. 2 (July 2019): 201–13.

Rauchway, Eric. *Why the New Deal Matters*. New Haven, CT: Yale University Press, 2021.

Rauchway, Eric. *Winter War: Hoover, Roosevelt, and the First Clash Over the New Deal*. New York: Basic Books, 2018.

Reagan, Patrick D. *Designing a New America: The Origins of New Deal Planning, 1890–1943*. Amherst: University of Massachusetts Press, 1999.

Reblando, Jason. *New Deal Utopias*. Heidelberg, Ger.: Kehrer Verlag, 2017.

"Report on the Rental Market in Relation to Project #000–0040, Farm Security Administration at Greenbelt, Maryland." Federal Housing Administration Division of Economics and Statistics, July 12, 1938. Marked "Confidential—not for publication." Federal Housing Administration records, National Archives and Records Administration, College Park, MD.

Resettlement Administration. *Greenbelt Towns*. Washington, DC: US Government Printing Office, September 1936.

Resettlement Administration. "Homes for Workingmen," n.d. John Scott Lansill Papers, University of Kentucky Special Collections and Digital Programs, University of Kentucky, Lexington, KY.

Resettlement Administration press release, dated October 11, 1935. Official file, OF 1568, box 1, "September–November 1935." Franklin D. Roosevelt Presidential Library, Hyde Park, NY.

Resettlement Administration. "Summary of Information, Greenhills, Hamilton County, Ohio," n.d. John Scott Lansill Papers, University of Kentucky Special Collections and Digital Programs, University of Kentucky, Lexington, KY.

Richards, Wallace, to Eleanor Roosevelt. November 6, 1937. Franklin D. Roosevelt Presidential Library, Hyde Park, NY.

Riggs, Austen Fox. *Play: Recreation in a Balanced Life*. New York: Doubleday, Doran, 1935.

Riis, Jacob. *How the Other Half Lives*. New York: Charles Scribner's Sons, 1890.

Robbins, Ira S. "Resettlement Administration Only Partially Unsettled: Greenbelt Project Held Invalid." *American City* 51 (June 1936): 5.

Rogers, Millard F. Jr. *John Nolen and Mariemont: Building a New Town in Ohio*. Baltimore: Johns Hopkins University Press, 2001.

Rogers, Sally Scott. "Community Planning and Residential Satisfaction: Case Analysis of Greenbelt, Maryland." PhD diss., University of Maryland, 1975.

Roosevelt, Eleanor. *It's Up to the Women*. New York: Frederick A. Stokes, 1933.

Roosevelt, Franklin D. Address before the American Country Life Conference on the Better Distribution of Population Away from Cities, Ithaca, New York, August 19, 1931. *The Public Papers and Addresses of Franklin D. Roosevelt*, Volume 1, *The Genesis of the New Deal 1928–1932*. New York: Random House, 1938.

Roosevelt, Franklin D. "Growing Up by Plan." *The Survey* 67 (February 1932): 483.

Roosevelt, Franklin D. Inaugural Address, March 4, 1933. *The Public Papers and Addresses of Franklin D. Roosevelt*, Volume 2, *The Year of Crisis 1933*. New York: Random House, 1938.

Roosevelt, Franklin D. Nomination Acceptance Speech, Chicago, July 2, 1932. *The Public Papers and Addresses of Franklin D. Roosevelt*, Volume 1, *The Genesis of the New Deal 1928–1932*. New York: Random House, 1938.

Roosevelt, Franklin D. "The Philosophy of Social Justice through Social Action." Campaign address, Detroit, MI, October 2, 1932. https://www.presidency.ucsb.edu/documents/campaign-address-detroit-michigan.

Roosevelt, Theodore. Special Message to the Two Houses of Congress. Speech, Washington, DC, February 9, 1909. *American Presidency Project*, https://www.presidency.ucsb.edu/documents/special-message-366.

"Roosevelt—Dictator?" Editorial, *Catholic World* (April 1934): 1–8.

Rosenbaum, Emily, and Laura E. Harris. "Low-Income Families in Their New Neighborhoods." *Journal of Family Issues* 22, no. 2 (March 2001): 183–210.

Rosenbaum, James E., Linda K. Stroh, and Cathy A. Flynn. "Lake Parc Place: A Study of Mixed-Income Housing." *Housing Policy Debate* 9, no. 4 (January 1998): 703–40.

Rosten, Leo C. *The Washington Correspondents*. New York: Harcourt, Brace, 1937.

Rutherford, Janice Williams. *Selling Mrs. Consumer: Christine Frederick and the Rise of Household Efficiency*. Athens: University of Georgia Press, 2003.

Schaffer, Daniel. *Garden Cities for America: The Radburn Experience*. Philadelphia: Temple University Press, 1982.

Schaffer, Daniel. "Resettling Industrial America: The Controversy Over FDR's Greenbelt Town Program." *Urbanism Past & Present* 8, no. 1 (Winter/Spring 1983): 18–32.

Schlesinger, Arthur M. Jr. *The Coming of the New Deal*. Boston: Houghton, Mifflin, 1958.

Schulman, Harry M. "A Study of Crime and the Community." *Report of the New York Crime Commission, 1930*. Albany, 1930. Quoted in John M. Gries and James Ford, eds., *The President's Conference on Home Building and Home Ownership*, Vol. 8, *Housing and the Community—Home Repair and Remodeling*, 130, 140. Washington, DC: National Capital Press, 1932.

"Semi-Dictator?" *Barron's* 13, no. 7 (February 13, 1933): 12.

Sharp, George. *City Life and Its Amelioration*. Boston: Richard G. Badger, 1915.

Sies, Mary Corbin. "North American Suburbs, 1880–1950: Cultural and Social Reconsiderations." *Journal of Urban History* 27, no. 3 (March 2001): 313–46.

"Site Plans of 'Greenbelt' Towns." *American City* (August 1936): 56–59.

Sitkoff, Harvard. *A New Deal for Blacks: The Emergence of Civil Rights as a National Issue: The Depression Decade*. New York: Oxford University Press, 2008.

Sklaroff, Lauren Rebecca. *Black Culture and the New Deal: The Quest for Civil Rights in the Roosevelt Era*. Chapel Hill: University of North Carolina Press, 2009.

Smith, Jason Scott. *Building New Deal Liberalism: The Political Economy of Public Works, 1933–1956*. New York: Cambridge University Press, 2006.

Soule, George. *The Coming American Revolution*. New York: Macmillan, 1934.

Sparkes, Boyden. "The Reckless Other Fellow." *Saturday Evening Post*, September 26, 1936, 33, 100–102.

Stapp, Peyton. *Urban Housing: A Summary of Real Property Inventories Conducted as Work Projects, 1934–1936*. Washington, DC: US Government Printing Office, 1938.

Stegner, Mabel J. "Cooking Is a Continuous Pleasure." *Better Homes and Gardens* 10 (May 1932): 36, 68–69.

Stein, Clarence. "The Conception of Greenbelt." Typewritten paper, July 24, 1947. Tugwell Room, Greenbelt Public Library, Greenbelt, MD.

Stein, Clarence. "Dinosaur Cities." In *Planning the Fourth Migration: The Neglected Vision of the Regional Planning Association of America*, ed. Carl Sussman, 67. Cambridge, MA: MIT Press, 1976. Originally published in *Survey Graphic* 7 (May 1925): 134–38.

Stein, Clarence. "Housing and Common Sense." *Nation*, May 11, 1932, 541–44.

Stein, Clarence. *Toward New Towns for America*. Liverpool: University Press of Liverpool, 1951.

Stein, Clarence, and Catherine Bauer. "Store Buildings and Neighborhood Shopping Centers." *Architectural Record* 75 (February 1934): 174–87.

Steiner, H. Arthur. "Fascism in America?" *American Political Science Review* 29 (October 1935): 821–30.

Steiner, Jesse Frederick. *Americans at Play: Recent Trends in Recreation and Leisure-Time*. New York: McGraw-Hill, 1933.

Steiner, Jesse Frederick. "Challenge of the New Leisure." *Recreation* 27 (February 1934): 517–22.

Steiner, J[esse]. F[rederick]. "Recreation and Leisure Time Activities." In *Recent Social Trends in the United States: Report of the President's Research Committee on Social Trends*, vol. 2, 912–57. New York: McGraw-Hill, 1933.

Steiner, Ralph, and Willard Van Dyke, dirs. *The City*. American Institute of Planners, 1939.

Stephenson, Flora C. "Greenbelt Towns in the United States." *Town and Country Planning* 10, no. 40 (Winter 1942–43): 121–22.

Sternsher, Bernard. *Rexford Tugwell and the New Deal*. New Brunswick, NJ: Rutgers University Press, 1964.

Stevenson, Katherine Cole, and H. Ward Jandl. *Houses by Mail: A Guide to Houses from Sears, Roebuck, and Company*. Washington, DC: Preservation Press, 1986.

Stokes, Sally Sims. "God, Government, and Greenbelt: Lived Religion and the Cultural Politics of (In)Tolerance in the Social Engineering of a Cooperative New Deal Resettlement Town, 1937–1940." In *Lived Religion and the Politics of (In)Tolerance*, edited by R. Ruard Ganzevoort and Srdjan Sremac, 135–70. Palgrave Studies in Lived Religion and Societal Challenges. Cham, Switzerland: Palgrave Macmillan, 2017.

Strong, W. A., to Justin Hartzog. August 10, 1936. Justin Hartzog Papers, Cornell University, Ithaca, NY.

Strasser, Susan. *Never Done: A History of American Housework*. New York: Henry Holt, 2000.

"A Study of the Characteristics, Customs and Living Habits of Potential Tenants of the Resettlement Project in Cincinnati," February 1936. Justin Hartzog Papers, Cornell University, Ithaca, NY.

"Summarized History of Greenbrook." Tugwell Room, Greenbelt Public Library, Greenbelt, MD.

Surdam, David George. *Century of the Leisured Masses: Entertainment and the Transformation of Twentieth-Century America*. New York: Oxford University Press, 2015.

Swing, Raymond Gram. *Forerunners of American Fascism*. New York, J. Messner, 1935.

Szylvian, Kristin. *The Mutual Housing Experiment: New Deal Communities for the Urban Middle Class*. Philadelphia: Temple University Press, 2015.

Teaford, Jon. *City and Suburb: The Political Fragmentation of Metropolitan America, 1850–1970*. Baltimore: Johns Hopkins University Press, 1979.

This Is Greendale. Tenth anniversary booklet. Greendale, WI: Greendale Historical Society, ca. 1947 or 1948.

Thomas, Lenore, file. Undated summary of Thomas's work for Greenbelt. Greenbelt Museum, Greenbelt, MD.

Thompson, John Giffen. *Urbanization: Its Effects on Government and Society*. New York: E. P. Dutton, 1927.

Thompson, Warren S[impson]. "Movements of Population." *American Journal of Sociology* 40, no. 6 (May 1935): 713–19.

Thompson, Warren Simpson. "On Living in Cities." *American Mercury* 20 (June 1930): 192–201.

Tigner, Hugh Stevenson. "Will America Go Fascist?" *Christian Century*, May 2, 1934, 592–94.

Tobey, James A. "The Hazard of the Automobile." *Scientific Monthly* 32, no. 6 (June 1931): 519–21.

Tugwell, Rexford G. Address to the Regional Planning Association of Hamilton County, Ohio, February 5, 1936. Tugwell Papers Collection, Franklin D. Roosevelt Presidential Library, Hyde Park, NY.

Tugwell, Rexford G. *The Battle for Democracy*. New York: Columbia University Press, 1935.

Tugwell, Rexford G. "Design for Government." *Political Science Quarterly* 48, no. 3 (September 1933): 321–32.

Tugwell, Rexford G. *FDR: Architect of an Era*. New York: Macmillan, 1967.

Tugwell, Rexford G. "Government in a Changing World." *Review of Reviews and World's Work* (May 16, 1933): 33–34, 56.

Tugwell, Rexford G. "The Meaning of the Greenbelt Towns." *New Republic*, February 17, 1937, 42–43.

Tugwell, Rexford G. Personal diary, March 14, 1935. Tugwell Papers Collection, Franklin D. Roosevelt Presidential Library, Hyde Park, NY.

Tugwell, Rexford G. "Our Philosophy of Despair." *University Journal of Business* 2, no. 4 (September 1924): 428–431.

Tugwell, Rexford G. "The Progressive Tradition." *Atlantic Monthly* (April 1935): 409–18.

Tugwell, Rexford G. "The Resettlement Idea." *Agricultural History* 33, no. 4 (October 1959): 159–164.

Tugwell, Rexford G. Speech delivered in Olympic Auditorium, Los Angeles, October 28, 1935. Tugwell Papers Collection, Franklin D. Roosevelt Presidential Library, Hyde Park, NY.

"Unemployed Arts." *Fortune* 15 (May 1937): 109–17, 168, 171–72.

US Census Bureau. *1930 Census*. Volume 3, *Population, Reports by States*. Washington, DC: US Government Printing Office, 1932.

US Census Bureau. *Historical Census Statistics on the Foreign-Born Population of the United States: 1850 to 1990*, Table 8, "Race and Hispanic Origin of the Population by Nativity: 1850 to 1990." https://www.census.gov/population/www/documentation/twps0029/tab08.html.

US Census Bureau. *Historical Statistics of the United States, 1789–1945: A Supplement to the Statistical Abstract of the United States*. Washington, DC: United States Department of Commerce, 1949.

US Census Bureau. *Ohio: 2010: Summary Population and Housing Characteristics,* Table 3, "Race and Hispanic or Latino Origin: 2010." https://www.census.gov/prod/cen2010/cph-1-37.pdf.

US Census Bureau. *QuickFacts*, "Greenbelt city, Maryland." https://www.census.gov/quickfacts/fact/table/greenbeltcitymaryland/PST045219.

US Census Bureau. *QuickFacts*, "Greendale village, Wisconsin." https://www.census.gov/quickfacts/fact/table/greendalevillagewisconsin/POP060210.

US Census Bureau. *Selected Historical Decennial Census Population and Housing Counts*, "Urban and Rural Populations, 1990." http://www.census.gov/population/www/censusdata/files/table-4.pdf.

US Census Bureau. *Sixteenth Census of the United States, 1940, Housing*: vol. 2, part 1. Washington, DC: US Government Printing Office, 1943.

US Census Bureau. *Statistical Abstract of the United States 1939*. Washington, DC: US Government Printing Office, 1940.

US Department of Agriculture. "Final Report of the Greenbelt Project of the Greenbelt Town Program." Washington, DC, 1938. John Scott Lansill Papers, University of Kentucky Special Collections and Digital Programs, University of Kentucky, Lexington, KY.

US Department of Agriculture. "Final Report of the Greenbrook Project of the Greenbelt Town Program." Washington, DC, 1938. John Scott Lansill Papers, University of Kentucky Special Collections and Digital Programs, University of Kentucky, Lexington, KY.

US Department of Agriculture. "Final Report of the Greendale Project of the Greenbelt Town Program." Washington, DC, 1938. John Scott Lansill Papers, University of Kentucky Special Collections and Digital Programs, University of Kentucky, Lexington, KY.

US Department of Agriculture. "Final Report of the Greenhills Project of the Greenbelt Town Program." Washington, DC, 1938. John Scott Lansill Papers, University of Kentucky Special Collections and Digital Programs, University of Kentucky, Lexington, KY.

Unwin, Raymond. "The Problem of Housing." In *America Can't Have Housing*, edited by Carol Aronovici, 9–10. New York: Committee on the Housing Exhibition by the Museum of Modern Art, 1934.

Walker, Hale J. "Some Major Technical Problems Encountered in the Planning of Greenbelt, Maryland." *Planners' Journal* 4, no. 2 (March–April 1938): 34–37.

Walker, John O. "A Demonstration in Community Planning." *Shelter* 3 (February 1939): 30.

Walker, John O. "Greenbelt Towns." *Shelter* 3 (January 1939): 20–24.

Warner, George A. *Greenbelt: The Cooperative Community: An Experience in Democratic Living.* New York: Exposition Press, 1954.

Watts, Jill. *The Black Cabinet: The Untold Story of African Americans and Politics during the Age of Roosevelt.* New York: Grove Press, 2020.

Whitaker, Charles Harris. "What Is a House?" In *The Housing Problem in War and in Peace.* Washington, DC: Journal of the American Institute of Architects Press, 1918.

White, Ann Folino. *Plowed Under: Food Policy Protests and Performance in New Deal America.* Bloomington: Indiana University Press, 2015.

Williamson, Mary Lou, ed. *Greenbelt, History of a New Town, 1937–1987.* Norfolk, VA: Donning, 1987.

Wiltse, Jeff. *Contested Waters: A Social History of Swimming Pools in America.* Chapel Hill: University of North Carolina Press, 2007.

Winfield, Betty Houchin. *FDR and the News Media.* Urbana: University of Illinois Press, 1990.

Winsten, Archer. "*The City* Goes to the Fair." In *The Documentary Tradition,* edited by Lewis Jacobs, 126–28. New York: W. W. Norton, 1979.

Wirth, Louis. "Urbanism as a Way of Life," *American Journal of Sociology* 44, no. 1 (July 1938): 1–24.

Wojtowicz, Robert. *Lewis Mumford and American Modernism: Eutopian Theories for Architecture and Urban Planning*. New York: Cambridge University Press, 1996.

Wolman, Leo, and Gustav Peck. "Labor Groups in the Social Structure." In *Recent Social Trends in the United States: Report of the President's Research Committee on Social Trends*, vol. 2, 801–56. New York: McGraw-Hill, 1933.

Wood, Edith Elmer. *The Housing of the Unskilled Wage Earner: America's Next Problem*. New York: Macmillan, 1919.

Wood, Edith Elmer. *Introduction to Housing: Facts and Principles*. Washington, DC: Federal Works Agency, United States Housing Authority, 1940.

Wood, Edith Elmer. *Recent Trends in American Housing*. New York: Macmillan, 1931.

Wood, Edith Elmer. *Slums and Blighted Areas in the United States*. Washington, DC: Federal Emergency Administration of Public Works, 1935.

"WPA Federal Art Project." *Current History* 48, no. 4 (April 1, 1938): 68–71.

Wright, Henry. *The American City: An Outline of Its Development and Functions*. Chicago: A. C. McClurg, 1916.

Wright, Henry. "Community Planning: 'Lo!' the Poor One-Family House." *Journal of the American Institute of Architects* 14, no. 3 (March 1926): 118–21.

Wright, Henry. "Housing—When, Where, and How?" *Architecture* 68, no. 1 (July 1933): 1–32.

BEST-LAID PLANS

INDEX

ABOUT THE AUTHOR

Julie D. Turner holds a doctorate in U.S. History from Miami University of Ohio and teaches at the University of Cincinnati. Her research focuses on early twentieth-century US culture and society, along with the history of cities and technology. Her personal interests include photography and design.

BEST-LAID PLANS